Wed.

This edition of *The Canterbury Tales* was originally pub-
lished by Simon and Schuster, Inc., at $2.95.

ACKNOWLEDGMENTS

THE USUAL statement that Chaucer's Middle English is not particularly hard to read is for the most part true. There are, however, quite a few words and passages in *The Canterbury Tales* which are extremely difficult to translate into Modern English, and the professional journals frequently carry controversial articles about such words and passages. To these articles and to the notes prepared by editors of the *Tales* I am indebted on almost every page of this translation.

I am especially grateful for the suggestions made by Dr. Henry W. Simon, Senior Editor of Simon and Schuster, Inc., which greatly improved the method of translation. Mrs. Robert Hellendale, of New York City, also contributed considerable help with the revisions.

It is a pleasure to acknowledge here my constant indebtedness to Professor George R. Coffman, of the University of North Carolina, who introduced me to the serious study of Chaucer's works.

R. M. LUMIANSKY

New Orleans, 1948

PREFACE

by Mark Van Doren

ONLY THE greatest poems can be translated without loss, or at any rate without the fatal loss which most poems suffer as soon as they try to breathe in another language. The life of most poems is in their language merely. And this can be a delicious life for those who know that language. But it is nothing like the life of Homer, say, and Dante, a life that was lived in the heart and mind, and that consequently can flourish wherever there are men to listen. The same thing is true, all countries tell us, of Shakespeare. And it is true of Chaucer, whose language—a foreign one even to readers and speakers of English today—is one of the most charming a man ever used but the life in whose poems is so much more charming still that it is impossible to imagine a person dull enough to resist it. All anybody needs is half a chance to hear the voice of Chaucer talking and telling stories.

But it should be half a chance at least. I am not sure that Chaucer has ever had that much of a chance till now. If, in Mr. Lumiansky's prose, he has that much and more, the reason is first of all the prose. I have long been convinced that verse is the heaviest disadvantage under which translations of great poetry can labor. I prefer Homer and Dante in prose; and I prefer Mr. Lumiansky's modernization of THE CANTERBURY TALES to any verse one now available.

This is not simply, of course, because Mr. Lumiansky has used prose. It is because his prose has found so natural a way to render the absolute plainness of Chaucer. It is Chaucer's unique secret, this absolute plainness, this pretense that he is no poet at all, this air of being no more than a man who has been everywhere and learned everything that anybody knows.

We love Chaucer instantly, and never cease to love him. And Mr. Lumiansky seems to guess why. He has got to the incorruptible center of a humorous, just, merciful man whose slyness has so little malice in it that we hasten to let it educate us in the ways of the absurd, unchanging world. Mr. Lumiansky's prose has found this man and given him to us with neither archaism nor adornment. Nor with a modernity that anywhere is modish. For Mr. Lumiansky keeps himself out of sight as well as Chaucer does. It is merely the stories that we get, as clear as sunlight and as live as human speech.

If we do not get Chaucer's wise, sweet verse—and it is our loss that we do not—there is at least no poor reminder of it in the shape of an impossible substitute. If we want it badly enough, we can go and learn Middle English, which indeed is an excellent thing to do. But short of that the best thing is to have what Chaucer becomes when by modernization he is deprived of his music. That he survives as he does in this book is the surest proof of his simple greatness, and of Mr. Lumiansky's wisdom in never obstructing our view of what there is to see. The whole of the world is here to see. I for one have never enjoyed it more.

TABLE OF CONTENTS

Some Introductory Observations
for the Modern Reader of

THE CANTERBURY TALES

A NEW TRANSLATION of Chaucer's CANTERBURY TALES *needs some explanation. The chief point to be made is that I believe this Human Comedy—as it is frequently subtitled—holds a great deal of enjoyment for the modern reader. It was not considered, when it was written, an "academic" book, although it now may seem to be one because of the difficulty of the language.*

Quite a few translations from the original Middle English versions of the TALES *have already been made. Several of these are in verse, some by very well-known poets; but even the poets have not been able to avoid a certain awkward and unnatural quality in their verse translations. Some translators of* THE CANTERBURY TALES *have followed a system of using archaic or out-of-date words and sentence structure to create the "flavor" of Middle English for a modern reader. But often this archaic language seems far stranger to the present-day reader than Chaucer's usually familiar Middle English did to his audience.*

In preparing this translation, I have tried to reproduce the tone in which THE CANTERBURY TALES *was written—the colloquial idiom of the day, using the humorous, direct, often slangy expressions which were heard on the busy streets of fourteenth-century London. Although this language is the direct ancestor of Shakespeare's English and of our own American idiom, the modern reader cannot appreciate or even un-*

derstand Chaucer's writings in the original without considerable study. And so, if his work is to have many modern readers, it must be made available in present-day English.

I have tried to reproduce Chaucer's phrases exactly, almost word for word, in natural, idiomatic, colloquial, modern English, which will convey to the modern reader the same effects that Chaucer's idiomatic Middle English conveyed to his audience. To accomplish this in rhymed or blank verse is, I think, almost impossible. Consequently, I have used prose, though in such a translation the rhyme and meter of the original are lost. This is the closest we can approach the language and spirit of Chaucer today.

THE CANTERBURY TALES was probably put together in the late 1380's and early 1390's. It was to be a collection of short stories told by a group of thirty-odd English pilgrims who are making the sixty-mile, four-day trip from Southwark, a suburb of London, to the shrine of St. Thomas Becket at Canterbury. Within the framework of their conversations, each pilgrim was to tell the company four stories. Chaucer completed only about one-fifth of this plan, and the part he did complete was left in great disorder. But in spite of these handicaps, the book is still very much alive today, appearing on most lists of "great books." And no one would remove Chaucer from the company of Shakespeare and Milton, in the familiar sequence of the masters of English literature. It will be the purpose of these introductory remarks to indicate to the prospective reader of the TALES why the book is worth his reading.

As I indicated above, the answer to this lies in the fact that Chaucer has written some excellent short stories which are fun to read. In the second place, not only are the pilgrims themselves people well worth meeting—as are a number of characters in the stories—but surely there are, as well, new ideas and attitudes toward our own twentieth-century world and the people in it which can come to us from thinking about the motives and actions of these people in THE CANTERBURY TALES.

THE CHARACTERS

After a lifetime of close association with all kinds of Englishmen in his daily official life, Chaucer hit upon an almost perfect plan for presenting a cross-section of English society as a framework for his cross-section of popular narratives. THE CANTERBURY TALES *is a record of a pilgrimage from London to the shrine of St. Thomas at Canterbury, during which the pilgrims tell stories "to shorten the way." In his choice of a pilgrimage, Chaucer came close to the very core of the life of his times. For in fourteenth-century England, which was completely Catholic, formal religion was an important factor for everybody, and pilgrimages were strongly advocated by the Church. The journey to Canterbury was the "best" pilgrimage possible in England, and this certainly accounts for the presence of such truly devout people as the Prioress and the Parson among the pilgrims. But, then, almost as important as this religious consideration, a pilgrimage was a social event. All through the hard winter people were kept close at home, feeding fires and bundling up in heavy clothes. With the spring, however, came the possibility of going on a pilgrimage—the kind of vacation which had the approval of the Church and which impressed one's neighbors. No doubt, the Miller and the Friar, among others, joined the pilgrims for this reason. It is the combination of these two motives for the pilgrimage—sincere devotion and a pleasure trip—which Chaucer skillfully introduces in the opening paragraph of the* TALES *and continues throughout the book.*

The choice of a pilgrimage as the framework for his collection of stories also allowed Chaucer to accomplish one very unusual thing: the storytellers, the pilgrims, because of their interest as people, often overshadow the tales which they tell. Chiefly by means of the "General Prologue" and the links, Chaucer brought to life these thirty-odd memorable characters. Especially is the "General Prologue" remarkable for its gallery of portraits. Here, making full use of the little human affectations and pretensions, as well as the more admirable traits, which he had so often observed while performing his duties as diplomat and civil servant, Chaucer presented the outstanding series of brief character sketches in English literature. It is difficult to say just how Chaucer, in these rapid portraits, created such real characters, people who seem familiar to readers in any century. One eminent scholar argued, as convincingly as the scarcity of records and the lapse of over five hundred years permit, that Chaucer chose models from among his acquaintances for many of his pilgrims. Be that as it may, Chaucer's method appears to have been the selection of characters who represent types of fourteenth-century society and who, at the same time, stand out as individuals. And the secret of his converting typical characters into living individuals seems to lie in his mastery of the pregnant phrase, the brief comment touching upon universal human actions or attitudes, which arose from his wide experience among all kinds of people, and which brings to the reader a host of associations based on his own experience among people. The outlines of his portraits Chaucer sketches factually; then, by means of these brief associative comments, the reader is led to fill in the many details of the character, until a living person steps forth from the page.

So it is with the Man of Law, "wary and wise," to whom Chaucer devotes only twenty-two lines. He has risen to high legal renown, and deservedly so, for he knows his business thoroughly. But then comes the telling comment: "There was nowhere so busy a man as he, and yet he seemed busier than he was." And with that the reader calls up pictures of the people he knows who "seem busier than they are." We find the same sequence with the Merchant, who gets only fifteen lines in the "General Prologue." From his clothes and manner, we know him to be a man of importance, or at least he considers himself so. But by several brief remarks Chaucer allows us to place this Merchant among people we have met. The Merchant is always talking about his profits, though he tells nobody about his debts; and he complains that the government is not doing enough for private enterprise. Then, in

the last line of this portrait, Chaucer gives a pretty clear in-
dication of his own feeling about the Merchant: "to tell the
truth, I don't know what people call him." Despite Chaucer's
usual sociability—witness the second paragraph of the "Gen-
eral Prologue"—he spent about ten days in close company
with this man and wasn't sufficiently interested in him to find
out his name!

There are many other instances of Chaucer's creating liv-
ing people by skillful use of the pregnant phrase—the Monk,
a square peg in a round hole; the Friar, a social snob; the
Franklin, a voluptuary. And such characterizations are by no
means limited to the "General Prologue," for Chaucer does
the same thing time after time in the individual stories. For
example, there is Absalom, "the village dandy" (as one critic
calls him), in "The Miller's Tale." But no doubt the reader
will enjoy finding other instances for himself. There is an-
other point, however, which should be mentioned in this
connection. Though Chaucer's characters often show the
range of his careful observation of human failings, he almost
never uses biting satire in the treatment of the people he cre-
ates. Along with his great knowledge of human beings, he,
like the Parson in the "General Prologue," possessed tolerant
understanding rather than a holier-than-thou attitude. Only
once—in the case of January in "The Merchant's Tale"—is
Chaucer ruthless; and in this instance the result is superb
irony directed at the rationalizing of an old man blinded by
lust.

Having created this group of living people in the "General
Prologue," Chaucer kept them alive throughout the book by
means of the links, the prologues and epilogues, between the
stories. Here we get glimpses of the pilgrims as they move
along on their journey, and throughout Chaucer treats them
as real human beings, not as stiff, literary figures. At one
point, probably because he felt that his audience would ap-
preciate new faces in the group, two latecomers, the Canon
and the Canon's Yeoman, join the pilgrims.

From almost the beginning of the narrative Chaucer took
advantage of another possibility afforded him by the choice

of a pilgrimage as unifying device. Being members of a small group for a number of days brought the pilgrims into close contact with one another, and it is to be expected that antagonisms would spring up among them. Frequently these antagonisms heighten the dramatic interest for the reader and serve as motivating forces for the tales. Thus it is that the Reeve, who as an overseer of a farm has grain to be ground, and the Miller, who makes his living from reeves, are suspicious of each other; and it is quite understandable that each tells a story aimed at the other. The Friar and the Summoner form another such pair. In their unsavory work, both prey upon the same gullible people, and their two stories bear witness to their animosity.

Another method Chaucer used to make his pilgrims real people is to suit the tale and the teller. The Knight's story is of chivalry, the Squire's of romantic love, and the Second Nun relates the legend of St. Cecilia. Then there are several even more complicated arrangements whereby the portrait of a particular pilgrim in the "General Prologue" fits into the prologue to that pilgrim's story, and the story itself complements its prologue. All three together serve to characterize the pilgrim in great detail. The Wife of Bath and the Pardoner are treated in this fashion.

The Wife of Bath certainly deserves a paragraph here all to herself. The marriage question was as much debated in the fourteenth century as it is today, and in this matter the Wife claims to be the greatest expert of her time. She believes that in any well-run family the wife should have the upper hand, and she has managed to establish this relationship with each of her five husbands. But Chaucer's Wife is by no means interested in just the home. She is very proud of her position in her community and has a great deal of experience which she gained in her extensive travels—three trips to Jerusalem, and pilgrimages to Rome, Boulogne, Galicia, and Cologne. Also, the Wife is no stranger to books. She takes a firm stand against the widespread antifeminism of contemporary churchmen, and she can quote the Bible and other authorities in support of her arguments. Along with her advancing years, *which restrict the continued satisfying of her great lust for living, the Wife has developed a kind of practical philosophy which finds expression in her statement: "But, Lord Christ! when I think back upon my youth and my gaiety, it tickles me to the roots of my heart, and does my heart good to this very day, that I have had the world in my time." Though her beauty and vitality are fading, the Wife can still manage to be "right merry," and her prologue and tale will always have a place among the great performances in English literature.*

Throughout the book, there is that remarkable man, Harry Bailly, the Host, who is guide and governor for the pilgrims and reporter and judge for the stories. Wholly unabashed by his numerous responsibilities, he conducts the storytelling and manages the pilgrims in a masterful fashion, rising to his place among the really memorable characters of literature. But not even Harry is without a weak spot. Though he usually acts as lordly as a king on this pilgrimage, he can't hide the fact that he is very much henpecked at home by Goodlief, his wife.

THE TALES

We hear frequently that the twentieth century is "the age of the short story." Of course, short narratives have been popular in all ages, but it does seem, probably because of the speeding up of our way of living and the consequent cutting down in the time we have for reading, that the short story is our most popular form of literature. Hundreds of magazines offering short stories appear each week, and each year there are several collections of the year's "best" short stories. Now, as I said before, THE CANTERBURY TALES *is a collection of short stories grouped around the central idea of a pilgrimage from London to the shrine of St. Thomas Becket at Canterbury, and into this collection it seems that Chaucer planned to put representatives of the various types of short narratives which were popular in his day. Some of these types have remained popular through the centuries, while others, chiefly*

*those containing extensive moralizing, appeal less to modern
taste.*

*Since the book was left unfinished, we are by no means
sure about Chaucer's intentions; but, as we have it, the col-
lection consists of a "General Prologue," twenty-four tales,
and numerous links—the short conversations, usually between
the Host and some one or more of the pilgrims—which join
the stories. Of the twenty-four stories, three are incomplete:
the Cook's story of Perkin, the idle apprentice, who has all
the appearance of an interesting character; the Squire's tale
of Canace, which sounds much like a story from* THE ARA-
BIAN NIGHTS; *and Chaucer's own story of Sir Thopas, a bur-
lesque of the widely read metrical narratives about chivalrous
knights and their ladies, which Harry Bailly will not allow
Chaucer to complete. There has been a great deal of arguing
about why Chaucer left these three stories unfinished; what-
ever the reason, most readers will feel some regret that two
of these tales—the Cook's and the Squire's—are fragments.
And, for anyone familiar with the romances which were so
plentiful in the Middle Ages, there is great fun in "Sir
Thopas."*

*The longest of the twenty-one complete stories, "The
Knight's Tale," can be compared to a modern novelette bet-
ter than to a short story. In retelling this story of Palamon
and Arcite, the two young knights who fall in love with the
beautiful Emily, Chaucer stressed spectacle and movement.
In the descriptions of the building of the lists for the tour-
nament and of the burial of Arcite, the reader feels almost
that Chaucer had pictures before him as he wrote. And in
the account of the tournament itself, we are reminded of an
important football game in a large stadium. Also there is
careful differentiation in character between the two suitors
for Emily's hand: it seems that Arcite is much more given to
introspection and to pondering over causes and results than
Palamon, who drives more directly toward what he wants, at
least until Arcite's death. Throughout the story, Theseus
serves as a kind of master of ceremonies; using standard
medieval philosophical ideas, he urges making a virtue of*

necessity and brings the events to a happy end by marrying Emily to Palamon. As the Host says, the Knight has got the storytelling game off to a fine start.

Though we don't know just what sequence for the stories Chaucer would have decided upon if he had completed the TALES, *we can see that contrast was one of the guiding principles which he had in mind. There is an alternation in types of stories in order to avoid monotony. After the Knight's tale of chivalry, the kind of story most popular among the nobility, we find the stories of the Miller and the Reeve. These two stories belong to a type less "elevated," and many critics think that they show Chaucer at his best as a storyteller. Certainly there is in them an inevitability of sequence of events and a deftness of situation which can hardly be rivaled by short stories in any age. The fun reaches its highest point, I think, when the superstitious and gullible carpenter in "The Miller's Tale," hearing clever Nicholas scream for water to cool his scorched flesh, thinks that a second flood has arrived, cuts the ropes which hold his tub to the ceiling, and falls headlong to the cellar. Almost as entertaining is the scene in "The Reeve's Tale" in which the miller's proud wife beats her husband over the head with a stick, thinking him one of the "false students." Later the Shipman tells a story which is similar in type to the Miller's and the Reeve's. In it, the stinginess of the merchant of St. Denis brings him both cuckolding and loss of a hundred francs.*

Several of the stories in THE CANTERBURY TALES *concern the supernatural. The Wife of Bath, the liveliest and most argumentative of the pilgrims, tells of a young and handsome knight who, as punishment for a wicked deed, must answer the question "What do women most desire?" in order to save his life. He learns the answer from an old hag, whom he is forced to marry. Though he has escaped death, he is still sad, for his wife is old, poor, and of low birth. Everything turns out satisfactorily, however, when the old hag, after sternly lecturing the knight about his snobbishness, becomes young and beautiful. The Franklin's story also hinges upon a magical act. A scholar from the University of Orleans, a*

*school noted in the Middle Ages for its courses in magic, re-
moves some hideous black rocks from the coast of Brittany.
This act makes it possible for all four of the main people in
the story to reveal their nobility of character. But the most
likable of the supernatural figures in the* TALES *is the yeoman
in "The Friar's Tale." This yeoman is really a devil, and the
reader is delighted when, in his disguise as a yeoman, he
forces the greedy summoner to consign himself to Hell.*

Only one story in THE CANTERBURY TALES *seems to be
based on contemporary events. A great many people in
Chaucer's day were cheated by men who claimed to know
the secret of the philosopher's stone. Had these men lived in
the 1900's, they probably would have sold stock in fictitious
gold mines with equal success. In "The Canon's Yeoman's
Prologue and Tale" we meet the Canon's Yeoman, who has
worked for such a swindler, and who gets a great deal of
satisfaction out of telling how a priest was cheated by an
alchemist.*

*Mickey Mouse, Donald Duck, and Porky Pig will bear
witness to our enjoyment of beast fables, and in this respect
we differ little from Chaucer's audience. There are two such
fables in the* TALES. *The Nun's Priest's story of the rooster,
the hen, and the fox is probably the most widely known of
Chaucer's writings. So well drawn are these characters, and so
full of human quirks, that the reader sometimes forgets that
they are not people. And when Chanticleer almost comes to
grief because of his wife's hold over him, we find hints of the
Nun's Priest's dislike of "petticoat rule" as represented by his
boss, the Prioress. The Manciple's tale of the Crow is by no
means so good a beast fable as the Nun's Priest's, but it will
strike most of us as a sophisticated version of such old favorites
as "How the Rabbit Lost His Tail."*

*As I said earlier, the medieval audience was fonder of
moralizing stories than most of us are today. For this reason
I have chosen to present only brief summaries of three of
Chaucer's tales in this volume—the Monk's series of tragedies,
the long "Tale of Melibeus," and the Parson's sermon on
penitence.*

Several other tales have distinctly medieval characteristics. The Man of Law's story of the steadfast Constance seems almost an earlier exaggerated version of "The Perils of Pauline," and modern wives will probably feel very little sympathy for patient Griselda, whom the Cleric learned about from Francis Petrarch. The Second Nun fittingly tells the legend of St. Cecilia, and from the Physician we have the pathetic story of Virginia, whose beauty causes her death.

Critic after critic has praised the Pardoner's story of the three rioters as Chaucer's finest work as a storyteller. This little tale is like a modern short-short-story. One cannot find a flaw in Chaucer's motivation of the characters or his arrangement of the action, and the ironic figure of the old man, who shows the rioters the way to the heap of gold and thus to death, is unforgettable. This story perfectly illustrates the Pardoner's text: "The root of all evil is greed."

 ## THE SOURCES

Like Shakespeare, Chaucer felt no hesitancy in borrowing materials for his stories from earlier writers. In THE LEGEND OF GOOD WOMEN he tells us that he owned sixty books old and new—an impressive library in the fourteenth century— and there is plentiful evidence in his works that he read and re-read a considerable number of the best-known books of his day. His use of these books in his writing takes various forms. Sometimes he borrows a complete plot, sometimes a long passage, and then at times only a brief phrase or figure of speech. At times he seems to be writing with his source-book in front of him; again his borrowings seem to come from his memory. Frequently, he appears to have used translations of well-known books, but often he works from original versions. As a general rule, we can say that Chaucer's works, when examined in their probable chronological order, show a steadily increasing complexity of sources; that is, the earlier works follow their sources fairly faithfully, while the later *ones include extensive original elements plus borrowings from many different sources.*

Since the twenty-four stories in THE CANTERBURY TALES were not all written at the same period of Chaucer's life, we are not surprised to find wide variety in his use of source material in the TALES. It should be borne in mind that many of the tales represent complications of sources too detailed for presentation here, while for others no sources have been found, though that does not mean necessarily that Chaucer did not have a source before him. Also, in quite a few instances there is not general agreement among scholars about exactly what source Chaucer did use. Nevertheless, one thing which seems certain is that Chaucer did not borrow the idea of a pilgrimage as the framework for a collection of tales. This device, which results in the "General Prologue" and the links—to many critics the outstanding element of the TALES—is Chaucer's original contribution, though within these sections there are numerous short borrowings. A brief description of the materials which went into four of the tales will give some idea of the variety in Chaucer's "literary method."

First of all, there are a number of tales, most of them written, we think, when Chaucer was at the height of his powers, for which no source has been discovered. For example, "The Miller's Tale" is made up of three motifs skillfully put together. These three motifs have been named "The Flood," "The Misdirected Kiss," and "The Branding," and a number of analogues (tales which contain similar incidents, but which Chaucer did not certainly know) have been found. Probably, Chaucer worked from a lost French tale in which these three motifs were already combined. At any rate, a reader of "The Miller's Tale" will be struck by the artistry with which Chaucer has welded these three incidents together.

Next, some of Chaucer's tales are close translations of their sources. Typical of these is the Cleric's tale of patient Griselda. Chaucer found this story told in Latin by Francis Petrarch, and he knew it also from a rather literal anonymous translation of Petrarch's Latin into French prose. Except for numerous expansions and an occasional omission, Chaucer's story follows these two versions almost sentence for sentence, though we can see that he depended more on the French source than on the Latin. But, even in this close translation, we find alterations that furnish evidence of the story-telling ability which Chaucer exhibits so liberally in his later and better tales. Walter becomes more obstinately cruel; Janicula is a more realistic father; and Griselda is more pathetically and courageously meek.

Third, we find that there are several tales in which Chaucer has greatly altered and improved the principal source from which he was writing. For "The Knight's Tale" he used Boccaccio's TESEIDA as basic source, but his tale is by no means a translation of the Italian poem. Where the latter has roughly ten thousand lines, "The Knight's Tale" has something over two thousand, and only about a third of these are from the TESEIDA. In general, Chaucer speeds up the narrative by condensing lengthy sections of Boccaccio's poem; thus, the whole first book of the TESEIDA is covered in the opening twenty-five lines of "The Knight's Tale." Also, the tone of Chaucer's tale differs considerably from that of the Italian poem by reason of philosophical passages in the tale which Chaucer borrowed from Boethius' CONSOLATION OF PHILOSOPHY.

Last, and most difficult to describe, come those tales probably written late in Chaucer's career which show a multiplicity of borrowings. An example of this method is "The Wife of Bath's Prologue and Tale." Her "Prologue" is practically an anthology of borrowings from the antifeminist ecclesiastical writers, to whose attitudes the Wife is so vigorously opposed. In her tale, for which no source has been found, Chaucer joined two well-known narrative motifs: "the hag transformed through love" and "the man whose life depends on the correct answer to a question." These two motifs are welded into the perfect "clincher" for the Wife's claim, advanced in her "Prologue," that in any well-run marriage the wife must have the upper hand.

This, then, is a glimpse of the methods Chaucer used in his handling of the materials from which he made his stories. One often-stated conclusion emerges: whatever his method of putting a given story together, Chaucer always added something of his own, and, particularly in his later tales, that something represented an immortal touch.

THE AUTHOR

There is of course no explaining where or how Chaucer acquired his ability as a great storyteller. However, the fact that he was a man of affairs as well as a man of books, a civil servant who dealt frequently with people from all walks of life, seems to have had great influence on the writing he did at night when he returned home from the office. Chaucer left us a picture of his double life—the office and the study— in a poem called THE HOUSE OF FAME. *There the Eagle, one of the most entertaining of all Chaucer's characters, jokingly scolds the poet for overwork. He says: "For when your work is all done and you have finished all your accounts, instead of resting or doing different things, you go home to your house at once and sit as dumb as any stone with another book until your eyes are completely dazed." We can be sure that many of the realistic details and the keen insights into people which we find in Chaucer's stories came, not from the books he read at night, but from his daily contact with the world in carrying on his various jobs.*

From birth (somewhat after 1340, probably) it seemed certain that Chaucer would take an active part in the affairs of his world. His father and grandfather had prospered as wine-merchants and had held positions as officials of the Crown. Our first record of the poet is as a page in the household of Prince Lionel. Then in 1359 Chaucer was taken prisoner by the French near Rheims, and the King contributed to his ransom. Somewhat later he seems to have entered the service of King Edward III, who, in 1367, granted him a pension for life. It is also believed that in 1366 Chaucer married Philippa Roet, who served the Queen.

Between 1368 and 1374 Chaucer traveled steadily back and forth between England and the Continent in the King's service, and in the latter year the King granted him a daily pitcher of wine as a reward for his good diplomatic work. Of considerable importance is his trip to Italy to help select a harbor in England for Genoese ships, for during this mission Chaucer is supposed first to have come in contact with Italian literature.

After this period of diplomatic service, Chaucer settled in London. In 1374 the City gave him a house rent-free, and he was appointed Controller of Customs. Various records from this period show that he had become a wealthy and important man, and between 1376 and 1378 he was called back into diplomatic work, serving Richard II, who came to the throne in 1378, just as he had served Edward III. Then followed seven years' work at the Customs House. In 1385 he was living in Kent, in which county he held public offices, but there is evidence that he was in difficult financial circumstances during his stay there.

In 1389, Chaucer was appointed Clerk of the King's Works, an important post which he held for almost two years, and which he probably gave up voluntarily in 1391. In the same year he received his next appointment—deputy forester of a royal forest in Somerset. He continued to travel about England a great deal and was still very much in favor with the King. This same appointment was renewed in 1398 and seems to have been Chaucer's last regular job. In 1399, Henry IV was crowned, and he, like Edward III and Richard II, held Chaucer in high esteem. Though some authorities think that Chaucer was poverty-stricken during his last years, he was able in 1399 to lease a house near Westminster Abbey for fifty-three years. Less than a year, however, was left to him; he died on October 25, 1400.

This brief listing of dates and events is enough to show the fullness and variety of Chaucer's life as diplomat and civil servant. His success in public affairs under three kings is

*proof of his ability, tact, and understanding of his fellow
men. But what of his first love, the writing for which he is
remembered today?*

THE WRITING OF THE TALES

*Actually we don't know a great deal about the order of or
the circumstances surrounding the composition of Chaucer's
writings. There is clear evidence in them that Chaucer was
familiar with a considerable number of the great books of
his time, and it is fairly well established that his writings
show a steady increase in his literary skill. The earlier pieces,
such as* THE BOOK OF THE DUCHESS *and* THE HOUSE OF
FAME, *are highly imitative of the popular French poetry of
the period. Then come such works as* THE PARLIAMENT OF
BIRDS *and* THE LEGEND OF GOOD WOMEN, *in which there is
evidence of Chaucer's profiting from the materials he had
encountered on his diplomatic missions to Italy. Shortly after-
ward he wrote his longest single piece,* TROILUS AND CRI-
SEYDE, *a love poem based on the same story which Shake-
speare later used for a play. Finally, as most critics put it,
Chaucer reached the height of his powers in* THE CANTER-
BURY TALES. *This statement, however, is a bit misleading, for
not all the stories for the* TALES *were written late in Chaucer's
career. There is no doubt that in the tales of the Miller and
the Reeve, the Nun's Priest and the Wife of Bath, among
others, we see Chaucer at his best; but it is also certain that
such stories as the Manciple's and "The Tale of Melibeus"
were done much earlier. The whole situation is further con-
fused by the fragmentary nature of the* TALES *and the fact
that the book has come down to us in manuscripts which
Chaucer himself never saw.*

There is one fact about Chaucer's writings in general and
THE CANTERBURY TALES *in particular which we should not
fail to appreciate—Chaucer wrote in English. Latin was the
standard literary language all over western Europe in the four-
teenth century and, though his choice of English may have*

been influenced by Dante's having used Italian, we can see in the choice Chaucer's desire to write for the English people as a whole, rather than for just the learned few. And when we come to examine the English which Chaucer used, we are impressed by the great effect which his official life—his rubbing shoulders with people of all ranks and occupations—had upon his literary life. For his English is not the language of the universities or the court, except when he wants it to be; usually it is the highly colloquial, everyday language of the streets. One of the really remarkable things about THE CANTERBURY TALES is that within the rigid requirements of Middle English verse Chaucer managed to reproduce the rhythms of natural conversation.

Such in brief are the stories and the background of THE CANTERBURY TALES. Chaucer himself, in the prologue to "The Miller's Tale," wrote the perfect advice to the reader: If you do not like one story, "turn over the page and choose another tale. . . . Don't blame me if you choose amiss."

—THE TRANSLATOR

THE CANTERBURY TALES

GENERAL PROLOGUE

HERE BEGINS THE BOOK OF THE TALES OF CANTERBURY: When April with its gentle showers has pierced the March drought to the root and bathed every plant in the moisture which will hasten the flowering; when Zephyrus with his sweet breath has stirred the new shoots in every wood and field, and the young sun has run its half-course in the Ram, and small birds sing melodiously, so touched in their hearts by Nature that they sleep all night with open eyes—then folks long to go on pilgrimages, and palmers to visit foreign shores and distant shrines, known in various lands; and especially from every shire's end of England they travel to Canterbury, to seek the holy blessed martyr who helped them when they were sick.

One day in that season when I stopped at the Tabard in Southwark, ready to go on my pilgrimage to Canterbury with a truly devout heart, it happened that a group of twenty-nine people came into that inn in the evening. They were people of various ranks who had come together by chance, and they were all pilgrims who planned to ride to Canterbury. The rooms and stables were large enough for each of us to be well lodged, and, shortly after the sun had gone down, I had talked with each of these pilgrims and had soon made myself one of their group. We made our plans to get up early in order to start our trip, which I am going to tell you about. But, nevertheless, while I have time and space, before I go farther in this account, it seems reasonable to tell you all about each of the pilgrims, as they appeared to me; who they were, and of what rank, and also what sort of clothes they wore. And I shall begin with a Knight.

There was among us a brave KNIGHT who had loved chivalry, truth, and honor, generosity and courtesy, from the time of his first horseback rides. He had performed admirably in his lord's wars, during which he had traveled as widely as any man, in both Christendom and heathen countries, and he had always been cited for his bravery. He had been at Alexandria when it was conquered, and had sat at the head

1

of the table many times in Prussia, above all the foreign knights. He had fought successfully in Lithuania and in Russia more frequently than any other Christian knight of similar rank. Also he had been in Granada at the siege of Algeciras, and had fought in Benmarin. He had been at Ayas and Attalia when they were won, and had taken part in many an armed expedition in the Mediterranean. He had fought in fifteen large battles, in addition to the three times he had defended our faith in lists in Algeria, and each time he had killed his opponent. This same brave Knight had once been with the lord of Palathia to fight against another heathen in Turkey, and he had always been given valuable loot. But though he was brave, he was prudent, and as meek in his conduct as a maid. He had never yet in all his life spoken discourteously to anybody. He was a true and perfect gentle Knight. But let me tell you of his clothing and equipment: his horses were good, but he was not gaily dressed. He wore a thick cotton coat, which was all stained by his breastplates, for he had just returned from his travels and had set out at once on his pilgrimage.

With him there was his son, a young SQUIRE, a lover and a lusty bachelor, with hair as curly as if it had been set. He was about twenty years old, I would say, and he was of average height, remarkably agile, and very strong. He had already been on cavalry raids in Flanders, in Artois, and in Picardy, where he had borne himself well for one so young, in an effort to win favor with his lady. His clothes were as covered as a meadow with white and red flowers. All day he sang or played the flute; in fact, he was as joyful as the month of May. His cloak was short, with long, wide sleeves, and he sat his horse well and rode excellently. He could compose the words and music for songs, joust and also dance, and draw and write very well. So ardently did he love that he slept no more at night than a nightingale. He was courteous, humble, and helpful, and carved at the table for his father.

The Knight had brought along only one servant, for he wished to travel that way, and this YEOMAN was dressed in a green coat and hood. He carefully carried a sheaf of bright, keen peacock arrows attached to his belt, and a strong bow in his hand. He knew very well how to care for his equipment, and the feathers on his arrows never drooped. His hair was cut short, and his complexion was brown. He understood all the tricks of woodcraft. He wore a bright leather wristguard, and carried a sword and a small shield on one side, and a fine ornamented dagger, as sharp as the point of a spear, on the other. A Christopher hung on his breast, and he had a hunter's horn with a green cord. In my opinion he was a real forester.

There was also a Nun, a PRIORESS, whose smile was very quiet and simple. Her harshest curse was "by St. Loy," and she was named Madam Eglantine. She sang the divine service very well, with excellent nasal intonation, and spoke French fluently and carefully with the accent of the school at Stratford-Bow, for the French of Paris was unknown to her. Her table manners were admirable: she allowed no crumb to fall from her lips, nor did she wet her fingers deeply in her sauce; she knew exactly how to carry the food to her mouth and made sure that no drops spilled upon her breast. She was very much interested in etiquette. So carefully did she wipe her lips that no trace of grease could be seen in her cup when she had drunk from it. She reached for her food very daintily, and truly she was very merry, with a pleasant disposition and an amiable manner. She took pains to imitate court behavior, to be dignified in bearing, and to be considered worthy of respect. But to tell you of her tender feelings: she was so kind and so full of pity that she would weep if she saw a dead or bleeding mouse caught in a trap. She had several small dogs which she fed with roasted meat or milk and fine bread; if one of her dogs died, or if someone beat it with a stick, she cried bitterly. Indeed, with her everything was tenderness and a soft heart. Her wimple was very neatly pleated, her nose shapely, her eyes blue, and her mouth very small, soft, and red. But, truly, she had a fair forehead; it was almost a hand's-breadth wide, I swear, for, to tell the truth, she was not particularly small. I noticed that her cloak was very well made. On her arm she wore a coral rosary with large green beads for the paternosters, from which hung a brightly shining golden brooch. And on this brooch was first inscribed a capital *A*, surmounted by a crown, and after that *Amor vincit omnia.* This Prioress had another NUN, who was her chaplain, and three priests with her.

There was a MONK, an outstanding one, whose job it was to supervise the monastery's estates, and who loved hunting. He was a manly person, quite capable of serving as abbot. He had many excellent horses in his stable, and when he rode you could hear his bridle jingling in the whistling wind as clearly and also as loudly as the chapel bell at the subordinate monastery where this lord was prior. Because the rule of St. Maurus or of St. Benedict was old and somewhat stringent, this monk let old-fashioned things go and followed new-fangled ideas. He didn't give a plucked hen for that text which says that hunters are not holy, and that a monk who is irresponsible is like a fish out of water—that is to say, a monk out of his cell. For he thought that text not worth an oyster; and I said his reasoning was good. Why should he study and drive himself crazy, always poring over a book in his cloister, or work and slave with his hands as St. Augustine orders? How shall that serve the world? Let Augustine have his labor for himself! Therefore this monk was a true hunter: he had greyhounds as swift as birds in flight; his greatest pleasure, for which he would spare no cost, was to ride and hunt the hare. I saw his sleeves edged at the wrist with fur, and that the finest in the land; and he had a very rare pin made of gold, with a love knot in the larger end, to fasten his hood under his chin. His head was bald and shone like glass, as did his face also, as if he had been oiled. He was a fine, fat lord, and in good shape. His protruding eyes rolled in his head and gleamed like coals under a pot. His boots were supple, and his horse richly equipped. Now surely he was a fair prelate; he was not pale as a tormented ghost. Of all roasts he loved a fat swan best. His horse was as brown as a berry.

There was a wanton, merry FRIAR, a licensed beggar and a very gay man. No member of all four orders knew so much of gossip and flattering talk. He had found husbands for many young women at his own expense. A noble representative he was of his order. Among the franklins all over his district, and also among the respectable women in the towns, he was well liked and intimate, for he had, as he said himself, more power of confession than a parish priest, since he was licensed by his order. He heard confession very agreeably, and his absolution was pleasant. When he thought he would get a good present, he was an easy man in giving penance. For to give a present to a poor order is a sign that a man is well shriven. He even boasted that he knew that a man who contributed was repentant, for there are many men with hearts so stern that they cannot weep, even when they are contrite. Therefore, instead of weeping and praying, people could give silver to the poor friars. His cloak was always stuffed full of knives and pins to be given to pretty women. And, certainly, he had a pleasant voice: he could sing and play the fiddle excellently. At ballad-singing he won the prize hands down. His neck was as white as the lily, but he was as strong as a champion wrestler. He knew the taverns well in every town, and cared more for every innkeeper and barmaid than for a leper or a beggar; it was not fitting, as far as he could see, for such an important man to be acquainted with lepers. It is not honest, and it will not advance a man, to deal with such poor folks; rather, he should deal with the rich and with the food-merchants. And, above everything, wherever there was a chance for profit, this Friar was courteous and humbly helpful. There was no man anywhere more capable at this work. He was the best beggar in his order, and paid a certain sum for his grant so that none of his brethren came into his district. And even if a widow did not own a shoe, his greeting was so pleasant that before he left he would have got a coin. The money which he picked up on the sly amounted to more than his regular income. And he could frolic just like a puppy. During court meetings he could be of great help, for then he was not like a cloisterer with a coat as threadbare as a poor scholar's but like a master or a pope. His short coat was of double worsted, as neat as if it were freshly pressed. He intentionally lisped a bit in his joking, in order to make his English roll sweetly from his tongue, and when he played the harp after singing, his eyes twinkled in his head just like the stars on a frosty night. This worthy licensed beggar was named Hubert.

There was a MERCHANT with a forked beard, dressed in clothes of varied colors and sitting proudly on his horse; he wore a beaver hat from Flanders, and his boots were neatly fastened. He spoke his opinions very pompously, talking always about the increase in his profits. He wished the sea were kept open at all costs between Middelburg and Orwell, and was expert in selling money on the exchange. This responsible man kept his wits about him: so closemouthed was he about his dealings in bargaining and in borrowing and lending that no one knew when he was in debt. Nevertheless, he was really a worthy man; but, to tell the truth, I don't know what he was called.

There was also a CLERIC from Oxford, who had long ago applied himself to the study of logic. His horse was as thin as a rake, and he himself, I assure you, was by no means fat, but looked hollow and solemn. His overcoat was threadbare, for as yet he had found no benefice, and he was not worldly enough to hold a secular position. For he would rather have twenty books of Aristotle and his philosophy bound in red or black at the head of his bed than rich clothes, or a fiddle, or a gay psaltery. But though he was a philosopher, he still had but little gold in his chest, for he spent all he could get out of his friends on books and on schooling, and prayed earnestly for the souls of those who gave him money with which to go to school. He was most concerned and occupied with studying. He spoke not one word more than was necessary, and that which he did say was correct and modest, brief and to the point, and filled with worthwhile meaning. His talk centered on moral themes, and gladly would he learn and gladly teach.

A Lawyer, careful and wise, a most excellent man long practiced in legal discourse, was also there. He was discreet and well thought of—at least he seemed so, his words were so wise. Many times he had served as justice at assizes, appointed by letters from the King and also in the regular way. He had earned many large fees and presents of clothes as a result of his skill and his wide reputation. There was nowhere so able a buyer of land: he always sought unentailed ownership, and his papers were never invalidated. No man was so busy as he, and yet he seemed busier than he was. He had all the cases and decisions which had occurred since the time of King William at the tip of his tongue. He could compose and draw up a legal paper so that no one could complain about his phrasing, and he could recite every statute by heart. He rode unostentatiously in a coat of mixed color, with a silk belt on which there were small bars—I shall tell no more about his dress.

A Franklin was with the Lawyer. His beard was as white as a daisy, and he was sanguine by nature. Dearly did he love his bread dipped in wine in the morning. He had the habit of living for pleasure, for he was a true son of Epicurus, who held that pure pleasure was truly perfect bliss. He was a substantial landowner, St. Julian in his part of the country. Always his bread and ale were of the best, and nobody had a better cellar. His house was never without baked fish and meat in such quantity that it snowed food and drink, the choicest that you could imagine. His menus changed in accordance with the various seasons of the year. Many a fat bird was in his coop, and many a bream and pike in his fishpond. Woe to his cook unless the sauce were pungent and sharp and all the equipment in order. All day long his table stood ready laid in the hall. He was lord and sire of the sessions and had frequently served as member of parliament from his shire. A short dagger and a pouch of silk hung from his milk-white belt. He had served as administrator and as auditor for his shire. Nowhere was there such a worthy sub-vassal.

A Haberdasher and a Carpenter, a Weaver, a Dyer,

and a TAPESTRY-MAKER were with us, all clothed in the uniform of a great and important guild. Their equipment was all freshly and newly decorated: their knives were mounted with silver, not with brass; their belts and pouches were in every respect well and cleanly made. Indeed, each of them seemed suited to sit on a dais in the guildhall as burgess. Each, because of his wisdom, was able to serve as alderman. For they owned sufficient goods and money, as even their wives had to agree, or else they certainly would be blameworthy. It is a very fine thing to be called "Madam," to go in first to evening services, and to have a train carried like royalty.

These guildsmen had a COOK with them for the trip to boil chickens with the bones and with the flavoring powder and the spice. He could easily recognize a draught of London ale, and could roast and boil, broil, fry, make stew, and bake good pies. But it was a shame, I thought, that he had a large sore on his shin. For he could make blancmange with the best.

There was a SAILOR who lived far in the west; for all I know he was from Dartmouth. He rode upon a nag as best he could, in a coarse gown which came to his knees. Under his arm he had a dagger which hung down on a cord about his neck. The hot summer sun had tanned him heavily, and certainly he was a good fellow. Often while the wine-merchant slept, he had tapped the wine casks he brought from Bordeaux. He gave no heed to scruples. When he fought and had the upper hand, he made his prisoners walk the plank. But in his business—the correct reckoning of tides and streams; the handling of the ship's controls; the knowledge of the harbors, the moon, and the compass—there was none so good from Hull to Carthage. He was bold and wise in any undertaking. His beard had been shaken by many a tempest. He knew the condition of all the anchorages from Gotland Isle to Cape Finisterre, and every creek in Spain and Brittany. His ship was called the "Magdalen."

With us there was a PHYSICIAN; in all the world there was not another like him for talk of medicines and of surgery, for he was trained in astrology. He skillfully and carefully observed his patient through the astrological hours, and was quite able to place the waxen images of his patient so that a fortunate planet was ascendant. He knew the cause of every disease—whether hot, cold, moist, or dry—and how it developed, and of what humour. Indeed, he was the perfect practitioner: the cause and root of the disease determined, at once he gave the sick man his remedy. He had his apothecaries quite ready to send him drugs and syrups, for each of them worked to the other's profit—their friendship was not newly begun. This Physician knew well ancient Aesculapius and Dioscorides, and also Rufus, Hippocrates, Haly and Galen, Serapion, Rhazes, Avicenna, Averroes, Damascenus and Constantine, Bernard, Gatesden, and Gilbertine. His diet was moderate—not too much, but that little nourishing and digestible. But little time did he devote to the study of the Bible. He was dressed in red and blue cloth lined with taffeta and with silk; and yet he was not quick to spend his money. He held on to that which he gained during a plague. For, in medicine, gold is healthful in drinks; therefore, he especially loved gold.

There was a good WIFE from near Bath, but she was somewhat deaf, which was a shame. She had such skill in cloth-making that she surpassed the weavers of Ypres and Ghent. In all her parish there was no woman who could go before her to the offertory; and if someone did, the Wife of Bath was certainly so angry that she lost all charitable feeling. Her kerchiefs were of fine texture; those she wore upon her head on Sunday weighed, I swear, ten pounds. Her fine scarlet hose were carefully tied, and her shoes were uncracked and new. Her face was bold and fair and red. All of her life she had been an estimable woman: she had had five husbands, not to mention other company in her youth—but of that we need not speak now. And three times she had been to Jerusalem; she had crossed many a foreign river; she had been to Rome, to Bologna, to St. James' shrine in Galicia, and to Cologne. About journeying through the country she knew a great deal. To tell the truth she was gap-toothed. She sat her gentle horse easily, and wore a fine headdress with a hat as broad as a buckler or a shield, a riding skirt about her large hips, and a pair of sharp spurs on her heels. She knew how to laugh and joke in company, and all the remedies of love, for her skill was great in that old game.

There was a good man of the church, a poor parish PRIEST, but rich in holy thoughts and works. He was also a learned man, a cleric, who wished to preach Christ's gospel truly and to teach his parishioners devoutly. He was benign, wonderfully diligent, and extremely patient in adversity, as he had proved many times. He did not at all like to have anyone excommunicated for non-payment of tithes; rather, he would give, without doubt, a portion of the offering and also of his salary to his poor parishioners. He needed little to fill his own needs. His parish was wide and the houses far apart, but he never failed, rain or shine, sick or well, to visit the farthest in his parish, be he rich or poor, traveling on foot with a staff in his hand. To his congregation he gave this noble example: first he practiced good deeds, and afterward he preached them. He took this idea from the gospels and added to it another: if gold rust, what shall iron do? For if a priest whom we trust is not worthy, it is no wonder that an ignorant man sins. And it is a shame, if a priest only realizes it, to see a wicked priest and a godly congregation. Surely a parson should set an example by his godliness as to how his parishioners should live. This Priest did not hire out his benefice and leave his people in difficulties while he ran off to St. Paul's in London to look for an endowment singing masses for the dead, or to be retained by a guild. He stayed at home and guarded his parish well so that evil did not corrupt it. He was a pastor and not a mercenary. And yet, though he himself was holy and virtuous, he was not contemptuous of sinners, nor overbearing and proud in his talk; rather, he was discreet and kind in his teaching. His business was to draw folk to heaven by fairness and by setting a good example. But if any sinner, whether of high or low birth, was obstinate, this Parson would at once rebuke him for it sharply. I don't believe there is a better priest anywhere. He cared nothing for pomp and reverence, nor did he affect an overly nice conscience; he taught the lore of Christ and His twelve Apostles, but first he followed it himself.

With him there was a PLOWMAN, his brother, who had hauled many a load of manure. He was a good and true laborer, living in peace and perfect charity. With all his heart he loved God best at all times, whether it profited him or not, and next he loved his neighbor as himself. He would thresh and also ditch and dig, free of charge, for the sake of Christ, to help a poor neighbor, if it were at all possible. He paid his tithes promptly and honestly, both by working himself and with his goods. Dressed in a laborer's coat, he rode upon a mare.

There were also a Reeve, a Miller, a Summoner, and a Pardoner, a Manciple, and myself—there were no more.

The MILLER was a very husky fellow, tremendous in bone and in brawn which he used well to get the best of all comers: in wrestling he always won the prize. He was stocky, broad, and thickset. There was no door which he could not pull off its hinges or break by ramming it with his head. His beard was as red as any sow or fox, and as broad as a spade. At the right on top of his nose he had a wart, from which there grew a tuft of hairs red as the bristles of a sow's ears, and his nostrils were wide and black. A sword and a shield hung at his side. His mouth was as huge as a large furnace, and he was a jokester and a ribald clown, most of whose jests were of sin and scurrility. He knew quite well how to steal grain and charge thrice over, but yet he really remained reasonably honest. The coat he wore was white and the hood blue. He could play the bagpipe well and led us out of town to its music.

There was a friendly MANCIPLE of an Inn of Court whom other stewards might well imitate in order to buy provisions wisely. For no matter whether he bought for cash or on credit, he always watched his purchases so closely that he was constantly solvent and even ahead. Now isn't that a fine gift from God, that such an uneducated man can outwit a whole heap of learned men? He had more than thirty masters, who were expert and deep in legal matters; a full dozen of them were capable of serving as steward of the moneys and the lands of any lord in England, and of making that lord live within his own income and honorably out of debt (unless he were crazy), or just as sparingly as he wished. And these lawyers could take care of any emergency that occurred in the administration of a shire; and yet this Manciple made fools of them all.

The REEVE was a slender, choleric man. His beard was shaved as close as possible, and his hair was cut round by his ears and clipped short in front like a priest's. His legs were as long and lean as sticks, completely lacking calves. He knew fully how to keep a granary and a bin; there was no accountant who could get the best of him. From the drought and from the rainfall he could tell the expected yield of his seed and grain. His lord's sheep, cattle, dairy, swine, horses, equipment, and poultry were wholly under this Reeve's care, and his word had been accepted on the accounting ever since his lord was twenty years old. There was no one who could find him in arrears. There was no bailiff, no sheepherder, nor any other laborer, whose petty tricks and stealings were not known to the Reeve; they were as afraid of him as of death. His house was well placed upon a heath and shadowed by green trees. He was better able to buy than was his lord. He had privately accumulated considerable money, for he knew very well how to please his lord subtly, to give and lend him money from the lord's own stock and therefore to receive thanks, plus a coat and hood. As a youth he had learned a good trade: he was a very fine woodworker, a carpenter. This Reeve rode upon a large, fine, dappled-gray horse called Scot. He wore a long blue topcoat, and carried a rusty sword by his side. This Reeve that I am telling about was from Norfolk, near a town called Bawdswell. His coat was tucked up like a friar's, and he always rode last in our procession.

There was a SUMMONER with us there who had a fiery-red babyish face, for he was leprous and had close-set eyes. He

was as passionate and lecherous as a sparrow, and had black
scabby brows and a scraggly beard. Children were frightened
by his face. There was no quicksilver, litharge, or brimstone,
borax, white lead, or any oil of tartar, or ointment which
would rid him of his white pimples or of the bumps on his
face. He really loved garlic, onions, and also leeks, and to
drink strong wine, red as blood, after which he would speak
and shout like a madman. Then, when he had drunk his fill
of the wine, he would speak no word but Latin; he knew a
few phrases, two or three, that he had learned out of some
church paper—that is not unusual, for he heard Latin all
day; and you know very well how a jay bird can say "Wat"
as well as the Pope. But if anyone attempted to discuss other
learned matter with the Summoner, it was at once evident
that he had spent all of his philosophy; he would always
cry: "The question is what is the law?" He was a friendly
and a kind rascal; you couldn't find a better fellow. For a
quart of wine, he would allow a good fellow to have his
mistress for a year, and excuse him fully. And he could pull
the same trick quite expertly on someone else. If he came
across a good companion, he would teach him to have no fear
of the archdeacon's excommunication, unless that man's soul
was in his purse; for the punishment was sure to be in his
purse, since, as the Summoner said, "The purse is the arch-
deacon's Hell." But I know very well that he certainly lied;
every guilty man ought to be afraid of excommunication,
which will as surely kill the soul as absolution will save it,
and a man should also beware of a *Significavit.* This Sum-
moner controlled all the young people of the diocese in his
own way, and he knew their secrets and was their favorite
adviser. He had placed a bouquet on his head, large enough
to decorate an alehouse signpost. He had made himself a
shield of a cake.

With him there rode an amiable PARDONER from Roun-
civalle, his friend and colleague, who had just come from the
court at Rome. Loudly he sang, "Come hither, Love, to me!"
The Summoner, singing bass, harmonized with him; never
was there a trumpet with half so loud a tone. This Pardoner

had hair of a waxy yellow, but it hung as smoothly as strands of flax, and he wore what hair he had gathered into small bunches on top but then thinly spread out over his shoulders. But for sport he did not wear his hood, for it was tied up in his bag. He affected to ride all in the new fashion, uncovered except for his little cap. He had eyes which glared like those of a hare. A religious talisman was sewn to his cap. He carried his bag, stuffed full of pardons hot from Rome, before him in his lap. His voice was small and goatlike. He had no beard, and never would have; his face was as smooth as if freshly shaven. I believe he was a eunuch. But in his business, there was not another such pardoner from Berwyck to Ware. For in his bag he had a pillowcase which he said had served as the veil of Our Lady; he claimed to have a piece of the sail with which St. Peter went to sea until Jesus Christ caught him. He had a metal cross embedded with stones, and also he had pig's bones in a jar. And with these same relics, when he found a poor parson living out in the country, he made more money in one day than the parson made in two months. And thus, with feigned flattery and tricks, he made monkeys of the parson and the people. But, finally, to tell the truth, he was in church a noble ecclesiastic. He could read a lesson or a parable very effectively, but best of all he could sing the offertory; for he knew very well that, when that service was over, he must sweeten his tongue and preach to make money as best he could. Therefore, he sang merrily and loud.

Now I have told you very briefly about the rank, the dress, and the number of these pilgrims, and also why this group was assembled in Southwark at this good inn called the Tabard, close to the Bell. But the time has come to tell you what we did that same night we arrived at the inn, and afterwards I shall tell you about our trip and all the rest of our pilgrimage. But, first, I beg you in your kindness not to consider me vulgar because I speak plainly in this account and give you the statements and the actions of these pilgrims, or if I repeat their exact words. For you know just as well as I that whosoever repeats a tale must include every word as nearly as he possibly can, if it is in the story, no matter how crude and low; otherwise, he tells an untrue tale, or makes up things, or finds new words. He cannot spare even his brother's feelings; he must say one word just as well as any other. Christ himself spoke quite crudely in Holy Writ, and you know very well that there is no vulgarity in that. Even Plato says, to those who can read him, that the words must be cousin to the deeds. Also I ask you to forgive me for not arranging the people in my tale by their rank as they should be. My wit is short, as you can well imagine.

Our Host made each of us very comfortable and soon sat us down to supper. He served us with the best food; the wine was strong, and we were glad to drink. Our Host was a seemly man, fit to serve as major-domo of a banquet hall. He was a large man with protruding eyes—no more impressive burgess is to be found in Cheapside—frank in his speech, wise, and well schooled, and nothing lacking in manliness. Also, he was a very merry man, and after supper began to play and told many jokes, among other things, after we had paid our bills. Then he said: "Now, ladies and gentlemen, truly you are heartily welcome here, for by my troth, if I do not lie, all this year I haven't seen so gay a group together in this inn as now. I would like to make you happy if I knew the way; in fact, I just now thought of a way to please you, and it shall cost you nothing.

"You are going to Canterbury—God speed you, and may the blessed martyr give you your reward! And I know very well that as you go along the road you plan to tell tales and to play, for truly, there's no fun or pleasure in riding along as dumb as a stone. Therefore, I shall make you a proposition, as I said before, and do you a favor. And if you are unanimously agreed to stand by my judgment and to do as I shall suggest, tomorrow when you ride along the road, by the soul of my dead father, if you don't have fun I'll give you my head! Hold up your hands without more talk."

It didn't take us long to reach a decision. We didn't think the matter worth much careful discussion, and we voted his way without debate. Then we told him to explain his plan as he wished.

"Ladies and gentlemen," he said, "now listen carefully; but,
I beg you, don't be contemptuous. Here is the point, to be
brief and plain: that each of you, to make our trip seem short,
shall tell two tales of old adventures on the way to Canter-
bury—I mean it that way—and two more coming home. And
the one of you who tells the best tales of all, that is to say,
those greatest in moral teaching and in entertainment value,
shall have a supper at the expense of all of us here in this
inn, right by this column, when we come back from Canter-
bury. And, to make your trip more enjoyable, I will ride with
you myself, at my own expense, and be your guide; and
whoever will not accept my judgment along the way will have
to bear the full expense of the trip for everybody. Now, if
you agree to this plan, say so at once, without any more talk,
and I shall immediately get myself ready."

We agreed, and gladly gave our oaths to obey; then we
asked him also to agree to serve as our manager, and to
judge and report our tales, and to arrange for a supper at a
set price. Also, we agreed to be ruled in all things as he saw
fit. Thus unanimously we accepted his suggestion, and at
once the wine was fetched. We drank, and everyone went to
bed without further loitering.

The next morning, when the day began to dawn, our Host
got up, roused us, and gathered us all together in a bunch.
Then we rode the short distance to the Well of St. Thomas,
where the Host halted his horse and said:

"Ladies and gentlemen, listen, if you please; you remem-
ber your agreement, and I remind you of it. Now let's see
who shall tell the first story. Just as surely as I hope always
to drink wine and ale, whoever rebels against my judgment
shall stand the whole expense of this trip. Now draw straws,
before we go farther; whoever draws the shortest shall be
first. Sir Knight," he said, "my master and my lord, now draw
a straw, for that is my wish. Come near, my lady Prioress," he
said, "and you, Sir Cleric, don't be bashful or think too hard.
Fall to, everyone!"

We all immediately drew straws, and, to make a long story
short, either by luck, or chance, or fortune, the truth is that

the draw fell to the Knight, for which everyone was content and glad; and in accordance with our promise and agreement, as you have heard, he must tell his tale. What need is there to say more?

When this good man saw the situation, since he was wise and willingly held to his promise, he said: "Well, since I must start the game, I welcome the decision, in the name of God! Now, let's ride on, and listen to what I say."

After those words we rode ahead on our way, and he at once very cheerfully began his tale, and spoke in the following manner.

THE KNIGHT

HERE BEGINS THE KNIGHT'S TALE: Once upon a time, as old stories tell us, there was a Duke named Theseus. He was lord and governor of Athens, and in his day was such a conqueror that there was none greater under the sun. He had conquered many a rich country. Through his wisdom and his powerful army he conquered the whole country of the Amazons, once called Scythia, and married Queen Hippolyta, whom he brought home with him to his country amid great pomp and splendor, together with her young sister Emily. And here I shall leave this noble Duke, victorious and happy, riding towards Athens, surrounded by his army.

Certainly, if it were not too lengthy to listen to, I would have told you fully how the realm of Scythia was conquered by Theseus and his knights; of the great battle on that occasion between the Athenians and the Amazons; how Hippolyta, the fair, brave Queen of Scythia, was besieged; of the feast at their wedding; and of the tempest at their home-coming. But all those things I must now let pass. I have, God knows, a large field to till, and weak are the oxen in my plow. The rest of the tale is long enough. Also, I don't want to hinder anyone of this company; let everyone tell his tale in turn, to see who will win the supper. And now I shall begin again where I left off.

When this Duke whom I mentioned had almost reached the city in all his prosperity and his great pride, he noticed as he looked about that a company of ladies kneeled two by two in the highway, each pair behind another pair, and all were dressed in black. But they uttered such cries and lamentations that no one in the world had ever heard the like, and they would not stop crying until they had grasped his bridle.

"Who are you people who want to upset the celebration of my home-coming with crying?" asked Theseus. "Do you envy my success so much that you cry and complain this way? Or has someone insulted or offended you? Tell me if the trouble can be remedied and why you are clothed this way in black."

The oldest lady of the group, after fainting in such a death-like way that it was pitiful to watch, spoke: "Lord, to whom Fortune has given victory and the right to live as conqueror, we do not grieve because of your honor and glory; rather, we seek your mercy and aid. Take pity on our woe and our distress! Let fall a drop of pity, through your courtesy, upon us wretched women. For truly, lord, there is not one of us all who was not a duchess or a queen. Now we are captives, as you plainly see, thanks to Fortune and her false wheel which assures no one continuance of prosperity. And actually, lord, we have awaited you here in the temple of the goddess Clemency for a fortnight. Now help us, lord, since it is within your power.

"I, wretch, who weep and wail so, was once the wife of King Cappaneus, who died at Thebes—cursed be that day! And all of us in this group who utter such laments lost our husbands during the siege of that city; yet old Creon, ruler now of Thebes, is filled with wrath and iniquity. Out of hatred and tyranny and in order to dishonor the dead bodies of all our slain husbands, he had all the corpses piled in one heap and will in no way allow them to be either buried or burned, but out of spite makes dogs eat them."

With these words, without pause, all the women fell prostrate and begged piteously: "Have mercy on us wretched women, and let our sorrow sink into your heart."

The kind Duke, filled with pity, dismounted when he heard them speak. He thought that his heart would break when he saw these ladies who once had ranked so high and were now so pitiable and so poor. With his own hands he lifted each of them, and comforted them with good intentions. He swore his oath that he, as a true knight, would wreak such vengeance on the tyrant Creon that all the people of Greece would talk about how Creon, who justly deserved death, was repaid by Theseus. At once, without waiting, he unfurled his banner and rode toward Thebes, followed by his whole army. He would not go nearer Athens, nor enjoy half a day's rest, but continued on his way that night. He sent Hippolyta, the Queen, and Emily, her beautiful younger sister, to Athens, and rode toward Thebes.

On Theseus' banner the red figure of Mars with spear and shield shone in such contrast to the white background that all the surrounding fields were illuminated. Next to his banner was borne his pennant of rich gold on which the Minotaur he killed in Crete was embroidered. So this Duke, this conqueror, rode forward with the best knights in the world in his army, until he came to Thebes. There he dismounted in the middle of the field in which he planned to fight. But to be brief—he fought with Creon, King of Thebes; killed him in knightly fashion in open battle; put his followers to flight; then took the city by assault; and tore down all the walls, pillars, and rafters. Then he restored to the ladies the bones of their slain husbands to be buried according to the customs in those days. But it would be too long to tell you all the great clamor and the lamentation of the ladies at the funeral pyre, and the high honor that Theseus, the noble conqueror, did the ladies when they parted from him. My intention is to be brief.

When this worthy Duke, Theseus, had thus killed Creon and won Thebes, he remained on the battlefield that night to rest, and dealt with that country as he wished.

After the battle, the pillagers began their work of ransacking the heap of dead bodies to strip them of their equipment and clothing. It happened that among the bodies they found two young knights very badly wounded lying side by side; both bore the same coat of arms, expensively made; one of these two knights was named Arcite and the other Palamon. They were neither fully alive nor fully dead, but the heralds knew from their coats of arms and from their equipment that they were of the royal house of Thebes, sons of two sisters. The pillagers pulled them out of the heap of bodies and gently carried them to Theseus' tent. He at once sent them to Athens to be kept perpetually in prison—he would not allow them to be ransomed. When the worthy Duke had done this, he immediately rode homeward, with all his army, crowned with laurel as a conqueror. From then on he lived all his life in joy and honor; what need is there for more talk? And in a tower Palamon and his companion Arcite were doomed to live for evermore, in anguish and in woe; no amount of gold could free them.

Day after day and year after year passed until it happened one May morning that Emily, who was more beautiful to look at than the lily upon its green stalk and fresher than May with its new flowers—for her complexion so rivaled the color of the rose that I do not know which was the fairer of the two—arose and dressed herself before daybreak, as was her custom; for May will permit no sluggishness in rising. That season touches every sensitive heart and forces a person to leap from bed by saying, "Arise, and pay homage to me." This caused Emily to remember to honor May and to get up early. She was freshly dressed, and her yellow hair was twined into a braid which hung down her back, a yard long, I guess. She walked up and down in the garden as the sun rose, and gathered the flowers she desired, some red, some white, to make a pretty garland for her head; meanwhile, she sang divinely as an angel. The great tower, thick and strong, the chief dungeon of the castle, in which the knights whom I spoke about before and will speak about again were imprisoned, adjoined the wall of this garden in which Emily took her walk. The sun was bright and clear that morning, and Palamon, the poor prisoner, as was his custom by per-

mission of his jailer, rose and walked about in his high cell.
He saw all the noble city and also the garden, full of green
branches, in which the beautiful Emily walked, roaming up
and down. Palamon walked sorrowfully back and forth, com-
plaining to himself about his situation; often he cried alas,
that he was born! And so it happened by chance or luck
that he glanced through the thickly-barred square window at
Emily, and at that he turned white and cried "Ah," as if he
were badly stung. Upon hearing that cry Arcite jumped up
at once and said, "My cousin, what's the matter with you
that you are so pale and faint? Why did you cry out? What
bothers you? For love of God, take our imprisonment with
patience, for our life cannot be otherwise. Fortune sent us
this adversity. The unfavorable position of Saturn in the ar-
rangement of the heavenly bodies caused our trouble, al-
though we had sworn otherwise; the heavens were so ar-
ranged at our birth. We must endure it; that's the plain
truth."

Palamon answered: "Cousin, truly, you have completely
misunderstood. It is not our imprisonment which caused me
to cry out, but I was just now struck to the heart through my
eye, and will die of the wound. The beauty of the lady whom
I see wandering back and forth in the garden below was the
cause of my cries and my sadness. I cannot tell whether she
is a woman or a goddess; surely, it's Venus, I think." Then he
fell upon his knees and said: "Venus, if it is your desire to
transfigure yourself this way in the garden before me, a sor-
rowful wretched creature, help us to escape from this prison.
But if it is my foreordained destiny to die in prison, take pity
on our family, which is brought so low by tyranny."

Meanwhile, Arcite began to cast glances at the lady walk-
ing below, and her beauty so struck him that, if Palamon was
sorely wounded, Arcite was equally touched or more. With a
sigh he sadly said: "The fresh beauty of her who walks be-
low slays me instantly, and unless she is kind enough to agree
that I may see her frequently, I am as good as dead; there is
no more to say."

Palamon, when he heard these words, angrily looked around and asked, "Do you say that jokingly or in earnest?"

"No," said Arcite, "in earnest, by my faith! God help me, there's no joke in this."

Palamon knitted his brows. "It is not," he said, "a great honor for you to be false or a traitor to me, your cousin and your sworn brother; we have solemnly sworn to each other that never until death parts us shall either of us hinder the other in a love affair or in any other situation, though we die of the pain. Rather, in every emergency we must help each other —that was your oath, and mine also; I know it well, and you cannot deny it. You are accordingly without doubt my counselor, and now you treacherously plan to love my lady, whom I now love and serve and shall until I die. No, certainly, false Arcite, you shall not do that. I loved her first and told you my situation, in an effort to have your counsel and help as my sworn brother. You are therefore bound as a knight to help me if it lies in your power. Otherwise, you are a false knight, I swear."

Arcite replied with great formality, "You will be the false one, not I," he said. "And you are false, I tell you plainly, because I loved her as a woman before you. What will you say? You don't know yet whether she is a woman or a goddess! Your feeling is an affectation of holiness, while mine is love for a fellow creature. For that reason I told you, my cousin and sworn brother, about this love. What if we consider the problem from the point of view that you did love her before me? Don't you know the old saying of the clerics: 'All's fair in love'? Love transcends, I swear, all laws made by mortal man. Therefore, man-made laws of all kinds are broken regularly for love. A man must needs love, whatever happens. He cannot run away from it, though it means his death, whether his lady is a maid, a widow, or a wife. Furthermore, it is unlikely that you will be her favorite all your life; nor shall I, either; for you know very well that both of us are condemned to life imprisonment. We cannot be ransomed. Our quarrel is like that of the hounds for the bone: they fought all day but got no part of the bone, because a hawk came while they were fighting and stole the bone away from both of them. Therefore, dear brother, you see that around a king's court it is every man for himself; there is no other way. Love her, if you like, as I do and always shall. Truly, dear brother, that is all I have to say. We must remain here in this prison, and each of us must take his chances."

The argument raged long and loud between them, as I should tell you if I had the time. But let's get to the point. It happened one day—to make it as short as possible—that an important duke named Perotheus, a friend of Duke Theseus since the time that they were small children, came to Athens to visit his friend and to have his usual vacation. For nowhere in the world could one find better friends than these two. They loved each other so well, the old books say, that when one of them died the other actually journeyed down into Hell to look for him—but I don't want to write about that story. Duke Perotheus had known Arcite in Thebes for many years and thought very highly of him. Finally, at Perotheus' request, Duke Theseus let Arcite out of prison without any ransom; he was free to go wherever he liked, within certain conditions that I shall now tell you.

Here was the agreement, plainly stated, between Theseus and Arcite: If ever Arcite were found by day or night for one hour in any country ruled by Theseus, and were caught, it was agreed that his head would be cut off with a sword. Arcite could not change this decision, but immediately left and traveled homeward. Let him be careful; his neck is pledged!

What great sorrow Arcite now endured! He felt death strike his heart. He wept, wailed, cried pitifully, and planned to kill himself secretly. He said: "Cursed be the day that I was born! My present prison is worse than my former one. Now I am doomed to live eternally not in Purgatory but in Hell. Alas, that I ever knew Perotheus! Otherwise, I should have lived on with Theseus as a permanent prisoner. Then I would have been happy, not sorrowful. Just the sight of her whom I love, even though I never could have won her favor, would have sufficed for me. Oh, dear cousin Palamon," he said, "you have won the victory in our struggle. You can happily stay in prison—in prison? Certainly not, but in Paradise! Fortune has caused the dice to favor you, for you can look at Emily while I must be absent. And it is possible, since you, a worthy and able knight, are near her, that changeable Fortune by some chance may bring you fulfillment of your desire. But I, exiled and lacking all favor, am in such great despair that there is no particle of earth, air, fire, or water, or any creature formed of them, which can help me or comfort me in this matter. Surely I must die of hopelessness and grief. Good-by to life, hopes, and happiness!

"Alas, why is it that so many people complain about the foresight of God or of Fortune, when often they have so many better things than they could have arranged for themselves? One man longs for money which, when possessed, results in his murder or great misfortune. And another man wishes to be free from his prison, but is then slain by a member of his household. Untold difficulties lie in this question. Surely we do not know exactly what we pray for; we behave like a man as drunk as a mouse. A drunk man knows very well that he has a home, but he does not know the right way to it; in addition, any road is slippery for a drunk man. Certainly, in this world we behave similarly. We try hard for happiness, but we very often go wrong. We may all say this, but chiefly I who once had the strong opinion that if I could only escape from prison I would then be thoroughly happy and in perfect health; but now I am exiled from all my good fortune. Since I cannot see you, Emily, I am as good as dead; there is no help for it."

On the other hand, Palamon, when he learned that Arcite had left, gave vent to such grief that the great tower resounded with his crying and clamoring. The very irons on his legs were wet by his bitter salty tears. "Alas," he said, "my cousin Arcite, God knows you have the best of our quarrel. You now walk at liberty through Thebes with little concern for my woe. Since you are wise and brave you will be able to assemble all the members of our family and wage such bitter war against this city that by some chance or treaty you may win the girl, for whom I must die, as your lady or wife. For, as far as your opportunities are concerned, certainly you, who are at liberty and a noble man, have a great advantage over me, dying here in this cage. All I can do as long as I live is weep and wail from sorrow at being a prisoner and also from the pain of being in love, which doubles my torment and my sorrow."

With these words he became so completely overwhelmed by the fire of jealousy that he looked like the white flowers of the box tree or dead ashes. Then he said: "Oh, cruel gods who govern this world by your eternal word and who write your opinion and decision on a tablet of stone, wherein is mankind held in higher esteem by you than is the sheep crouching in the fold? For man is slain just like any other beast; he dwells always in prison or arrest, and suffers sickness and great adversity. Moreover, he is often guiltless.

"What reason is there in your foreknowledge which torments guiltless innocents? And the situation seems even worse to me when I consider that man is bound for the sake of God to restrain his desires, while a beast may fulfill his every lust. Also, when a beast is dead he experiences no suffering, but man after death, though he had cares and woes on earth, must weep and wail. Without doubt it must be so. I leave the answers of these questions to the churchmen, but I know very well that there is great suffering in this world. Alas, I can look upon a serpent or a thief who has done great harm to many a true man, yet is allowed to go at liberty and wander where he pleases. But I must stay in prison just because Thebes was conquered by warfare, as a result of Saturn and the jealous wrath of Juno, which has destroyed nearly all the royal family of Thebes, whose wide walls are now crumbled. And moreover, Venus causes me to die from fear and jealousy of Arcite."

Now I shall leave Palamon for a while in his prison, and tell you about Arcite.

The summer passed and the long nights doubled the sharp pain of both the lover and the prisoner. I don't know which has the sorrier lot: Palamon is condemned to imprisonment in chains and fetters until death; Arcite is exiled from that country forever, and can never see his lady again.

You lovers, I now ask you this question: Which has the worse situation, Arcite or Palamon? The one may see his lady every day, but must live always in prison; the other may ride or walk wherever he pleases, but can never again see his lady. Now judge as you like, you who know, and I shall continue as I planned. THE FIRST PART ENDS.

THE SECOND PART FOLLOWS: When Arcite arrived at Thebes, he fainted many times each day and sighed, "Alas!" because he would never see his lady again. To sum up, his grief was so great, one might say that nobody ever had, has, or will have so much sorrow while the world lasts. Sleep, food, and drink were impossible for him, and he grew thin and dry as a stick. His eyes became hollow and terrible to look at; his complexion turned yellow and pale as cold ashes. He became solitary and was always alone, wailing and moaning all night long. And if he heard a song or a musical instrument, then he would weep and no one could stop him. His spirits grew so feeble and low and he changed to such an extent that no one could recognize his voice or speech even if they could hear it at all. In his behavior he acted for all the world as if he had not only the malady of love, but in addition a mania arising from the melancholy humour in the imaginative cell of his brain. Soon his habits and disposition were completely distorted: this woeful lover, Sir Arcite.

Why should I speak all day about his grief? When he had endured this cruel torment and this pain and woe for a year or two in his own country, Thebes, as I have said, one night as he lay asleep he dreamed that the winged god Mercury stood before him and commanded him to be merry. Mercury carried his wand upright in his hand, and wore a hat upon his shining hair. The god was dressed, Arcite noticed, as he had been when he put Argus to sleep. Mercury then said, "Go to Athens; the end of your grief is prepared for there." At these words Arcite awoke and jumped up. "Now, truly," he said, "no matter how I suffer for it, I will go immediately to Athens; I will not fail because of fear of death to see the lady I love and serve. I don't care if I die, so long as I am in her presence."

With these words he caught up a large mirror and saw that his complexion was so completely changed that he appeared to be another person. At once it occurred to him that, since his face was so disfigured by the malady which he had endured, he could easily live in Athens unrecognized in some lowly position and see his lady almost every day. Immediately he dressed himself as a poor laborer, and all alone, except for a squire who knew his secrets and all the circumstances and who was disguised as humbly as he, he set off for Athens by the shortest route.

One day he arrived at the court there, and at the gate he offered his services to do whatever drudgery he should be ordered to do. To make the story short: he got a job helping the chamberlain who served Emily, for Arcite was wise and could soon tell which of the servants worked for her. He could cut wood and carry water well, for he was young and strong; he was tall and big-boned and could do whatever anyone ordered. He held this job for a year or two, page of the chamber of fair Emily, and he said his name was Philostrate. There was never a man of his rank in any court half so well beloved; he was so courteous that his reputation spread throughout the court. Everyone said that Theseus should raise his rank and put him in a respectable position where he might use his abilities fully. Thus, after a while he became so well known because of his deeds and his good speech that Theseus made him squire of his own chamber and gave him gold to maintain his rank. In addition, each year men secretly brought him his income from his own country. But he spent it suitably and prudently so that no one wondered how he got it. He passed three years of his life in this fashion and conducted himself so well in peace and also in war that there was no man whom Theseus held dearer. I shall now leave Arcite in this happy state, and speak a little of Palamon.

For seven years Palamon sat in the horrible, dark, strong prison, tortured by woe and distress. Who could feel double sorrow and sadness like Palamon, so distraught by love that he went out of his mind with grief? And also he was a prisoner not for just a year but forever. Who could recount his martyrdom adequately in English verse? Truly not I; therefore I pass over it as lightly as I can.

It happened during May of the seventh year—the old books which tell this tale more plainly specify the third night of May—either by chance or destiny (for whatever must be shall be) that shortly after midnight, Palamon broke out of prison with the help of a friend, and fled from the city as fast as he could go. He had given his jailer a drink made of a certain wine mixed with narcotics and fine opium of Thebes; as a result, the jailer slept all night and could not be roused even when he was shaken. Now Palamon was fleeing as fast as possible. Since the night was short and the dawn near, it was necessary for him to hide. He fearfully made for a grove close by. His plan was to hide in this grove during the day, and when night came he would start again toward Thebes to ask his friends to help him make war against Theseus. Either he would be killed or would win Emily for his wife. This was his straightforward intention.

Now I shall turn again to Arcite, who little realized how close trouble was to him until Fortune had caught him in her snare.

The busy lark, messenger of day, saluted the azure morning with song, and fiery Phoebus rose so clear that all the east shone golden as the sunlight dried the silvery dew from the leaves in the thickets. Then Arcite, the principal squire in the royal court of Theseus, rose and looked out upon the lovely day. In order to observe May Day as he had planned, he rode on a spirited horse into the fields to wander around a mile or two from the court. By chance he took the path that led to the grove which I told you about earlier, in order to make a garland of twigs, woodbine, or hawthorn, and he sang loudly to the shining sun: "May, with all your flowers and shrubs, welcome to you, fair fresh May, in the hope that I may get some greenery." Getting down from his horse, he went happily and hastily into the grove and wandered up and down a path next to where Palamon happened to be hidden in the bushes so that no one could see him, for he was terribly afraid of death. Palamon did not realize that it was Arcite; God knows it would have been difficult for him to believe. Nevertheless, as the true old saying goes: "Fields have eyes, and the woods have ears." It is wise for a man to conduct himself carefully, for at any unexpected time of day he may meet others. Little did Arcite realize that his former companion was near by to listen to all that he said, for Palamon sat very quiet in the bushes.

When Arcite had had his fill of wandering about and had gaily sung the complete song, he fell into a brown study, as lovers have the quaint habit of doing; sometimes their spirits are up in the tops of trees and sometimes down in the briers, now up and now down, like a bucket in a well. They are just like Friday, when, to tell the truth, it sometimes rains and it sometimes shines; in the same way changeable Venus can cast shadows over the hearts of her followers; her day is as changeable in weather as she is in dress. Seldom is Friday like the rest of the week.

When Arcite had finished singing, he grew sad and sat down to ponder. "Cursed be the day that I was born!" he said. "How long, cruel Juno, will you make war against the city of Thebes? Alas, the royal house of Cadmus and Amphion has been brought to utter confusion. I am of the royal blood of Cadmus, the founder of Thebes, its beginner and its first crowned king, and I am of his lineage and his true offspring, of royal stock, and now I have descended to so wretched and lowly a state that I serve as humble squire to my mortal enemy. And yet Juno shames me further, for I dare not make known my real name; whereas I was once called Arcite, I am now called Philostrate—completely worthless. Alas, dreadful Mars; alas, Juno! In this way your wrath has ruined our family, except for me and wretched Palamon, whom Theseus martyrs in prison. In addition to all this, in order to kill me without fail, Love has shot his fiery arrow so burningly through my true, troubled heart, that my death was predestined before I owned my first shirt. Emily, you kill me with your eyes! You are the cause of my death. I would care absolutely nothing for all my other troubles if I could please you in any way." After these words he lay for a long time in a trance; upon awakening, he jumped up.

Palamon felt as if an icy sword had suddenly pierced his heart; he shook with anger and could wait in hiding no longer. After hearing Arcite's tale, he rushed from the thick bushes with a face as pale and set as a madman, and said, "Arcite, wicked false traitor, you who love the lady that causes all my pain and woe are now caught, you, my kinsman and sworn brother, as I have often called you in the past. You have made a fool of Duke Theseus by falsely changing your name! Either you or I must die. You shall not love my lady Emily, for I alone will love her. For I am Palamon, your mortal foe. And though I have no weapon here with me, since I just escaped by good luck from prison, I do not doubt that you must die or else give up your love for Emily. Choose which it shall be; you shall not escape!"

Arcite, when he had heard this speech and had recognized Palamon, with hatred in his heart drew his sword as fiercely as a lion, and said: "By God who sits above, if it were not that you are ill and crazed by love and also without any weapon, you would never leave this grove, for you would die by my hand. For I deny the promise and bond which you say I made you. Bear well in mind, great fool, that love is free; I will love her in spite of all your efforts! Since you are a brave knight and are willing to decide the right to her by battle, you now have my promise that I will come here without fail tomorrow, unknown to anyone, and that, as I am a knight, I will bring battle equipment for both of us. And you may choose the better equipment and leave me the worse. I will bring sufficient food and drink for you tonight, together with bedding. If you can kill me here in this wood and win the lady, you are welcome to her, for all of me."

Palamon answered, "I agree." Then they parted until the next day, each having pledged himself.

Oh, Cupid, lacking in all mercy! Oh, monarch, who will have no companion! It is truly said that love does not willingly recognize either authority or fellowship. Arcite and Palamon have seen that fact clearly.

Arcite rode immediately into town, and before daylight the next morning he secretly prepared two sets of equipment sufficient and fitting for the battle to be held in the fields between the two of them. Completely alone, mounted on his horse, he carried all this equipment. Then Palamon and Arcite met in the grove at the appointed time and place. Their complexions began to change, as is the case with the Thracian hunters who stand with spears at an opening in the forest when the lion or bear is hunted and hear the beast come rushing through the brush toward them, crushing boughs and twigs; then they think, "Here comes my deadly enemy! He or I must surely be killed. For I must kill him at the gap, or, if things go wrong, he will kill me." Such thoughts caused the two knights to change color as soon as they recognized each other.

There was no "good morning," no greeting at all; but at once without a word each began to help arm the other, as courteously as if they were brothers. And after that, they thrust at each other for an amazingly long time with sharp strong spears. You would have thought that Palamon as he fought was a crazed lion and Arcite a cruel tiger. They began to strike each other like wild boars which from insane anger cover themselves with white froth. They fought in blood up to the ankles, and I leave them fighting in this fashion. Now I shall tell you about Theseus.

Destiny, the great executor, which carries out all over the world the providence which God has foreseen, is so strong that no matter whether the world wishes a thing or not, that thing will occur on the appointed day, though it will not happen again in a thousand years. For, truly, our desires on earth, whether war, peace, hate, or love, are arranged by some heavenly vision.

I say this with respect to mighty Theseus, who was so fond of hunting the great stag in May that no day dawned that he was not dressed and ready to ride with hunter, horn, and hounds. He took such delight in hunting that his only joy and desire was to kill the stag. For, after Mars, he served Diana.

This particular day was clear, as I have said earlier, and Theseus was completely happy; he rode royally on the hunt with Hippolyta, the fair Queen, and Emily, all in green clothing. He took the shortest route to the nearby grove, in which men had told him that there was a stag. And he rode straight for a clearing which the stag was accustomed to traverse before crossing a brook in his flight. The Duke wished to have a try or two at him with the hounds which he had brought along.

When the Duke reached the clearing, he shaded his eyes from the glare and immediately saw Arcite and Palamon, who fought as fiercely as two boars. The bright swords swung back and forth so dreadfully that it seemed as if the lightest blow would have felled an oak. But he did not know who they were. The Duke struck spurs to his horse and in one jump was between the two, and pulled out his sword and shouted, "Stop! No more of this, upon threat of losing your head! By mighty Mars, whoever strikes another blow shall die at once. But tell me what manner of men you are who are so bold as to fight here just as if this were a royal tournament, though without a judge or other official."

Palamon hastily answered: "Sire, there is no need for explanations. We both deserve death. We are two woeful wretches, two prisoners tired of our own lives. And as you are a righteous lord and judge, show us no mercy or pity; just kill me first in holy charity! But also kill my companion as well as me, or kill him first, for though you don't know it, he is Arcite, your mortal enemy, who was banished on pain of death from your kingdom; therefore, he deserves death. For it was he who came to your house and said that he was named Philostrate. In this way he has tricked you for many years, and you have made him your chief squire; and this is the man who loves Emily. Since the day of my death has arrived, I hereby make full confession that I am the same poor Palamon who has wickedly broken out of your prison. I am your mortal enemy, and I love the fair Emily so dearly that I wish to die in her sight. Therefore, I ask my sentence and death; but kill my fellow in the same fashion, for we both deserve death."

The good Duke at once replied: "This decision is easily reached. By your own confession you have condemned yourself, and I shall remember it. There is no need to force your confession by torture. You shall die, by mighty Mars the red!"

At once the Queen, in feminine fashion, began to weep, and so did Emily and all the ladies in the company. It seemed a great pity to all of them that such a misfortune should occur. For these were two noble gentlemen, whose only quarrel was for love; and the women looked at their deep bloody wounds and cried, "Have mercy, lord, upon all us women!" They fell upon their bare knees as if to kiss Theseus' feet as he stood there, until at last his anger cooled, for pity comes easily into a tender heart. And though at first he quivered with anger, he had soon calmly considered their misdeeds and what had caused them. Although his wrath still forced him to consider them guilty, his reason excused them both. He thought: "Any man in love will surely help himself in any way he can, even to freeing himself from prison." Theseus was also moved by the women, for they continued to weep. His tender heart was soon touched, and he whispered softly to himself: "Fie upon a lord who has no mercy, but is like a lion both in word and deed, just as much toward a man who is repentant and fearful as toward one who is proud and contemptuous and continues his error. That lord has little discretion who can see no difference between such cases, but judges pride and humility similarly." Soon, when his anger had thus passed away, he looked up with shining eyes and vigorously spoke these words:

"The god of love, ah, bless him! How mighty and great a lord he is! No obstacles can stand against his might. He may be called a god because of his miracles, for he can make of any individual in his own way whatever he desires. Consider Arcite and Palamon, who were freed from my prison and who might have lived royally in Thebes; they knew that I was their mortal enemy and that their death lay within my power. And yet love has, in spite of their foresight, brought them here to die. Now, look, isn't that great folly? Is there any true fool except one in love? Look, for the sake of God who sits on high, how they bleed! Aren't they well decorated! In this way their lord, the god of love, has paid them their wages and their fees for their services! And yet those who serve love claim to be wise, whatever may happen. But here is the best joke of all: she who is the cause of this entertainment can thank them for it in the same manner as I. She knew no more of all this strange affair, by God, than did a cuckoo or a rabbit! But everything must be experienced, hot or cold; a man must be a fool, old or young—I learned that myself long ago, for in my time I have been love's servant. Therefore, since I know love's pain and how sorely it can trouble a man—as one who has been often caught in its snare —I completely forgive you your misdeeds, at the request of the Queen, who kneels here, and of Emily, my dear sister. You must both at once swear to me that you shall nevermore make war upon my country or me by day or night, but be my friends in every way. I forgive you completely." Then they swore fairly and well that which he had requested, assured him of their allegiance, and begged him for mercy. He granted them grace and said:

"Now to speak of royal families and riches. Each of you is certainly worthy to marry Emily when the time comes, though she were a queen or a princess. Nevertheless, I shall speak for my sister about whom you have this quarrel and jealousy. You yourselves know that she cannot marry two of you at once, although you were to fight forever. One of you, whether he likes it or not, must go whistle up a tree; that is to say, she cannot have both, no matter what jealousy or anger exists. Therefore, I propose to you that each of you shall accept his answer as it is destined for him in the following way. Listen to my plan for you.

"My plan is for a final decision from which there can be no appeal—if you like that idea, accept it for the best. Each of you shall go where he pleases freely without ransom or supervision, and fifty weeks from today, whether you are far or near, each of you shall return with a hundred knights properly armed for a tournament, ready to do battle for Emily. And I promise you without fail, upon my honor as a knight, that whichever one of you is more powerful—that is to say, whichever one, with his hundred knights whom I specified a while ago, can kill his opponent or drive him from the lists— to him whom Fortune favors I will give Emily as a wife. I shall prepare the lists here in this place, and God have pity on my soul unless I prove a fair and true judge. You shall not make other terms with me than that one of you must be dead or overcome. If this seems to you well planned, say so and consider yourselves pledged. This is your final judgment."

Who but Palamon appears happy now? Who but Arcite jumps up for joy? Who could tell or write about the joy that occurred in that place when Theseus had made so fair a proposal? Everyone present fell on his knees and thanked him with all his heart and might, and chief among them were the two Thebans. Thus with good hope and blithe spirits these two take their leave and ride home to Thebes, with its ancient wide walls. THE SECOND PART ENDS.

THE THIRD PART FOLLOWS: I think that my listeners would consider me negligent if I failed to tell of the arrangements Theseus made as he busily prepared the royal lists; it was such an impressive theater that I dare say that there was never another like it. It was a mile in circumference, with a stone wall and then a moat around it. The shape was circular, sixty yards high, with divisions like a compass, and there were tiered stands, so arranged that those who sat in one tier did not prevent those sitting in the tiers behind from seeing.

To the east there was a white marble gate, and opposite it to the west was a similar gate. In short, there was no other theater like this one in the world, for there was no man in the country who was skilled in geometry, mathematics, painting, or sculpture whom Theseus did not employ to work on his theater. And in order to observe the religious proprieties, he had an altar and an oratory made above the eastern gate for the worship of Venus, goddess of love. Above the western gate he had a similar expensive structure prepared in honor of Mars. And to the north he had a noble rich oratory of alabaster and coral built in a turret on the wall and consecrated to chaste Diana.

But I almost forgot to describe the magnificent sculpture and the paintings—their shape, appearance, and structure— which were in these three oratories.

First, in the temple of Venus you could see movingly depicted on the walls the interrupted sleep, the deep sighs, the bitter tears, the wailing, and the burning lust which the servants of love endure on earth. Also there were the solemn oaths which lovers swear; Pleasure and Hope; Desire; Folly; Beauty and Youth; Vulgarity; Wealth; Charm and Power; Lies; Flattery; Generosity; Gossip; and Jealousy, with a garland of yellow gold and a cuckoo perched on her hand. There were successively shown there feasts, musical instruments, carols, dances, lust, and costumes, and all the circumstances of love which I can or shall call to mind; in fact, there were more things represented on the walls than I can mention. Truly, the whole mountain of Mt. Cythera, Venus' principal home, was painted on the wall, with its garden and the sensuous scenery. Nor were Idleness, the porter; nor Narcissus, the fair one of ancient days; nor the folly of King Solomon; nor even the great strength of Hercules; nor the magic spells of Medea and Circe; nor the hardy courage of Turnus; nor the cowardly service of rich Croesus, forgotten. Therefore, you could see that neither wisdom nor wealth, beauty nor magic, strength nor courage, could rival Venus, who guides the world according to her desires. See, all these people were so caught in her snares that they very often

could only moan, "Alas!" Though I could illustrate this point
with a thousand examples, one or two will suffice here.

The glorious statue of Venus was naked, bathing in the
sea, covered by the bright green waves from the navel down.
She had a stringed instrument in her right hand and an at-
tractive garland of fresh and fragrant roses on her head;
doves flew about over her head. Her son Cupid stood in front
of her, with two wings upon his shoulders; he was blind, as
he is usually portrayed, and carried a bow and sharp, bright
arrows.

Why should I not tell you also about the paintings upon
the walls within the temple of the mighty Mars the red? The
wall was completely painted like the inside of that terrible
palace called the great temple of Mars in Thrace, in the cold
region where Mars had his chief home.

First, a forest was painted on the wall, uninhabited by man
or beast, with ancient, gnarled, knotty, barren trees and sharp,
hideous stumps, through which the wind rushed with great
noise, as if a storm would break every bough. And under the
slope of a hill stood the temple of Mars, the all-powerful,
wrought all of burnished steel. The entrance was long and
straight, frightening to behold. Such a great sound of rush-
ing wind came forth that it made the gate tremble. The
northern light shone in through the doors, for there was no
window through which any light appeared. The door was
made of everlasting stone, bound horizontally and vertically
with iron bars; in order to make the temple strong, each pil-
lar which supported the roof was like a large cask, of bright
and shining iron.

I saw in the temple, first, Felony with dark and wicked
plots; cruel Anger, red as any coal; the petty thief; also pale
Dread; the smiling villain with a knife beneath his coat; the
stable burning with black smoke; treasonable murder in the
bed; open warfare, with the wounded covered with blood;
Strife, with bloody knife and dangerous threats. That hor-
rible place was filled with confused cries. I even saw a man
there who had committed suicide—his hair was bathed in his
heart's blood; the nail driven into the temple by night—a cold

death, with gaping mouth exposed. In the center of the temple sat Misfortune, with an unpleasant and ugly face. Also I saw Insanity, laughing though angry; armed Complaint; Pursuit; and fierce Outrage; the carrion in the bushes with slit throat; a thousand dead, not by sickness; the tyrant with his prey gained by force; the sacked town with nothing left. In addition, I saw the dancing ships burning; a hunter strangled by wild bears; the sow eating the child right in the cradle; the cook scalded in spite of his long spoon. No one of the horrors associated with Mars was forgotten. The carter, overrun by his cart, lay crushed beneath its wheel. Among Mars' followers were also the barber-surgeon, the butcher, and the blacksmith who makes sharp swords on his anvil. And above the rest, depicted in a tower, I saw Conquest sitting in great honor, with a sharp sword hanging by a thread above his head. The murders of Caesar, great Nero, and Antony were portrayed; though at the time of our story they were not yet born, their future deaths were planned by Mars. In these paintings, it was shown as clearly as in the stars above who will be killed or else die for love. Let one example from ancient stories suffice. I could not retell them all, even if I wanted to.

The armed statue stood upon a chariot and looked as grim as if he were insane with anger. Above his head, two arrangements of stars shone, which are called in the book Puella and Rubeus—the god of war was presented this way. A wolf with glaring eyes, eating a man, stood between his legs. This scene was done with a subtle brush to enhance the glory of Mars.

Now for the temple of chaste Diana; as briefly as I can, I hasten to give you the description. Scenes of hunting and modest chastity covered all the walls. There I saw how sad Callisto was changed from a woman to a bear and afterwards became the North Star, because Diana was displeased with her. It was painted that way; there is no more for me to tell. Her son is also a star, as one may observe. There I saw Daphne turned into a tree—I do not mean the goddess Diana, but the daughter of Peneus who was called Daphne. There I saw Actaeon turned into a deer because he saw Diana naked; I saw how his hounds caught and ate him, not knowing who he was. A little farther along were scenes showing Atalanta hunting the wild boar, and Meleager, and many others to whom Diana brought trouble and woe. I saw there many other wonderful stories which I don't want to recite from memory.

Diana sat upright on a deer with small hounds about her. Beneath her was a moon, waxing but soon to wane. Her statue was clothed in light green, with a bow in hand and arrows in a case. Her eyes were downcast towards Pluto's dark region. A woman in labor was in front of Diana; so delayed was childbirth that the woman began piteously to call upon Lucina, saying, "Help, for you can help more than anyone!" The artist had represented this very realistically; he must have spent a great deal of money for his paints.

Now the lists have been completed and Theseus, who had spared no cost in preparing the temples and the theater, was highly pleased. But I shall leave Theseus for a while, and speak of Palamon and Arcite.

The day for their return drew near, when, with one hundred knights each, they must come to Athens for the tournament, as I told you earlier. Each of them, to keep his promise, brought the hundred knights correctly equipped for war to Athens. Truly, many observers believed that never since the world began, wherever on land or sea knighthood was customary, had there been so noble a group brought together. For every knight who loved chivalry and wished to increase his reputation had begged to take part in this tournament, and those who had been chosen were indeed proud. And you know very well that if tomorrow such a tournament were announced every powerful knight who represents a lady, in England or elsewhere, would be eager to be present to fight for his lady—ah, me, that would be a wonderful sight!

Just that sort were the many knights who came with Palamon. Some preferred to be armed in a habergeon, a breastplate, and a light head-covering; some wished a pair of large plates; some desired a Prussian shield or a targe; some preferred only strong leg-coverings and an ax; others wanted a steel mace—there is no new fashion which is not really old. They were armed, as I have told you, each according to his preference.

There you could see Lycurgus himself, the great King of Thrace, accompanying Palamon. His beard was black and his countenance manly. His eyes, of a color between yellow and red, shone from his head, and, with shaggy hair over his strong brows, he glanced about like a griffon. His legs were large, his muscles strong and hard, his shoulders broad, his arms long and round. After the custom of his country, he stood high in a chariot of gold drawn by four white bulls. Instead of a tunic over his armor, he wore the skin of an aged black bear with yellow talons bright as gold. His long hair was combed down his back; it shone as black as a raven's wing. He wore on his head a wreath of gold, as large as your arm, of great weight and set with fine rubies and diamonds. Around his chariot ran white hunting dogs, more than twenty, as large as bulls, for hunting lions or deer; their tightly fixed muzzles were gold-colored, with smoothly filed swivel rings. He had a hundred well-armed, stern, and brave lords in his retinue.

With Arcite—one learns from the stories—was the great Emetreus, King of India. He rode like Mars, the god of war, upon a bay horse with steel trappings, and he was dressed in a cloth of gold which had an attractive pattern. His outer tunic was of rich silk decorated with large white round pearls; his saddle was of gold, newly beaten and burnished. The mantle which fell from his shoulders was covered with red rubies sparkling like fire. His crisp, yellow, curly hair glittered like the sun, and his nose was well formed, his eyes light brown, his lips full, and his complexion florid. A few freckles, brownish-black in color, were sprinkled over his face. His glances seemed as fierce as a lion's. I judge he was twenty-five years old. His beard had begun to grow, and his voice was like a trumpet's thunder. Upon his head he wore a fresh green garland of laurel, and upon his hand for pleasure he carried a tame white eagle. He also had a hundred lords with him there, all fully armed, except for their heads, and

rich in all respects. For you can be sure that dukes, earls, and
kings had gathered in this noble company because of love and
desire for fame. All around Emetreus ran many a tame lion
and leopard. In this fashion these lords, one and all, came
to the city early on a Sunday morning and dismounted from
their horses.

Duke Theseus, the worthy knight, when he had led them
into his city and billeted them, each according to his rank,
gave them a banquet. He worked so hard to honor them and
to make them comfortable that people still say that no one at
all could have improved upon his arrangements.

Of the entertainment, the service at the banquet, the fine
gifts for great and small, the rich decoration of Theseus'
palace, who sat at the head of the table, what ladies were
the fairest or the best dancers, who could sing and dance
best, who spoke most feelingly of love, what sorts of hawks
sat on the perches, what types of hounds lay on the floor—of
all these things I make no mention, except to say that every-
thing seemed to me of the best. Now we come to the point;
listen if you will.

That Sunday night, before dawn, when Palamon heard the
lark sing (although there was still two hours before dawn, the
lark sang and Palamon also), he rose with a pious and hope-
ful heart to go on his pilgrimage to the temple of the blessed
Cytherea—I mean Venus, honorable and respected. During
the hour consecrated to her, he walked to her temple in the
theater, knelt down, and with troubled heart and humble
manner, he spoke as you shall hear:

"Fairest of the fair, oh, my lady Venus, daughter of Jove
and wife of Vulcan, you bright light of Mt. Cythera, for the
sake of the love you felt for Adonis take pity on my bitter
tears and heed my humble prayer. Alas! I have no words to
explain properly the torment of my hell; my heart cannot re-
veal my difficulties. I am so confused that I can only say,
'Mercy, fair lady, who knows well my thoughts and sees what
fears I experience!' Consider all these things and have pity
upon me, and henceforth I shall be your true servant to the
full extent of my ability and shall make war always against

chastity. That is my vow, so help me! I don't care about
boasting of military feats, nor do I ask to have the victory to-
morrow, or an increased reputation in this matter, or the vain-
glory of deeds of arms broadcast widely. But I do desire to
have full possession of Emily and to die in your service. You
determine the method and manner to accomplish this. I don't
care whether I or my opponents win the victory, so long as I
have my lady in my arms. For, although Mars is god of war,
your power is so great in heaven that if you so desire I shall
surely have my love. In your temple I will worship ever-
more, and whenever I travel I will make sacrifices and light
fires at your altar. And if you will not do this, my sweet lady,
then I pray you that Arcite shall pierce my heart with a spear
tomorrow. When I am dead, I shall not care at all whether
or not Arcite wins her for his wife. This is the point and the
conclusion of my prayer: Give me my love, you blessed dear
lady."

When Palamon completed this morning prayer, he immedi-
ately made dutiful sacrifices, carefully observing all the cere-
monies. I shall not tell all the details, but at last the statue
of Venus shook and made a sign whereby he understood
that his prayer was that day accepted. For though the sign
had been delayed, he knew that his request had been grant-
ed; and with a happy heart he went straight home.

About the third hour after Palamon went to Venus' temple,
the sun rose. Then Emily got out of bed and went to the
temple of Diana. Her maidens who accompanied her brought
the fire, the incense, the ceremonial robes, and all the things
necessary to the sacrifice. Not even the customary horns
filled with mead were lacking. While the richly decorated
temple was perfumed with sweet incense, Emily gaily washed
her body with well water. But I dare not tell the details of
this rite, though it would be enjoyable to hear it all. It would
not harm one who meant well, for it is good for a man to
speak freely. Her bright hair was unfastened and combed,
and a crown of evergreen oak was neatly set upon her head.
She kindled two fires on the altars and performed her rites as
men may read in Statius of Thebes and other old books.

When the fires were kindled, she spoke with a sad face to Diana as you may hear:

"Oh, chaste goddess of the green woods, to whom heaven, the earth, and the sea are visible, queen of the deep, dark realm of Pluto, goddess of maidens, for many years you have known my heart and my desire; keep me now from your wrath which Actaeon cruelly experienced. Chaste goddess, you know very well that I wish to be a maiden all my life; never do I want to be a mistress or a bride. You know that I am still a maid among your followers and that I love hunting, the chase, and walking in the wild forests better than being a wife and having children. I do not want to know the company of men. Now help me, lady, since you may and can, in the name of your triple deity. My only request to you is that you arrange peace and friendship between Palamon and Arcite, who bear me such great love, and turn their love away from me, so that all their lust, desire, trouble, and passion is quieted or turned in another direction. But if you will not do me this favor, and if my destiny is such that I absolutely must have one of the two, send me the one who most desires me. Behold, goddess of pure chastity, the bitter tears which fall upon my cheeks. Since you are a maid and the guardian of all maidens, guard and preserve my virginity, and as long as I live I will serve you as a maid."

The fires burned clearly upon the altar as Emily prayed, but suddenly she saw a strange breath of air quench one of the fires momentarily; that fire revived, but immediately afterwards the other fire was completely quenched. And as it went out, it whistled like wet wood when it burns, and from the end of the sticks of wood what looked like many bloody drops ran out. Emily was almost insane with fear at this and began to cry, for she did not know what this meant. She cried only because of the fear she felt, and wept in a manner pitiful to hear.

Then Diana appeared with her bow in hand, just like a huntress, and said, "Daughter, stop worrying. It has been affirmed among the gods on high and written in the eternal word that you shall be married to one of those who have suffered such troubles and woe because of you; but I cannot tell you which one of them. Farewell, I may not stay longer. The fires which burn on my altar will make known your future in love, as far as the present situation is concerned, before you go home." With these words the goddess vanished, her arrows ringing and clattering in their case.

Emily was amazed and said, "What does this mean, alas? I put myself wholly in your care and at your disposition, Diana." Then she immediately went home by the shortest route. This is the conclusion; there is no more to say.

At the next hour consecrated to Mars, Arcite walked to the temple of that fierce god to sacrifice with all the rites of pagan custom. With contrite heart and deep devotion he said his morning prayer directly to Mars:

"Oh, strong god, who is honored and respected in the cold realm of Thrace, who holds in his hands the reins of all warfare in every land and kingdom, and who gives good or evil fortune as he desires, accept from me my devout sacrifice. If my youth is deserving, if my skill is worthy to serve your godhead, and if I may be one of your followers, then I pray you to take pity upon my pain. Because of this pain, the same hot desire with which you once burned when you enjoyed the beauty of fair, fresh, young Venus and took her in your arms at will—although things once went wrong for you, when Vulcan caught you in his trap and found you sleeping with his wife, alas—because of the torment which was then in your heart, have some pity upon my pain. I am young and inexperienced, as you know, and, I believe, more wronged by love than anybody ever was: she for whom I suffer all this trouble doesn't care whether I sink or swim. And I am sure that before she will promise to be kind to me, I must win her by force in the tournament; and I know that without help and kindness from you my strength will not be sufficient. Therefore, help me, lord, tomorrow in my battle, for the sake of the desire which once burned within you, as well as for that which now burns within me, and arrange that I shall have the victory tomorrow. Mine will be the work, and yours will be the glory! I will honor your mighty temple more than any other place, and I will always work hard for your pleasure at your strong skills. In your temple I will hang my banner and the arms of all my company, and evermore until the day I die I will provide eternal fire before your altar. And also I will bind myself to the following vow: I will give you my beard and my hair which hangs long, neither of which has ever felt razor or scissors; and I will always be your true servant. Now, lord, take pity upon my dire sorrow. Give me the victory; that is all I ask of you."

When the prayer of Arcite the strong was ended, the rings hanging upon the temple doors and also the doors themselves began to clatter loudly, at which Arcite was somewhat awe-stricken. The fires burned so brightly upon the altar that all the temple was illuminated. A sweet smell at once rose from the ground, and Arcite immediately cast more incense into the fire and observed additional rites. Then at last the hauberk on the statue of Mars jingled, and Arcite heard a murmuring, low and faint, saying, "Victory!" For this, he gave the honor and glory to Mars, and with joy and optimism he soon went to his inn, as happy as a bird in the bright sun.

But because of the granting of Arcite's request, such quarreling immediately broke out in the heavens between Venus, goddess of love, and Mars, stern god of war, that Jupiter had to intervene. At last, pale, cold Saturn, who had been through so many adventures, drew from his great experience a plan which immediately pleased all sides. It is truly said that age has a great advantage; in age there is both wisdom and practical value. Men may outrun the aged, but not outwit them. At once Saturn, to stop this quarreling, found the remedy for the difficulty, though such peace-making was contrary to his nature. "My dear daughter Venus," said Saturn, "my authority, which extends so widely, is greater than anyone realizes. I have supervision over drowning in the pale sea; over prisoners in dark dungeons; over strangling and hanging by the throat; over workers' complaints and rebellions; over grumbling and secret poisoning. I carry out revenge and strict punishment while I am in the sign of the Lion. I cause the ruin of impressive buildings and the collapse of towers and

walls upon miners or carpenters. I slew Samson, who shook
the pillars. I bring about deadly maladies, dark treachery, and
devious plots. My glance is the father of pestilence. Now
don't cry any more; I will make sure that Palamon, who is
your own knight, shall have his lady as you have promised.
Even though Mars must aid his knight, nevertheless there
must be eventual peace between you two, who are now so far
from being of the same opinion that there is constant quarrel-
ing. I am your grandfather, ready to help you. Now stop cry-
ing; I will carry out your wishes."

Now I shall stop speaking of the gods, of Mars and of
Venus, goddess of love, and tell you as fully as I can about the
outcome, for which I began this story. THE THIRD PART ENDS.

THE FOURTH PART FOLLOWS: The feast in Athens that day
was magnificent, and also the fresh May season made every-
one so joyous that all that Monday there was jousting, danc-
ing, and serving of Venus. But because it was necessary to get
up early the next day to see the great tournament, everyone
went to bed early. Then, in the morning, at daybreak, there
was great noise and clatter of horses and equipment in all the
inns. And many groups of lords rode upon their horses to the
palace. There you could see rich and strange arrangements
of equipment, with skilled work of goldsmiths, embroidery,
and steelwork. There were bright shields, headpieces, and
trappings, golden helmets, hauberks, tunics, lords in fine robes
on their horses, knights in retinue, and also squires nailing the
spears and buckling helmets. There was adjusting of shields
with straps (whatever needed doing was done); foamy steeds
gnawing on their golden bridles; and armorers quickly mov-
ing back and forth with file and hammer; yeomen on foot;
and commoners with short staves thick as flies; pipes, trum-
pets, kettledrums, clarions, which make stirring sounds dur-
ing battle; the palace filled with people from top to bottom—

here three, there ten, debating and speculating about the two Theban knights. Some said one thing; others said, "It shall be so." Some agreed with the man with the black beard, some with the bald man, and some with the brawny shepherd. Some said he looked grim and would fight. "He has a battle-ax weighing twenty pounds." The hall was full of this kind of speculation long after the sun began to rise.

The great Theseus, who was awakened by music and the general noise, stayed in his rooms within the rich palace until the Theban knights, both equally honored, were shown into the palace. Duke Theseus sat in a window seat, dressed like a god on his throne. The people immediately crowded there to see him, to honor him, and also to listen to his commands and instructions. A herald on a scaffold sounded a note until the people were quieted, and then he announced the mighty Duke's wishes, when he saw that everybody was listening.

"The lord has decided with his usual excellent judgment that it would be a foolish waste of noble blood to fight as if in mortal battle in this tournament. Therefore, to avoid all deaths, he has modified his first plans. Consequently, no man, upon threat of death, may bring or send into the lists any sort of arrow, poleax, or short knife; nor may anyone draw or carry by his side a short sword with a sharp point. No man shall ride against his opponent more than once with a sharply ground spear; let him thrust, if he likes, while on foot to defend himself. And anyone who is captured shall not be slain, but led to a prisoner's stake planted on each side; but he must be brought there by force and shall remain there. And if it happens that the leader of either side is captured or his opposite slain, the tournament will be considered finished. God bless you! Go forth, and do your best! Fight your fill with long swords and maces. Go your way now; this is the Duke's desire."

The shouts of the people reached the heavens, so loudly did they say with merry voices, "God save a lord who is so good that he desires no deaths of noble knights!" The trumpets and bands played, and the company rode to the lists in good order through the great city decorated with cloth of gold rather than with serge.

In every respect like a lord, noble Theseus rode with the two Thebans, one on each side. Next came the Queen and Emily, and behind rode the other groups, one by one, according to their rank. They passed through the city this way and came in good time to the lists. It was not yet six o'clock when Theseus was seated in his splendid box, with Queen Hippolyta, Emily, and other ladies about him. The crowd pushed on toward their seats. Then from the west, through the gates beneath Mars' temple, Arcite entered with his red banner and his hundred supporting knights. At the same moment Palamon entered through the eastern gate, under Venus' temple, with a white banner and a defiant face. You could search the world over and never find two companies so equally matched at every point. For no one was wise enough to be able to say that either had the advantage in any respect over the other in bravery, or rank, or age, so equal had been the selection. Then they arranged themselves in two rows. When each knight's name had been called out, to see that no trickery was going on, the gates were shut and the cry rang out: "Do now your duty, young proud knights!"

The heralds stopped spurring up and down, and the trumpets and pipes sounded loudly. There is no more to say, except that on both sides spears went firmly into place, and sharp spurs were thrust into the horses' flanks. The time had come to see who could joust and who could ride. Spear shafts shattered on thick shields; one man felt the thrust through the breastbone. Spears shot twenty feet into the air; out came the swords bright as silver to hew and hack the helmets. Out rushed the blood in thick red streams; bones were crushed by mighty maces. One knight tried to thrust through the throng at its thickest; the strong horses stumbled, and down went everyone. One knight rolled underfoot like a ball; another, afoot, thrust with his sword; and one crashed to the ground with his horse. One man was wounded in the body, and then captured in spite of all he could do, and led to the prisoner's stake. At intervals Theseus arranged a rest period to refresh the knights, if they so desired. Many times the two Thebans came against each other, and each caused harm to the other. Each of them also unhorsed the other. No female tiger in Gargaphia, whose small cub had been stolen, was so vicious toward the hunter as jealous Arcite was toward Palamon. And there was no terrible lion in Benmarin, insane from hunger or from being chased, who desired blood as Palamon desired to kill his enemy Arcite. Their angry blows bit into their helmets, and the red blood of both ran out freely.

But all things must have an end. Before the sun had set, powerful King Emetreus attacked Palamon, who fought against Arcite, and his sword bit deeply into Palamon's flesh. Then Palamon was captured, held, and dragged to the prisoner's stake by twenty knights. In an effort to rescue Palamon, brave King Lycurgus was overcome, and King Emetreus, in spite of his power, was thrown a sword's length from his horse by a blow which Palamon gave him before his capture. But all was in vain; Palamon was taken to the stake. His brave heart was of no help to him, and he was compelled by force and also by the rules to stay there after his capture.

Who was so sorrowful as poor Palamon, who could not go back again into the fight? And when Theseus saw the situation, he called out to all the fighters: "Stop! no more; for the tournament is over! I will be a true judge and not partial. Arcite of Thebes shall have Emily; it has been his destiny to win her fairly." At once the crowd began to shout for joy, so long and loud that it seemed the lists must collapse.

Now what could fair Venus up in heaven do? What could she say? What did she do, the queen of love, but weep so bitterly because she had not had her way that her tears fell into the lists? She said, "I am thoroughly ashamed."

Saturn said, "Daughter, hold your peace! Mars had his way; his knight won the reward, but, by my head, you shall soon have some comfort."

The trumpets, the loud music, and the heralds who yelled and shouted loudly celebrated the success of Sir Arcite. But stop the noise a bit, and listen to my story of the great miracle which occurred before long.

Fierce Arcite had taken off his helmet and, in order to let the crowd see his face, he rode on a warhorse all around the large theater, looking up at Emily. And she glanced down at him in a friendly fashion (for women, generally speaking, allow their opinions to be formed by Fortune). Arcite was greatly delighted in his heart by this fact.

A terrible noise suddenly rose out of the ground, sent by Pluto at Saturn's request. At this, Arcite's horse reared from fright, leaped to one side, and stumbled as he leaped. Then before Arcite knew what had happened, he was thrown upon his head and lay there as if dying, with his chest crushed by the saddle. So much blood rushed into his face that he turned as black as a coal or a crow. At once he was sadly carried from the theater to Theseus' palace. There he was cut out of his armor, and quickly placed in a bed. He was in good spirits, for he was still alive and in possession of his senses, and he kept asking for Emily.

Duke Theseus, with all his retinue, came home to Athens in great happiness and pomp. In spite of the accident, he did not want to sadden the company. Also, the people said that Arcite would not die, but would be healed of his injury. And the knights were glad about another fact: that no one of them all was slain. But many were sorely wounded, especially one whose breastbone was pierced by a spear. Some had salves and charms for other wounds and for broken arms; they drank medicines and also mixtures of herbs, for they wished to recover their strength. The noble Duke, knowing their difficulties, comforted and honored everyone, as best he could, and made the visiting lords merry all night long, as was proper. No grudges were held, but everything was looked upon as a joust or tournament; and, truly, there were no hurt feelings. For one person unaided to have been unhorsed, captured by twenty knights, and dragged to the stake by the arms and feet, while yeomen and servants drove his horse away with sticks, should not be held a disgrace. No man may call that cowardice. Therefore Duke Theseus soon announced that all rancor and jealousy should stop; he praised the excellent feats of both sides, one exactly like the other, gave gifts according to rank, and held a feast for three full days. Then he formally accompanied the visiting kings one day's march out of his city, and every man went to his home by the shortest route. There was no more to be said except "Farewell; good day!" I shall speak no more of the tournament, but turn to Palamon and Arcite.

Arcite's breast swelled, and the pain from his injury increased more and more. The blood clots festered, in spite of all surgery, and polluted his body. Neither bloodletting nor medicinal herbs helped him, nor were the natural curative powers sufficient to throw off and expel the poison. His lungs began to swell, and every muscle below his chest was overcome by poison and infection. His recovery was not aided by either vomiting or movements resulting from laxatives. His body was torn apart; nature had no more power over it. And it is certain that where nature cannot work, good-by to medicine! Carry the man to the church! It was clear, therefore, that Arcite must die.

As a result, he sent for Emily and Palamon, his dear cousin, and spoke to them as you shall hear: "I am so sad at heart that I can in no way declare to you, my most beloved lady, the sorrow which I feel. Since I cannot live any longer, I swear that my spirit shall serve you above all other creatures. Alas, the great woe and the sharp pains that I have suffered on account of you for so long a time! Alas, my Emily! Death forces us to part company. Alas, queen and lady of my heart, my wife, dearest one of my existence! What is this world? What do men want? One minute a man is with his beloved, the next he is in his cold grave alone. Farewell, sweet one, my Emily! Now take me gently in your two arms, for the love of God, and listen to what I say.

"Because of my love for you and my jealousy, I have had strife and rancor with my cousin Palamon for many a day. Now may Jupiter wisely guide my soul so that I may speak of a lover properly and of all his true characteristics—that is, truth, honor, knighthood, wisdom, humility, position, noble birth, generosity, and all that pertains to greatness. As I hope Jupiter will have my soul, I do not now know in this world another so worthy to be loved as Palamon, who serves you and will do so all his life. If you ever decide to marry, do not forget Palamon, that noble man."

With these words his speech began to fail, for the cold hand of Death moved from his feet to his chest and overcame him; moreover, his arms lost all their vital strength. Even his feelings, which dwelt in his sick heart, began to fail when his heart felt Death. His two eyes darkened and his breathing stopped, but he still kept his eyes on Emily. His last words were "Mercy, Emily!" His spirit left his body and went away; since I was never there, I cannot say where it went. Therefore, I stop; I am no cleric. I find no account of souls in my book, and I have no desire to recount the opinions of those who claim to know the soul's destination. Arcite is cold; may Mars guide his soul to its rest! Now I shall speak about Emily.

Emily shrieked and Palamon cried. Theseus at once bore his fainting sister away from the corpse. What help would it be to spend the day telling you how she wept morning and evening? For in such cases women have so much sorrow when their husbands leave them that usually they grieve in this fashion, or else they sicken and finally must die.

Infinite were the sorrow and the tears of the old and young people throughout Athens over the death of this Theban. Men and children wept for him. Certainly, there was not so much weeping when Hector was brought freshly slain to Troy. Alas, the grief that was felt: scratching of cheeks and also tearing of hair. "Why did you have to die," cried the women, "when you had gold enough and also Emily?"

No man could cheer up Theseus except his old father Aegeus, who knew the transitory quality of this world; for he had seen it change up and down, from woe to joy and back to woe again, and he gave them illustrations of this fact.

"Just as no man ever died," said Aegeus, "who had not to some extent lived on earth, so no man ever lived in this world who is not at some time destined to die. This world is only a thoroughfare filled with woe, and we are pilgrims who pass back and forth. Death puts an end to every earthly care." And in addition he said much more in the same vein, wisely trying to urge the people to be comforted.

Duke Theseus, in spite of his many duties, concerned himself with the question of where the tomb of brave Arcite might best be placed in order to do him the greatest honor. And at last he concluded that at the same spot in the sweet, green grove on which Arcite and Palamon had fought because of love, and where Arcite had felt the desires, torment, and the hot fire of love, he would build a fire with which he might accomplish all the ceremonies of the funeral. He at once commanded that the old oaks be cut down and laid all in a row in well-arranged piles for burning. His officers ran with swift feet to carry out his commands. Then Theseus sent for a bier and spread a cloth of gold over it, the richest that he had. In similar cloth he clothed Arcite, with white gloves on his hands, a crown of green laurel on his head, and a bright keen sword in his hand. He placed him with his face uncovered upon the bier and wept pitifully. In order that all the people could see Arcite, Theseus carried him at daybreak into the hall, which resounded with the weeping.

Then the woeful Theban, Palamon, came with ragged beard and shaggy hair sprinkled with ashes, in black clothing spotted with tears; and Emily was there, weeping more bitterly than all the others, the saddest of the group. In order that the funeral service might be noble and rich, befitting Arcite's rank, Duke Theseus had three large white warhorses led forth, glittering with steel trappings and bearing Sir Arcite's arms and equipment. The rider of one of these horses bore Arcite's shield; another held his spear upright; the third carried his Turkish bow (the case and also the decorations were of burnished gold). The funeral party rode sorrowfully toward the grove, as you shall hear. The noblest of the Greeks then carried the bier on their shoulders, with slow steps and eyes red and wet, through the main street of the city, the length of which was covered with a deep black carpet so that the street was completely hidden. On the right walked old

Aegeus, and on the other side Duke Theseus, who each carried golden vessels full of honey, milk, blood, and wine. Palamon was also there, among other notable company, and behind the bier walked sad Emily, with a torch in her hand, as was the custom then, to perform the ceremonies of the funeral service.

Great pomp and ceremony were observed at the funeral and at the making of the great fire, from which the flames sprang up toward the heavens. The logs were so broad that the fire extended forty yards. Many loads of straw formed the first layer. But how the succeeding layers for the fire were laid; and also the names of the trees used, whether oak, fir, birch, aspen, alder, evergreen, poplar, willow, elm, plane, ash, box, chestnut, linden, laurel, maple, thorn, beech, hazel, yew, or dogwood, and how these trees were cut—these things I shall not tell. Nor shall I relate how the gods of the forest— nymphs, fauns, and dryads—ran up and down, deprived of the homes in which they had long dwelt in peace and quiet; nor how the frightened beasts and all the birds fled when the trees were felled; nor how the ground, which was not accustomed to seeing even sunlight, was frightened by the firelight; nor how the fire was first bedded in straw, then divided into three parts, first with dry sticks and then with green wood, spices, gold cloth, gems, garlands of flowers, and sweet-scented myrrh and incense; nor how Arcite lay in the center of all this; nor how rich were the articles surrounding him; nor how Emily, as was then customary, lit the fire for the service; nor how she fainted as the fire was built up; nor how she spoke her feelings; nor what jewels men threw into the fire when it burned satisfactorily; nor how some cast their shields, their spears, their clothing which they wore, and cups full of wine, milk, and blood into the fire, which burned insanely; nor how a huge crowd of Greeks rode three times all around the fire counterclockwise with a great shouting, and three times with their spears rattling; nor how the ladies wept three times in succession; nor how Emily was led homeward; nor how Arcite burned to cold ashes; nor how the wake was held all that night; nor how the Greeks conducted the funeral games. I do not care to tell who was best at wrestling with a greased body, nor who managed to avoid all difficulties. I shall not tell how they went home to Athens when the games were over, but I shall soon come to the point and put an end to my long tale.

With the normal passing of the years, all mourning and weeping was discontinued by unanimous agreement among the Greeks. Then, I think, a parliament was held in Athens to discuss certain questions. Among the questions raised was the formation of alliances with certain countries, and the supervision of conquered Thebes. Therefore, noble Theseus at once sent for Palamon, who came in haste without knowing why, sadly dressed in black. Then Theseus sent for Emily. When these two were seated and the parliament was quiet, Theseus waited a short time before speaking his words of wisdom; then, as usual, he closed his eyes, sighed deeply, and with a grave face gave voice to his opinion:

"Our first creator brought into being the beautiful chain of love, with a high purpose and intention. He knew well why he did this and what he hoped to accomplish, for with that fair chain of love he placed within bounds, so that they might not flee, fire, air, water, and land. This same prince and creator," he said, "has allotted to each person and thing created on this wretched earth a certain length of days beyond which they may not go, though they may shorten their time. One needs no authority to prove this fact, for it is evident from experience; yet I wish to express my opinion. Now men can see from this arrangement that this creator is stable and eternal. A man may know surely, unless he is a fool, that every part is derived from its whole. Thus, nature did not begin from any divided thing but from a perfectly unified whole, and descended in scale until it became mortal. And, therefore, by his wise providence he has so well ordered the progress of the various species that they shall truly endure by successive generations and not eternally. You can see and understand this point at a glance.

"Behold the oak; it has an extended growth and long life from the time it first begins to sprout; yet in the end it dies.

"Consider also how the hard stone beneath our feet, upon which we constantly tread and walk, wears away by the roadside. The broad river sometimes dries up; we can observe the great towns pass away. From this you can see that all things come to an end.

"When we consider man and woman, we see that either in youth or old age one must die, the king as well as the page. Some die in bed, some in the deep sea, some in the large fields in the sight of others. There is no avoiding it; all go the same way. Therefore, I can say that everything dies.

"What true explanation is there for this situation except that Jupiter, the king and creator of all things, thereby converts all to that substance from which it was derived? And it will not avail any creature alive, no matter what his rank, to argue against this fact.

"Thus it is wisdom, it seems to me, to make a virtue of necessity and accept that which we may not avoid, especially that which comes to us all. And whoever grumbles is foolish and a rebel against the creator, who directs everything. Certainly a man who dies in the flower of his excellence, when he is sure of his good name, has the greatest honor; then he brings no shame upon himself or upon his friend. Therefore, his friend should be happier that he died in such circumstances than if he had died when his name had grown pale with age and his accomplishments were all forgotten. Thus it is best, from the point of view of fame, to die when one's name is best known.

"To hold any other view but this one is willfulness. Why do we grumble and feel sad because brave Arcite, the flower of chivalry, has left the foul prison of this life with duty and honor? Why do his wife and cousin who loved him well mourn over him? Can he thank them? No, God knows, not a bit. They offend both his soul and themselves; yet they cannot better their lot.

"What conclusion is there for my long discourse except that I urge that we leave our woe and be merry, and thank Jupiter for all his kindness? And before we leave here, let me urge that from two sorrows we derive one perfect and everlasting joy. Consider now where there is the greatest sorrow; there we must begin to make amends.

"Sister," he said, "here is my decision, reached with the advice of my parliament: that you take pity upon brave Palamon, your own knight, who has served you with his will, heart, and power ever since you first knew him, and accept him as your lord and husband. Give me your hand, for this is our decision. Let's now see your feminine mercy. He is indeed the son of a brother to a king, but even though he were a poor squire, the trouble which he has suffered for so many years in your service would deserve your consideration, believe me. For true pity should go beyond mere justice."

Then Theseus spoke to Palamon: "I do not think I need give you a lengthy sermon in order to win your assent to this suggestion. Draw near, and take your lady by the hand."

At once the bond of matrimony was made between them by the assembled council and barons, and Palamon married Emily in all happiness and harmony. God, who wrought this wide world, sent love to the man who had so dearly paid for it, for Palamon was in all ways content, living in happiness, in wealth, and in health. Emily loved him so dearly, and he served her so courteously, that there was never any word of jealousy or any other difficulty between them.

Thus end Palamon and Emily. May God save all this fair company! Amen. HERE ENDS THE KNIGHT'S TALE.

THE MILLER

HERE FOLLOW THE WORDS BETWEEN THE HOST AND THE MILLER: When the Knight had finished his tale there was nobody in the whole company, young or old, who did not say it was a noble story, worth remembering, and every one of the gentlefolk thought so particularly. Our Host laughed and swore: "As I hope to prosper, things are going well; the bag is open. Now let's see who will tell the next tale, for, certainly, this game is off to a fine start. Now, Sir Monk, you tell a tale, if you know something to match the Knight's."

The Miller, who was so drunk that he had turned white, could scarcely sit on his horse; he wouldn't take off his hood or hat, nor act politely toward anyone. But in Pilate's voice he shouted and swore: "By the arms, the blood, and the bones of Christ, I know a noble story for this occasion, with which I'll match the Knight's."

Our Host saw that he was drunk on ale and said: "Wait, Robin, my dear brother; let some better man tell us a story first. Wait, and let's proceed sensibly."

"By God's soul," said the Miller, "I will not. I will speak or else go my own way."

Our Host answered: "Tell away, to the devil with you! You're a fool; drink has got the better of you."

"Now listen," said the Miller, "one and all! First, I want to declare that I am drunk; I know it from the noise I'm making. And, therefore, if I speak improperly, blame it on the ale of Southwark, I beg you. I shall tell a legend of a carpenter and his wife, and of how a cleric made a fool of the carpenter."

The Reeve spoke up and said: "Stop your chattering! Stop your ignorant, drunken vulgarity. It is a sin and great folly besides to speak ill of any man or defame him, or to bring wives into such gossip. There are enough other things you can tell about."

The drunken Miller at once replied: "Dear brother Oswald, whoever has no wife is not a cuckold. But I do not therefore say that you are one. There are a great many good wives, always a thousand good ones to one bad; you know that yourself, unless you are crazy. Why are you already angry at my tale? I have a wife, by God, as well as you; yet I would not, for the oxen which pull my plow, take on trouble by deciding that I am a cuckold; I will believe that I'm not one. A husband should not be inquisitive about God's secrets or his wife's. So long as he finds God's plenty there, he should not ask questions about the rest."

Why should I say any more than that this Miller would not yield to any man, but told his vulgar story in his own way. I regret to retell it here. And therefore, I ask every well-brought-up person, for God's love, not to consider that I speak with evil intention, but that I must recount all their tales, good or bad, or else falsify my material. Whoever doesn't want to hear it, therefore, can turn over the page and choose another. For he will find plenty of stories, long and short, which deal with courtesy, morality, and holiness. Don't blame me if you choose poorly. The Miller is a low fellow; you know that very well. So are the Reeve and many others, and both of them told vulgar stories. Think about this, and don't blame me. And also one must not make the game too serious.

HERE BEGINS THE MILLER'S TALE: Once upon a time there lived at Oxford a rich fellow, a carpenter by trade, who took boarders into his home. A poor scholar, who had studied the liberal arts but whose inclination was wholly toward learning astrology, boarded with him. This scholar knew how to work out a number of problems: he could give an answer if men asked him at certain times whether there should be drought or showers, or what would happen in any given situation; I cannot recount each one.

This cleric was called clever Nicholas. He knew about secret love affairs and pleasure, in which he was most sly and cautious, appearing to be as meek as a maiden. He had a room all to himself in that boardinghouse, neatly decorated with sweet herbs, and he himself smelled as sweet as licorice root or ginger. His *Almageste,* his other books large and small, his astrolabe, which was part of his astrological equipment, and his counters for calculations, were all neatly arranged on shelves at the head of his bed. His closet was covered in heavy red cloth, and above it lay a gay psaltery on which he played at night so sweetly that the whole room rang. He sang *Angelus ad virginem* and, after that, the "King's Note." His merry voice was often praised. And so this sweet cleric spent his time, living upon his own income supplemented by borrowing from his friends.

The carpenter had just married a girl whom he loved better than his life. She was eighteen years old. He was jealous and kept close watch upon her, for she was wild and young, while he was old and thought himself likely to be cuckolded. Being ignorant, he did not know of Cato's advice that a man should marry a woman similar to him. Men should wed their contemporaries, for youth and age are often at odds. But since he had fallen into the trap, he had to bear his burden like other people.

The young wife was pretty, with a body as neat and graceful as a weasel. She wore a checked silk belt, and around her loins a flounced apron as white as fresh milk. Her smock was white also, embroidered in front and in back, inside and outside and around the collar, with coal-black silk. The strings of her white hood were of the same material as her collar; her hair was bound with a wide ribbon of silk set high on her head. And, truly, she had a wanton eye. Her eyebrows were plucked thin and were arched and black as any sloe. She was even more delightful to look at than a young, early-ripe pear tree, and she was softer than lamb's wool. A leather purse, with a silk tassel and metal ornaments, hung from her belt. In all the world there is no man so wise that, though he looked far and near, he could imagine so gay a darling or such a wench. Her coloring was brighter than that of a coin newly forged in the Tower, and her singing was as loud and lively as a swallow's sitting on a barn. In addition, she could skip about and play like any kid or calf following its mother. Her mouth was as sweet as honey or mead, or a pile of apples laid up in hay or heather. She was as skittish as a young colt, and tall and straight as a mast or wand. On her low collar she wore a brooch as broad as the boss on a shield. Her shoes were laced high on her legs. She was a primrose, a trillium, fit to grace the bed of any lord or to marry any good yeoman.

Now, sir, and again, sir, one day it happened that clever Nicholas began to tease and flirt with this young wife while her husband was at Oseney (for clerics are subtle and sly), and he slipped his hand intimately between her legs, and said: "Surely, unless I can fulfill my burning desire for you,

sweetheart, I will die." Then he grasped her roughly by the
hips and said: "Sweetheart, make love with me right now or
I will die, God save me!"

She sprang aside like a colt in the traces, quickly turned
her face away, and said: "I will not kiss you, by my faith!
Stop; let me alone, Nicholas, or I will call out for help. Take
your hands away! Where are your manners!"

Then Nicholas began to beg for mercy, and spoke so win-
ningly and offered himself so eagerly that she at last granted
his wish and swore by St. Thomas of Kent that she would do
his will as soon as she saw her opportunity. "My husband is
so jealous that unless you wait patiently and secretly I know
that I am as good as dead," said she. "You must be extremely
secretive about this matter."

"No, don't worry about that," said Nicholas. "A cleric has
surely spent his time badly if he cannot outwit a carpenter."
In this way they reached an agreement and swore to wait for
their chance, as I told you.

When Nicholas had for some time stroked her body, he
kissed her gently. Then he took down his psaltery and joy-
ously played many melodies.

It happened on a holy day that this good wife went to
worship Christ at the parish church. She had washed herself
so carefully after she had finished her work that her forehead
shone as clear as day. Now there was at that church a parish
clerk who was named Absalom. His curly hair shone like
gold; it was spread out like a large fan and parted straight
and evenly down the center. He had red cheeks and eyes as
blue as a goose, and he walked daintily in shoes of an open-
work design, like a window of St. Paul's. He was clothed
trimly and correctly in red stockings and a coat of light blue,
adorned with numerous handsome laces, and over this he
had a surplice as white as a blossom on a twig. He was a
gay young fellow, God save me, and knew how to let blood,
to clip and shave a beard, and to draw up a charter or a
quittance for land. He could dance in twenty different ways
after the Oxford manner, casting his legs to and fro, and

play songs on a small fiddle, sometimes singing an accompaniment in a loud, high treble. And he could play just as well on a guitar. There was not an alehouse or tavern in the whole town, where any gay barmaid worked, which he had not visited for his amusement. But, to tell the truth, he was rather squeamish about breaking wind and a bit fastidious in his speech.

On this particular holy day, gay, jolly Absalom passed among the wives of the parish with a censer, burning incense as he went by. And he cast many a longing look upon the wives, but chiefly upon the carpenter's wife. He could think of no greater pleasure than to gaze at her, she was so fair, so sweet, and so flirtatious. I dare say that if she had been a mouse and he a cat, he would have pounced on her at once. This parish clerk, this gay Absalom, had such a love-longing in his heart that he would accept no money from any of the wives; he said that his courtesy prevented him.

That night the moon shone brightly and Absalom took his guitar and went forth, gay and amorous, expecting to find a woman to sleep with. Shortly after cock-crow he came to the carpenter's house and took his stand below a window set in the wall.

He sang, gently and softly, "Now, dear lady, if it is your wish, I beg you to take pity on me," accompanying himself pleasantly on his guitar.

The carpenter awoke and, hearing the singing, at once said to his wife: "What! Alison, don't you hear Absalom, singing under our bedroom wall?"

Thereupon she answered her husband: "Yes, God knows, John, I hear the whole thing."

This went on; what can one wish for better than well enough? Day by day jolly Absalom wooed her until he became completely woebegone. He could not sleep, night or day; he combed his flowing hair and dressed elegantly; he wooed her by go-betweens and messengers and swore that he would serve as her page; he sang, faltering like a nightingale; he sent her sweet wine, mead, spiced ale, and cakes, piping hot from the oven; and, since she was city-bred, he offered her money. For some people are won by rich gifts, others by blows, and still others by courtesy.

Once, in order to show his gaiety and versatility, he acted the role of Herod upon a high stage. But what good could it do him in this case? Alison loved clever Nicholas so much that Absalom could go blow his horn elsewhere; he got only scorn for his efforts. Indeed, she made a monkey of Absalom, and turned all his seriousness into a joke. This proverb, so frequently heard, is surely true: "Always the sly one near by causes the one far away to be loathed." For no matter how insane or angry Absalom got, because he was far from her sight the nearby Nicholas overshadowed him. Now, make the most of your chances, you clever Nicholas, for Absalom must wail and cry "Alas."

So it happened one Saturday that the carpenter went to Oseney, and Alison and Nicholas agreed that Nicholas should prepare a trick to deceive the poor jealous husband. Then, if all went well, she would sleep in his arms all night, for this was what they both wanted. Nicholas needed no further urging, but immediately put the plan into action. He quietly took food and drink for a day or two up to his room and instructed her to tell her husband, if he asked about him, that she did not know where he was and that she had not laid eyes on him all day; but that she thought he must be sick, because he would not give any answer to the calls of the servant girl.

This went on all that Saturday; Nicholas remained quietly in his room, eating, sleeping, or doing what he liked, until Sunday at sunset. The stupid carpenter was greatly astonished by this and wondered what might be ailing Nicholas. He said: "I'm afraid, by St. Thomas, that things go badly with Nicholas. God forbid that he should die suddenly! This is surely a ticklish world now. Today I saw a corpse carried to church, and last Monday I saw that very man at work. Go upstairs," he said to his houseboy. "Call at the door, or knock with a stone. See what's happening and tell me frankly."

The boy clumped up the stairs and, standing outside the door, he called and knocked like a madman: "What! Ho! What are you doing, Master Nick? How can you sleep all day long?"

But all was in vain, for not a word did he hear. The boy found a hole low down in the door, through which the cat was accustomed to creep. And through this hole he peeped into the room until at last he caught sight of Nicholas. He was sitting gaping steadily upward as if he were gazing at the new moon. Down the boy ran and at once told his master in what state he had seen this Nicholas.

The carpenter began to bless himself and said: "Help us, St. Frideswide! A man little knows what shall happen to him. Nicholas has fallen into some insanity or trance because of his astrology. I always thought this would happen! Men should not pry into God's secrets; yea, ever blessed is the ignorant man who knows only his creed! It happened like this to another cleric who practiced astrology. He walked in the fields in order to determine future events by gazing at the stars, and he fell into a fertilizer pit; he didn't see that. And yet, by St. Thomas, I'm very sorry about friend Nicholas. I shall scold him about his studies, if I can, by Jesus, King of Heaven! Go get me a strong stick so that I can pry up the door while you push, Robin. He'll come out of his studying, I'll bet."

Then he began to get busy with the door to Nicholas' room. The houseboy was unusually strong, and he pushed so hard that the door soon came off its hinges and fell on the floor. Nicholas sat there as still as a stone, steadily gaping up into the air.

The carpenter thought Nicholas was crazy, and grabbed him firmly by the shoulders, shook him mightily, and cried out: "What! Nick, what, ho! what, look down! Wake up and think about Christ's sufferings! I will cross you against the spells of elves and spooks." With that he recited the magic night-spell at each of the four corners of the house and at the threshold of the door:

Jesus Christ and St. Benedite,
Bless this house from each evil wight;
For the night-hag, the white paternoster!
Where did you go, St. Peter's soster?

At last clever Nicholas began to sigh deeply and said: "Alas, shall all the world be now once more destroyed?"

"What did you say?" the carpenter answered. "What! Have faith in God, as we men who work do."

Nicholas answered, "Bring me a drink, and afterwards I shall speak in private of a certain thing which concerns you and me. I certainly will not tell it to any other man."

The carpenter went downstairs and returned with a large jug of strong ale. When each of them had drunk his share, Nicholas closed the door tightly and sat down beside the carpenter.

He said, "John, my kind and dear landlord, you must swear to me here upon your honor that you shall not give away this secret to any man; for this is Christ's secret that I shall reveal, and if you tell it to anyone, you are doomed. If you betray me, your punishment shall be to go insane."

"Nay, Christ forbid that, by His holy blood!" said this simple man. "I am no blabber; no, though I say it myself, I don't like to gossip. Say what you will; I won't ever repeat it to woman or child, by Him that harrowed hell!"

"Now, John," said Nicholas, "I will not lie; I have found in my astrology, by looking at the bright moon, that next Monday night at nine o'clock there shall fall a rain so wild and furious that Noah's flood was not half so large. This world," he said, "shall be inundated in less than an hour, so terrible will be the downpour. Thus everyone shall drown and die."

The carpenter answered, "Alas, my wife! And shall she drown? Alas, my Alison!" Overcome by this, he almost collapsed. "Is there no way out?" he asked.

"Why, yes, before God," said clever Nicholas, "if you will be guided by learning and advice. You must not act upon your own ideas, for, as Solomon truly says, 'Follow advice and you will not be sorry.' And if you wish to follow good advice, I guarantee that without mast or sail I will save Alison, you, and myself. Haven't you heard how Noah was saved when our Lord warned him ahead of time that all the world would be destroyed by water?"

"Yes," said the carpenter, "a long time ago."

"Have you not heard also," said Nicholas, "about the troubles Noah and his companions had before they could get his wife aboard the ship? I'll guarantee that then Noah would have given all his black sheep for his wife to have had a ship all to herself. And so do you know what must be done? This problem demands speed, and, where speed is necessary, one cannot waste time talking.

"Go at once and bring here quickly a kneading trough or a barrel for each of us, but be sure that they are large enough for us to float on, as if on a barge. Put enough food in each for one day only—don't worry about anything else! The water will recede and go away about nine o'clock the next morning. But Robin, your houseboy, must not know about this, nor may I save Jill, your maid; don't ask why, for even though you ask me, I will not tell God's secrets. It should be enough for you, unless you are insane, to have the same good fortune Noah had. I shall save your wife, without doubt. On your way now, and make haste.

"But when you have found the three kneading tubs for the three of us, then you must hang them high up under the roof, so that no one will spy upon our arrangements. And when you have done as I have said and have placed the food safely in the tubs, together with an ax with which we can cut the cords to free the tubs when the water rises, and when you have also cut an opening high in the gable over the shed facing the garden, so that we may go forth easily on our way when the great flood has passed, then you shall be ready to float as merrily, I swear, as a white duck following her drake. Then I shall call, 'How goes it, Alison? and you, John? Be merry, for the flood will soon pass.' And you will answer, 'Hail, Master Nick! Good morning, I see you clearly for it is day.' Then for the rest of our lives we shall be lords of the world, like Noah and his wife.

"But about one thing, however, I strictly warn you: be very sure that on the night we go aboard ship none of us speaks a single word, or calls, or cries out, except in prayer; for that is God's own particular command. Your wife and you must hang far apart, so that there will be no carnality between you, no more in look than in act. This rule is strict. Go, God speed you! Tomorrow night, when all men are asleep, we shall creep into our kneading tubs and sit there awaiting God's mercy. Go on your way now; I have no more time to talk longer about this. Men say, 'Send the wise man forth and say nothing.' You are so wise, you require no instruction. Go, save our lives, I beseech you."

The simple carpenter went on his way, with many an "Alas," and "Woe unto us," and told his secret to his wife. She was fully aware, far better than he, of what all these strange doings meant. Nevertheless, she acted as if she would die and said: "Alas! Go about your business at once; help us to escape or we will all be dead! I am your own true wedded wife; go, dear husband, and help save our lives."

See what a great thing feeling is! Men can die of imagination, so deep may impressions be made upon them. This stupid carpenter began to shake; it seemed to him that he actually saw Noah's flood come surging in like the sea to drown Alison, his honey-dear. He wept, wailed, and grieved sorely; he sighed many a deep sigh; he went and got a kneading trough, then a barrel, and then a tub. And secretly he had them delivered at his house, where he hung them from the roof. With his own hand he made three ladders for climbing up to the tubs hanging from the rafters; then he put in the food—bread, cheese, and good ale in a jug, enough for one day. But before he did any of these things, he sent Robin and Jill away to London upon an errand. Then on Monday, as night approached, he closed his door and, lighting no candle, prepared everything as it should be. All three shortly climbed up and sat quietly each some distance from the other.

"Now, say a paternoster, and then keep mum!" said Nick; and "Mum," said John; and "Mum," said Alison. The carpenter said his prayers and sat still, waiting to hear the rain-drops.

The sleep of the dead, from weariness caused by his recent labors, overcame the carpenter just about curfew time, I guess, or a bit later. Because of a troubled spirit he groaned pitifully, and frequently he snored, for his head was in an uncomfortable position. Down his ladder crept Nick, and Alison slipped quietly down hers. Without wasting words they went into the same bed in which the carpenter usually slept. Then there was great sport and merriment! They lay there in mirth and pleasure until the bell rang for early morning services and the friars began to sing in the chancel.

The parish clerk, amorous Absalom, who was still woebe-gone with love for Alison, had been that Monday to Oseney with a group of people, merrymaking and having fun, and had secretly asked a cloisterer there about John, the carpenter. The cloisterer drew Absalom aside out of the church and said, "I don't know; I haven't seen him here at work since Saturday. I think he has gone for timber to a place our abbot sent him. For it is his habit to go for timber and to stay at the barn a day or two. Otherwise, he is surely at his house. But I can't tell you exactly where he is."

Absalom was gay and lighthearted, and thought, "Now is the time to stay up all night, for truly I haven't seen John stirring around in his yard since daybreak. As I hope to thrive, I shall knock very quietly tonight at the low window in his bedroom wall. I shall now tell all my love-longing to Alison, for at least I can't miss kissing her. I swear I ought to get something out of it. All day long my mouth has itched, and that is a sign of kissing, at least. Also, I dreamt all night that I was at a banquet. Therefore, I shall go sleep for an hour or two, and then I shall stay awake all night and have fun."

About midnight this jolly lover Absalom got up quickly and dressed himself in all his finery. But, first, before he combed his hair, he chewed grain and licorice in order to smell sweet. Under his tongue he put a true-love talisman, hoping to be lucky. He then went to the carpenter's house and stood quietly

by the low window which reached only up to his chest.
Softly he coughed under his breath: "What are you doing,
honeycomb, sweet Alison, my fair bird, my sweet cinnamon?
Awake, my love, and speak to me! You don't care about my
troubles, but for love of you I sweat wherever I go. It's no
wonder that I burn and sweat; I cry like a lamb for the teat.
Indeed, sweetheart, I am so lovelorn for you that my mourn-
ing is like a turtledove's. I cannot eat any more than a girl."

"Get away from the window, you Jack-fool," she said. "So
help me God, it won't be 'come kiss me.' I love another better
than you, by Jesus, Absalom; I would be a fool if I didn't.
Go away and let me sleep, or I'll throw a stone, as sure as
the devil!"

"Alas," said Absalom, "woe and wellaway! That true love
should ever be so evilly repaid! At least kiss me, since it can
be no better, for love of Jesus and for love of me."

"Will you go away immediately, then?" she asked.

"Yes, certainly, love," said Absalom.

"Then, get ready," she said. "I will come at once." And
she whispered to Nicholas, "Now be quiet, and you shall
laugh your fill."

Absalom got down on his knees and said: "At any rate I
am fortunate, for from this kiss I hope more will come. Love,
give me your favor; sweet bird, be kind to me!"

She opened the window hastily. "Be quiet," she said, "stop
talking and hurry, lest the neighbors see you."

Absalom wiped his lips dry. The night was dark as pitch,
as black as coal, and she thrust her ass out the window.
Absalom, knowing no better, kissed it enthusiastically before
he realized the trick. He jumped back and thought some-
thing was wrong, for he knew very well that a woman has
no beard. He felt something rough and hairy, and said, "Fie,
what have I done?"

"Teehee!" she said, and slammed the window shut.
Absalom had come to a sorry pass.

"A beard, a beard!" shouted clever Nicholas. "By God's
body, this goes merrily and well."

Poor Absalom heard all of this and began to bite his lip in anger. He said to himself, "I'll get even with you."

Who now scrubbed his lips with dirt, with sand, with straw, with cloth, with bark? Who but Absalom, who kept repeating, "Alas, may Satan take my soul if I wouldn't rather have revenge for that insult than own this whole town. Alas," he said, "that I did not turn away!" His hot love was now cooled and extinguished, for from the time he had kissed her ass he did not care for lovemaking. Now he was cured of his malady. He began to curse lovers and to weep like a beaten child. Quietly he went across the street to a blacksmith called Gervase, who forged equipment in his shop for plowing. This smith was busily engaged in sharpening shares and colters. Absalom knocked quietly at the door and said, "Open up, Gervase, at once."

"Who's there?"

"It's I, Absalom."

"What! Absalom, by Christ's dear cross, why are you up so early? Ah, bless me, what ails you? Some gay girl, God knows, has got you on the move this way. By St. Neot, you know very well what I mean."

Absalom didn't care a bean about this teasing; he didn't even reply. He had more knitting to attend to than Gervase knew, and said: "Dear friend, lend me that hot colter there in the chimney. I have something to do with it; I shall return it to you very soon."

"Certainly," Gervase answered. "Even if it were gold or a bag of uncounted coins, you could have it, as I am a true smith. Aye, Christ's foot, what will you do with it?"

"Let that be as it may," replied Absalom. "I shall tell you tomorrow." With that he grabbed the colter by the cool handle and went quietly out of the door across to the carpenter's house. First he coughed, then knocked upon the window just as he had done before.

Alison answered, "Who knocks there. I'll bet it's a thief."

"Why no," said Absalom. "God knows, my sweet one, I am your Absalom, darling. I have brought you a gold ring," he said. "My mother gave it to me, so help me God. It is very fine and well engraved. I will give it to you if you kiss me."

Nicholas had risen from the bed to urinate, and thought he would put the finishing touch to the joke; Absalom should kiss his ass without fail. So Nicholas quickly raised the window and thrust his ass far out. Then the clerk Absalom said, "Speak, sweet bird, I do not know where you are."

At this Nicholas let fly a fart with a noise as great as a clap of thunder, so that Absalom was almost overcome by the force of it. But he was ready with his hot iron and he smote Nicholas in the middle of his ass.

The skin came off a hand's-breadth across, the hot colter had so scorched his buttocks, and Nicholas thought he would die of the pain. Like a mad man, he began to shout, "Help, water! Water, help, for God's sake!"

The carpenter started out of his sleep and heard someone madly shouting "Water!" He thought, "Alas, here comes Nowell's flood!" He sat up at once and cut the cords in two with his ax. Down went everything, without a stop on the way, until it hit the floor, and there the carpenter lay unconscious.

Alison and Nick rushed out in the street crying, "Help!" All the neighbors, high and low, ran in to stare at the unconscious man. He lay pale and wan, for his arm had been broken by the fall. But he had to stand the blame for his own hurt, for when he tried to explain he was shouted down by clever Nicholas and Alison. They told everyone he was crazy; his imagination had made him so afraid of "Nowell's" flood that he had foolishly brought three kneading tubs and hung them from the roof, and he had begged them, for God's love, to sit under the roof with him to keep him company.

The folks began to laugh at the carpenter's delusion. They poked about the roof and gaped and turned all his injuries into a joke. No matter what the carpenter answered, it counted for nothing; no one would listen to him. He was sworn at with great oaths and held to be crazy by the whole town, for one cleric will naturally stand by another. They

THE REEVE

THE PROLOGUE OF THE REEVE'S TALE: When the people had laughed at this silly adventure of Absalom and courteous Nicholas, different ones gave different opinions, but for the most part they laughed and joked about it. The only one I saw who was distressed by this tale was Oswald, the Reeve. Since he was a carpenter by trade, a little irritation lingered in his heart, and he began to grumble and find fault.

"So help me," he said, "I could very well pay you back with an account of the hoodwinking of a proud miller, if I chose to speak in a vulgar way. But I am old; my age has overcome my desire to joke. My grass time is over; my fodder is now forage. This white top bears witness to my advanced years; my passion is as moldy as my hair, unless I turn out to be like the medlar, that fruit which grows worse as it grows older, until it rots in muck and straw, and then becomes edible. With us old men, I'm afraid it's like this: we cannot rot until we are thoroughly ripe. We continue to dance as long as the world will pipe for us. There is always some stumbling block to our desire to have a white head and a green tail, like a leek. For, though our virility is gone, we still desire folly. That which we cannot do, we want to talk about. The fire still smolders in our burnt-out ashes.

"Four coals burn us, by my count—boasting, lying, anger, and covetousness. These four sparks belong to old age. Though our old limbs may be unwieldy, our desire still remains with us, that's the truth. I still have a colt's tooth, though many a year has passed since my tap began to run. Truly, when I was born, death immediately opened the tap of life and let it run, and it has run ever since, until the barrel is now almost empty. The stream of life now drips upon the rim. The poor old tongue may well chatter about misery which occurred long ago; for old folk, nothing remains except dotage!"

When the Host heard this discourse, he began to speak as pompously as a king. "What is the good of all this wisdom?" he said. "Why should we speak all day of Holy Writ? The Devil made a preacher out of a reeve, just as he made a shipman or a doctor of a cobbler. Tell your tale; don't waste time. Look there's Deptford, and it's half-past seven! Look, there's Greenwich, where there's many a shrew. It's high time for you to begin your tale."

"Now, sirs," said Oswald, the Reeve, "I ask all of you not to be grieved, when I answer this Miller and to some extent make a fool of him; it is quite legal to repulse attack with counterattack.

"This drunken Miller has told us here how a carpenter was deceived; perhaps he told his tale in mockery, for I am a carpenter. By your leave, I shall at once repay him; I will speak in his own vulgar terms. I hope to God he breaks his neck. He can very well observe a stick in my eye, but he can't see a beam in his own."

HERE BEGINS THE REEVE'S TALE: At Trumpington, not far from Cambridge, there runs a brook with a bridge over it, and by this brook stands a mill. Everything that I am telling you is the exact truth. For many years a miller lived there, and he was as proud and gay as a peacock. He could play the pipes, fish, mend nets, turn cups on a lathe, and wrestle and shoot well. In his belt he always carried a long knife and a sword with a sharp blade. He carried a pretty dagger in his pouch, and no man, on peril of his life, dared touch him. In his hose he wore another knife from Sheffield. This miller's face was round, his nose flat, and his skull was as hairy as an ape's. In fact, he was a full-fledged market-bully. No one dared lay a hand on him, for the miller swore he would at once repay him. He was a thief of grain and meal, truly a sly one, who made a habit of stealing. He was called Scornful Simkin. He had a wife with relatives among the nobility; her father was parson of the town. For her dowry he gave many a brass piece, so that Simkin would marry into the family. She had been brought up in a nunnery. Simkin had often said that he would not have a wife who was not well reared and a virgin, worthy of his position as a yeoman. She was proud and as pert as a magpie. Truly, these two made a fine sight on holy days. He would walk in front of her with the tail of his hood wound about his head, and she came behind in a red dress. Simkin's hose were of the same color. No one dared call her anything but "madam" then. No man in the vicinity once dared to trifle or play with her, unless he wished to be killed by Simkin with a knife or dagger or bodkin. Jealous folk are always dangerous; at least they want their wives to think so. And she, because she was of a somewhat dubious reputation, was as standoffish as water in a ditch, and full of scorn and mockery. She thought all ladies should treat her respectfully because of her family and the education she had gained in the nunnery.

These two had a daughter who was twenty years old, and no other children except a baby of six months which lay in its cradle and was a fine-looking child. The daughter was stout and well developed, with a pug nose, blue eyes, broad buttocks, and round, high breasts. Her hair was very pretty; I do not lie.

Because she was pretty, the town parson planned to make her his heir, both of his movable property and of his house, and he made difficulties about her marriage. His purpose was to marry her well into some noble family. Holy Church's goods must be kept in a family descended from Holy Church; therefore, he wanted to dignify his holy blood even though he harmed Holy Church.

This miller got large profits, without a doubt, in wheat

and malt all over the district. Especially, the great college which is called King's Hall at Cambridge had its wheat and malt ground at his mill. One day it happened that the steward suffered an attack of illness and was sick in bed; it was thought that he would surely die. Because of this, the miller stole a hundred times more meal and grain than usual. Before he had stolen sparingly, but now he stole outrageously. For this the warden scolded and made a fuss, but the miller didn't care a straw. He made loud boasts and swore it was not so.

There were two young, poor students who lived in the college of which I speak. They were high spirited and eager for any kind of sport. In the hope of having some fun, they eagerly begged permission from the warden to be absent a short while in order to go to the mill and watch the grain being ground. They boldly wagered their necks that the miller would not rob them of so much as a half-peck of grain, either by cunning or by force. At last the warden gave his assent. One student was named John and the other Allan. They were both born in the same place—a town called Strother, far in the north; I don't know where it is.

This student, Allan, got everything ready and put the sack on a horse's back. Then he and John started out, with swords and shields by their sides. John knew the way—they needed no guide—and upon arriving at the mill they threw down the sack. Allan spoke first. "Hail, Simon! How is your fair daughter and your wife?"

"Welcome, Allan," said Simkin, "and you also John; what are you two doing here?"

"Simon," answered John, "by God, necessity knows no law. As the clerics say, he who has no servant must serve himself or else he is a fool. I fear our manciple is going to die, judging from the way he gnashes his teeth. Therefore Allan and I have come to bring the college's grain to be ground and to carry it back home. Please help us to get back as quickly as possible."

"It shall be done," said Simkin, "by my faith! What would you like to do while the work is in progress?"

"By God, I want to stand next to the hopper," said John, "and watch how the grain goes in. I never yet have understood, by my father's cows, how the hopper goes back and forth."

"John, do you want to do that?" asked Allan. "Then by my father's head, I'll go down below and watch how the meal falls down into the trough; I'll pass the time that way. John, you know I'm just like you: I don't know any more than you about the job of a miller."

The miller smiled at their naïveté and thought: "All this is just a trick. They think no one can outwit them, but, by my soul, I'll hoodwink them, in spite of all the cunning in their philosophy. The more sly tricks they play, the more I will steal from them. Instead of flour, I'll give them bran. 'The greatest clerics are not the wisest men,' as the wolf said to the mare. I don't care a straw for all their book learning."

When he saw his opportunity, he slipped quietly out of the door. He looked up and down till he spied the students' horse where it stood tied behind the mill under an arbor. He went softly up to the horse and quickly took off the bridle. As soon as the horse was free, he started through the underbrush with loud whinnies, heading for the marsh, where there were wild mares running loose.

The miller went back inside and, without a word about the horse, attended to his work, joking meanwhile with the students, until all the grain was completely ground. When the meal was sacked and tied, John went outside and found their horse gone. He began to shout "Help!" and "Alas! Our horse is lost, Allan; for God's sake, get a move on. Come here at once, man. The warden's saddle horse is lost." Allan forgot all about the meal and the flour; his thrifty intentions went clean out of his mind. "What? Which way did he go?" he cried.

The wife came running out. She said, "Alas, your horse has gone to the marsh as fast as he can, to join the wild mares. Curses on whoever tied him; the bridle should have been tied better!"

"Alas," said John. "Allan, for the pain of Christ, put down

your sword and I'll do the same. I can run as fast as a deer, God knows; the horse won't get away from us. Why didn't you put the nag in the barn? Bad luck to you, Allan; by God, you're a fool!"

And both poor students, Allan and John, ran quickly into the marsh.

When the miller saw that they were gone, he took a half-bushel of their flour and bade his wife make a cake with it. He said: "I believe these students were afraid of what might happen. But a miller can get the best of clerics, in spite of their learning. Let them go ahead now. Look where they've gone! Yes, let those children play; they won't catch that horse so easily, by my crown."

The poor clerics ran up and down, shouting, "Stop, stop! Whoa, whoa! Here; look out behind; you whistle; I'll catch him here!" But, in brief, in spite of their efforts, their horse ran so fast that it was black night before they at last caught him in a ditch.

Weary, and as wet as beasts in the rain, poor John and Allan started back. "Curse the day that I was born!" said John. "Now we will have to put up with mockery and jokes. Our meal is stolen; people will call us fools—the warden and our friends, and particularly the miller. Alas!"

Thus John complained as he and Allan proceeded to the mill, leading Bayard. They found the miller sitting by the fire. It was night, and they could go no farther. They begged the miller, for the love of God, to furnish them food and lodging, for which they would pay.

The miller replied, "If there is anything to eat you shall have a share, such as it is. My house is small, but you two have book learning: by logic, you can create a space a mile wide where there are only twenty feet. Let's see if this place will do; otherwise, make it larger by talking, as is your custom."

"Now, Simon," said John, "by St. Cuthbert, you are a great joker and that was a good answer. I have heard it said, 'A man must choose one of two things: that which he finds or that which he brings.' But I beg you especially, dear host, bring us some food and drink and make us comfortable; we will pay you generously. Men with empty hands catch no hawks; look, here is our money, ready to be spent."

The miller sent his daughter to the village for bread and ale, roasted a goose for them, and tied their horse so that it could not run away again. He also prepared a bed for them himself, with sheets and blankets carefully arranged, not more than ten or twelve feet away from his own bed. His daughter had a bed all to herself near by in the same room. The students could do no better; there was no more spacious lodging in the place. They ate supper and talked, trying to comfort themselves, and steadily drank the best strong ale. About midnight they all went to bed.

The miller was extremely well oiled. He was so drunk that he was pale, not red. He hiccoughed, and he spoke through his nose as if he were hoarse or had a cold. He went to bed, and his wife went with him. She was gay and frisky as a jay bird, so well was her jolly whistle wet. The baby's cradle was placed at the foot of their bed, so that the mother could rock and suckle the child. When all that was in the jug had been drunk, the daughter at once went to bed. Allan and John also went to bed; there was no more to drink—no one needed a sleeping potion. The miller had drunk so much that in his sleep he snorted like a horse and unconcernedly broke wind. His wife accompanied him with a full strong bass; one could hear her snoring a quarter of a mile away. The daughter snored also, to keep them company.

Allan, hearing this music, poked John, and said, "Are you asleep? Did you ever hear such a song before? A plague on people who make such harmony! Whoever heard such a fantastic thing? Yes, they must come to the worst of bad ends. I won't be able to sleep this whole night long. But, nevertheless, things will turn out for the best, for, John, as I hope to prosper, I'm going to sleep with that wench. Surely, John, we are legally entitled to some compensation. There is a law which says that if a man suffers a grievance in one way he shall be repaid in another. Our grain is stolen, there's no doubt about that; and we've had a bad time all day. Since we are not going to be repaid for our loss, I will arrange my own compensation. By God's soul, it shall not be otherwise!"

John answered, "Allan, listen; the miller is a dangerous man. If he wakes up, he may do us both harm."

Allan replied, "I don't care a fly for him." And he got up and crept into bed with the daughter. She lay fast asleep on her back and didn't know what was happening until it was too late to call for help. In brief, they were soon hard at it. Now play, Allan, for I want to speak of John.

John lay still a few minutes, feeling very sorry for himself. "Alas," he said. "This is a cruel joke; I see clearly that I am nothing but a fool. My friend now has something for the harm he suffered: he is in bed with the miller's daughter. He took a risk and has got what he wanted, while I lie like a sack of straw in my bed. In the future, when this adventure is told, I'll look like a fool, a sissy! I will get up and try my chances too, by my faith! 'Nothing ventured, nothing gained,' they say." He got up and went quietly to the cradle, and, taking it in his hands, moved it softly to the foot of his own bed.

A bit later, the wife stopped her snoring, woke up, went to urinate, and, upon returning, missed the cradle. She groped here and there without finding it. "Alas," she said, "I almost made a mistake—I almost got into bed with the students. Oh! bless me, then I would have been in a bad spot." She groped about until she found the cradle, and from the cradle she felt her way to John's bed, which she thought was her own because the cradle stood at its foot. She didn't know where she was because it was pitch-dark. She crept softly into bed with John, lay still, and would have gone to sleep. Soon John jumped up and began to make love most vigorously to the good woman. She had not had so much fun in many a year! John penetrated hard and deep, as though he were mad. These two students continued their jolly sport until about dawn.

Allan, who had worked hard all night, grew weary shortly before dawn and said, "Farewell, Molly, sweet one! Daylight is here; I can stay no longer. But in the future, wherever I go, I am your own scholar, as long as the soul is in my body!"

"Now, dear lover," she said, "go, farewell! But before you go I want to tell you one thing: when you pass by the mill on the way home, if you look behind the front door you will find a cake made from a half-bushel of your own flour which I helped my father steal. And, beloved, God save you and guard you!" With these words she almost began to cry.

Allan got up and thought, "Before dawn comes I'll slip into bed with John." He soon found the cradle with his hand. "By God," he thought, "I'm completely lost. My head is dizzy from my night's work; that's what's making me go wrong. I know by the cradle that I have gone astray. The miller and his wife are in this bed." Accordingly, he made his way—twenty devils' luck!—to the bed in which the miller slept. He thought the miller, whom he got in next to, was John and grabbed him by the neck and whispered, "John, you hog's head, wake up for Christ's soul, and hear a great joke. By St. James, three times during this short night, I have laid the miller's daughter flat on her back, while you have stayed here like a coward."

"Oh, have you, false knave?" cried the miller. "False traitor, false scholar! You shall die, by God's worth! How dare you brazenly insult my daughter, who comes of such a noble family?" He grabbed Allan by the Adam's apple, and he, in return, roughly grabbed the miller and hit him on the nose with his fist. The blood streamed down on the miller's breast while the two wallowed on the floor, their noses and mouths crushed, like two pigs in a poke. First they were up and then they were down again, until the miller stumbled on a stone and fell backwards upon his wife, who had heard nothing of this ridiculous fight. She had fallen into a short doze, after making love with John all night. When the miller fell on her, she started up out of her sleep and shouted, "Help! Holy cross of Bromholm, I'm in your hands! Lord, I call to you! Wake up, Simon, the devil has fallen on me! My heart is crushed; help, I'm as good as killed! Somebody is lying on my stomach and my head. Help, Simon, the false scholars are fighting!"

John jumped up as quickly as he could and groped back and forth around the walls in search of a stick. She got up also and, since she knew the interior of the house better than John, she soon found a stick by the wall. She saw a ray of light, where the moon shone in through a hole in the wall, and by this light she saw the two on the floor, but she couldn't tell for certain who was who; they appeared to her as a white something. When she caught sight of this white thing, she supposed it was a nightcap which one of the students wore, and drew nearer with the stick, thinking to hit Allan squarely. Actually she beat the miller on his hairy skull. He fell flat and cried, "Help, I die!" The two students beat him thoroughly and let him lie there. They dressed themselves, took their horse and meal, and went on their way. At the mill they picked up the cake baked with the half-bushel of their meal.

In this way, the proud miller was well beaten; he lost the money for grinding the wheat and he paid for every bit of supper for Allan and John, who beat him thoroughly and who slept with his wife and daughter. See what happens to a miller who is false! Therefore the proverb is true which says: "He who does evil must not expect good." A cheat himself will be outwitted. And God, who sits on high in majesty, save all this company, great and small! Now I have repaid the Miller with my tale. HERE ENDS THE REEVE'S TALE.

THE COOK

THE PROLOGUE OF THE COOK'S TALE: While the Reeve was speaking, the Cook of London seemed as though he would claw him on the back for joy. "Ha! ha!" he said. "By Christ's passion, that miller got a bitter experience from giving a night's lodging. Solomon told the truth: 'Do not bring just any man into your house.' Giving lodgings is a dangerous business. A man should consider very carefully whom he brings into his home. May God give me sorrow and trouble if I ever heard, since I was named Hodge of Ware, about a miller more beautifully put in his place. He had a malicious trick played on him in the dark. But God forbid that we stop here. Therefore, if you are willing to hear a tale from a poor man like me, I shall tell you as best I possibly can about a funny little affair which happened in our city."

Our Host answered: "I grant your request. Now tell away, Roger, but be sure it's good. For you have sold many a juiceless pasty and many a twice-warmed-over meat pie. You have had Christ's curse from many pilgrims who got sick from your parsley, which they ate with your stubble-fed goose. There are plenty of flies loose in your shop. Now tell away, dear Roger, as you're called, but I beg you, don't be angry at my teasing; a man may speak the exact truth in playful jest."

"By my faith," said Roger, "you do speak the truth! But 'true joke is no joke,' as the Flemings say. And so, Harry Bailly, by your faith, don't you be angry before we leave here, even though my tale is about an innkeeper. Nevertheless, I won't tell that one yet; but before we part, you certainly shall be repaid."

With that, he laughed merrily and told his tale, as you shall hear.

HERE BEGINS THE COOK'S TALE: An apprentice once lived in our city who belonged to a guild of food merchants. He was as gay as a bullfinch in the woods, brown as a berry, and a handsome, short fellow, with black hair very neatly combed. He could dance so well and merrily that he was called Perkin the Reveler. He was as full of love and adultery as a hive is full of sweet honey. Any wench who could meet him was lucky. He sang and danced at every wedding, and he loved the tavern better than the shop. For whenever there was a parade in Cheapside, he would run to it out of the shop—he would not return until he had seen all the sights and danced his fill—and gather a crowd of his companions to dance, sing, and generally make merry. There they would set a time for a meeting in such-and-such a street to roll dice. For in the whole town there was no apprentice who could roll a pair of dice more skillfully than Perkin. And, too, he was generous with his money in private. His master discovered this easily in his business, for many times he found his strongbox completely empty. And truly, the master of a reveler apprentice who loves dice, riotous living, and wenches will pay for it out of his shop, even though he has no part in the fun. For theft and riotous living go hand in hand, even though the apprentice plays well on the guitar or fiddle. Revelry and truth, in a man of low rank, are completely at odds, as anyone can see.

This jolly apprentice stayed on with his master until he had almost finished his apprenticeship, though he was scolded both early and late and was sometimes led behind musicians to Newgate jail. But at last, when his master went over the account book one day, he remembered a proverb which says these words: "It is better to cast a rotten apple out of the storehouse than to let it rot all the others." So it is with a riotous servant; it is certainly less harm to let him go than to have him ruin all the servants in the place. Therefore, his master gave him his discharge papers and told him to leave, and sorrow and bad luck to him. And this jolly apprentice lost his job. Now let him revel all night if he likes.

Since there is never a thief without an accomplice who helps him embezzle and squander all that he can steal or borrow, this apprentice at once sent his bed and his clothing to the house of a companion of his own sort who loved dice, revelry, and play, and who had a wife that kept a shop for appearances' sake, but who whored for her living.

[*Chaucer did not complete this tale. The inconsistencies and the lack of continuity which the reader will notice at times in* THE CANTERBURY TALES *result from Chaucer's leaving the collection of stories unfinished.*]

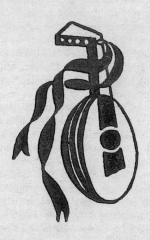

THE MAN OF LAW

THE WORDS OF THE HOST TO THE COMPANY: Our Host realized that the bright sun was more than a half-hour beyond a fourth of its daily course, and, though he was not expert in such matters, he knew that it was the eighteenth of April, the month preceding May. He also observed that every tree's shadow was the exact length of the tree which caused it. Therefore, he concluded from the shadows that, since the bright clear sun had climbed forty-five degrees in the sky, it was for that latitude on that day ten o'clock. And quickly he pulled his horse around.

"Ladies and gentlemen," he said, "I warn everyone of this company: the day is one-fourth over. Now, for the love of God and St. John, waste no more time than absolutely necessary. Ladies and gentlemen, while we sleep or are negligent during our waking hours, time passes and creeps away from us day and night like a river which never turns back in its descent from mountain to plain. Seneca and many other philosophers may well bewail wasted time more than wasted gold, as he said, for 'money lost may be recovered, but loss of time defeats us.' It will not come again, surely, any more than a slut's virginity which she has lost in her wantonness. Let's not mold this way in idleness.

"Sir Man of Law," he said, "as you hope for bliss, tell us a tale at once, as you agreed. You are committed through your own free assent to being guided in this matter by my judgment. Make good your promise now; then, at least you will have done your duty."

"Host," the Man of Law replied, "by God, I agree; my intention is not to break my promise. A promise is a debt, and I certainly wish to keep all my promises to the letter; I can give no better advice. It is only right that a man himself follow the rules he sets for other people's behavior. Let's agree to that text. But, nevertheless, I really don't know any worthwhile tale to tell, except those of olden times which Chaucer, though he is ignorant of metres and skillful rhyming, has told in English as best he could, as everybody knows. If he didn't tell them in one book, dear friend, he told them in another. He has told in various places of more lovers than Ovid, an ancient writer, made mention of in his *Heroides*. Why should I repeat them, since they have already been told?

"When he was young, Chaucer told of Ceÿx and Alcyone, and since then he has spoken of almost all noble wives and their lovers also. Whoever will look up his large volume called *The Legend of Cupid's Saints* may see there Lucrece's large, wide wounds and those of Babylonian Thisbe; Dido's sword used because of false Aeneas; Phyllis' hanging herself on the tree because of love for Demophon; the complaints of Dejanira, Hermione, and Hypsipole; Ariadne on a barren isle in the sea; Leander drowned because of Hero; the tears of Helen; the woe of Briseis and of Laodamia; the cruelty of Queen Medea, whose little children hanged because of the false love of Jason! Oh, Hypermnestra, Penelope, Alcestis—he praises your wifeliness as the best.

"However, he certainly did not write a word of that wicked story of Canace who loved her own brother sinfully—I don't approve at all of such wicked tales. Neither did he write about Apollonius of Tyre, how the cursed King Antiochus raped Apollonius' daughter; that's a horrible tale to read, especially the part where she is thrown upon the pavement. And, therefore, Chaucer was truly very wise never to write about such unnatural abominations in any of his tales; nor will I rehearse them if I can avoid it.

"But for my tale—what shall I tell today? I am surely unwilling to be likened to the Muses whom people call the Pierides—the *Metamorphoses* explains what I am talking about. But yet, I don't care a bean if my story is plain in comparison to Chaucer. I speak in prose; let him make the rhymes."

And with these words the Man of Law began his tale in a serious manner, as you shall hear.

HERE BEGINS THE MAN OF LAW'S TALE: Once upon a time there lived in Syria a company of rich merchants, very serious and dependable, who exported their spices, gold cloth, and rich-colored satins far and wide. Their merchandise was so satisfactory and unusual that everyone wished to buy from them, and also to sell goods to them. Now it happened that the leading men of this company had planned to take a trip to Rome; whether their purpose was trade or pleasure, they decided definitely not to send a messenger but to go to Rome themselves. Upon arrival they took lodgings in an inn which they thought best for their purpose.

After they had been in Rome for a certain time, as they planned, it happened that the excellent reputation of the emperor's daughter, Lady Constance, was reported day after day to these Syrian merchants in detail, as I shall explain to you. This was the general opinion of all people: "Our Emperor of Rome—God bless him!—has a daughter so endowed with goodness and beauty that there never was another like her since the world began. Pray God to protect her honor. If only she were queen of all Europe! She has great beauty without pride, youth without ignorance or folly; in all her activities virtue is her model; humility has overcome all tyranny in her; she is the mirror of all courtesy; holiness itself dwells in her heart; her hand is the agent of generous charity." And all these comments were as true as God. But now let us turn back to our story. These merchants had their ships reloaded and, after having seen this remarkable princess, they returned eagerly to Syria. And there they took up their business as before and lived in prosperity. I can say no more about that.

Now it happened that these merchants were in favor with the Sultan of Syria. For whenever they returned from their travels in foreign countries, he would entertain them royally with great kindness and eagerly inquire for news of the various kingdoms, in order to learn of the wonders which they had seen and heard. This time the merchants told him, among other things, particularly about Lady Constance; they so emphasized her noble qualities that the Sultan wanted to see her very badly; his only desire and concern was to love her as long as he lived.

Perhaps when he was born it was written in the stars in that large book which men call the heavens that he would die because of love, alas; for, God knows, it is true beyond doubt that the death of every man is written clear as glass in the stars for whoever can read it. In the stars, many winters before they were born, the deaths of Hector, Achilles, Pompey, and Julius were written, as were the Theban War and the deaths of Hercules, Samson, Turnus, and Socrates. But men's wits are so dull that no one can really read these things fully.

The Sultan sent for his privy council and, to make a long story short, he told them his purpose and insisted that unless he could have Constance in the near future he was certainly as good as dead; then he ordered them to work out a plan to save his life. Various men said various things; they debated and argued up and down; many a subtle argument was advanced; they spoke of magic and deceit. But finally, to conclude, they could see no other possible satisfactory solution except marriage. Many obvious difficulties at once became apparent in this plan; plainly, there were such differences in the religions of the Sultan and Constance that the counselors declared: "No Christian prince would be eager to have his daughter marry according to our excellent laws laid down for us by Mohammed, our prophet."

The Sultan answered, "Rather than lose Constance, I will certainly turn Christian; I must be hers; I cannot choose another. I suggest that you stop your arguments. Save me and do not fail to get this girl who holds my life in her hands; for I cannot endure this suffering very long."

What need is there for further elaboration? I will simply say that by treaty, by ambassadors, and by the mediation of the Pope, the church, and all knighthood, an agreement was reached—to the harm of Mohammedanism and to the profit of Christ's dear laws, as you shall hear: The Sultan, his barons, and all his followers were to be christened; in return, the Sultan was to have Constance for his wife, plus certain moneys, I don't know the exact amount. Pledges were sworn to this agreement by each side, and security was put up. Now, fair Constance, let almighty God be your guide!

Now I guess some people will no doubt expect me to tell of all the extensive arrangements the noble emperor made for his daughter, Lady Constance. But everyone knows that the great preparations which were made for so important an event cannot be described briefly by anyone. In short, bishops, lords, ladies, famous knights, and many other people were selected to accompany Constance on her journey. Notice was served that everyone in the city should pray Christ, with great devotion, to receive this marriage with good will and to speed the voyage.

The day came for Constance's departure; I repeat, that woeful, fatal day beyond which there could be no further postponement arrived. Everyone was ready. Constance, pale and overcome with sorrow, rose and dressed herself for the trip. She saw clearly that there was no way out. Alas! Is it a wonder that she wept, she who was being sent to a strange land far from her friends who cherished her, to be bound in servitude to one of whose qualities she knew nothing? Husbands are all good, and it has always been so; wives know that. I dare not say any more.

"Father," she said, "and you, my mother, my greatest joy of all except Christ on high, your wretched child, Constance, your young, tenderly brought-up daughter, commends herself to your grace, for I go to Syria and shall never lay eyes on you again. Alas, I must leave at once for the land of Barbary, since that is your decision; but Christ, who died to redeem us, give me strength to carry out his commands. I am a wretched woman; it does not matter if I die. Women are born to servitude and penance, and to be under the control of men."

I do not believe that such pitiful weeping as now went on in the palace at Constance's departure was heard at Troy when Pyrrhus broke through the wall before the city burned, or at Thebes, or at Rome when Hannibal had conquered the Romans three times. But, whether she sang or wept, she had to leave.

Oh, cruel prime-moving sphere, which in your diurnal travel forces and hurls all things from east to west which naturally should go in the opposite direction, your juggling set the heavens in such an arrangement at the beginning of this dire voyage that cruel Mars ruined this marriage. Oh, unfortunate, obliquely ascending Aries; alas, your lord, Mars, has helplessly fallen from his angle into the most unfavorable position! Oh, Mars, you were an evil influence in this affair! Oh, feeble moon, your motion was unhappy; you were in conjunction where you were not welcomed! Then you moved away from a favorable position. Alas, imprudent emperor of Rome! Was there no philosopher in all your city to advise you? Did you not know that one time is better than another for such arrangements and that, especially for those of noble birth whose horoscope is known, a propitious time for a journey should be picked? Alas, you were too ignorant or stupid!

The poor beautiful Constance was led to the ship in pomp, as befitted her station. "Now Jesus Christ be with all of you!" she said. That's all, except the reply: "Farewell, dear Constance!" She tried hard to appear cheerful. I shall let her sail away while I turn again to my story.

The mother of the Sultan, well of vices, saw clearly that her son planned definitely to divorce himself from his traditional religion. At once she sent for her advisers, who immediately came to find out what she wanted. When all had assembled, she took her seat and spoke as you shall hear:

"Lords, each one of you knows that my son is on the point of giving up the holy laws of our Koran, left to us by God's agent Mohammed. But one oath I swear to almighty God: the breath shall leave my body before Mohammed's law leaves my heart! What shall we find in this new religion except servitude and penance because of our bodies? And afterwards we shall be drawn through hell because we renounced our faith in Mohammed. But lords, if I can show you a way to make us safe for eternity, will you give your assent to what I propose?"

They swore their assent, every man, to live and die with her and to stand by her. And each one promised to do his best to win followers for her among his friends. She took full charge of the proceedings which I shall explain to you. To all of them she said:

"We shall first pretend to accept Christianity—cold water will not cause us much grief! Then I shall prepare a great feast and revelry, during which I promise you I shall repay the Sultan. His wife, no matter how white she is from baptism, will need to bring more than a fountain full of water with her to wash away her red stains."

Oh, Sultaness, root of all evil! Virago, second Semiramis! Oh, serpent in female guise, just like the serpent bound deep in hell! Oh, deceitful woman, nest of every vice; there is everything within you which your malice can breed against virtue and innocence! Oh, Satan, envious since the day you failed to conquer mankind, you know the most effective approach to women! You caused Eve to lead us into bondage, and you will doom this Christian marriage. Alas, in this way you make women your agents when you wish to cause trouble.

The Sultaness, whom I blame and curse in this fashion, quietly dismissed her counselors. Why should I draw out this story? One day she went to the Sultan and told him that she would renounce her religion and receive Christianity from the hands of the priests, repenting that she had been a heathen so long. She begged him to allow her the honor of having a feast for all the Christians—"I will work hard to please them." The Sultan replied, "I grant your request," and thanked her on his knees for making it. He was so pleased he did not know what to say. She kissed her son and went home. THE FIRST PART ENDS.

THE SECOND PART FOLLOWS: The Christians arrived in the land of Syria with a huge, impressive procession. The Sultan at once sent his messenger to his mother and all around the kingdom to say that there was no doubt but that his future wife had arrived. He asked his mother to ride out to meet the future queen, to uphold the honor of his realm. The crowd was great and rich when the Syrians and Romans met. The mother of the Sultan, richly and gaily dressed, received Constance as happily as any mother might welcome her dear daughter. Then, with fitting pomp, they rode the short distance to the nearest city. I do not think that the triumph of Julius Caesar, of which Lucan speaks so boastingly, was more royal or unusual than the assembly of this happy group. But that scorpion, that wicked spirit, the Sultaness, in spite of her flattery, planned secretly to sting mortally. The Sultan himself arrived shortly thereafter, in a splendid manner wonderful to describe, and greeted Constance with all joy and happiness. I leave them there in their mirth and gladness; the outcome of all this is what I am interested in. After a time everyone thought it best to halt the revelry and go to bed.

When the time came, the old Sultaness set the date for the feast of which I spoke. And all the Christians, young and old, prepared to attend. At this feast one could eat dainties more numerous than I can tell, and look upon royalty also. But they paid much too dearly for all this before they left the table.

Oh, sudden woe, that always succeeds worldly happiness, which is nourished in bitterness! You are the end of the joy of our earthly labors; our happiness always ends in sorrow. Listen to this advice for your own good: on your day of happiness bear in mind that unexpected woe or harm follows behind.

To make the story brief, the Sultan and every one of the Christians were hacked and stabbed at the table, except Constance. The old Sultaness, cursed crone, accomplished this horrible deed with the help of her friends, for she wished to rule the whole country herself. There was not a single Syrian who had been converted at the urging of the Sultan, who was not murdered before he could get up. And, post haste, the conspirators took Constance and put her into a boat without any rudder, God knows, and told her to learn how to sail from Syria to Italy. They gave her, it is true, the money which she had brought with her, a gracious plenty of food, and also sufficient clothes. And thus she set sail on the salty sea. Oh, my Constance, kind one, oh, dear young daughter of an emperor, may He who is lord of Fortune be your star.

Constance crossed herself, and with a very sorrowful voice she prayed to the cross of Christ: "Oh, clear beneficent altar, holy cross, red with the piteous blood of the Lamb which washed ancient evil from the world, protect me from the devil and his claws on the day that I drown in the sea. Victorious tree, protection of the faithful, the only tree which was worthy to bear the King of Heaven with his fresh wounds, the White Lamb, who was pierced with nails—expeller of devils from the men and women over whom your limbs faithfully spread, protect me and give me the power to amend my life."

This unfortunate creature floated for years through the Mediterranean Sea and finally came by chance to the Straits of Gibraltar. She had to eat many a scanty meal, and she expected death many times before the wild waves drove her to a landing place. One might ask why she was not also slain at the feast. Who saved her? And I answer that question with another: Who saved Daniel in that terrible den where every person but him, master and man, was eaten by the lion before escape was possible? No one except God, whom Daniel had in his heart. God wished to exhibit His miraculous power through Constance so that we could observe His mighty deeds. Christ, who is the balm for every hurt, often does things through various means for a certain end not clear to mankind because in our ignorance we cannot perceive His wise providence—clerics know this very well. Now, since she was not slain at the feast, who saved her from drowning in the sea? Who protected Jonah in the whale's belly until he was spouted up at Nineveh? Everybody knows very well that it was no one except the same Being who kept the Hebrew people from drowning when they passed with dry feet through the sea. Who gave this command to the four winds which have the power to harass on land and sea, north, south, east, and west: "Harass neither sea, nor land, nor any tree"? Truly, the giver of that command was He who steadily guarded this woman from the tempest, both when she woke and when she slept. Where could this woman find food and drink for three years and more? How did her supplies last? Who fed Mary the Egyptian in the cave or in the desert? No one but Christ, without doubt. It was an equally great miracle to feed five thousand folk with five loaves and two fishes. God sent His plenty to fill her great need.

She sailed forth into our Atlantic Ocean and through our wild English Channel, until at last the waves cast her up in distant Northumberland, near a stronghold which I cannot name. Her ship stuck so fast in the sand that even the full tide could not move it. It was Christ's will that she should stay there. The warden of the castle came down to see the wreck. He searched the whole ship and found this weary troubled woman; he also found the treasure she brought. In her own language she begged him in his mercy to kill her in order to deliver her from her sorrow. She spoke a sort of corrupt Latin; but, nevertheless, she was thereby understood. The warden, having completed his search, led the poor woman to the land. She knelt down and thanked God for his help. But she would tell no one, despite threats or promises, who she was, though she should be killed for it. She swore that she had been so bewildered on the sea that she had lost her memory. The warden and also his wife felt such great pity for her that they broke into tears. She was so diligent, so tireless in her efforts to serve and please everyone in that place, that all who saw her loved her.

This warden and his wife, Dame Hermengild, and all the occupants of that country were pagans. However, Hermengild loved Constance as her own life; and when Constance had lived here, with prayers and pious tears, for a long time, Christ through His grace converted Dame Hermengild, the wife of the warden, to Christianity. The Christians throughout all that country did not dare gather together; all Christian people had fled from that land because of the pagans who had conquered by land and sea all the districts of the north. The old Britons who were Christians and who had lived in the island had fled to Wales, which served for the time as their refuge. Yet the exile of the Christian Britons was not so strict but what some in secret honored Christ and outwitted the pagans, and three such people lived near the castle. One of them was blind, but it is with the spirit's eye that blind men see.

One bright, sunny summer's day the warden, his wife, and Constance walked the short distance to the seashore to frolic and roam back and forth. While walking they met this blind man, old and bent, with his eyes tightly closed.

"In the name of Christ," cried this blind man, "Dame Hermengild, give me back my sight!" The lady grew frightened at this for fear her husband, having learned that she was a Christian, would at once kill her. But Constance encouraged Hermengild and urged her to perform the will of Christ as a daughter of His church.

The warden was taken aback thereat and said, "What is all this about?" Constance answered, "Sir, it is the power of Christ which helps people to escape the devil's snares." Then she began to advocate our religion so convincingly that before evening she had converted the warden to a belief in Christ.

The warden was not really the lord of this district of which I speak, and in which he had found Constance. But for many winters he had held it securely under the rule of Aella, king of all Northumberland, a very wise man, who had fought bravely against the Scots, as is well known. But I must return to my story.

Satan, who always lies in wait to deceive us, saw the perfection of Constance and plotted how he might betray her. He filled a young knight of that village with such hot love and foul desire for her that the knight actually thought he would die if he could not possess her body at least once. He wooed her, but in vain. She would not sin in any way. Out of spite he planned to bring about a shameful death for her. He waited until the warden was away from home and then one night he secretly crept into Hermengild's chamber while she slept. Weary and tired from their frequent prayers, Constance and Hermengild both slept soundly. This knight, tempted by Satan, slipped stealthily to the bed and cut Hermengild's throat; and then he laid the bloody knife by Lady Constance and went away. May God bring him to a bad end!

Shortly afterwards, the warden returned home, accompanied by Aella, ruler of that country. He saw his wife cruelly slain, for which he often wept and wrung his hands. And in the bed he found the bloody knife by the side of Lady Constance. Alas, what could she say? For pure grief, her wits left her.

All these events were told to King Aella—how, when, and where this Constance was found in the ship, as you have already heard. The King's heart was shaken with pity when he saw so gracious a creature fallen into distress and misfortune. For the innocent Constance stood before the King like a lamb led forth to death. The false knight, who had committed this treachery, swore that she had done this deed. Nevertheless, there was great mourning among the people, who said that they could not imagine that she had done so wicked a thing. For, they had observed her great virtue and her sincere love for Hermengild. Everyone present testified in this manner except the knight who killed Hermengild. The noble King was impressed by the testimonies and thought it best to inquire further into the case in order to learn the truth.

Alas, Constance, you have no champion and you cannot fight for yourself, so wellaway! But He who died to redeem us and who bound Satan so that he still lies there must be your mighty champion today! For unless Christ performs a clear miracle, you will surely be slain in spite of your innocence. Constance knelt and prayed: "Immortal God, who saved Susannah from false blame, and you, merciful Virgin Mary, daughter of St. Anne, before whose child the angels sing 'hosannas,' if I am guiltless of this crime, save me; else shall I die!"

Haven't you at times seen in a crowd the pale face of one who is led to death and who can hope for no pardon? His face has such a troubled look that men can pick his out of all the faces in the crowd. So stood Constance and looked about her. Oh, queens living in prosperity, duchesses, and all you ladies, take some pity on her troubles! An emperor's daughter stands alone; she has no one to whom she can turn. Oh, royal blood, standing thus in fear, far are your friends in your hour of great need!

King Aella felt such compassion that the tears ran from his eyes; a kind heart is ever full of pity. "Now, have fetched immediately a book," he said, "and if the knight will swear that she killed Hermengild, we will then decide who shall serve as our judge." A book of the Gospels in British was brought, and the knight at once swore on this book that she was guilty. But meanwhile, a hand smote him so hard upon the collarbone that he immediately fell down like a rock, and both his eyes burst from his head in the sight of everyone present.

A voice was heard by all: "Thou hast slandered an innocent daughter of the holy Church in the presence of God. Thus hast thou done, but still I hold my peace!" The entire crowd was aghast at this miracle. All except Constance stood stunned by the fear of vengeance.

Great was the fear and also the repenting of those who had wrongly suspected this poor innocent Constance. And, finally, because of the miracle and because of Constance's efforts, the King and many others were there converted; glory to the grace of God.

Aella immediately decided that the false knight should be killed for his treachery. Yet Constance was greatly saddened by his death. And later Christ, in His mercy, caused Aella to marry this holy maiden, so bright and shining, with full ceremony. In this way, Christ made Constance a queen.

Who, to tell the truth, was sad at this wedding except Donegild, tyrannical mother of Aella? It seemed to her that her wicked heart would burst in two over what her son had done, for she considered it a disgrace that he had taken so strange a creature for his wife.

I do not care to dwell as long in my tale upon the chaff and straw as upon the grain. Why should I tell of the royal personages at the marriage, or of the steps in the procedure, or of who blew a trumpet and who a horn? The fruit of every story is to say: they ate, they drank, they danced, they sang, and they played. The new couple went to bed, as was right and reasonable. For although wives are extremely holy, they must patiently bear at night the necessary acts which please those who gave the wedding rings, and for a short time put aside their holiness—there is no help for that. Constance became pregnant. Her husband left her with a bishop and the warden as guardians, while he went towards Scotland to fight his enemies. Constance, fair, humble, and meek, was so near childbirth that she stayed in her room awaiting Christ's will. In due time she gave birth to a boy whom they baptized Maurice. The warden wrote the happy news to King Aella, together with other cheerful reports, and gave the letter to a messenger who rode forth on his way.

This messenger, hoping to receive a gift, rode quickly to the court of the King's mother. In courteous language he addressed her. "Madam," said he, "you will be very happy at my news and will thank God a hundred thousand times: my lady, the Queen, has borne a child; the whole kingdom will rejoice. See, here is a sealed letter containing this news which I must bear to the King, as fast as possible. If you wish to send anything to the King, I am your servant night and day."

Donegild answered, "Not right now; I wish, however, that you would remain here overnight, and tomorrow I shall tell you what I have decided."

The messenger drank heavily, both ale and wine, and while he slept like a pig, his letter was secretly stolen from his pouch. Another letter, wicked in purpose, was forged and substituted; it seemed to give an account of this matter, written directly by the warden to the King, as I shall tell you. The letter said that the Queen had given birth to so horrible and devilish a creature that there was no one in the castle brave enough to stay with it. The mother must surely be an elf, come to earth by chance, charms, or magic; and everyone now hated her company.

The King was grief-stricken when he had seen this letter, but he told his dire troubles to no one. Rather, with his own hand he answered the letter, saying: "The will of Christ shall always be welcome to me, now that I know His teachings! Lord, your desires and pleasures are welcome; I place my own desires fully under your supervision. Protect this child, fair or foul, and also my wife, until I return home. Christ, when He so desires, may send me a more agreeable and pleasing heir." He sealed the letter, weeping quietly, and sent it at once to the messenger, who started his return trip. There is no more to be done.

Oh, messenger, slave of drink, your breath is foul, your steps always falter, and you give away all secrets. Your memory is lost, you chatter like a jay bird, your face is constantly contorted. Wherever drunkenness prevails in any group, no secrets are possible.

Oh, Donegild, I lack English fit to describe your malice and tyranny! Therefore, I consign you to the devil; let him tell of your treachery! Fie, human—no, by God, I lie—fie, devilish spirit; for I dare to state that though you walk on earth, your spirit is in hell!

The messenger returned and dismounted at the court of the King's mother. She was most cordial to him and did all she could to please him. He drank and had to loosen his belt several notches; he slept and snored in his disgusting way all night until the sun rose. Once again his letters were stolen and forged ones substituted, which said: "The King commands that at once his warden, upon pain of hanging after strict judgment, shall refuse absolutely to allow Constance to remain longer than three days and three hours in this realm; he shall put her into the same ship in which she arrived, together with her young son and all her equipment, and shove her out to sea, and command her never to return." Oh, my Constance, your spirit has good reason to be afraid and to dream of hardship, for Donegild planned all this treachery.

Upon awakening the next day, the messenger took the shortest road to the castle and gave the letter to the warden. When the latter had read the sad news, he kept repeating, "Alas and woe to me!" "Lord Christ," he said, "how can this world endure when there is so much sin within all creatures? Oh, mighty God, if it is within Thy power, since Thou art a righteous Judge, how canst Thou allow innocent people to die while the wicked rule prosperously? Oh, good Constance, alas, I am sad that I must either be your tormentor or die a shameful death; I have no other choice."

Young and old throughout the district wept because the King had sent this accursed letter. And on the fourth day, Constance, with a face deathly pale, went to her ship. But yet she bore the will of Christ patiently, and, kneeling on the strand, she said:

"Lord, Thy will is ever welcome. He who kept me from false blame when I was here on land among you will guard me from harm and also from shame on the salty sea, though I cannot see how He will do it. He is still as strong as He ever was. I trust in Him and in His dear Mother, who is my sail and also my star to steer by."

Her little boy lay weeping in her arms; kneeling, she spoke to him pityingly: "Peace, little son, I will do you no harm." With that she untied the kerchief from her head and placed it over his little eyes; and she lulled him fast asleep, and cast her eyes up to heaven.

"Mother," she said, "shining Virgin Mary, it is true that

through the instigation of a woman mankind was lost and doomed to die, for which thy Child was torn on the cross. Thy blessed eyes viewed all His torment; there is therefore no comparison between thy woe and any woe suffered on earth. Thou sawest thy Child killed before thine eyes, yet now my little child still lives. Now, bright Lady, to whom all who suffer appeal, glory of womankind, fair Virgin, haven of refuge, bright star of day, take pity on my child, thou whose gentleness takes pity on all the pitiful.

"Oh, little child, alas, wherein lies your guilt who indeed never yet has sinned? Why does your cruel father wish you killed? Mercy, dear warden," she said, "let my little child live here with you. Yet if you dare not save him because of fear, kiss him once in his father's name!"

With that she looked back at the land and said, "Farewell, cruel husband!" Then she rose and walked down the strand to the ship, with the crowd following her, and she kept begging her child not to cry. And so she took her leave, piously crossed herself, and entered the ship.

The ship was abundantly supplied for a long period; all things necessary to her were there in great plenty, praised be the grace of God! May God control the wind and waters and bring her home! I can only say that she sailed away across the ocean. THE SECOND PART ENDS.

THE THIRD PART FOLLOWS: King Aella returned home to his castle, which I spoke about before, shortly after this and asked for his wife and child. The warden was chilled with fear, and at once told him all that had been done—you have heard it once; I cannot better the story by repeating it. The King was shown the letter with his own seal, and the warden said, "I have done exactly that which you commanded me to do upon pain of death." The messenger was tortured until he confessed fully and exactly where he had passed each night of his trip. And thus through wise and subtle questioning it was evident who was at the bottom of this treachery. The handwriting in the letter was recognized, and all the venom of this wicked deed came to light, though I do not know exactly how. The result was certainly that Aella killed his mother—anyone can easily read that fact—because she was a traitor to her country. Thus ends old Donegild; curses on her!

No tongue can tell the sorrow which Aella felt night and day for his wife and child. Therefore, I shall now turn to Constance, who floated on the sea wherever Christ willed, in pain and sorrow, for more than five years before her ship approached land.

At last the sea washed up Constance and also her child on land near a heathen castle, the name of which I do not find in my text. Almighty God, who saves all mankind, take care of Constance and her child! They have again fallen into heathen hands and are at the point of death, as I shall immediately explain to you.

Many people came down from the castle to stare at the ship and at Constance. But a few nights later, the steward of the lord of the castle—God curse him, a thief who had renounced our faith—came alone to the ship and said she must be his mistress, whether she wished to do so or not. Poor Constance was then really woebegone. She cried piteously and her child cried also. But blessed Mary soon helped her, for Constance wrestled so strongly and well that the thief suddenly fell overboard and drowned in the sea, as he deserved. In this way Christ kept Constance pure.

Oh, foul sin of lust, observe your end! Not only would you weaken man's mind, but you wish completely to enslave his body. The end of your deeds or blind desires is lamentation. How many we see around us who, not for sometimes doing this sin but merely for the intention of doing it, are killed or ruined! How could this weak woman have the strength to defend herself against such a ruffian? Oh, great Goliath, gigantic in stature, how could young unarmed David conquer you? How dared he look at your terrible countenance? One can easily see it was only by the grace of Christ. Who gave Judith the courage or strength to slay Holofernes in his tent and to deliver God's people from misery? I say, in this connection, that just as God sent strength to these people to enable them to save themselves from evil, so He sent power and might to Constance.

Constance's ship sailed straight out through the narrow mouth of Gibraltar and Ceuta, heading sometimes west, sometimes north, sometimes south, and sometimes east for many weary days until Christ's mother—blessed be She ever—arranged with Her unending kindness to put an end to all Constance's troubles.

Now let us leave Constance for a little while and speak of the Roman emperor, who learned by letters from Syria of the slaughter of the Christians and of the dishonor done his daughter by a false traitor. I mean the accursed evil Sultaness who murdered both high and low at the feast. Therefore, the emperor at once sent his agent, a senator, accompanied by many other lords, God knows, with a royal order to take strict vengeance upon the Syrians. These Romans burned, killed, and in general brought troubles to the Syrians for many days; and then, finally, they prepared to return to Rome.

The victorious senator set sail ceremoniously for Rome and met the ship in which poor Constance sat—so the story says. He knew nothing about who she was or why she was in such circumstances; neither would she tell her true position, though she should die for it. The senator took her to Rome and gave her and also her young son to his wife. She became a member of the senator's household; in this way Our Lady led poor Constance out of trouble, as She has led many others. And, for a long time, Constance lived there, always busy with holy deeds for which she was distinguished.

The senator's wife was Constance's aunt, though she did not at all recognize her niece. I shall not dwell on these details, but shall return to King Aella, of whom I spoke before, who wept and sighed bitterly for his wife. I shall leave Constance in the senator's care.

King Aella, who had killed his mother, one day became so repentant that—to get to the point—he came to Rome to receive penance. He put himself under the Pope's orders in all things and prayed Jesus Christ to forgive his wicked deeds. The news of King Aella's coming to Rome on a pilgrimage was soon brought to the city by couriers who preceded him. Therefore, the senator, accompanied by many of his relatives, as was customary, rode out to meet Aella, as eager to display his own splendid magnificence as he was to honor a visiting king.

Both the noble senator and Aella showed each other many courtesies. So it happened that a day or two later this Roman was invited by Aella to a feast, and Constance's son—I tell no lie—went with him. Some men will say that it was at Constance's own request that her child was taken to the feast. I personally am not able to tell all the details—be that as it may, the child was certainly there. The truth is that at his mother's command the child stood in front of Aella between the courses and stared at the King's face.

King Aella wondered greatly about this child and soon asked the senator, "Who is that fine-looking child standing over there?" "By God and by St. John, I do not know," the senator replied. "He has a mother, but no father that I know of"—and briefly, in a few sentences, he told Aella how the child was found. "But God knows," he concluded, "never in my life have I seen or heard of so virtuous a woman on earth —spinster or wife—as is his mother. I dare say she had rather have a knife thrust through her breast than be a wicked woman. There is no man who could seduce her."

Now, this child looked as much like Constance as any living creature could. Aella clearly remembered Lady Constance's face and therefore, sighing quietly, he wondered if his wife might be the child's mother. And as soon as he could he left the table. "By my faith," he thought, "ghosts are in my head! Reason bids me conclude that my wife drowned in the sea." But he afterwards argued to the contrary: "How do I know but that Christ has led my wife here by sea, just as He led her to my country, from which she sailed away?"

And that afternoon Aella accompanied the senator to the latter's home in order to see this wonderful woman. The senator received Aella with great ceremony and at once sent for Constance. But you can be sure that she did not want to dance when she learned why she was summoned; she could scarcely keep her feet. When Aella saw his wife, he greeted her eagerly and wept in a way pitiful to watch. For from his first glance at her, he knew that she was really his wife. And she, sorrow-stricken, stood as silent as a tree, because her heart so pained her at the thought of his former cruelty. Twice she fainted before him; he wept and piteously explained his past behavior. "By God and all His shining angels who have taken mercy on my soul," he said, "I am as innocent of causing you harm as is my son Maurice, whose face is so like yours! If I lie, may the devil take me at once!"

Long was the sobbing and the cruel pain before the bitter pangs left their hearts. It was indeed touching to hear their laments, which caused Constance's woe to increase steadily. I beg you, however, to excuse me; I am so weary of talking about grief that I shall have to postpone until tomorrow a recital of her woes. But, finally, when it became certain that Aella had had no part in causing her tribulations, they kissed a hundred times, I swear; and they were so happy at being reunited that, except for eternal bliss, nobody had ever experienced similar joy, or ever will so long as the world lasts. Then Constance meekly begged Aella, in view of her long terrible suffering, to urge her father strongly to do him the great honor of condescending to dine with him someday. She requested also that Aella mention no word of her to her father.

Some men would claim that the child Maurice was sent to present this invitation to the emperor; but, it seems to me, Aella was not so discourteous to one of royal rank who was the flower of Christendom as to send a child. It is better to say that Aella went himself; that way is more seemly.

The emperor courteously accepted the invitation to dinner

which Aella extended, and I read in the book that he stared at the child and thought about his daughter. Aella went to his inn and fittingly arranged for this feast, carrying out every detail as best he could.

The next day arrived, and Aella and his wife dressed to meet the emperor. Then they rode out in joy and gladness. And when Constance saw her father approaching, she dismounted and fell at his feet. "Father," she said, "you have completely forgotten your young child Constance. But I am your daughter Constance, whom you long ago sent to Syria. It was I, Father, who was sent to sea alone and condemned to death. Now, good father, I beg your mercy! Do not send me again into heathendom, but give thanks to my lord here for his kindness."

Who can describe the touching happiness among these three who were united? But I shall make an end to my tale; the day goes by rapidly, and I shall tarry no longer. These happy people sat down to dinner. I leave them eating in joy and happiness a thousand times greater than I can relate.

The child Maurice was later named emperor by the Pope and lived in true Christian fashion. He showed great honor to Christ's church, but I shall not concern myself with his story—my tale deals especially with Constance. You can find Maurice's story in the old Roman histories; I do not have it fresh in mind.

When King Aella saw his opportunity, he returned to England by the shortest route with his sweet, holy wife, Constance; there they lived in happiness and peace. Yet, I tell you, happiness is short lived in this world; it cannot endure time, and it changes night and day like the tide. Who has ever lived in great delight for one day and was not then troubled by conscience, wrath, longing, family troubles, envy, pride, lust, or insult? My only reason for stressing this point is that the great happiness of Aella and Constance lasted only a little while.

For when a year had passed, I think, Death, which takes both high and low, seized King Aella from this world; then Constance grieved terribly. Now let us pray God to bless his soul! Finally Lady Constance set out for Rome. Upon arrival there, this holy woman found her friends hale and hearty. Now she has escaped from all her adventures. And when she found her father, she fell upon her knees. Weeping with the joy she felt in her tender heart, she praised God a hundred thousand times. They lived thus together, without parting, in virtue and holy works, until death separated them.

And now, farewell! my tale is ended. May Jesus Christ, who has the power to send joy after woe, keep us in His grace and protect all who are here! Amen. HERE ENDS THE MAN OF LAW'S TALE.

THE EPILOGUE TO THE MAN OF LAW'S TALE: Our Host immediately stood up in his stirrups and said, "Good people, listen, every one of you! That was a worth-while tale for this occasion! Sir Parish Priest," he said, "by God's bones, tell us a tale, as you have already agreed to do. I see clearly that you men who are learned know much that's good, by God's dignity!"

The Parson answered him, "Bless me! What ails this man that he curses so sinfully?"

Our Host answered, "Oh, Jenkin, are you there? I smell a Lollard in the wind! Now, good people, listen to me," said our Host. "Pay close attention, for the sake of God's suffering; for we shall hear a real sermon; this Lollard here will preach to us somewhat."

"No, by my father's soul, that shall not be," said the Shipman. "He shall not preach here; he shall not comment upon the Gospels or try to teach us. We all believe in the mighty God," he said. "He will start some trouble or put some cockleburs in our clean grain. And, therefore, Host, I give you fair warning, I, the jolly one, shall tell a tale, and I shall jingle so merry a bell for you that I'll awaken all this company. But it will not be about philosophy, nor medicine, nor full of strange legal words. There is but little Latin in my mawl"

lowed as much freedom in the house as any friend could possibly have. For inasmuch as the merchant and the monk whom I just mentioned had been born in the same village, the monk claimed the merchant as a cousin. And the merchant did not once say no, but was as pleased with it as a bird is with the dawn, for in his heart this friendship made him very happy. Thus the two were bound in an eternal alliance, and each of them assured the other of brotherhood as long as he lived.

Don John was generous, especially with his money, in that house, and very eager to please, no matter what the cost. He did not forget to tip the lowliest page in that house; when he came to visit he gave some appropriate gift to the lord and then to all his staff, each according to his position. Therefore, they were as glad to see him come as a bird is to see the sunrise. No more of this now, for this is enough.

It so happened that one day this merchant planned to make ready for a trip to Bruges to buy some goods there. He therefore sent a message to Don John in Paris, urging him by all means to come to St. Denis for a visit with him and his wife a day or two before he left for Bruges. The noble monk, about whom I am telling you, because he was a man of high prudence and also an official in his monastery, had his abbot's permission to ride out whenever he wished to see about their farms and their large barns; so at once he came to St. Denis. Who was so welcome as my lord Don John, our dear cousin, so extremely courteous? He brought with him a jug of malmsey, another jug full of fine white wine, and some wild fowl, as was his custom. And now I leave the merchant and the monk eating, drinking, and playing, for a day or two.

The third day, the merchant rose, gravely considered his business matters, and went up to his countinghouse to count up, as well as he could, how he stood for that year, how he had spent his money, and whether he had made a profit or not. He laid his books and his many money bags before him on his counting-table. His hoard of treasure was very large; therefore, he shut tight the door to his countinghouse. Also, he did not want anyone to bother him while he checked his accounts. In this way he sat there until after nine o'clock.

Don John had also risen early that morning and was walking back and forth in the garden, properly saying his devotions. The goodwife quietly entered the garden where he was pacing quietly and greeted him as she had often done. She had a little maidservant with her, whom she governed and guided as she wished, for the child was still under the rod. "Oh, Don John, my dear cousin," she said, "what ails you that you rise so early?"

"Cousin," he answered, "five hours' sleep a night ought to be enough for anyone, unless he is an old, weak fellow, like these married men who lie and crouch in the bed like a tired rabbit sitting in its burrow, frightened by large and small hounds. But, dear cousin, why are you so pale? Indeed, I think that your husband worked you so hard last night that you are badly in need of rest." And with these words he laughed very merrily and turned all red at his own thought.

The pretty wife shook her head and replied: "Well, God knows everything. No, my cousin, it's not that way with me, for, by that God who gave me soul and body, there isn't a wife in the whole kingdom of France who gets less enjoyment from that silly game. I can sing 'Alas and woe is me that I was born,' " she said, "but I dare tell no one how things stand with me. Therefore, I am thinking about leaving this country, or else killing myself, I am so filled with fear and worries."

The monk stared at the wife and said: "Alas, my cousin, God forbid that you should kill yourself because of any sorrow or fear. But tell me your troubles. Perhaps I can advise or help you in your difficulty. So, tell me everything; I shall keep it secret. For I swear on my breviary that never in my life, willingly or unwillingly, will I give away any of your secrets."

"I say the same to you," she replied. "By God and by this breviary, I swear to you that I will never, though men tear me all to pieces or I go to hell for it, reveal a word of what you honestly tell me. I say this not for our kinship and family spirit, but truly for love and trust." They pledged themselves in this way and kissed upon it, and each one told the other whatever he wished.

"Cousin," she said, "if I had time, as I have not, and particularly not in this place, I would tell you the story of my life—how I have suffered since I married my husband, even though he is your cousin."

"No," replied the monk, "by God and St. Martin, he is no more my cousin than this leaf hanging on the tree! By St. Denis of France, I only call him cousin to have a better reason for friendship with you, whom I have especially loved above all other women truly. I swear this to you on my profession. Tell me your troubles before he comes down; hurry now, and leave right afterwards."

"My dear love," she said, "oh, my Don John, I would like to conceal my secret, but it must come out; I can wait no longer. My husband is the worst man towards me that ever was since the world was made. But since I am his wife, it is not fitting that I discuss our private affairs, either in bed or elsewhere, with anyone; God in His grace forbid that I should tell tales. It seems to me that a wife should say nothing but good of her husband. Only this much shall I tell you: so help me God, he is not in any way worth the value of a fly. But most of all, his stinginess grieves me. And you know that women naturally desire the same six things as I; they want their husbands to be brave, wise, rich, generous with money, obedient to the wife, and lively in bed. But, by the same Lord who died for us, in order to dress myself properly next Sunday, to do credit to my husband, I must pay a hundred francs; or else I am lost. But I would rather never have been born than do a disgraceful or vulgar thing; yet, if my husband should find me out, it would be my undoing. Therefore, I beg you, lend me this sum or else I must die. Don John, I say, lend me this hundred francs. By God, I will not fail in my gratitude if you will do what I ask. On a certain day I will repay you, and I will give you whatever pleasure and service I can, whatever you decide upon. Unless I do, may

God take as foul vengeance on me as ever Ganelon got from France."

The courteous monk gave this answer: "Now truly, my own dear lady," he said, "I feel such great pity for you that I swear and give you my word that when your husband has left for Flanders I will deliver you from this trouble; for I will bring the hundred francs to you." And with these words he caught her by the hips, embraced her hard, and kissed her several times. "Now, go away quietly," he said, "and let's dine as soon as possible. For, according to my sundial, it is nine o'clock. Go now, and be as faithful as I shall be."

"God forbid it be otherwise, sir," she replied, and went out as gay as a magpie. She told the cooks to bestir themselves so that everyone might dine at once. She went up to her husband and knocked boldly at his countinghouse.

"*Qui est là?*" he asked.

"By Peter, it's I," she answered. "What, sir, how long are you going to fast? How long are you going to add up and juggle your figures and your books and accounts? The devil take all such reckonings! You have enough, Heaven knows, of God's gifts; come down today and let your moneybags alone. Aren't you ashamed to cause Don John to fast miserably all day? How now! Let's hear a Mass and then go dine."

"Wife," the man answered, "little can you understand of the difficult business we conduct. For among us merchants, so help me God and that lord named St. Ive, there are scarcely two out of twelve who prosper continually until old age. It is true that we act cheerful and put a good face on things, while we let the world go as it wishes and keep our own affairs secret until we die; or else we feign a pilgrimage or go off somewhere. But it is very necessary for me to keep up with events in this strange world; for we merchants must always fear chance and fortune in our business.

"Tomorrow at daybreak I must go to Flanders; I shall return as soon as possible. Therefore, I beg you, my dear wife, be obedient and meek to everyone while I am away, keep a close watch over our property, and govern our household virtuously and well. You have enough in every way to suffice a thrifty household easily. You lack no clothes or provisions; you will not run out of money." And with these words, he closed his countinghouse door and came down without longer delay. A Mass was hastily said; then the tables were quickly set, and they went in at once to dinner. The merchant fed the monk richly.

After dinner Don John gravely led the merchant aside and privately said to him: "Cousin, I see it stands that you plan to go to Bruges. May God and St. Augustine speed you and guide you! I pray you, cousin, ride carefully. Also be moderate in your diet, especially in this heat. There is no need for ceremony between us two; farewell, cousin; God keep you from worries! And if there is anything, day or night, which you wish to ask of me, if it lies in my power and abilities, it shall be done just as you wish.

"One thing I should like to ask of you, before you leave, if it is possible: lend me a hundred francs for a week or two, for I must buy certain animals to stock one of our places. So help me God, I wish you owned it! I surely shall not fail to repay you on the appointed day, not for a thousand francs, not by an hour. But, I beg you, keep this matter secret, for I still have to bargain for these animals tonight. And now, farewell, my own dear cousin; thank you for your generosity and good cheer."

The noble merchant answered at once and said courteously: "Oh, my cousin, Don John, now truly that is a small request. My gold is yours whenever you wish it, and not only my gold but my merchandise. Take what you please; God forbid that you should stint yourself. But there is one thing about merchants, as you know well enough: their money is their plow. We may have credit as long as we have a reputation, but it is no joke to be without gold. Repay it when it is convenient; I am glad to do what I can to please you."

The merchant at once brought out the hundred francs and secretly gave them to Don John. No one in the world knew of the loan except the two of them. They drank, talked, strolled for a while, and played, until Don John rode back to his abbey.

The morning came and the merchant rode off for Flanders. His apprentice guided him well, and he reached Bruges in good spirits. Then he went about his business rapidly and industriously, buying and borrowing. He neither played dice nor danced, but, in a word, conducted himself exactly like a merchant; and there I leave him.

The Sunday after the merchant had left, Don John came to St. Denis with his head and beard all freshly shaven; there was not the smallest boy, or anyone else, in the entire household who was not very happy to see Don John return. And—to come quickly to the point—the fair wife agreed with Don John that, in return for the hundred francs, he could have her lying in his arms all night. And this agreement was carried out to the letter. All night they worked merrily away until dawn; then Don John left, bidding the staff, "Farewell; good day!" For none of them, or anyone in the town, had the least suspicion of Don John. So he rode off to his abbey, or wherever he pleased; I shall speak of him no more.

The merchant returned to St. Denis when the market-fair was over, and feasted and celebrated with his wife. Then he told her that his purchases had been so costly that he now needed to borrow money, for he was legally bound to pay twenty thousand coins at once. The merchant therefore went to Paris to borrow a sum of money from certain of his friends; and he took some money with him. When he arrived in town, he went first, out of great kindness and affection, to Don John, to make him a friendly visit; not to ask for money or to borrow from him, but to learn about his welfare and to tell him the news of business, as friends do when they meet. Don John gave him a feast, with much celebration, and the merchant told him repeatedly in detail how he had conducted his buying trip successfully, thank God, except that now he was forced for his own good to arrange in some way for a loan; then he would be in joy and peace.

Don John answered: "Truly, I am glad to see that you have returned home prosperous. And if I were rich, as I hope for salvation, you should not lack your twenty thousand shields, because you were so kind the other day in lending me money. With all my heart, by God and by St. James, I thank you! And, incidentally, I left that same gold on your bench at home with your wife. She will surely remember it well, by certain facts which I can recall to her. Now, with your permission, I can remain here no longer. Our abbot is going to leave town immediately, and I must accompany him. Greet my own sweet cousin, your wife, and farewell, dear cousin, until we meet again!"

The merchant, who was very wary and wise, borrowed his money and paid the sum he owed in Paris into the hands of certain Lombards, in return for which they gave his note back to him. Then he went home, merry as a popinjay, for he knew well that his affairs were such that he stood to gain a thousand francs from that trip, above all his expenses.

His wife met him eagerly at the gate, as it had long been her custom to do. And all that night they worked merrily, for he was rich and clearly out of debt. When dawn came, the merchant started embracing his wife all over again; he kissed her on the mouth and gave her a vigorous tussling.

"No more," she said. "By God, you've had enough!"

Then she gaily teased him again, until at last the merchant said: "By God, I'm a little angry with you, wife, although it grieves me. Do you know why? By God, it seems to me that you have caused some kind of misunderstanding between my cousin Don John and me. You should have warned me before I left that he had paid you a hundred francs, and had a receipt for it. He considered himself mistreated because I spoke to him about borrowing—so it seemed to me from his expression. But, really, by God, our King of Heaven, I had no idea of asking him for anything. I pray you, wife, never do that again. Always tell me, before I leave you, if any debtor has paid you in my absence; or, through your negligence, I might ask him for money he has already paid."

The wife was not shaken or frightened; rather, she at once replied boldly: "By the Virgin, I defy that false monk, Don John! I care nothing for his talk of receipts. I know very well that he paid me a certain sum—ill luck to his monk's snout! For, God knows, I thought surely that he gave it to me because of you, from a cousinly desire to honor and benefit me, and also in return for the fine hospitality he has enjoyed here so many times. But since I see that I stand in this pickle, I will answer you right to the point. You have far slacker debtors than I, for I will repay you promptly and well day by day; and if I happen to fail, I am your wife: put it on my account, and I shall pay as soon as ever I can. For, on my word, I spent every bit of that money for clothes; I did not waste it. And, since I spent it so carefully to do you credit, I say for God's sake don't be angry; let's laugh and frolic. You shall have my fair body in pledge; by God, I won't repay you except in bed! Forgive me, my own dear husband; turn over this way and cheer up."

The merchant saw that there was no remedy and that scolding would only be foolish, since the mistake could not be amended. "Now, wife," he said, "I forgive you. But, on your life, don't be so generous again. Take better care of my money, I charge you."

Thus ends my tale; and may God send us credit enough to the end of our lives. Amen. THUS ENDS THE SHIPMAN'S TALE.

THE PRIORESS

Behold, the merry words of the host to the shipman and to the lady prioress: "Well said," cried our Host, "by *corpus dominus*. Now long may you sail up and down the coast, good master, noble mariner! God send the monk a thousand cartloads of bad years! Aha, fellows! Beware of such a trick! The monk made a monkey of that man and of his wife too, by St. Augustine. Take no more monks into your house.

"But now let's pass on and look about to see who in this group is going to tell the next tale." And with these words he continued, as courteously as a maiden: "My lady Prioress, with your permission, if I thought it would not grieve you, I should decide that you must tell the next tale, if you care to do so. Now, will you so honor us, my dear lady?"

"Gladly," she replied, and spoke as you shall hear.

The prologue of the prioress' tale: *Domine dominus noster.* "Oh, Lord, our lord, how marvelously is Thy name spread throughout this great world," she said. "For Thy high praise is sung not only by men of dignity, but Thy excellence is extolled by the mouths of children, who sometimes, even when they are sucking at the breast, show Thy praise. Therefore, in praise of Thee and of the white lily-flower who bore Thee and is forever a virgin, I will try to tell a story as best I am able. Not that I think to increase Her honor, for She is honor

Herself and the root of excellence, next in order to Her Son, and the comfort of souls.

"Oh, virgin Mother! Oh, gracious virgin Mother! Oh, un-burned bush which burned in the sight of Moses, Thou who drew forth from the Deity through Thy humility the Spirit which alighted in Thee, from whose power, when He illuminated Thy heart, the Wisdom of the Father was conceived, help me to tell this story in Thy honor! Lady, Thine excellence, Thy nobility, Thy virtue, and Thy great humility cannot be properly expressed by any tongue or any wisdom. For sometimes, Lady, before people pray to Thee, Thou goest before in Thy great kindness and procurest for us through Thy prayers the light to guide us to Thy dear Son.

"My ability is so much too weak, oh, blessed Queen, to declare Thy great worth adequately that I cannot sustain the burden. But I shall do just as a child of twelve months or less who can scarcely utter one word; and, therefore, I pray Thee, guide this song which I shall sing of Thee."

HERE BEGINS THE PRIORESS' TALE: In Asia, in a large city populated mainly by Christians, there was a Jewry established by a lord of that land for evil purposes of usury and excessive gain, which are hateful to Christ and His people. One was able to ride or walk right through this ghetto, for it was open and unlocked at either end. A little school for Christians stood at the farther end, attended by many children of Christian descent, who year after year learned in that school such teachings as were needed in this land; that is, to sing and to read, as small children are accustomed to do.

Among these children there was a widow's son, a little

choirboy seven years old, who day after day attended the school; and he had been taught the habit, whenever he saw an image of Christ's Mother as he went on his way, of kneeling down and repeating his *Ave Maria*. The widow had thus instructed her little son always to worship our blessed Lady, Christ's dear Mother, and he never forgot, for happy children learn very quickly. Whenever I recall this situation, St. Nicholas seems to stand before me, for he as a child did reverence to Christ.

This little boy, studying his small book as he sat in the school with his primer, heard other children singing the *Alma Redemptoris* as they were taught from their anthem-book. As soon as he dared, he crept closer and closer to them, and listened closely to the words and the music until he knew the first verse by heart. He did not understand what the Latin meant, for he was too young and of too tender an age. But one day he begged a schoolmate to explain this song to him in his own language, or to tell him for what purpose this song was used. Many times upon his bare knees he begged his comrade to explain this and make it clear to him.

His schoolmate, who was older than he, answered in this fashion: "This song, so I have heard, was made for our blessed, generous Lady, to salute her and also to pray her always to be our help and succor when we die. I cannot explain this matter any better; I do learn to sing, but I do not know much grammar."

"Then this song was made in reverence of Christ's mother?" asked this innocent boy. "Now, certainly, I shall work my hardest to memorize it all before Christmas is over. Though I may be punished for not learning my primer, and even may be beaten three times in one hour, I am going to learn it in honor of our Lady!"

Day after day his schoolmate secretly taught him as they went home from school, until he knew the whole song by heart. Then he sang it clearly and well, word by word in keeping with the music. Twice a day it filled his throat: as he went to school, and as he returned home. His complete attention was fixed on Christ's Mother. As I have said, this little boy, when he passed through the Jewry, going back and forth, would regularly sing *O Alma Redemptoris* happily and loudly. The sweetness of Christ's Mother had so pierced his heart that in order to pray to her he could not choose but sing to her as he walked along.

The serpent Satan, our primal enemy, who has his wasp's nest in Jewish hearts, swelled with anger and said, "Oh, Hebrew people, alas! Is this a thing which is worthy of you, that such a boy shall go along as he pleases, spiting you by singing a song which does dishonor to your religion?"

From that time on, the Jews plotted to rid the earth of this innocent child. Consequently they hired a murderer, who had a hiding-place in an alley. And as the boy walked by there, this cursed Jew grabbed him, held him tightly, cut his throat, and threw him in a pit. Threw him, I say, into a privy, where these cursed Jews emptied their bowels. Oh, cursed people of Herod, born again, how can your evil intention help you? Murder will out—it never fails, especially where God's glory shall thereby spread. The blood cries out against your cursed act.

Oh, martyr, confirmed in virginity, now may you sing forever in the company of the white Lamb celestial—said the Prioress—concerning whom the great evangelist St. John wrote in Patmos. He said that those who never experience women in the flesh go before this Lamb and sing a song ever new.

The poor widow waited all that night for her little child, but he did not return. Therefore, as soon as it was daylight, she sought him at school and elsewhere, her face pale with fear and her thoughts busy. Finally, she was able to learn that he was last seen in the Jewry. Her breast full of a mother's sorrow, and half out of her mind, she visited every spot where she thought there was any likelihood of finding her little child. And steadily she cried out to Christ's Mother meek and kind, who at last caused her to seek him among the cursed Jews. She asked and begged pitifully every Jew who lived in that place to tell her if her child had passed through there. They told her "No"; but after a time Jesus in his grace so guided her that she called out to her son from a spot near where he was thrown into the pit.

Oh, great God, whose praise is effected through the mouths of innocents, herein we see your might! This gem of chastity, this emerald, and also the bright ruby of martyrdom, lying there upright with cut throat, began to sing *Alma Redemptoris* so loudly that the entire place resounded. The Christian people passing through the street gathered to marvel at this fact, and sent at once for the provost. He came immediately without delay, and praised Christ, the King of Heaven, and also his Mother, the glory of mankind. After that, he had all the Jews imprisoned.

The child was taken up with piteous lamentation, steadily singing his song; and, honoring him with a great procession, the people carried him into the nearby abbey. His mother lay fainting beside the bier; scarcely could the people there lead this second Rachel from his side.

Without loss of time the provost had all the Jews slain who knew of this murder, with torture and a shameful death for each. He would not tolerate such evil-doing. "Evil shall have what evil deserves." Therefore he had them drawn by wild horses, and afterwards he hanged them according to law.

The innocent child lay on his bier before the high altar while mass lasted. Then the abbot and his convent hastened to bury him quickly. When they cast the holy water upon him, the child still spoke; when they sprinkled him with holy water, he still sang *O Alma Redemptoris Mater*.

The abbot, who was a holy man—as monks are, or else should be—began to implore the young boy and said, "Oh, dear child, I beg you, by virtue of the Holy Trinity, tell me how you are able to sing when in my judgment your throat is cut?"

"My throat is cut down to the bone," said the boy, "and according to natural law I should indeed have died some time ago. But Jesus Christ, as you may find written, wishes that his glory shall last and shall be remembered; for the honor of his dear Mother I am still able to sing *O Alma* loudly and clearly. This well of mercy, Christ's sweet Mother, I always loved according to my ability. When it happened that I lost my life, she came to me and bade that I should sing this song even as I died, as you have heard me do. And when I began to sing, it seemed to me that she placed a kernel upon my tongue. Therefore I sing, and certainly I must sing, in honor of that blessed, generous Maid until the kernel is taken from my tongue. Later she spoke thus to me: 'My little child, I shall come for you when the kernel is taken from your tongue. Be not afraid; I shall not forsake you.' "

This holy monk—I refer to the abbot—drew forth the boy's tongue and lifted off the kernel. Then his spirit left him peacefully. When the abbot beheld this miracle, his salty tears trickled down like rain. He fell down prostrate upon the ground and lay as still as if he had been tied there. The convent lay also weeping upon the pavement, praising Christ's dear Mother. Later they rose and went out bearing this martyr from his bier. They placed his small sweet body in a tomb of clear marble. There he remains now—God grant that we meet him!

Oh, young Hugh of Lincoln, also slain by cursed Jews—as is well known, since it happened not long ago—pray for us who are unstable sinful folk, that in his mercy the merciful God shall multiply his mercy upon us, in reverence of his Mother Mary. Amen. HERE ENDS THE PRIORESS' TALE.

BEHOLD, THE MERRY WORDS OF THE HOST TO CHAUCER: When this miraculous legend had been completed, everyone was so quiet that it was a wonder to behold, until our Host began to joke; and then at last he looked at me and said: "What kind of man are you? You look as if you are searching for a rabbit, for I see you staring steadily at the ground. Come nearer and look up merrily. Now watch out, folk; give this man a place! He's got as noble a waistline as I; wouldn't he make a fine armful for any pretty little woman? I'd say from his face that he's full of mischief, though he hasn't chatted with any of us. Tell us something now, since it's your turn; tell us a merry tale at once!"

"Host," I said, "don't be disappointed, for I only know a tale in rhyme which I learned a long time ago."

"Yes, that's good," said the Host. "Now I'll bet we shall hear some rare tale, judging by the look of him."

HERE BEGINS CHAUCER'S TALE OF THOPAS. THE FIRST FIT: Listen, lords, with good will, and I shall truly tell you a story of mirth and joy, all about a knight who was fair and graceful in battle and in tournaments. His name was Sir Thopas. He was born in a distant land, Flanders, far across the sea at Poperinghe. His father was a bountiful man, lord of that district, by the grace of God. Sir Thopas grew into a sturdy youth; his face was as white as fine white bread and his lips were red as a rose bud; his complexion was like unfading scarlet, and I tell you truly that he had a seemly nose. His hair and his beard were like saffron and reached to his waist. His shoes were of Cordovan leather, and his brown hose were from Bruges; his robe was of silk which cost many a coin. He could hunt the wild deer and ride ahawking by the river with a gray goshawk on his hand. He was good at archery, and there was not his equal at wrestling for the prize ram. Many a lovely maiden sighed passionately in her boudoir for him when she would have done better to sleep. But he was chaste and no lecher, and as pure as the bramble flower which bears the red fruit.

And so one day it happened, as truly as I can tell it, that Sir Thopas decided to ride forth. He got on his gray steed, with his short lance in his hand and a long sword by his side. He spurred his horse through a green forest wherein there was many a wild beast—yes, even bucks and hares. And as he rode northeast, I tell you that a terrible thing befell him. Along his way there grew many herbs great and small: the licorice, the ginger, the clove, and the nutmeg, which is put into stale or fresh ale, or placed in the clothes chest. The birds sang, there was no doubt; the sparrowhawks and the jays—it was a pleasure to hear them. The throstle also made his song, and the wood-dove on the branch sang loud and clear.

Sir Thopas fell into love-longing when he heard the throstle sing, and he spurred forward as if he were insane. His fine steed sweated so from running that one could have wrung him out; his sides were all bloody. Sir Thopas also was so weary from riding across the soft grass—so fierce was his spirit—that he flung himself down on the spot to give his steed some rest, and gave him good fodder.

"Oh, St. Mary, bless you! What ails this love that it binds me so sorely? I dreamt all last night, by God, that an elf-queen would be my mistress and sleep under my robe. Truly, I will love an elf-queen, for there is no woman in any town in this world worthy of being my mate. I hereby forsake all other women and will seek an elf-queen over valley and also over plain!"

Soon he clambered into his saddle and rode rapidly over fence and stones to spy out an elf-queen, until, after much riding and walking, he came to a secret retreat and found the wild Fairyland. In that country there was no one who dared approach him, neither wife nor child. But at last a great giant named Sir Oliphant, a very dangerous man, came forth. "Knight," he said, "by Termagant, unless you ride at once out of my territory, I will slay your steed with my mace. The Queen of Fairyland dwells here, with harp and pipe and tabor."

The knight answered: "As I hope to prosper, I will meet you tomorrow when I have my armor; and I hope, by my faith, that you shall pay for this bitterly at the point of this lance. I shall pierce your stomach before nine o'clock, if I can, for here you shall die."

The giant cast stones at him from a terrible sling-shot, but Sir Thopas fell back quickly and, through God's grace and his own courageous manner, managed to escape.

Keep listening, lords, to my story, which is merrier than the nightingale; for now I shall whisper to you how Sir Thopas with his trim flanks rode over hill and dale and arrived again in town. He commanded his merry men to prepare games and feasts for him, for he must needs fight a giant with three heads for the love and embraces of a beautiful, shining someone.

"Summon my minstrels and storytellers," he called. "Let them tell tales of royal romances, of popes and cardinals, and also of love-longing, while I arm myself."

First, they brought him sweet wine and mead in a wooden bowl, then fine spiced gingerbread and licorice and cumminseed with fine sugar. Next to his white body he put on shirt and breeches of fine clear linen. And over his shirt he put on a tunic, and over that a coat of mail to prevent the piercing of his heart; then over that he placed a fine breastplate, all the work of a Jew, of strong plate, and over that his coat armor, white as the lily, in which he would fight. His shield was all of red gold, and on it was the head of a boar with a precious stone beside it. Then he swore on bread and ale that, come what may, the giant would die! His leg-pieces were of hard leather, his sword-sheath of ivory, and his helmet of bright copper; his saddle of whale-ivory, and his bridle shone like the sun or like moonlight. His spear was of fine cypress and proclaimed war, not peace, with the point ground sharp. His steed was dappled gray and ambled across the country quietly and gently.

Behold, lords, here ends the Fit; if you wish any more of this, I shall be glad to tell on.

THE SECOND FIT: Now hold your tongues, for charity's sake, gentlemen and gracious ladies, and listen to my tale; I shall soon tell you of battles and of chivalry and of the passionate love of ladies. People talk about famous romances—of Horn Child, of Ypotis, of Beves, of Sir Guy, of Sir Libeus, and of Pleyndamour—but Sir Thopas was really the flower of royal knighthood!

He mounted his good steed and glided forth on his way like a spark from a burning brand. His crest was a tower into which a lily was stuck. God shield his body from harm! And since he was a knight adventurous, he would not sleep within doors, but lay wrapped in his cloak. His bright helmet was his pillow, and his charger grazed beside him on fine, sweet herbs. He himself drank water from the well, as did the Knight Percival, who looked so handsome in his clothes; then one day—

HERE THE HOST INTERRUPTS CHAUCER'S TALE OF THOPAS: "For God's sake, no more of this," said our Host, "for you make me so tired by your plain stupidity that, as I hope God will bless my soul, my ears ache from your filthy chatter. Now, I say to the devil with such a rhyme! This is just like rhyme-doggerel."

"Why so?" I asked. "Why do you stop me in my tale more than another man, since it is the best rhyme I know?"

"By God," he said, "because, to speak plainly, to be brief, your filthy rhyming is not worth a turd! All you do is waste time. Sir, in a word, you shall no longer rhyme. Let's see whether you can tell something historical in rhyme, or at least tell something in prose, in which there is some gaiety or some instruction."

"Gladly," I replied, "by God's sweet pain! I shall tell you a little thing in prose which should please you, I think; otherwise, you are certainly too particular. It is a virtuous moral tale, though it is sometimes told differently by different people, as I shall explain to you. It's like this: you know that each Evangelist who tells us of Jesus Christ's sufferings does not agree with the next one in every detail; but, nevertheless, their substance is all true, and they all agree as to their meaning, though their manner of telling differs. For some of them say more and some say less, when they tell of His piteous crucifixion—I mean Matthew, Mark, Luke, and John. But, no doubt, the meaning is all the same. Therefore, ladies and gentlemen, I beg you, if you think that I vary in my speech in that I include more proverbs in this little treatise, to support the point of my material, than you have heard before, and if I do not use the same words which you are accustomed to, I beg all of you not to blame me. For, in my meaning you shall find no difference from the meaning of the little treatise which serves as the model for this merry tale I shall tell. Therefore, listen to what I shall say, and, I beg you, let me tell my tale through."

THE TALE OF MELIBEUS: [*True to his promise, Chaucer tells a moral tale in prose. It is the lengthy story, filled with quotations from the authorities, of the young, powerful, and rich Melibeus, who accepted the counsel of his wise wife, Prudence.*

Melibeus returns home one day, after roaming pleasantly in the fields, and finds that his enemies have broken into his house in his absence and have beaten and wounded his wife and his daughter, Sophie. He is almost insane with anger and vows to avenge his wrongs, but his wife urges him to be patient, to call together all his friends, ask them whether he should make war or remain at peace, and be guided by their counsel. Melibeus calls the assembly but receives contradictory advice. He is still determined to make war. Prudence then marshals her authorities and manages to win Melibeus' consent to a plan whereby she will hold a secret conference with his enemies. When these enemies meet with her, she stresses the advantages of peace and the righteousness of Melibeus' anger. The enemies are convinced and put their fate into her hands. Upon Prudence's return home, Melibeus accepts the confession of guilt from his enemies in the spirit in which it was offered. Prudence at once summons all her relatives and old friends to hear the case. They decide for peace. The enemies place themselves wholly at the mercy of Melibeus, who accepts his wife's advice and forgives them.]

THE MONK

THE MERRY WORDS OF THE HOST TO THE MONK: When my tale of Melibeus and of Prudence and her kindness was ended, our Host said: "As I am a faithful man, and by the precious body of Madrian, I had rather than a barrel of ale that Goodlief, my wife, had heard this story! For she is by no means of such patience as was this Melibeus' wife, Prudence.

"By God's bones! When I beat my servingboys, she brings me the great knotted clubs and shouts, 'Kill every one of those dogs, and break their backs and every bone in their bodies!' And if any of my neighbors will not bow to my wife in church, or is so bold as to offend her, when she gets home she roars in my face and screams, 'False coward, avenge your wife! By God's bones, I will take your dagger and you can have my distaff and go spin!' Day and night she carries on just that way. 'Alas,' she says, 'that I was ever created to marry a milksop or a cowardly ape who is intimidated by everybody! You dare not stand up for your wife's rights!'

"This is my life, unless I pick a quarrel. And I must take myself out of the house as fierce and foolhardy as a lion, or else I am lost. I know quite well that on some occasion she will cause me to kill some neighbor and run away. For I am dangerous when I have my knife in hand, although I dare not stand up to her, for she is big in the arms, by my faith; whoever says or does anything against her shall find that out. But let's pass on from this subject.

"My lord Monk," he said, "cheer up, for really you must

134

tell a tale. See, we are close to Rochester! Go ahead, my own lord, don't spoil our sport. But, by my faith, I don't know your name. Shall I call you my lord Don John, or Don Thomas, or Don Alban? Of what order are you, by your father's soul? I vow to God, you have a very handsome complexion. It must be a fine pasture where you feed. You are not like a penitent or a ghost; upon my faith, you are some official, some worthy sacristan, or some cellarer, for, by my father's soul, the way I see it you are a master when you are at home—not a poor cloisterer or novice, but a wily and discreet governor, and, with all that, a very handsome man in brawn and bone. I pray God to send confusion to the man who first led you into the religious life! You would have ridden chickens, all right. If you had had as much freedom as you have strength to do all you wanted in procreation, you would have begotten many a child. Alas, why do you wear so wide a coat? If I were Pope, as God may send me sorrow, not only you but every vigorous man, no matter how close his head was shaven, would have a wife. All the world is lost, for religion has taken in all the men best at child-getting, and we laymen are but shrimps. Wretched limbs come from feeble trees. That's why our heirs are so skinny and weak that they cannot easily have children. That's why our wives turn to religious men, for you can make Venus' payments better than we can; God knows, you pay with no counterfeit coins! But don't be angry, my lord, because I make jokes. Many times I have heard truth spoken in jest!"

The worthy Monk took all this patiently, and said: "I shall do my very best, as far as is within the limits of virtue, to tell you a tale, or two, or three. And if you care to listen, I shall tell you the life of St. Edward—or better, I shall first tell you some tragedies, of which I have a hundred in my cell. A tragedy means a certain story, such as those preserved for us in old books, concerning one who stood in great prosperity, but who fell from that high station into misery and ended wretchedly. They are usually written in verses of six feet which are called hexameters. Many are also written in prose and in various sorts of meters. This definition should suffice.

"Now listen, if you care to hear. But, first, I beseech you in this matter to excuse me for my ignorance if I do not tell these stories about popes, emperors, and kings in their proper chronological order, as one finds them written, but tell them some before and some behind, just as they come to my memory."

ERE BEGINS THE MONK'S TALE OF THE FALL OF ILLUSTRIOUS PERSONS: "I will bewail, in the manner of tragedy, the hardships of those who held high place but fell so far that there was no way of bringing them out of their adversity. For, certainly, when Fortune wishes to run away, no man can check her course. Let no man trust in blind prosperity; be warned by these old and true examples."

[*The Knight does not permit the Monk to recount all of the hundred tragedies which he has in his cell, but the latter does manage to present seventeen examples to fit his definition of tragedy and to warn the company against placing blind faith in prosperity. The list of celebrated individuals whose downfall the Monk treats is as follows: Lucifer, Adam, Samson, Hercules, Nebuchadnezzar, Belshazzar, Zenobia, King Pedro of Spain, King Peter of Cyprus, Barnabo of Lombardy, Count Ugolino of Pisa, Nero, Holofernes, Antiochus, Alexander, Julius Caesar, and Croesus. A translation of the Monk's account of Ugolino is given below as representative of this collection of tragedies.*]

CONCERNING UGOLINO, COUNT OF PISA: No tongue, for pity, can tell about the wasting away of Earl Ugolino of Pisa. A tower stands just a little way outside of Pisa; he was put into this tower as a prisoner, and with him his three small children, the eldest of whom was scarcely five years old. Alas, Fortune! It was great cruelty to put such birds into that kind of a cage! He was condemned to die in that prison because Roger, Bishop of Pisa, had accused him falsely. As a result, the people rose against Ugolino and put him into prison, just as you have heard. He had so little food and drink—and that little was poor and bad—that it scarcely sufficed.

Then one day it happened, at the usual hour for his food to be brought, that the jailer shut the gates to the tower. Ugolino heard them close, but said nothing. Yet the suspicion that his enemies wished to kill him by hunger at once came into his mind. "Alas," he said, "alas, that I was born!" And the tears fell from his eyes.

His young son, who was three years old, said to him: "Father, why are you crying? When will the jailer bring our soup? Is there no little piece of bread which you have kept back? I am so hungry that I cannot sleep. Now would God that I might sleep forever! Then hunger would not creep into my stomach; there is nothing, except bread, which I would rather have."

Thus, day by day, this child cried, until he sank down upon his father's bosom and said, "Farewell, Father, I must die!" And he kissed his father and died the same day.

And when the woebegone father saw the child dead, he began to bite his arms in grief, saying, "Alas, Fortune, woe unto me! I blame your false wheel for all my woe."

His children thought that he gnawed his arms from hunger rather than from grief, and said: "Father, don't do that, alas! Eat our flesh instead. You gave us our flesh; take our flesh and eat enough." They spoke to him thus, and then, within a day or two, they lay down in his lap and died. He himself died from despair and hunger; thus ended the mighty Earl of Pisa.

Fortune cut this man away from his high station. That should be enough of this tragedy; whoever wishes to learn further details of it can read the great Italian poet named Dante, who has explained it fully, point by point, without missing one word.

THE NUN'S PRIEST

THE PROLOGUE OF THE NUN'S PRIEST'S TALE: "Stop," said the Knight, "no more of this, good sir! You have said entirely enough, and even more, for a little sadness is quite sufficient for most people, I think. As for me, I say it is extremely painful to hear about the sudden fall, alas, of men who have had great wealth and luxury. But the contrary is a joy and a great comfort, as when a man who has been in poor circumstances climbs upward, becomes prosperous, and stays that way. Such a thing is cheering, it seems to me, and it would be a good idea to tell such a tale."

"Yes," said our Host. "By St. Paul's bell, you speak the truth; this Monk talks too much. He told how Fortune covered I know not what with a cloud; and also you heard just now about a tragedy. By God, it is no remedy to bewail and lament what's done. And, besides, it is painful, as you have said, to hear about sad things.

"Sir Monk, no more of this, as God may bless you! Your tale annoys everyone in this group. Such talk is not worth a butterfly, for there is no gaiety or fun in it. Therefore, Sir Monk, or Don Peter, as you are called, I beg you sincerely to tell us something else. For truly, if it had not been for the jingling of the bells which hang on every side of your bridle, by the King of Heaven who died for all of us, I would have fallen down before now because of sleep, though the mud had been never so deep. Then your tale would have been told all in vain. For certainly, as these clerics say, if a man has no audience, there is no use in his giving his opinions. And I know very well that I have it in me to appreciate anything that is well told. Sir, tell something about hunting, I beg you."

"No," said the Monk. "I have no desire to joke. Let someone else tell a tale now, as I have told mine."

Then our Host at once spoke plainly and boldly to the Nun's Priest, saying, "Come near, you priest; come hither, you Sir John! Tell us something to make our hearts glad. Be gay, even though you ride upon a nag. What if your horse is both dirty and thin? If he can serve you, you shouldn't care a bean. See that your heart is always merry."

"Yes, sir," said the Nun's Priest. "Yes, Host, as I hope to prosper, unless I act merry, I am certainly to be blamed."

And at once he began his tale, and he spoke in the following way to us all, this kind priest, this good man Sir John.

HERE BEGINS THE NUN'S PRIEST'S TALE OF THE COCK AND THE HEN, CHANTICLEER AND PARTLET: Once upon a time a poor widow, getting on in years, lived in a small cottage beside a grove which stood in a little valley. This widow, about whom I shall tell you my tale, had patiently led a very simple life since the day her husband died, for her possessions and her money were limited. By careful management of that which God sent her, she was able to take care of herself and also her two daughters.

She had only three large sows, three cows, and also a sheep called Molly. Her "drawing room" was very sooty, as was her "boudoir," in which she ate many a scanty meal. She had not a bit of need for sharp sauce; no tasty morsels passed her lips, for her fare matched her coat. She was never sick from overeating; a moderate diet, exercise, and a contented heart were her only medicines. The gout in no way kept her from dancing, nor did apoplexy harm her head. She drank no wine, neither red nor white; her table was set most often with white and black—milk and dark bread, of which there was no shortage—broiled bacon, and sometimes an egg or two; for she was, as it were, a kind of dairywoman.

She had a yard, fenced all around with sticks, with a dry ditch beyond that, in which she had a rooster named Chanticleer. For crowing there was not his equal in all the land. His voice was merrier than the merry organ that plays in church for Mass, and his crowing from his resting place was more trustworthy than a clock or an abbey timepiece. Instinctively he knew each revolution of the equinoctial circle in that region, for when fifteen degrees were ascended, then he crowed in a way which could not be bettered. His comb was redder than fine coral and turreted like a castle wall, his bill was black and shone like jet, and his legs and toes were like azure. His nails were whiter than the lily, and his feathers were like burnished gold. This fine rooster had seven hens in his service to do all his bidding; they were his sisters and his paramours, all colored exceedingly like him. The hen with the throat of fairest color was called fair Demoiselle Partlet. She was polite, discreet, debonair, and companionable, and she had conducted herself so well since the time that she was seven nights old that, truly, she held the heart of Chanticleer all tightly locked. His love for her accounted for his own well-being. It was a great joy to hear them sing in sweet harmony when the bright sun began to rise: "My love is gone away!" For in those days, so I'm told, beasts and birds could talk and sing.

And it so happened, one day at dawn, as Chanticleer sat on his perch in the hall, surrounded by all his wives and with Partlet right next to him, that he began to groan in his throat, like a man sorely troubled by his dreams. When Partlet heard him moaning this way, she was frightened and said: "Dear heart, what ails you that you groan in such a manner? You are a good sleeper; fie, shame on you!"

And he answered, saying: "Madam, I beg you not to take this amiss. By God, I dreamt just now that I was in such danger that my heart is still sorely troubled. Now, God, interpret my dream favorably and keep my body out of a wretched prison! I dreamt that I roamed up and down within our yard, when I saw a beast like a hound which tried to grab my body and would have killed me. His color was between yellow and red, and his tail and both ears were tipped with black, different from the rest of his fur. His snout was small and his two eyes glowed. I almost died of fear at the sight of him; doubtless that's what caused my groaning."

"Go on!" she said. "Shame on you, faint heart! Alas," she said, "for by God above, you have now lost my heart and all my affection. I cannot love a coward, by my faith! Certainly, no matter what any woman says, we all desire, if possible, to have husbands brave, wise, generous, and trustworthy, not niggardly, not foolish, not afraid of every weapon, and no boaster, by God on high! How dare you say, for shame, unto your love that anything could make you afraid? Haven't you a man's heart, and haven't you a beard?

"Alas, and can it be that you're afraid of dreams? God knows, there is nothing but vanity in dreams. Dreams are caused by overeating, and often by gases and combinations of the elements within the body, when humours are too abundant within a person. Certainly this dream which you had tonight comes from a great superfluity of your red bile, you may be sure, which causes folk to fear arrows in their dreams, and fire with red flames, red beasts that will bite them, strife, and large and small dogs. In the same way, the humour of melancholy causes many a man to cry out in his sleep for fear of black bears, or of black bulls, or else that black devils will get him. I could tell you also of other humours that bring woe to many a man in his sleep, but I will pass over it as lightly as possible. Look at Cato, who was so wise a man; didn't he say: 'Take no heed of dreams'?

"Now, sir," said she, "when we fly down from these rafters,

for the love of God, take a laxative. On peril of my soul and of my life, I counsel you for the best—I will not lie—that for both choler and melancholy you should purge yourself. And, so that you shan't put it off, since there is no apothecary in this town, I myself shall teach you about herbs which will work for your health and profit. I shall find those herbs in our yard which are naturally capable of purging you beneath and also above. Do not forget this, for the love of God! You are quite choleric in temperament; beware that the sun at its height does not find you overfull of hot humours. For if it does, I would be willing to bet a groat that you will have a fever coming on every other day, or an ague which may cause your death. For a day or two you must take digestives of worms before taking your laxative—laurel, century, and fumitory, or else hellebore, which grows here, or caper, or dogwood berries, or ground ivy from our pleasant yard. Pick them right where they grow and swallow them down. Be merry, husband, for your father's soul! Do not fear dreams; I can tell you no more."

"Thank you, madam," he said, "for your learned advice. But, nevertheless, regarding Master Cato, who has such a great reputation for wisdom, even though he says not to fear dreams, by God, a man may read in old books, by many authors of higher authority than Cato ever was, as I may prosper, quite the reverse of his opinion. They hold it to be well founded on experience that dreams are significant of joy as well as of trouble which people go through in this present life. There is no need to argue about this; the true proof lies in facts.

"One of the greatest authors read by men says that once upon a time two fellows went on a pilgrimage with pious intentions. And it happened that they came to a town where there was such a crowd of people, and also such scarcity of lodgings, that they could not find so much as a cottage where they both might be taken in. Therefore, they were forced to part company for the night; each of them went to his inn and took whatever lodging he could find. One of them was put in a stall, far away in a yard with plow-oxen, while the other chanced, by luck or the Fortune which governs all our lives, to be well enough lodged.

"And so it happened that long before dawn the second man dreamt as he lay in his bed that his friend began to call to him, saying, 'Alas, tonight in an ox's stall I shall be murdered in my sleep. Now help me, dear brother, or I shall die. Come to me in all haste!'

"The dreamer was frightened and started out of his sleep, but, upon awaking, he turned over and took no notice of his dream, thinking it to be only foolishness. He dreamt this same thing twice, and then the third time his friend seemed to appear and say, 'I am now slain. Behold my bloody wounds wide and deep! Get up early in the morning and at the west gate of the town,' he said, 'you shall see a cart full of manure in which my body will be secretly hidden. Boldly halt this cart. My money caused my death, to tell the truth.' And with a pitiful, pale face his friend told him every detail of how he was killed. And, believe me, he found his dream to be exactly true. For at dawn the next day he went to his friend's inn and, when he reached the ox's stall, began to call for his friend.

"The innkeeper answered him at once and said, 'Sir, your friend is gone. As soon as it was day, he left town.'

"The man became suspicious, remembering the dreams he had had, and went on without stopping any longer to the west gate of the town. There he saw a manure cart, going as if to spread manure over some land, which was arranged exactly as you have heard the dead man explain.

"Then with a bold heart he began to shout for vengeance and justice for this crime. 'My friend was murdered last night; he lies stark dead in this cart. I call upon the officials,' he said, 'who should guard and rule this city. Help! Alas! Here lies my friend murdered!' Why should I add more to this story? The people ran out and turned the cart over, and in the middle of the manure they found the dead man, freshly murdered.

"Oh, blessed God, so just and true, how you always bring murder to light! Murder will out; we see that every day.

Murder is indeed so loathsome and abominable to God, who is so just and reasonable, that He will not suffer it to be concealed, though it is quiet for a year or two or three. Murder will out; that is my conclusion. Immediately, then, the officials of that town arrested the carter and so sorely tortured him and the innkeeper, whom they put on the rack, that these two soon confessed their crime and were hanged by the neck.

"From this story one can see that dreams are to be feared. Indeed, I read in the same book, right in the very next chapter—I don't talk idly, as I hope for joy and bliss—about two men who wished to cross the sea, for a certain reason, into a foreign country. But the wind was not favorable and they had to wait in a city which was agreeably situated by a harbor. Then, one day toward evening, the wind began to change and blew in just the direction they desired. They went to their beds jolly and glad, and planned to get up early and sail. But a miraculous thing occurred to one of the men: as he slept he had a strange dream about the next day. It seemed to him that a man stood by his bedside and commanded him to wait, saying, 'If you sail tomorrow, you shall be drowned; my tale is at an end.'

"He awoke and told his companion what he had dreamt, begging him to delay his trip and not to sail that day. His companion, who lay in the next bed, began to laugh and poke fun at him. 'No dream,' he said, 'may so frighten me that I will give up my plans. I don't care a straw for your dreams, for dreams are but foolishness and jokes. Men dream all day of owls and apes and many other complicated things; men dream of things that never were and never shall be. But since I see that you wish to stay here and thereby wilfully miss the favorable tide, God knows I am sorry; good luck to you!'

"Then he left to go on his journey. But before he had sailed half his course—I don't know why or what mishap occurred— the bottom of his ship accidentally burst open, and ship and man went down in sight of other nearby ships which had sailed on the same tide. And, therefore, fair Partlet so dear, from such ancient examples you can learn that no man should be too careless about dreams; for I tell you, beyond doubt, many a dream is greatly to be feared.

"Look, I read in the life of St. Cenhelm, the son of Cenwulf, that noble king of Mercia, how Cenhelm dreamt of an event. One day, shortly before he was murdered, he saw his murderer in a vision. His nurse explained to him every detail of his dream, and told him to guard himself carefully against treason. But he was only seven years old and therefore paid little attention to any dream, he was so holy in heart. By God! I would give my shirt for you to have read his story, as I have.

"Dame Partlet, I tell you truly, Macrobius, who wrote of the vision of the noble Scipio in Africa, affirms dreams, and says that they are warnings of things that men shall see in the future. And furthermore, I beg you, look carefully into the Old Testament and see if Daniel held dreams to be foolish. Read also about Joseph, and there you shall see where dreams can sometimes—I don't claim always—be warnings of future events. Look at lord Pharaoh, King of Egypt, his baker, and also his butler, and see if they did not have results from dreams. Whoever will look up histories of various kingdoms can find many wonderful things about dreams. Look at Croesus, who was king of Lydia; didn't he dream that he sat in a tree, which signified that he would be hanged? There is also Andromache, the wife of Hector; on the day that Hector was to lose his life, she dreamt the night before that if he went into battle the next day he should be killed. She warned him, but to no avail; he nevertheless went to fight and was soon killed by Achilles. But this tale is much too long to tell, and also it is almost day; I must stop. Briefly, I say in conclusion that trouble shall come to me from this dream; and I say furthermore that I put no stock in laxatives, for they are poison, I know very well. I defy them; I do not like them at all!

"Now let's stop all this and talk of gayer things. Madam Partlet, as I hope to be saved, God has been very kind to me in one respect; for when I see the beauty of your face, all scarlet red about the eyes, all my fears die away. For it is as true as gospel, *Mulier est hominis confusio*—madam, the meaning of this Latin is, 'Woman is man's joy and all his bliss.' For when at night I feel your soft side, even though the narrowness of our perch prevents my riding you, I am so full of joy and comfort that I defy both dreams and visions!"

And with these words he flew down from the rafter, along with all his hens, for it was day, and with a clucking called them all to some grain which he found lying in the yard. He was regal and no longer afraid. He feathered Partlet twenty times before nine o'clock, and rode her as often. He looked like a grim lion as he roamed up and down on his toes; he barely condescended to set foot to the earth. When he found some grain he clucked, and all his wives came running to him. I shall leave this Chanticleer in his yard, as regal as a prince in his palace, and later I shall tell of his adventure.

The month called March, in which the world was begun and in which God first made man, was over, and also thirty-two days had passed in addition. Chanticleer, walking in all his pride with his seven wives beside him, cast up his eyes at the bright sun, which had traveled a bit more than twenty-one degrees in the sign of Taurus. Knowing by instinct alone that it was nine o'clock, he crowed with a happy voice. "The sun," he said, "has climbed forty-one degrees in heaven, and more. Madam Partlet, bliss of my world, listen how the happy birds sing, and look how the fresh flowers grow; my heart is full of gaiety and joy!"

But suddenly a sorrowful event overtook him. Happiness always ends in sorrow. God knows that worldly pleasure passes quickly; and if a rhetorician could write well, he might safely put this thought into a chronicle as a profound truth. Now let every wise man listen to me; this story is as true, I'll be bound, as is the book of Lancelot of the Lake, which women hold in such great reverence. Now I shall turn again to my account.

A fox, tipped with black, full of sly wickedness, who had lived in the grove three years, put there by divine foreknowledge, burst through the hedges that same night into the yard where fair Chanticleer and his wives were in the habit of going. And this fox lay quietly in a bed of herbs until past noon of that day, waiting for his chance to attack Chanticleer, as all murderers usually do who lie in wait to kill people.

Oh, false murderer, lurking in your den! Oh, second Iscariot; another Ganelon, false dissembler! Oh, Greek Sinon, who brought Troy to its utter ruin! Oh, Chanticleer, cursed be that morning on which you flew into the yard from your rafters! You were fully warned by your dreams that this day was dangerous for you. But what God has foreordained must come to pass: such is the opinion of certain churchmen. Yet any perfect cleric will bear witness that there is in the schools great altercation and dispute about this matter, and it has been so among a hundred thousand men. But I cannot sift the matter to the bottom, as the holy doctor Augustine can, or Boethius, or Bishop Bradwardine: whether God's noble foreknowledge forces me of necessity to do a certain thing—by "necessity" I mean simple necessity—or whether free choice is granted me to do that same thing or not to do it, although God had foreknowledge of it before it was done; or whether His foreknowledge forces me only by conditional necessity. I will not have anything to do with such debates; my tale is of a rooster, as you can hear, who took the advice of his wife, worse luck, to walk in the yard on that morning after he had had the dream that I have told you about.

Women's counsel is very often comfortless. Women's counsel first brought us misfortune and forced Adam to leave Paradise, where he had been very happy and quite comfortable. But I don't know whom I might offend, if I find fault with women's counsel; pass over it, for I said it as a joke. Read the authors who treat of such matters, and you will hear what they have to say about women. These are the words of the rooster, not mine; I can imagine no harm in woman.

Partlet, with all her sisters near by, lay merrily bathing in the sand, with her back to the sun, and the lordly Chanticleer sang more joyfully than the mermaid in the sea; for the Latin book, *Physiologus*, certainly claims that mermaids sing merrily and well. And it happened that, as he cast his eye upon a butterfly among the herbs, he became aware of the fox lying low there. He had no desire to crow then, but at once cried "Cok! cok!" and started up like a man frightened in his heart. For it is instinctive for a beast to want to flee from his enemy, if he can see it, even though he has never laid eyes on such a creature before.

Chanticleer, when he spied the fox, would have fled, if the fox had not said at once: "My dear sir, alas, where are you going? Are you afraid of me, your friend? Now, truly, I would be worse than a devil if I tried to harm you or do you wrong! I haven't come to spy on your secrets; actually, the reason I came was only to listen to you sing. For, truly, you have as merry a voice as any angel in heaven. There is more feeling in your music than in that of Boethius, or of anyone who can sing. My lord your father—God bless his soul—and also your courteous mother did me the great honor of visiting my house; and certainly, sir, I am very eager to please you. But speaking of singing, I shall say, as I hope to enjoy my two eyes, that except for you I have never heard anyone who could sing as your father did in the morning. Without doubt, it came from his heart, all that he sang. In order to make his voice stronger, he made such an effort that he found it necessary to close both his eyes, so loudly would he cry. And he would stand on his tiptoes meanwhile, and stretch forth his long and slender neck. And his judgment was so good, also, that there was no one in any country who could surpass him in song or wisdom. I have read carefully in *Sir Brunellus the Ass*, among the verses, that there was a rooster who caused a priest to lose his benefice because the son of the priest, when young and foolish, gave the rooster a knock on the leg. But, certainly, no comparison can be made between the wisdom and judgment of your father and the subtlety of this rooster. Now sing, sir, for holy charity; let's see whether you can imitate your father."

Chanticleer began to beat his wings, like a man who cannot see his betrayal because he is so entranced by flattery.

Alas, you lords, many a false flatterer is in your courts, and many a smooth-tongued rascal who pleases you much more, by my faith, than the man who speaks the truth to you. Read Ecclesiasticus on flattery; be wary, you lords, of the treachery of flatterers.

Chanticleer stood up high on his toes, stretched his neck, closed his eyes, and began to crow loudly for this occasion. Then Sir Russell, the fox, at once jumped up, grabbed Chanticleer by the throat, and carried him on his back towards the woods, for as yet no one had pursued him.

Oh, Destiny, there is no escaping you! Alas, that Chanticleer flew down from the rafters! Alas, that his wife took no heed of dreams! And all this trouble came on a Friday.

Oh, Venus, goddess of pleasure, since Chanticleer was your servant and did all he could in your service, more for delight than to propagate the race, why would you allow him to die on your day?

Oh, Geoffrey, dear sovereign master, who mourned so bitterly when your noble king Richard was shot, why do I not have the ability and learning to blame Friday as you did? For on a Friday, truly, he was killed. Then I would show you how I could mourn for Chanticleer's fear and pain.

Truly, such a cry or lamentation was never made by the ladies when Troy was conquered, and when Pyrrhus with drawn sword had grasped Priam by the beard and slain him, as the *Aeneid* tells us, as was made by all the hens in the yard when they saw Chanticleer captured. For queenly Partlet shrieked louder than Hasdrubal's wife when her husband had been killed and the Romans burned Carthage. She was so full of torment and rage that she jumped into the fire intentionally and burned herself with a steadfast heart.

Oh, woeful hens, you cried just as the wives of the senators did when Nero burned the city of Rome, because their husbands were killed, slain guiltless, by Nero. Now I shall return to my tale.

The poor widow and her two daughters heard the woeful cries of the hens and at once ran out of doors. They saw the fox going toward the grove, carrying the rooster away on his back. "Out! help! woe is me! Look, a fox!" they screamed,

and ran after him, as many other people did with sticks.
Colle, the dog, and Talbot, and Garland, and Malkin, with
her distaff in her hand, ran after him. The cow, the calf, and
even the hogs, so frightened were they by the barking of the
dogs, and also by the shouting of the men and women, ran
after him. All of them ran so hard they thought their hearts
would burst. They yelled like fiends in hell; the ducks
quacked as if they were to be killed; the geese, from fear,
flew over the trees; the noise was so terrible that the bees
swarmed from their hive. Ah, bless me! Truly, Jack Straw and
his crew never gave shouts half so shrill when they wanted to
kill a Fleming as were made this day after the fox. They
brought trumpets of brass, wood, horn, and bone, into which
they blew and puffed; and, meanwhile, they shrieked and
whooped. It seemed that heaven would fall.

Now, good people, I beg you all to listen. See how Fortune
suddenly overturns the hope and pride of her enemy! This
rooster, who lay across the fox's back, spoke to the fox in
spite of his fear, saying: "Sir, if I were you, so help me God,
I would say, 'Turn back, all you proud peasants! May bitter
plague take you! I have reached the edge of the wood now;
the rooster shall stay here; in spite of you I will eat him, in
faith, and not be long about it!'"

"In faith," the fox answered, "it shall be done." As soon as
he spoke the words, the rooster nimbly broke away from his
mouth and flew at once high into a tree.

When the fox saw that the rooster was gone, he said:
"Alas! Oh, Chanticleer, alas! I have done you a bad turn, in
that I frightened you when I grabbed you and took you out
of the yard. But, sir," he said, "I did it without evil inten-
tion. Come down, and I shall tell you what I meant. So help
me God, I shall tell you the truth."

"Nay, then," said Chanticleer. "I curse us both; but mainly
I will curse myself, both blood and bones, if you trick me
more than once. Never again shall you with your flattery get
me to sing with my eyes closed. For he who closes his eyes
on purpose when he should watch, God let him never pros-
per."

"No," said the fox, "but God bring misfortune to him who is so careless about his self-control as to prattle when he should hold his peace."

See, that is the result of being careless and negligent and trusting in flattery.

But you good people who think that this tale is a piece of foolishness about a fox, or a rooster and a hen, take heed of the moral. For St. Paul says that all which is written is without doubt written for our instruction; take the fruit and let the chaff be.

Now, dear God, if it be your will, as says my lord, make us all good men and bring us to heavenly bliss! Amen. HERE ENDS THE NUN'S PRIEST'S TALE.

EPILOGUE TO THE NUN'S PRIEST'S TALE: "Sir Nun's Priest," our Host said at once, "blessings on your breeches and stones! This was a merry tale of Chanticleer. By my troth, if you were a layman, you would be a real cock. For if you have as much spirit as you have strength, you have need of hens, I think; yes, more than seven times seventeen. See how brawny this gentle priest is! What a neck, what a big chest! His eyes have a look like a sparrow-hawk's; he doesn't need to paint himself with red dye or with cochineal from Portugal. Now, sir, good luck to you for this tale!"

And after that the Host spoke very merrily to another, as you shall hear.

"Madam, if I dared I would pray you to tell us a tale; thereby you could do us a great favor."

"Gladly," she said; "in order that I might please you—you and this worthy company."

Then she very soberly began her tale, as follows.

THE PROLOGUE OF THE WIFE OF BATH'S TALE: "My experience
gives me sufficient right to speak of the trouble there is in
marriage, even if there were no other authority in the world;
for, ladies and gentlemen, since I was twelve years old I have
had five husbands, eternal God be thanked—if it is legal
to have been married so often—and all were fine men in their
way. But not long ago I was certainly told that since Christ
attended only one wedding, in Cana of Galilee, He therefore
taught me by example to be married only once. And listen
also to the sharp words Jesus, God and man, spoke beside
the well to scold the Samaritan about this matter: 'You have
had five husbands,' he said, 'and that man whom you now
have is not your husband.' Certainly He said this; what He
meant by it I can't say. But I ask why the fifth man was
not husband to the Samaritan? How many was she allowed
to marry? In my time I never yet heard of a limitation of
number. Men can interpret and gloss the text up and down,
but I know surely without doubt that God expressly told
us to increase and multiply; that pleasant text I can easily
understand. I also know very well that He said my husband
should leave his father and mother and live with me. But He
made no mention of number, of bigamy, or of octogamy.
Why then should men call it wickedness?

"Look at the wise King, Lord Solomon: I believe he had
more than one wife. I wish to God it were possible for me
to be refreshed half as often as he was! What a gift from
God he had for all his wives! No man now living has the
same. God knows, this noble King must have had many a
merry bout with each of them the first night, to my think-
ing. He was well fixed for a lifetime! Thank God that I
married five! The sixth, whenever he comes, shall be wel-
come. Truly, I don't want to remain chaste at all. When my

husband has gone from this world, some Christian man shall marry me at once, for then, so says the Apostle, I am free to wed in God's name wherever I please. He says that it's no sin to be married; it's better to marry than to burn. What do I care if folks speak of cursed Lamech and his bigamy as wicked? I know very well that Abraham was a holy man, and Jacob also, as far as I can tell; and each of them had more than two wives, and many another holy man did, too. Where can you find in any period that the high God expressly forbade marriage? I beg you, answer me. Or where did He demand chastity? I know as well as you—it's no secret—that in speaking of virginity the Apostle said that he had no rules for it. People may advise a woman to be a virgin, but advice is not a commandment. God left it to our own judgment, for if He had commanded chastity, then He would have thereby condemned marriage. And, surely, if no seed is sown, where will virgins come from? Paul, at least, did not dare to command a thing for which his Master laid down no rules. The prize is set up for chastity; whoever is able can win it; let's see who runs the best race.

"This ideal chastity was not meant for everyone, but only when God in His power desired to bestow it. I know quite well that the Apostle was a virgin; but, nevertheless, though he wrote and said that he wished everyone would take him as an example, he only advises virginity. And he gave me full permission to be a wife; therefore, it is no sin, even of bigamy, to marry me if my husband dies. Though he said it is good for a man not to touch a woman, he meant in bed or on the couch, for it is dangerous to bring fire and tinder together— you all know what this comparison means. This is the sum of it: he considered chastity preferable to the weak compromise of marriage. I call men and women weak to marry only if they wished to remain chaste all their lives.

"I grant the right, without envy, of those who prefer chastity to bigamy. It pleases them to be spotless in body and spirit; about my own state I won't boast. A lord, as you all know, doesn't have all the dishes in his household of gold; some are wooden, yet they are very serviceable. God calls folks to Him in various ways, and each has a special gift from God, some this, some that, as He desires.

"Chastity is the perfect state, and continence, and devotion; but Christ, who is the well of perfection, did not instruct everyone to sell all his belongings and give the proceeds to the poor, and so to follow in His footsteps. He spoke to those who wish to live perfectly; and, ladies and gentlemen, by your leave, that's not me. I will bestow the flower of all my years on the acts and fruits of marriage.

"Tell me, also, why do we have organs of reproduction, and why were we created as we are? You can be sure they were not made for nothing. Let anybody interpret who wishes, and talk unendingly of how those organs are only for urinating and for distinguishing male from female—don't you disagree? Experience shows clearly that this is not so. In order to keep the clerics from being angry with me, I say that those organs were created for two purposes; that is, for business and for the pleasure of conception, whereby we do not displease God. Otherwise, why should the authors put down in their books that a husband should pay his debt to his wife? And with what can he make this payment except through the use of his poor tool? Therefore, these organs were made part of an individual for urinating and also for conception.

"But I do not claim that everyone who has such equipment as I just mentioned is bound to go and use it for conception. If that were so, no one would pay any attention to chastity. Christ, though formed like a man, was a virgin, and so was many a saint since the world began; yet they always lived in complete chastity. I don't hold any grudge against chastity. Let those who want to be pure white bread, and let us wives be called barley bread; yet Mark tells us that our Lord Jesus refreshed many a man with barley bread. I will continue in that way of living for which God intended us. I'm not finicky. As a wife, I will use my instrument as freely as God gave it to me. If I am standoffish, may God send me sorrow! My husband shall have me both evening and morning, whenever he wishes to come forth and pay his debt.

I don't deny that I will have my husband both my debtor and my slave; and as long as I am his wife he shall suffer in the flesh. I will have command over his body during all his life, not he. That's just the way the Apostle instructed me, and he told our husbands to love us well. I am completely in agreement with that opinion."

The Pardoner started up quickly. "Now, Madam," he said, "by God and by St. John, you are a noble preacher on this subject. I was about to take a wife, alas! But why should I punish my flesh so harshly? I would rather never take a wife!"

"Wait!" she replied, "My story has not yet begun. No, you'll drink from another barrel before I'm through, that shall taste worse than ale. And when I have told you my story of the troubles in marriage, in which I have been expert all my life—that is to say, I have held the whip—then you can judge whether you will drink from this barrel which I shall open. Beware of it before you approach too near, for I shall give more than ten examples. 'He who will not be warned by others, from him shall other men be warned.' Ptolemy wrote these very words; read in his *Almageste,* and you'll find it there."

"Madam," said the Pardoner, "I would like to ask you, if it is your desire, to continue your story as you started it. Spare no man, and from your experience instruct us young men."

"Gladly," she replied, "since it pleases you; but I beg all this company not to be vexed by what I say if I speak according to my fancy, for my only purpose is to amuse. Now, sirs, I shall continue my story.

"As I ever hope to drink wine or ale, I'll tell you the truth: of the husbands that I have married, three were good and two were bad. The three good ones were rich and old; they could scarcely hold to the contract by which they were bound to me. You know very well what I mean by this, by God! So help me God, I laugh when I think how pitifully I made them work at night! And, by my faith, I gave them no credit for it. They had given me their land and treasures; there was no longer any need for me to be diligent or respect-

ful to them to win their love. They loved me so well that
before God I set no value on their affection. A wise woman
will constantly busy herself to get a lover when she has
none, but since I had them completely in my hand, and since
they had given me all their property, what need was there
for me to try to please them, unless for my own profit and
pleasure? I put them to work in such a fashion that many a
night, by my faith, they sang 'Woe is me!' I assure you that
they did not get the prize of bacon which some married men
get at Dunmow in Essex. But I managed them so well by
my own rules that each of them was blissfully happy and
glad to bring me gay things from the fair. They were over-
joyed when I spoke affectionately to them, for, God knows, I
nagged them unmercifully.

"Now, listen, you wise wives who can understand me, to
how sensibly I conducted myself. This is the way you should
speak to them and put them in the wrong, for there is no
man who can swear and lie half so boldly as a woman. I
don't say this for wise wives, except when they are ill-advised.
A wise wife who knows what's good for her will be able to
convince her husband that the little gossipy bird is crazy, and
arrange for her own maid to bear her witness. But listen to
how I did it:

" 'Is this your doing, you old fool? Why is my neighbor's
wife so gay? She is admired wherever she goes, while I sit
at home without a single good dress. What do you do at my
neighbor's house? Is she so pretty? Are you so affectionate?
What do you whisper to our maid? Bless me! You old lecher,
stop your tricks! Now if I, innocently, have a friend or an
acquaintance, you scold like the devil when I just walk to
his house or amuse myself there. You come home as drunk as
a mouse and preach from your bench, bad luck to you! You
tell me it's a great mistake to marry a poor woman because
of the expense; and if she is rich, of fine family, then you
say it is a torment to put up with her pride and her tempera-
ment. And if she is good looking, you old knave, you say that
every lecher can have her, since any woman so besieged from
all sides cannot remain chaste.

" 'You say some men want us for our money and some for our figures, some for our beauty, some for our singing or dancing, some for our breeding and charm, and some for our small arms and hands; so, according to you, we're all going to the devil. You say that a castle long besieged cannot hold out.

" 'And if a woman is ugly, you say that she wants every man she sees, and that she will fawn on men like a spaniel until she finds one who will do business with her. There is no goose on the lake so plain as to be willing to go without a mate, according to you. You claim it is a hard thing to control what no one will willingly have. That's what you say when you go to bed, you wretch—and that no wise man needs to marry, or any man who wants to go to heaven. May thunder and lightning break your warty neck!

" 'You say that falling houses, smoke, and nagging wives cause men to run away from their own homes; ah, bless me, what ails an old man who goes on like that?

" 'You say we wives try to hide our faults until we are secure, and then we let them show. That's surely a malicious person's proverb.

" 'You say that oxen, asses, horses, and hounds are tried out thoroughly before they are bought, and so are basins, bowls, spoons, stools, and all such household equipment, as well as pots, clothes, and finery; but men don't try out their wives until they are married. You rascally old idiot! And then, you say, we exhibit our faults.

" 'You say further that I am displeased unless you praise my beauty, gaze continually at my face, call me "fair lady" in public, arrange a banquet for my birthday, keep me in good spirits, cater to my nurse and chambermaid, and honor my father's relatives and friends—you say that, you old barrelful of lies!

" 'And yet you have become falsely suspicious of our helper Jenkin because of his curly hair, shiny as the finest gold, and because he escorts me up and down. If you died tomorrow, I wouldn't have anything to do with him!

" 'But tell me this: why do you hide the keys of your

strongbox from me, bad luck to you? It's my money as well as yours, by God! Do you think you can make an idiot of your wife? Now, by that Lord called St. James, even if you were crazy you couldn't be master both of my body and my money. Blast your eyes, you'll have to give up one of them. What good is it to question and to spy on me? I believe you would like to lock me up in your strongbox! You should say, "Wife, go where you please; have fun, I won't believe any gossip. I know that you are a true wife, Dame Alice." We don't like a man who keeps watch on where we go; we want to be at liberty.

" 'The wise astrologist, Ptolemy, should be blessed by everyone, for in his *Almageste* he has this proverb: "The wisest of all men is the one who does not care who rules the world." You should understand from this proverb: If you have enough, why should you worry or care how happy other folks are? For you can be sure, old dotard, by your leave, that you can have me all you want at night. The man who will not allow another to light a candle from his lantern is too stingy; his light will not be therefore less, by God. So long as you have enough, you shouldn't complain.

" 'You also say that if we dress up in finery and expensive clothes there is danger to our chastity; but, worse luck for you, you have to support your argument with these words from the Apostle: "You women should dress yourselves in accord with chastity and modesty, without elaborate hairdress and gay jewelry, such as pearls and gold, and not in rich clothes." I will not behave according to your text or your interpretation any more than a gnat.

" 'You said that I was like a cat, which will live with whoever singes her fur; if the cat's fur is slick and bright, she will not stay in the house half a day, but goes out before dawn to show off her fur and go caterwauling. That is to say, Sir Bad Temper, if I dress up I will run out to show off my clothes.

" 'You old fool, what's the good of your spying? Even though you got Argus with his hundred eyes to be my bodyguard to the best of his ability, in faith, he couldn't guard me unless I wanted him to. I could fool him, you can be sure!

" 'You also said that there are three things which trouble all this earth, and that no one can endure a fourth. Oh, dear Sir Idiot, may Jesus shorten your days! You preach and say that a hateful wife is counted one of these misfortunes. Isn't there any comparison you can make in your parables without using a poor wife as one of them?

" 'You also compare a woman's love to hell, to barren ground where water cannot stand, and to wild fire; the more it burns, the more it wishes to consume everything that can be burned. Just as worms destroy a tree, you say, so a wife destroys her husband, and any man tied to a wife knows this.'

"Ladies and gentlemen, that's the way I convinced my old husbands that they had said what you have heard while they were drunk, and it was all false. But Jenkin and my niece bore witness to it for me. Oh, Lord, the trouble and grief I caused those husbands, and they were absolutely guiltless, by God's sweet pain! For I could bite and whine like a horse. I could complain even though I was guilty; otherwise I would have been killed many a time. First come, first served: I complained first, and that ended the fight. They were glad enough to make hurried excuses for things they had never been guilty of in their lives.

"I would nag my husband about wenching when he was so sick that he could scarcely stand up. But that tickled his heart, for he thought it was a sign of my great regard for him! I swore that all my gadding about at night was in order to spy on the wenches he slept with. By that trick I had many a gay time; for all such cunning is our birthright. God has given a woman the instinctive ability to deceive, to weep, and to spin as long as she lives. And so I can boast of one thing: in the end I got the best of my husbands in every way, by tricks, by force, or by something else, such as constant complaining or grumbling. They had bad luck in bed, especially; there I nagged them and gave them no pleasure. I would not stay in the bed if I felt my husband's arm over me, until he had paid me his bribe; then I would allow him to do his business with me. And, therefore, I give everybody this advice: anyone can profit, for everything is for sale; with an empty hand a man lures no hawks. For profit, I would suffer through all his lust and pretend enjoyment, although I never did like old men; that's what made me nag them all the time. For, though the Pope sat beside them, I would not spare them at their own table. And, by my faith, I paid them word for word. So help me omnipotent God, if I had to make my last testament right now, I don't owe them a word that is not paid. I brought it about by my cunning that they considered it best to give up any argument, or else have no peace. For, though my husband glared like an enraged lion, in the end he failed to have his way.

"Then I would say: 'Dearest one, observe how meek our sheep Wilkin is! Come close, dear husband, let me kiss your cheek! You should be all meek and patient and have a sweet, tender disposition, since you preach so much about Job's patience. Endure always, since you can preach so well. And if you don't, I will surely teach you that it is a fine thing to have a wife in peace. Without doubt, one of us two must give in, and, since a man is more reasonable than a woman, you must be the one to suffer. What ails you that you grumble and groan so much? Is it because you want my body all to yourself? Why, take it all! Here, have every little bit! By St. Peter, I wouldn't bother with you, if you didn't love it so well! For if I wished to sell my *belle chose*, I would have money to keep myself fresh as a flower. But I'll keep it all for your sweet tooth. You're to blame, by God; that's sure!'

"That was the kind of words we had. Now I shall tell you about my fourth husband. He was a reveler; that is to say, he had a mistress. And I was young and very passionate, stubborn and strong, and gay as a magpie. How I could dance to the small harp, and sing just like a nightingale, when I had drunk a draught of sweet wine! Metellius, the dirty pig that took his wife's life with a stick because she drank wine—if I had been his wife, he could not have frightened me away from drink! And after drinking, my thoughts turned to Venus, for as surely as cold causes hailstones, a liquorous mouth makes a lecherous tail. Tipsy women are without resistance—lechers know this from experience.

"Lord Christ! When I think back upon my youth and my gaiety, it tickles the cockles of my heart. To this day it does my heart good to think that I have had the world in my time; but age, alas, which poisons everything, has robbed me of my beauty and my sap. Let it go, farewell! The devil take it! The flour is gone, there's no more to say; now I must sell the bran as best I'm able. But nevertheless, I'll manage to be happy enough. I shall now continue about my fourth husband.

"As I was saying, it made me very jealous that he took pleasure in another woman. But he was repaid, by God and by St. Joce! I made him a cross from the same wood; not by vulgar bodily sin, but I was really so pleasant to other men that it made him fry in his own grease with anger and pure jealousy. By God, I was his purgatory on earth, for which I hope his soul is now in glory. For, God knows, he often sat and sang when his shoe pinched him bitterly. There was no one except him and God who knew in how many ways and how cruelly I tormented him. He died when I got back from Jerusalem and he lies buried in church in a tomb not so elaborate as that which Apelles skillfully made for Darius; it would only have been a waste to bury him expensively. Let him fare well; may God rest his soul! He is now in his coffin and his grave.

"Now I shall tell you about my fifth husband. May God let his soul never enter hell! And yet he was the most vicious towards me, as I can feel now on all my ribs, one after the other, and shall to my dying day. But in our bed he was so lively and jolly, and he could also flatter me so well when he wanted my *belle chose,* that even if he had beaten me on every bone he could immediately win my love again. I believe I loved him best because he was standoffish towards me. We women have, if I tell the truth, a peculiar reaction in this matter: whatever thing we cannot easily have, for it we will cry and crave all day. Forbid us a thing, and we want it. Pursue us, and we run away. When we encounter disdain, we show all our wares. A great crowd at the market makes high prices, and too great a bargain is held in little value. Every wise woman knows these things.

"My fifth husband, God bless his soul, whom I married for love and not for money, was once a cleric at Oxford. He left school and came home to board with my good friend who lived in our town, God bless her soul; her name was Alison. She knew my heart and all my secrets better than our parish priest, as I hope to prosper! I revealed all my thoughts to her. For even if my husband had urinated on a wall, or had done a thing which would cost him his life, to her and to no other woman and to my niece whom I loved so well I would have told every detail. And so I did, often, God knows; so many times it made his face red and hot with shame. Then he blamed himself for telling me so important a secret.

"It happened once in Lent—I often went to visit my friend, for I always loved to be merry and to go walking in March, April, and May from house to house to hear the various stories—that this cleric Jenkin, my friend Dame Alison, and I went into the fields. My husband was in London all that Lent; that gave me more leisure to play, to see and also to be seen by willing bachelors. How did I know what or where my destiny was? Therefore, I made my appearance at vigils, at processions, at sermons, on these pilgrimages, at the miracle plays, and at weddings; and I always wore my gay scarlet clothes. I'll swear that insects, moths, and mites ate no holes in them, and do you know why? Because they were constantly worn.

"Now, I'll tell you what happened to me. I said that we walked in the fields, and, really, this cleric and I got along so well together that after a while I told him, with foresight, that if I were a widow he could marry me. For, truly, and I don't say it as a boast, I was never yet without foresight in marriage, or in other things. I think that a mouse which has only one hole to run into is not worth an onion; for if that fails, all is lost.

"I convinced him that he had enchanted me—my mother taught me that trick. And I said, also, that I had dreamed of him all night, that he had come to kill me as I lay on my back, and all my bed was full of blood; yet I hoped that he would bring me luck, for I was taught that blood signifies gold. And all this was false; I had dreamed nothing of the sort, but was only following my mother's instructions in this, as in many other things.

"And now, let me see, what shall I say? Oh, yes, by God, I have my story again.

"When my fourth husband lay on his bier, I wept and looked sad in the way all wives must, for it is the custom, and I covered my face with my kerchief. But since I had already arranged for another husband, I wept but little, I'll tell you.

"The next morning my husband was borne to the church, followed by the neighbors who mourned for him; and Jenkin, our cleric, was one of them. So help me God, when I saw him walking behind the bier, it seemed to me that he had a pair of legs and feet so clean and trim that I gave my whole heart into his keeping. He was, I think, twenty years old and I was forty, if the truth be known; but I always had a colt's tooth. I was gap-toothed and that was suitable, for St. Venus had given me her birthmark. So help me God, I was a lusty one, pretty and rich, young and well made. And truly, as my husbands told me, I had the finest *belle chose* possible. For certainly, my emotions all come from Venus and my spirit from Mars. Venus gave me my lust and passion, and Mars gave me my sturdy strength. When I was born, Taurus was ascendant and Mars was in it. Alas, alas, that love was ever sinful! I always followed the influences of the constellation under which I was born; consequently, I could never refuse my chamber of Venus to any good fellow. But I have the mark of Mars on my face and also in another private spot. As I hope God will be my salvation, I never made love from expediency, but only because I wanted to. I didn't care whether he was short or tall, black or white, how poor he was or of what rank. It didn't matter, so long as he pleased me.

"What should I say? At the end of a month this gay cleric,

Jenkin, who was so attractive, married me with great ceremony. And to him I gave all the lands and property which had been given to me previously. But afterward I regretted this bitterly; he would not agree to anything I wanted. Once, by God, when I tore a leaf from his book, he hit me so hard on the side of my head that I became deaf in that ear. I was as stubborn as a lioness and had the tongue of a true shrew, and I went about as before, visiting from house to house, though he had forbidden it. Because of that, he often preached to me and taught me from old Roman histories: how Sulpicius Gallus left his wife permanently just because he once caught her looking out of the door bare-headed. And he told me by name of another Roman who also left his wife because she went to a summer party without his permission. And then he would search in his Bible for that proverb in which Ecclesiasticus strictly forbids a man to allow his wife to go running around. Then he would always quote the following proverb: 'Whoever builds his house of twigs, and rides his blind horse over rough ground, and allows his wife to visit shrines, is worthy to be hanged from the gallows!' But it was all in vain; I cared not a berry for his proverbs or his old sayings, and I would not be corrected by him. I hate a man who tells me my faults, and so do other women than I, God knows. This made him thoroughly angry with me; I wouldn't put up with him at all.

"Now I shall tell you truly, by St. Thomas, why I tore that leaf from his book, for which he hit me and made me deaf. He had a book in which he was always eagerly reading day and night, for pleasure; he called it Valerius and Theophrastus and always laughed heartily when he read it. And also there was once in Rome a cleric, a cardinal named St. Jerome, who wrote a book against Jovinian. In this book, in addition, were Tertullian, Chrysippus, Trotula, and Heloise, who was an abbess not far from Paris, and also the *Parables* of Solomon, Ovid's *Art of Love,* and many others; all these books were bound in one volume. And every day and night it was his custom, when he had leisure and freedom from other worldly occupations, to read in this book about wicked wives.

He knew more stories and biographies of them than there are about good wives in the Bible. For you can be sure that it's an impossibility for any cleric to speak well of wives, unless in holy saints' lives, but not about other women. Who wrote the fable of the lion, tell me, who? By God, if women had written stories, as the clerics have done in their studies, they would have written more about the wickedness of men than all the sons of Adam could make good. The children of Mercury and Venus are opposite in their attitudes: Mercury loves wisdom and science, while Venus loves sport and abandon. And because of their opposite ways, each falls as the other rises. Therefore, God knows, Mercury is desolate in Pisces when Venus is exalted, and Venus falls when Mercury mounts. As a result, no woman is praised by any cleric. The cleric, when he grows old and can no longer do Venus' work worth an old shoe, then he sits down and writes in his dotage that women cannot keep their marriage vows!

"But back to my purpose in telling you why I was beaten for a book, by God! One night my husband Jenkin read in his book, as he sat by the fire, first about Eve, who brought misery to all mankind because of her wickedness, for which Jesus Christ Himself was slain in order to redeem us with His life's blood. See, here expressly you can discover that woman caused the loss of all mankind. Then he read me how Samson lost his hair: as he slept, his mistress cut it off with her scissors, through which treachery he lost both his eyes. Next he read me, if I'm not mistaken, about Hercules and his Dejanira, who caused him to set fire to himself. He did not forget to read about the troubles and the woes which Socrates had with his two wives: how Xantippe emptied a chamber pot on his head; the poor man sat as still as if he had died, wiped his head, and dared only to say, 'Before the thunder stops, the rain comes!' The story of Pasiphae, queen of Crete, he, in his cursedness, considered excellent—fie, I won't tell any more—it's a horrible thing, all about her disgusting lust and her lechery.

"He read very religiously the story of Clytemnestra, the adulteress who murdered her husband. He also told me why

Amphiaraus lost his life at Thebes. My husband had a story about his wife, Eriphyle, who, for a gold brooch, secretly told the Greeks where her husband had hidden himself; as a result, he was killed at Thebes. He told me about Livia and Lucilia; they both murdered their husbands, one for love, the other for hate. Livia poisoned her husband late one evening because she hated him; lustful Lucilia loved her husband so much that she gave him a kind of love-drink to make him think always of her; as a result he died before morning. And thus husbands suffer no matter what.

"Then he told me how Latumius complained to his friend Arrius that a certain tree grew in his garden on which his three wives had hanged themselves because of broken hearts. 'Dear brother,' said Arrius, 'give me a root from this blessed tree and I shall plant it in my garden.' He also read me about wives of later periods; some had slain their husbands in their beds and allowed their lovers to sleep with them all night while the corpses lay face up on the floor. Others had driven nails into their sleeping husbands' brains and killed them. Some had put poison into their husbands' drinks. Of such matters he told more terrible stories than you can imagine, and at the same time he knew more proverbs than there are blades of grass or herbs on earth.

" 'It is better,' he said, 'to live with a lion or a foul dragon than with a nagging woman'; or, 'It is better to live high up near the roof than down below in the house with an angry wife; such women are so wicked and contrary, they always hate whatever their husbands love.' Or he would say, 'A woman puts aside her modesty when she takes off her smock'; or else, 'A pretty woman, unless she is also chaste, is like a gold ring in a sow's nose.' Who can think or imagine the sorrow and pain I felt in my heart?

"When I saw that he would never stop reading all night in this cursed book, I suddenly ripped three leaves from it as he read, and I also hit him so hard on the cheek with my fist that he toppled over backwards into the fire. Then he jumped up like an angry lion, and hit me so hard on the head with his fist that I was stretched out on the floor as if I had been killed. When he saw how still I lay, he was frightened and would have fled, but I finally came out of my swoon and cried out, 'Oh, false thief, have you killed me? And have you murdered me for my land? Before I die, I wish to kiss you.'

"He drew near and kneeled down gently, saying, 'Dear Alice, so help me God, I shall never hit you again. You yourself are to blame for what I have done. Forgive me for it, I beg you!' Then I hit him on the cheek again, and said: 'Thief, I'm even with you that much; now I will die, for I can talk no longer.'

"But at last, after much trouble, we two made up. He put the reins in my hands to have complete control of our property and house, and of his tongue and acts also. And I made him burn his book right then and there. When, by this master stroke, I had gained the upper hand, and he had said, 'My own true wife, do as you wish all your days; you guard your honor and my position'—after that day we never had any more arguments. So help me God, I was as kind to him as any wife, from Denmark to India, and faithful to him too, as he was to me. I pray God, who sits in splendor, to bless his soul out of His dear mercy. Now I shall tell my tale, if you will listen."

※

BEHOLD THE WORDS BETWEEN THE SUMMONER AND THE FRIAR: The Friar laughed when he had heard all this. "Now, Madam," he said, "as I hope to have joy and salvation, that was a long preamble to a tale!"

But when the Summoner heard the Friar exclaim, he said, "Look by God's two arms, a friar will always be a meddler! See, good people, a friar, like a fly, will fall into every dish and every discussion. Why do you speak of preambulation? What's the difference—amble, or trot, or shut up, or go sit down! You are interrupting our enjoyment!"

"Oh, is that so, Sir Summoner?" said the Friar. "Now, my

faith, before I leave I will tell such a tale or two about a summoner that everyone here will laugh."

"Now, Friar," said the Summoner, "I curse your face, and I'll curse myself if I don't tell two or three tales about friars, before I arrive in Sittingbourne, that will make your heart burn. For I know your patience is all gone!"

"Peace!" our Host cried, "and right now! Let the woman tell her story. You act like people drunk on ale. Go ahead, Madam, tell your story; that's the best thing to do."

"All right, sir," replied the Wife. "Just as you wish, if I have the permission of this worthy Friar."

"Yes, indeed, Madam," the Friar said. "Tell away and I shall listen." HERE THE WIFE OF BATH ENDS HER PROLOGUE.

HERE BEGINS THE TALE OF THE WIFE OF BATH: In the old days of King Arthur, of whom the Britons speak with such respect, all this land was filled with the supernatural. The fairy queen with her jolly band danced often in many a green meadow. At least, I have read that this was the old belief; the time of which I speak was many hundred years ago. But now one can no longer see the elves, for all kinds of holy friars, as thick as dust in a sunbeam, with their great charity and prayers seek out every land and river, blessing halls, chambers, kitchens, bedrooms, cities, towns, castles, high towers, villages, dairies, barns, stables—this is why there are no fairies. For where an elf once walked there now walks a friar, mornings and afternoons, saying his prayers as he begs through his district. Nowadays women can safely travel past every bush and tree; there is no other evil spirit abroad but the friar, and he can only do us physical dishonor.

It happened that King Arthur had in his court a lusty squire who one day rode along the river where he saw a girl walking ahead of him, alone as she was born, and, despite her resistance, he ravished her. This misdeed caused such an outcry and such protest was made to King Arthur that the knight was condemned to death by a court of law. He would have lost his head—perhaps this was the law then—had not the Queen and other ladies begged so hard for mercy that the King granted him his life and gave him to the Queen to decide as she wished whether he would live or die.

The Queen heartily thanked the King, and then one day when she found the opportunity she spoke to the knight: "Your situation is still such that your life is not safe. I will grant you your life if you can tell me what it is that women desire most. Take care, now, and save your neck from the ax! And if you cannot give the answer now, I will give you leave to travel for a year and a day to seek and learn a satisfactory answer to my question. But before you go, I must have your pledge that you will return."

The knight was sad and sighed deeply, but what could he do? He was not able to do as he liked. At last he decided to go away and to return at the end of a year with whatever answer God might provide. He took his leave and went on his way.

He sought out every house and place in which he hoped he might have the luck to learn what it is that women love most. But he could in no way manage to find two creatures who were in agreement on this subject. Some said women loved riches best; some said honor; some said gaiety; some said finery; some said love-making and to be frequently widows and wives. Some said that our hearts are most comforted when we are flattered and pleased. I won't deny that those folk are very near the truth. A man can best win us by flattery; we are all caught by constant attentions and consideration. Some others said that we love our freedom best, and to do just as we please, so that no man will scold us for our faults, but rather say that we are wise and in no way foolish. Actually, there is no one of us that will not kick if anybody scratches us on a sore spot. Let a man try it, and he'll find that true; for no matter how evil we are inside, we wish to be thought wise and pure. Some said that we take great delight in being considered stable and discreet, steadfast in purpose, not giving away secrets told to us. But that answer is not worth a rake-handle. By God, we women can keep no secret; witness Midas—do you want to hear the story?

Ovid, among other details, mentions that Midas had two ass's ears growing on his head under his long hair, and that he was able to hide this defect cunningly from the sight of everyone except his wife; no one else knew of it. He loved her deeply and also trusted her, and he begged her to tell no one of his disfigurement. She swore that she would not tell for all the world; she would not be so low or wicked as to bring a bad name upon her own husband, nor, by telling, to bring shame upon herself. Nevertheless, she thought that she would die from keeping a secret so long. The desire to tell pained her heart so sorely that she thought the words would burst from her. Since she dared tell no one, she ran down to a nearby marsh—her heart seemed on fire until she got there —and, like a heron sputtering in the mud, she put her mouth to the water and said, "Don't betray me, water, with your sound; I'll tell you and no other: my husband has two long ass's ears! Now it is out, and my heart is whole. Truly, I could keep the secret no longer." You see by this that, though we women can keep a secret for a while, it must come out; we can hide nothing. If you want to know the rest of that story, read Ovid and learn it from him.

When this knight, who is the subject of my tale, saw that he could not learn what women love most, his spirit was sad within him. But home he went; he could not linger, for the day had arrived when he had to return. On his way he happened to ride, greatly troubled, by the side of a forest, where he saw more than twenty-four ladies dancing. He went eagerly toward the dancers, in the hope of learning something useful. But before he reached them the dancers vanished; he could not tell where. He saw nobody except a woman sitting on the grass—an uglier creature no one can imagine. This old woman rose to meet the knight and said: "Sir Knight, there is no path this way. Tell me truly what you seek. Perhaps I can help you; old folks know many things."

"Dear mother," he said, "I am really as good as dead, unless I can say what it is that women most desire. If you can inform me, I shall pay you well."

"Take my hand and swear," she said, "that you will do the next thing I ask of you if it is in your power, and before nightfall I will tell you the answer."

"You have my word," said the knight. "I consent."

"Then I can truly say that your life is saved," she said, "for I will stake my life that the Queen will agree with my answer. Let's see the proudest wearer of kerchief or headdress dare to disagree with what I shall teach you. Come, let us go, without more talk." Then she whispered a message into his ear and bade him be happy and not worry.

When they arrived at the court, the knight said that he had kept to the day that he had promised, and that he was ready with the answer. Many high-born wives and maidens, and many wise widows had assembled there, and the Queen herself sat as judge to hear his answer. Then the knight was told to appear. Silence was ordered, and the knight was instructed to tell the audience what thing mortal women love best. The knight did not stand like a dumb beast, but at once answered the question in a manly voice so that all the court heard: "My liege lady," he said, "in general, women wish to have complete control over both their husbands and love-affairs, and to be masters of their men. That is your greatest desire, though you kill me for saying so. Do what you will with me; I'm at your disposal."

In all the court there was not one wife or maid or widow who denied what he had said; all agreed that he deserved to live.

At that decision the old woman whom the knight had seen sitting on the grass jumped up and cried, "Mercy, my sovereign lady Queen! Before you go, do me justice. I taught this answer to the knight, and in return he swore to me that he would do the first thing I asked him if it lay in his power. Before this court, then, Sir Knight, I ask you to take me as your bride, for you know well that I've saved your life. If I lie, say no, upon your honor."

The knight answered, "Alas, woe is me! I know very well that that was my promise. For the love of God, ask something else! Take all my money, and let my body go."

"No," she replied, "in that case I'd curse us both. Not for all the metal and ore that lies on this earth or is buried under it would I give up being your beloved wife, though I'm old and ugly and poor."

"My beloved?" he exclaimed, "rather my damnation! Alas, that anyone of my birth should be so foully shamed!" But all was in vain; the conclusion was that he was forced to marry her and to take his old wife to bed with him.

Now some people will perhaps say that I did not take the trouble to tell you about all the gaiety and finery which was to be seen at the wedding feast that day. I will answer them briefly: there was no joy nor any feast at all; there was nothing but sadness and much sorrow. The knight married her secretly in the morning and then hid himself like an owl all day, so troubled was he by the ugliness of his wife.

The knight's thoughts were very miserable when he took his wife to bed; he tossed and turned back and forth. His old wife lay there with a steady smile, and said: "Bless me, dear husband; does every knight treat his wife as you do? Is this the law of King Arthur's court? Is every one of his knights so standoffish? I'm your own love and also your bride, the one who saved your life, and truly I've done you no wrong. Why do you treat me so on the first night? You act like a man who has lost his mind. What have I done? For the love of God, tell me and I will amend it if I can."

"Amend it!" replied the knight. "Alas, no, no! It will never be amended. You are so ugly, so old, and of such low birth, it's little wonder that I toss and turn. I wish to God my heart would burst!"

"Is this the cause of your discontent?" she asked.

"Yes, of course," he answered, "and no wonder."

"Now, sir," she said, "I could change all this, if I wanted to, within three days, if you conducted yourself properly toward me. But you say that nobility of character is inherent in riches; that you wealthy folk are therefore gentlemen. Such arrogance is not worth a hen. See who is most quietly and unostentatiously virtuous and most diligent in doing whatever kind deeds he can; take him as the greatest gentleman. Christ wishes us to claim our nobility of character from Him and not from our forefathers because of their wealth. Though they left us all their possessions and we claim therefore to be of a noble family, they cannot bequeath to any of us any part of the virtuous way of life which made them gentlemen, and which served as an example for us to follow.

"Dante, the wise poet of Florence, could speak well about this subject. His story runs something like this: 'Man rarely rises by his own little efforts, for God in His goodness wishes us to derive our nobility of character from Him.' We can receive only temporal things from our ancestors, things which hurt and harm man.

"Everyone knows as well as I that if nobility of character were the natural, exclusive inheritance of a particular family, the members of that family could never cease to be truly noble, because it would be impossible for them to do evil and to have faults.

"Take a torch and carry it into the darkest house between here and the Caucasus; shut the door and go away. The torch will still blaze and burn as brightly as if twenty thousand men watched it. It will carry out its natural function, I'll stake my life, until it burns out. You can clearly see from this that nobility is not connected with wealth, for people do not always act from natural causes as the torch does. God knows, one finds often enough a lord's son doing wicked and shameful deeds. The man who wishes to be considered gentlemanly because he is born of virtuous ancestors, and yet will not act virtuously as did his ancestors, is not a gentleman, even though he is a duke or an earl. For wicked deeds make a scoundrel. Nobility of character is not just the reputation of your ancestors, resulting from their noble deeds, for that is no part of you. Your nobility of character comes from God alone; from Him comes all our true distinction; it was not left to us along with our position.

"Look how noble Tullus Hostilius was, who rose, as Valerius relates, from poverty to high rank. Read Seneca and also Boethius; there you'll find it plainly stated that there is no doubt that the man is noble who does noble deeds. Therefore, dear husband, I conclude as follows: though my ancestors were lowly, God can, as I hope He will, grant me the grace to live virtuously. When I begin to live in that fashion and to give up sin, then I am a gentlewoman.

"You also scorned my poverty, but God in whom we trust chose to live His whole life in poverty. And surely every man, maid, or wife knows that Jesus, the King of Heaven, would not choose an evil way of living. Contented poverty is an honest thing, certainly; Seneca and other writers say that. I consider the man who is satisfied with his poverty rich, even though he does not own so much as a shirt. The covetous man is poor, for he desires more than he can have. But he who has nothing and covets nothing is rich, although you look down on him. True poverty sings happily. Juvenal speaks gaily of poverty: 'The poor man as he goes along the road can sing and play in front of thieves.' Poverty is a harsh virtue, but I believe it makes for industry. It also adds wisdom, if it is borne patiently. These things are true of poverty, even though it seems a wretched state no one should wish to be in. When a man is depressed by poverty he often comes to know his God and also himself. It seems to me that poverty is an eyeglass through which one may see his true friends. Therefore, since I do not trouble you, don't complain any more about my poverty.

"Now, sir, you reproached me for my age. Surely, even if there were no authority for it in any book, you honorable gentlefolk agree that one must be courteous to an old man and call him father, in order to be considered well-mannered. I think, also, that I could find support for that statement among the writers. Since you find me old and ugly, don't be afraid that I'll make you a cuckold, for ugliness and age, I'll warrant, are fine guardians of chastity. Nevertheless, since I know your pleasure, I'll satisfy your physical desire.

"Choose one of these two things," she said, "to have me ugly and old until I die, but a true and humble wife who will never displease you as long as I live; or to have me young and lovely and take your chances on the traffic there will be in and out of your house, or quite possibly elsewhere, on account of me. Take your choice; whichever you want."

The knight thought hard and sighed deeply. At last he replied, "My lady, my love, my dear wife, I put myself under your wise control. You yourself choose whichever you think will be more agreeable and honorable for both of us. I don't care which; whatever you like suits me."

"Then am I now your master," she asked, "since I can decide and do as I wish?"

"Certainly, wife," he said, "I think that will be best."

"Kiss me," she commanded, "we are no longer at odds, for, by my troth, I will be both things to you; that is to say, both lovely and faithful. I pray God that I may die insane unless I am as loyal as ever any wife since the world began. And if by tomorrow morning I am not as beautiful as any lady, empress, or queen between the east and the west, you may kill me or not as you wish. Lift up the curtain and see for yourself."

When the knight saw that she was truly beautiful and young, he joyfully clasped her in his arms, his heart filled with happiness. He kissed her a thousand times over, and she obeyed him in everything which might give him happiness or pleasure.

Thus they lived all their lives in perfect joy. May Jesus Christ send us husbands meek, young, and lusty abed, and the luck to outlast them. And I also pray Jesus to hasten the death of those who will not be ruled by their wives. And may God soon send a severe pestilence to old and stingy husbands!
HERE ENDS THE WIFE OF BATH'S TALE.

THE FRIAR

THE PROLOGUE OF THE FRIAR'S TALE: The noble Friar, that worthy licensed beggar, had been casting unpleasant glances steadily at the Summoner, but as yet, for courtesy's sake, he had made no uncivil remark to him. At last he said to the Wife of Bath: "Madam, may God send you a happy life! You have touched here upon a difficult problem, one fit for the schools, as I hope to prosper. I think that you have spoken truly of many things, but, Madam, there is no need for us, as we ride along the road here, to speak about any but gay matters; let's leave quotation of authorities to the preaching and schoolwork of the clergy, for God's sake. But, if it pleases this company, I shall tell you an amusing tale about a summoner. Faith, you can easily tell from his title that nothing good can be said about a summoner; I trust none of you will be offended. A summoner is a runner up and down with summonses for fornication, and is beaten at every village's end."

Our Host then spoke: "Ah, sir, you should be kind and courteous, as befits one of your station. We want no arguments in this company. Tell your tale, and leave the Summoner alone."

"No," said the Summoner, "let him say what he likes to me. When my turn comes, by God, I'll repay every groat. I shall tell him what a great honor it is to be a flattering licensed beggar, and I'll tell about a lot of other kinds of crime which it isn't necessary to rehearse now. I'll tell him what his job is, don't worry."

Our Host answered, "Peace, no more of this!" And then he said to the Friar, "Tell your tale, my dear master."

HERE BEGINS THE FRIAR'S TALE: Once upon a time there lived in my part of the country an archdeacon, a man of high position, who boldly executed his duty in punishing fornication, witchcraft, procuring, slander, and adultery, as well as church robberies, breaches of wills and contracts, neglect of the sacraments, usury, and simony. But, without doubt, he caused the greatest trouble to lechers; they must sing, if they were caught! And people in arrears with their tithes were cruelly punished, if any parson reported them to the archdeacon, who let no fine escape him. For scanty tithes and too small offering he made the people sing pitifully. Before the bishop caught them with his hook, they were marked down by the archdeacon, and then he had the power within his jurisdiction to punish them. He had a summoner always handy; there wasn't a slicker boy in England, for he secretly kept a group of spies who reported everything to him which he could use to advantage. He knew how to let one or two lechers go if they directed him to twenty-four others. Though this summoner was as mad as a hare, I shall not refrain from telling of his deviltry, for he has no power over us. Summoners have no jurisdiction over us friars, and they never shall, to the end of their lives.

"By St. Peter!" exclaimed the Summoner. "So are the prostitutes also beyond our power!"

"Peace!" cried our Host. "Hard luck and misfortune to you! Let him tell his tale. Now tell on, Friar, even if the Summoner complains. Omit nothing, my own dear master."

This false thief, this summoner (continued the Friar), always had bawds handy, as ready to do his bidding as any hawk in England is to come to the lure; they told him all their secrets, for their acquaintance with him was not new. They were his secret agents. He got great profits for himself thereby, of which his master was frequently ignorant. He could summon an ignorant man on pain of excommunication without a written summons, and such men were glad to fill his purse and buy him large dinners at the tavern. As Judas had a small purse and was a thief, just such a thief was this summoner; his master received only half his income. He was, if I give him his just due, a thief, a summoner, and a bawd. He also had wenches in his employ who whispered in his ear whether it was Sir Robert or Sir Hugh, or Jack or Ralph, or whoever it was who slept with them. Then, when the wench and he were in this partnership, he would get a forged paper which summoned both the wench and the man to the chapter court. There the man was fleeced and the woman freed. Then the summoner would say to the man: "Friend, for your sake I'll have your name stricken from the records. This case will trouble you no more. I am your friend; I will help you in any way possible."

Indeed, this summoner knew more about bribery than it is possible to tell in two years. For there is no hunting dog in the world better at telling an injured deer from a sound one than this summoner was at recognizing a sly lecher or an adulterer or a loose woman. And since he made his whole living in this way, he therefore devoted all his time to it.

It happened one day that this summoner, always watching for easy prey, rode to summon an old widow, a hag, pretending he had a case against her because he wanted to rob her. It chanced that he saw a gay yeoman riding ahead of him at the edge of the forest. The yeoman carried a bow with bright, keen arrows and wore a green short coat and on his head a hat with black fringe.

"Sir," said the summoner, "hail and well met!"

"Welcome," replied the yeoman, "to you and to every

good fellow. Where are you riding in this forest? Will you travel far today?"

The summoner answered him, saying: "No, my destination is nearby. I plan to collect some rent that is owed to my lord."

"Are you then a bailiff?" asked the yeoman.

"Yes," replied the summoner. He was ashamed to reveal that he was a summoner, so despised was that title.

"By God," said the yeoman, "dear brother, you are a bailiff and I am one, too. I am not known in this country. I would be glad to become better acquainted with you, and, if you wish, to swear brotherhood with you as well. I have gold and silver in my chest and, if you should happen to visit our district, everything shall be yours, whatever you want."

"Thanks, indeed!" said the summoner. Joining hands, each swore to be the other's brother until he died. Then, pleasantly talking, they gaily rode on.

The summoner was as full of chatter as a butcher-bird is full of spite, and he constantly asked questions about everything. "Brother," he said, "where is your home, in case some day I should look for you?"

The yeoman courteously replied, "Far in the north country, brother, where I hope some time to see you. Before we part, I'll give you such careful directions that you will not miss my house."

"Now, brother," said the summoner, "since you are a bailiff the same as I, I beg you to teach me some cunning as we ride along; tell me frankly how I can most profit in my job. Don't hold anything back because of conscience or sin, but tell me as a brother how you do business."

"Now, my troth, dear brother," replied the yeoman, "to tell you the truth my income is very meager and scanty. My lord is hard and overbearing to me, and my job requires a great deal of work; therefore, I make my living by extortion. Truly, I take all that men will give me. Everything that I spend, at least, I get from year to year by cunning and force. I can truly tell you no plainer."

"Now, actually," said the summoner, "I do the same thing. God knows, I only refrain from taking whatever is too heavy or too hot. My conscience does not trouble me about anything I can get by secret dealings. Were it not for my extortions, I could not live; and I do not wish to be shriven for such tricks. I have no weak stomach or conscience: I curse every one of these shrift-fathers. By God and by St. James, you and I are well met! But, dear brother, tell me your name."

The yeoman meanwhile began to smile a little and replied: "Brother, do you want me to tell you my name? I am a fiend; my dwelling is in hell, and on earth I ride about my holdings to find out whether men will give me anything. My pickings are the whole of my income. Observe that you ride abroad for the same reason: to get spoils, you don't care how. I do the same, for now I would ride to the end of the world to find a victim."

"Ah," said the summoner, "bless me! What did you say? I thought you were a yeoman, truly. You have the form of a man just like me. Do you have a specified form in hell when you are in your usual state?"

"Certainly not," said the yeoman. "We have no form there; but we can assume a form when we like, or else make it seem to you that we are at times shaped like a man or like an ape; or I can ride or walk like an angel. It's no miracle that this is so; a lousy juggler can deceive you, and certainly I have more magical skill than he."

"Why is it, then," the summoner asked, "that you ride or walk in various shapes and not always in one?"

"Because we wish to assume whatever form enables us most easily to take in our victims," replied the fiend.

"Why do you take all this trouble?"

"Many causes, dear Sir Summoner," answered the fiend. "But there is a time for all things; the day is short, it is already past nine o'clock, and I have so far got nothing today. I shall attend to gain, if I can, rather than to discussion of our opinions. In any case, my brother, your wit is far too small to understand such matters, even though I explained them to you. But you ask why we work so hard; sometimes, when it pleases Him, we are God's agents and the means for carrying out His commands, upon His creatures, by various methods and in various shapes. We have no power without Him, certainly, if He desires to stand against us. And, sometimes, at our request, we have permission to torment only the body and not to grieve the soul; witness Job, to whom we brought misery. And sometimes we have power over both, that is, soul and body alike. Then, sometimes, we are allowed to seek out a man and to bring unrest to his soul, but not to his body, yet everything is for the best; when a man withstands our temptation, it brings about his salvation, though it was not our intent that he should be saved, but that we should take possession of him. And sometimes we act as servants to a man, as to the archbishop, St. Dunstan, and as I was servant to the Apostles."

"But tell me truly," said the summoner, "do you make your new bodies always of the elements?"

The fiend answered: "No, sometimes we dissemble, and sometimes we rise in dead bodies in various ways and speak as reasonably and fairly and well as Samuel did to the Witch of Endor (yet some men say it was not he; I pay no heed to your divinity). But of one thing I warn you, I do not joke. You wanted at all costs to know how we are formed; hereafter you shall go where you won't need to learn that from me, my dear brother. For you shall be better able, from your own experience, to preach about this matter from a pulpit than Virgil was while he lived, or even Dante. Now, let's ride on at once, for I wish to keep company with you until it happens that you forsake me."

"No," said the summoner, "that shall not happen! I am a yeoman, widely known; I will keep my promise in this matter. For though you were the devil Satan, I would keep my promise to my brother, as I swore to do, and each of us should be a true brother in this situation. So we shall proceed with our looting together. You take your share, whatever people will give you, and I'll take mine; that way we can both live. And if either of us has more than the other one, let him be true and divide it equally with his brother."

"I agree," said the devil, "by my faith." And with these words they rode on their way.

Just at the entrance of the town to which the summoner had planned to go, they saw a cart, loaded with hay, stuck in the deep mud. The carter beat the horses and shouted, as if he were crazy, "Up, Brok! Get up, Scot! Why do you stop because of the rocks? The fiend take you, body and bones, as sure as you were foaled, such troubles I have suffered with you! The devil take everything, horses, cart, and hay!"

"We shall have some fun now," the summoner said. He quietly drew near to the fiend, as if nothing were happening, and whispered in his ear, "Listen, my brother, listen, by your faith! Didn't you hear what the carter said? Take it at once, for he has given it to you—both the hay and the cart, and also his three nags."

"No," said the devil, "not a bit of it, God knows! That is not his intention, believe me. Ask him yourself, if you do not trust me; or else wait a little and you will find out."

The carter whacked his horses on the rump and they began to tug and pull. "Hey! now," he said. "May Jesus Christ bless you and all His handiwork, both great and small! That was well pulled, my own gray rascal. I pray God and St. Loy to save you! Now my cart is out of the mud, by God!"

"See," said the fiend, "what did I tell you? You can see here, my own dear brother, that this fellow said one thing but he thought something else. Let's continue on our journey; I get nothing here to carry away."

When they had passed a little beyond the town, the summoner began to whisper to his brother: "Brother," he said, "an old woman lives here who had almost as soon lose her neck as to give away a penny of her money. I will have twelve pence from her even if she goes crazy, or else I will summon her to our court; and yet, God knows, I know no wrong of her. But since you seem unable to make your expenses in this country, watch how I do this."

The summoner knocked at the widow's gate. "Come out, you old hag!" he cried. "I believe you must have some friar or priest in there with you."

"Who knocks there?" said the wife. "Bless me! God save you, sir; what is your honorable desire?"

"I have here," said the summoner, "a writ of summons; under threat of excommunication, see that you come before the archdeacon tomorrow to answer for certain things to the court."

"Now," said the widow, "may Lord Jesus Christ, King of Kings, kindly help me, for I am helpless. I have been sick for many a day. I cannot walk or ride that far without dying from the pain in my side. May I not request a copy of the charges, Sir Summoner, and answer there through my agent to those things of which I am accused?"

"Yes," replied the summoner. "Pay me—let's see—twelve pence at once, and I shall acquit you. I shall have very little profit from it; my master makes the profit, not I. Come on; let me go quickly. Give me the twelve pence; I can't wait any longer."

"Twelve pence!" she cried. "Now, Lady St. Mary kindly help me out of this care and sin. If I were to own this wide world, I wouldn't have twelve pence in my house. You know very well that I am poor and old. Show your charity to me, a poor wretch."

"No," he said, "may the foul fiend take me if I excuse you, though you be destroyed!"

"Alas!" she said, "God knows I am not guilty."

"Pay me," he said, "or, by the sweet St. Anne, I will take away your new pot for the debt you have owed me for a long time. When you made your husband a cuckold, I paid the court for your fine."

"You lie!" she said. "By my salvation, I was never before summoned to your court in all my life, wife nor widow; and I was never guilty of bodily sin! I send your body and my pot both to the black, rough devil!"

When the devil heard her curse upon her knees, he spoke in this way: "Now, Mabel, my own dear mother, is what you are saying your true desire?"

"The devil take him before he dies, pot and all," she said, "unless he repents!"

"No, old hag," said the summoner, "it is not my intention to repent for anything I've had from you. I wish I had your smock and every bit of your clothing!"

"Now, brother," said the devil, "don't be angry. Your body and this pot are mine by rights. You shall go to hell with me tonight, where you will know more of our secrets than a master of divinity."

With these words the foul fiend grabbed the summoner; body and soul, he went with the devil to that place where summoners have their heritage. May God, who made mankind in His own image, guide and save us one and all, and cause these summoners to become good men!

Ladies and gentlemen (said the Friar), I could have told you, if this Summoner here had given me time, about such terrors as would make your hearts shiver, after the texts of Christ, Paul, John, and many of our other learned divines, though no tongue can adequately describe the torments of that cursed house of hell, even if I spoke for a thousand winters. But, in order that we may be saved from that horrible place, awake and pray Jesus for His favor, to keep us from the tempter Satan.

Listen to these words! Learn from them to beware: "The lion sits always in waiting to slay the innocent if he can." Dispose your hearts constantly to withstand the fiend who wishes to make prisoners and servants of you. He cannot tempt you beyond your power, for Christ will be your champion and knight. And pray that these summoners repent of their misdeeds before the fiend seizes them! HERE ENDS THE FRIAR'S TALE.

THE SUMMONER

THE PROLOGUE OF THE SUMMONER'S TALE: The Summoner stood up high in his stirrups. He was so enraged at the Friar that he shook with anger like an aspen leaf.

"Ladies and gentlemen," he said, "I ask only one thing: I beseech you, of your courtesy, since you have listened to this false Friar lie, to allow me to tell my tale. This Friar boasts that he knows hell, and, God knows, it's little wonder that he does. Friars and fiends are not far apart; by God, you have often heard how a friar's spirit was once snatched to hell in a vision. As an angel led him up and down to show him the torments there, he didn't see a single friar in the whole place, though he saw plenty of other folks in trouble. The friar then spoke to the angel:

"'Now, sir,' he said, 'have friars such grace that none of them come to this spot?'

"'Yes, they come here,' said the angel. 'Many a million!' Then he led the friar down to Satan. 'Now Satan has a tail broader than the sail of a boat,' continued the angel. 'Hold up your tail, Satan! Show your ass and let the friar see where friars nest in this place!' And in less than a minute, just as bees swarm from a hive, so twenty thousand friars rushed in a line from the devil's ass and swarmed all over hell; then they all returned as fast as they could and crept back into his ass. He clapped his tail down again and lay still.

"When this friar had looked his fill at the torments of that terrible place, God in his mercy restored his spirit to his body again, and he awoke.

"Nevertheless, he continued to shake with fright, so clearly did he remember the devil's ass, which is by nature the friar's true heritage.

"May God save all of you, except this cursed Friar! I shall end my prologue in this manner."

HERE BEGINS THE SUMMONER'S TALE: Ladies and gentlemen, there is, I believe, a marshy district in Yorkshire called Holderness. A licensed beggar went about this district preaching and also, doubtless, begging. It happened one day that this friar had preached in his usual manner at a certain church. He had particularly urged the people in his preaching above all else to contribute toward masses for souls in purgatory and, for God's sake, to give money for the erection of holy houses where divine service is honored and not where there is waste and reckless spending, or where it is not necessary to contribute to the endowed clergy, who can live, thank God, in wealth and abundance. "Such masses," said this friar, "deliver the souls of friends, young and old, from penance—yes, when the masses are rapidly sung and not used to make a priest who sings only one mass a day be thought jolly and frivolous. Deliver the souls at once!" he said. "It is hard to be clawed with flesh-hooks or with awls, or to be burned or baked. Now give quickly, for the love of Christ!" And when this friar had said all he meant to, he took his leave with a *qui cum patre.*

When the folk in church had given him whatever they wished, he left; he would not stay any longer. With his scrip and tipped staff, his robes tucked up, he began to peek and pry into every house, begging meal and cheese, or else grain. His companion had a horn-tipped staff, a pair of ivory tablets, and a carefully polished stylus. He always wrote down on the spot the names of all who contributed anything, as if he would pray for the givers.

"Give us a bushel of wheat, malt, or rye, a little cake, or a

bit of cheese, or whatever else you wish—we can't be choosy;
a God's halfpenny or a masspenny, or give us some of your
pork, if you have it; a piece of your blanket, dear madam,
our dear sister. Look, I'll write your name here; bacon or
beef, or anything you can find."

A sturdy rascal, a servant at their house, always followed
behind these two. He carried a sack on his back in which he
put whatever anybody gave them. As soon as the friar left a
house he erased all the names that he had written on the
tablets earlier. He served the people with mockeries and
fables.

"No, there you lie, you Summoner!" said the Friar.

"Peace," said our Host, "for Christ's dear Mother! Get on
with your tale, and don't leave any of it out."

"As I may thrive," said the Summoner, "that's how I'll tell
it!"

So the friar went along, house by house, until he came to
one house where he was accustomed to better refreshment
than he found in a hundred other places. The good man who
owned the place was sick; he lay bedridden on a low couch.

"God bless you, Thomas, my friend, good day!" said the
friar, courteously and mildly. "Many times, Thomas, God re-
pay you, have I fared well upon your bench. I have eaten
many a merry meal here." And he pushed the cat off the
bench, put down his staff, his hat, and his scrip, and sank
down comfortably. His companion had walked on into town
with the servant to the inn where he planned to spend that
night.

"Oh, master dear," said the sick man, "how have you fared
since March? I haven't seen you for a fortnight or more."

"God knows," said the friar, "I have worked very hard,
and especially I have said many valuable early prayers for
your salvation and for our other friends, God bless them! I
was at your church today for mass and preached a sermon
to the best of my simple ability. It was not completely ac-
cording to the text of Holy Writ, for that would be hard for

you to understand, I think; therefore, I will teach you the gloss. Glossing is certainly a glorious thing, for the letter kills, as we clerics say. There I taught them to be charitable and spend their money in a reasonable manner. And I saw your wife there—ah! where is she?"

"Yonder in the yard, I believe," said this man. "She will come soon."

"Aye, master, you're welcome, by St. John!" said the wife, "And how are you?"

The friar very courteously stood up and embraced her tightly in his arms, and kissed her sweetly, chirping with his lips like a sparrow. "Madam," he said, "very well, as one who is in every way your servant, thanks be to God, who gave you soul and life! For in all the congregation today I didn't see a woman as handsome as you, God save me!"

"Yes, may God amend faults, sir," she said. "Anyway, you are welcome, by my faith."

"Thanks, madam, I have always found it so. But of your great goodness, by your leave, I beg that you won't be annoyed if I speak with Thomas for a little while. These curates are very negligent and slow to probe a conscience tenderly in confession. My diligence lies in preaching and in studying the words of Peter and Paul. I walk and fish for Christian men's souls to render to Jesus Christ His just due. Spreading His word is my whole purpose."

"Now, by your leave, dear sir," she said, "scold him well, for Holy Trinity! Although he has everything that he could want, he is as angry as a pismire. Even though I wrap him up warmly at night and put my leg or arm over him, he groans like the boar which lies in our sty. I have no pleasure at all from him; I cannot please him in any way."

"Oh, Thomas, *je vous dis,* Thomas! Thomas! This brings the devil; this must be amended. Wrath is a thing which high God forbade, and I will speak a word or two about that."

"Now, master," said the wife, "before I go, what will you have for dinner? I shall go prepare it."

"Now, madam," said the friar, *"je vous dis sans doute,* I

shall have only the liver of a capon and a thin slice of your soft bread, and after that the head of a roasted pig—but I want no beast killed for me; then I shall have had a gracious plenty with you. I am a man of little appetite; my spirit is nourished by the Bible. The body is always so readily and painfully on guard that my hunger is destroyed. I beg you, madam, don't be offended when I tell you my private opinion as to a friend. By God, I would not tell it except to a few."

"Now, sir," she said, "only one word before I go. My child died not two weeks ago, soon after you left town."

"I saw his death by revelation," said the friar, "at home in our dormitory. I dare say that not a half-hour after his death I saw him borne to bliss in my vision, as God may guide me! So did our sacristan and our infirmary chief; they have been true friars fifty years, and they may now make their jubilee and walk alone, God be thanked for His gift. Then I rose up, as did all our group, with many a tear trickling down my cheeks, without noise or ringing of bells. *Te Deum* was our song, and nothing more, except that I said a prayer to Christ, thanking Him for His revelation. For, sir and madam, trust me well, our prayers are more effective and we see more of Christ's secret matters than do laymen, though they be kings. We live in poverty and in abstinence while laymen live in riches, with plenty of meat and drink, indulging their foul delight. We hold all worldly desires as worthless. Lazarus and Dives lived differently, and they had thereby different rewards. Whoever wishes to pray must fast and be holy, fatten his soul and make his body lean. We live as the Apostle said; food and clothing suffice for us even if they are not very good. The purity and fasting of us friars cause Christ to accept our prayers.

"Look how Moses fasted for forty days and forty nights before the high powerful God spoke to him on Mount Sinai. With empty belly, after many days of fasting, he received the Law that was written with God's finger. And Elijah, you know well, fasted and meditated for a long time on Mount Horeb before he spoke at all with the Lord God, who is the physician of our lives.

"Aaron, who supervised the temple, and also each of the other priests, would not touch any sort of drink which would make them drunk before going into the temple to pray for the people or hold services; rather, they prayed and watched there in abstinence, lest they should die. Take heed of what I say! Unless those who pray for the people are sober, let them beware—but no more; that will suffice. Our Lord Jesus Christ, as Holy Writ explains, gave us an example of fasting and prayers. Therefore we mendicants, we poor friars, are wedded to poverty, chastity, charity, humility, abstinence, persecution for righteousness, weeping, mercy, and holiness. Therefore, you can see that our prayers—I speak of us, we mendicants, we friars—are more acceptable to the Lord God than are yours, with your feasts at the table. Man was first chased out of Paradise, if I tell the truth, because of his gluttony; and man was chaste in Paradise, certainly.

"But now listen, Thomas, to what I say. I don't think I have a text for it, but I can find in a kind of gloss that our sweet Lord Jesus spoke about friars especially when He said, 'Blessed are the poor in spirit.' And so, all through the Gospel, you can see whether the teachings are more favorable to our profession or to that of those who swim in possessions. Fie on their pomp and on their gluttony! I distrust them because of their ignorance. They seem to me like Jovinian, fat as a whale, and walking like a swan, as fond of wine as a bottle in the buttery. Their prayer is full of great reverence when they repeat the psalm of David for souls; then they belch and say, *'cor meum eructavit!'* Who follows Christ's teaching and path except us who are humble and chaste and poor, workers of God's words, not just hearers? Therefore, just as a hawk rises into the air with one soar, so the prayers of the charitable, chaste, and industrious friars soar up to God's two ears. Thomas! Thomas! As I hope to ride and walk, and by that lord called St. Ives, if you were not our brother you would not prosper. In our chapter we pray day and night to Christ to send you health and strength to heal your body speedily."

"God knows," said Thomas, "I feel no benefit therefrom. So

help me, Christ, in a few years I have spent many a pound on all sorts of friars, yet I never get better. Truly, I have almost used up my money. Farewell to my gold, for it is all gone!"

The friar answered, "Oh, Thomas, is that true? Why do you need to seek out various friars? Why does a man who has a perfect physician need to seek other doctors in the town? Your infidelity has ruined you. Do you think it insufficient that I, or rather our group, should pray for you? Thomas, that trick is not worth a thing. Your disease comes from our having received too little. Ah, give that convent half a quarter of a bushel of oats! Ah, give this convent twenty-four coins! Ah, give that friar a penny, and let him go! No, no, Thomas, it won't work that way! Of what value is a farthing divided into twelve parts? Look, anything which is united in itself is stronger than when it is divided. Thomas, you will not be flattered by me; you wish to have our work for nothing. The high God, who created all this world, says that the workman is worthy of his hire. Thomas, I want none of your treasure for myself, but for our convent which is always so diligent in its prayers for you, and in order to build Christ's own church. Thomas, if you wish to learn to work, you can read in the life of Thomas of India whether the building up of churches is good. You lie here, full of anger and wrath with which the devil sets your heart afire, and you chide this poor innocent, your wife, who is so meek and patient. And therefore, Thomas, believe me if you wish; for your own good don't argue with your wife. And carry away these words now, by your faith, which the wise man says concerning such matters: 'Be not a lion within your own house; oppress not your subjects, nor make your acquaintances flee.' And, Thomas, once more I charge you, take heed of her who sleeps in your bosom; beware of the serpent that slyly creeps in the grass and stings subtly. Beware, my son, and listen patiently: twenty thousand men have lost their lives by arguing with their wives and mistresses. Now, since you have so holy and meek a wife, why must you, Thomas, cause trouble? Certainly, there is no serpent so cruel or half so dangerous when a man steps on its tail as a woman is when she is angry; vengeance is then all that they wish. Wrath is a sin, one of the seven greatest, abominable to God in heaven and destruction to oneself. Every ignorant vicar or parson can tell you how wrath causes homicide. Truly, wrath is the executor of pride. I could tell so many troubles that arose from wrath that my tale would last until tomorrow. I pray God day and night, therefore, that He grant but little power to a wrathful man! It is a great harm and a great pity to place a wrathful man in high position.

"Once there was a wrathful ruler, says Seneca. One day during his reign two knights rode forth and, as Fortune would have it, one of them came home and the other did not. At once the knight who returned was brought before the judge, who said, 'You have slain your companion, for which I condemn you to certain death.' And he commanded another knight, 'Go, lead him to his death, I charge you.' It happened, as they went along the road toward the place where he was to die, that the knight whom men had thought dead arrived. They then decided it was most sensible to take both back to the judge. They said, 'Lord, the knight did not slay his companion; he stands here alive and whole before you.' 'You ought to be dead,' said the judge, 'as I hope to prosper; all of you—one, two, and three!' And to the first knight he said, 'I condemned you; therefore, you must surely die. And you, also, must lose your head, for it is because of you that your companion dies.' And to the third knight he said, 'You have not done that which I commanded you.' Then, he had all three of them killed.

"The wrathful Cambyses was also a drunkard who always took great delight in being a scoundrel. It happened that a knight in his court who loved righteous morality said one day when they were alone together: 'A lord who is vicious is lost; and drunkenness also makes a foul record for any man, especially for a lord. There is many an eye and many an ear watching a lord, and he doesn't know where. For God's love, drink more temperately! Wine causes a man to lose his mind disgustingly, as well as all the physical powers of his limbs.'

'You shall immediately observe the opposite,' replied Cambyses, 'and prove it by your own experience; wine does no such harm to people. There is no wine which robs me of my power of hand and foot, nor of my eyesight.' Then, for spite, he drank a hundred times more than he had drunk before. Soon this wrathful, cursed wretch had the son of the knight brought there, and commanded the boy to stand before him. Then, suddenly, he took up his bow, pulled the string to his ear, and with an arrow killed the child right there. 'Now, have I a steady hand or not?' he asked. 'Is all my strength and mind gone? Has wine robbed me of my eyesight?' Why should I relate the knight's answer? His son was slain; there is no more to tell. Beware, therefore, how you deal with lords. Sing *Placebo*, and 'I shall, if I can,' unless it is to a poor fellow. We can tell a poor man about his lord, but not a lord, even if he is going to hell.

"Look at wrathful Cyrus, the Persian, and how he destroyed the river of Gyndes because one of his horses was drowned in it when he went to conquer Babylon. He caused that river to shrink so much that women could wade across it. For what did he say who teaches so well?—'Be not a companion to a wrathful man, nor walk along the road with a madman, lest you be sorry.' I shall say no more.

"Now, Thomas, dear brother, give up your wrath; you will find me as just as a carpenter's square. Do not hold the devil's knife always at your heart—your anger troubles you too sorely—but show me your complete confession."

"No," said the sick man, "by St. Simon! I have been shriven today by my curate. I have told him all about my condition; there is no further need to speak of it, unless I care to from my own humility."

"Then give me some of your gold to build our house," said the friar, "for we have eaten many an oyster and many a mussel when other men have fared far better, in order to build our cloister. And yet, God knows, scarcely has the foundation been finished, and there is not yet one tile of our pavement in our house. By God, we owe forty pounds for stone! Now, Thomas, help us, for His sake who harrowed hell! For,

otherwise, we will have to sell our books. And if you are
without our preaching, then all the world will go to destruc-
tion. Whoever robs the world of us, Thomas, by your leave,
takes away the sun from the universe, so help me God. For
who can teach and work as we do? And that has been so not
just recently, but from the time of Elijah or Elisha there have
been friars in charity, so I find in the records, thank the Lord!
Now, Thomas, help, for Holy Charity!" And the friar got
down on his knees.

The sick man nearly went crazy with anger; he wished the
friar in flames burning, with his false dissembling. "Only such
things as I have can I give you," he said, "and nothing else.
You have told me that I am your brother, haven't you?"

"Yes, certainly," replied the friar, "trust in that. I took
your wife the letter with our seal."

"Well, then," said Thomas, "I shall give something to your
holy convent while I am alive, and you shall have it in your
hand at once, upon this condition and no other: that you so
divide it, my dear brother, that every friar will have an equal
share. This you must swear upon your faith, without fraud or
cavil."

"I swear it," said the friar, "by my faith!" And with that he
gave his hand to Thomas. "See, here is my promise; I shall
not fail you."

"Now, then, put your hand down my back," said the sick
man, "and grope around carefully. Beneath my buttocks you
will find a thing which I secretly hid there."

"Ah," thought the friar, "this thing shall go with me!" And
he reached his hand all the way down in hope of finding a
gift there. But when the sick man felt the friar groping here
and there around his hole, he broke wind in the middle of
the friar's hand; there is no nag drawing a cart that could
have broken wind so loudly.

The friar jumped up like an angry lion. "Ah, false fellow,"
he said. "by God's bones, you have done this on purpose out
of spite! You shall regret this fart, if I can arrange it!"

Thomas' servants, who heard the commotion, came rushing
in and chased the friar out. He went away very angry and

found his companion, who was with the loot. The friar looked like a wild boar. He gritted his teeth, he was so angry. At a fast pace he went to the manor, where there lived a man of great honor to whom the friar was always confessor. This worthy man was lord of that village. The friar came in as if in a frenzy to where the lord sat at his table, eating. The friar could scarcely speak a word, but at last he said, "God save you!"

The lord looked up and said: "Bless you! What, Friar John, what kind of world is this? I can plainly see that something is wrong. You look as if the woods were full of thieves. Sit down at once and tell me your trouble; it shall be amended, if I can help."

"I," said the friar, "have been insulted this day down in your village, God reward you; in all this world there is no page so poor that he would not despise what I got in your town. And yet nothing grieves me so bitterly as that this old fellow with white hair has blasphemed our holy convent also."

"Now, master," said the lord, "I beg you—"

"Not master, sir, but servant," said the friar, "though I had that title in school. God is not pleased when people call us 'Rabbi,' either in the market-place or in your great hall."

"It doesn't matter," said the lord. "Tell me all your grievance."

"Sir," said the friar, "an odious injury was done today to me and to my order, and therefore to every rank in Holy Church, may God soon amend it!"

"Sir," said the lord, "you know what has been done. Don't vex yourself. You are my confessor; you are the salt of the earth and the flavor. For God's love, keep your patience! Tell me your grievance." At once the friar told him that which you have heard before—you well know what.

The lady of the house remained sitting quietly until she had heard what the friar said, "Aye, God's mother," she said. "Blessed Maid! Is that all; tell me truly?"

"Madam," said the friar, "what do you think of this?"

"What do I think of it?" she said. "So help me God, I say

a knave has done a knave's trick. What should I say? May God never let him prosper! His sick head is full of vanity; I hold him somewhat insane."

"Madam," said the friar, "By God, I shall not lie, unless I am avenged in some way I shall discredit him everywhere I speak, this false blasphemer who charged me to divide that which cannot be divided equally among all, hard luck to him!"

The lord sat still as if in a trance, and in his heart he debated back and forth: "How could that fellow have had the imagination to offer the friar such a problem? Never before have I heard of such a thing. I believe the devil put it in his mind. No one could have discovered such a problem in mathematics before today. Who could make a demonstration of how every man should have an equal share of the sound or odor of a fart? Oh, foolish, proud fellow, I curse his face!" "Look, sirs," said the lord, "bad luck to him! Whoever heard of such a thing before? To everyone alike—how, tell me? It is impossible; it cannot be. Aye, foolish fellow, may God never let him prosper! The rumbling of a fart, like every sound, is but the reverberation of air which constantly decreases, little by little. There is no man who can judge, by my faith, if it is equally divided. Why look, my fellow, look, how shrewdly he spoke today to my confessor! I consider him surely possessed by a devil! Now eat your dinner, and let the fellow be; let him go hang himself, in the devil's name."

THE WORDS OF THE LORD'S SQUIRE, HIS CARVER, ON DIVIDING THE FART INTO TWELFTHS: Now the lord's squire who carved his meat stood by the table and heard, word by word, all the things which I have told you. "My lord," he said, "don't be ill-pleased; for enough cloth to make a suit, I could tell you,

Sir Friar, if you will not be angry, how this fart could be evenly divided among your convent, if I wanted to."

"Tell," said the lord, "and you shall at once have the cloth for a suit, by God and by St. John!"

"My lord," said the squire, "when the weather is good, without wind or disturbances in the atmosphere, have a cartwheel brought here into this hall. But see that it has all its spokes—a cartwheel normally has twelve spokes. Then bring me twelve friars; do you know why? Because thirteen makes a convent, I think. Your confessor here, because of his worth, shall fill out the number of his convent. Then they shall kneel down all together, and in this manner one friar shall firmly place his nose at each spoke's end. Your noble confessor— may God save him!—shall hold his nose upright under the axle-hole. Then shall this Thomas, with his belly as stiff and tight as a drum, be brought here and seated exactly over the axle-hole of the cartwheel, and he shall be made to break wind. And you shall see, upon peril of my life, by demonstrable proof, that the sound, and also the stink, will go equally to the ends of the spokes, except that this worthy man, your confessor, because he is a man of great honor, shall have the first fruit, as is fitting. It is the noble custom of friars that the worthiest of them should be served first, and certainly he has well deserved it. He taught us so much good today, with his preaching from the pulpit, that I personally would grant him the first smell of three farts; and so would all his convent, surely, he conducts himself so fairly and holily."

The lord, the lady, and everyone except the friar said that Jenkin spoke as reasonably in this matter as Euclid or Ptolemy. Concerning old Thomas, they said that craftiness and quick wit caused him to speak as he had spoken. He was not a fool, or possessed by a devil. And Jenkin has won a new suit.

My tale is done; we are almost in town. HERE ENDS THE SUMMONER'S TALE.

THE CLERIC

HERE FOLLOWS THE PROLOGUE OF THE CLERIC OF OXFORD'S TALE: "Sir Cleric of Oxford," our Host said, "you ride along as quiet and demure as a newly-married girl sitting at the table; I haven't heard a word from your tongue all day. I think you must be pondering over some sophistry; but Solomon says, 'There is a time for everything.' For God's sake, cheer up! This is no time for meditation. Tell us some merry tale, by your faith! For whoever enters into a game must follow the rules. But don't preach as the friars do during Lent, in order to make us weep over our past sins; and don't let your tale put us to sleep. Tell us some gay story about adventures; save your rhetorical terms and images and figures of speech for when you write in the high style, as when people write to kings. Speak plainly now, we beg you, so that we can understand what you say."

The good Cleric answered pleasantly. "Host," he said, "I am at your command; you have control of us now. Therefore, I shall certainly obey you in all that is reasonable. I shall tell you a tale which I learned from a cleric at Padua whose words and deeds proved him noble. He is dead now and nailed in his coffin. I pray God to give rest to his soul! Francis Petrarch, the poet laureate, was this cleric's name, whose sweet rhetoric illumined all the glory of Italian poetry, as John da Legnano did for philosophy, law, and other learned subjects. But death, which will not allow us to remain on earth for more than a twinkling of an eye, has killed both of these men, and all of us shall die.

"But to continue as I started about this worthy man who taught me this tale. I say that first, before he composed the body of his story, he wrote in the high style a prologue to his tale in which he describes Piedmont and the district of Saluzzo, and speaks of the high Apennine mountains, which

199

are the boundaries of West Lombardy, and he speaks especially of Mount Viso, where the Po River first rises and has its source in a small well, which grows steadily in its course eastward toward Emilia, Ferrara, and Venice—all that would take too long to explain. And anyway, I think it an irrelevant matter, except that he wanted to introduce his subject. But here is his tale, which you may hear."

HERE BEGINS THE TALE OF THE CLERIC OF OXFORD: On the western side of Italy, at the base of cold Mount Viso, there is a fertile plain, abounding in crops, where you can see many a castle and village founded in the time of our forefathers, together with many other pleasant sights. This fine country is called Saluzzo.

At one time a Marquis was ruler of this land, as were his worthy ancestors before him. All his subjects, both great and small, were always obedient and ready to do his bidding. In this way he lived happily for a long time, loved and respected, through Fortune's favor, both by his nobles and his commoners. He was descended from the noblest family in Lombardy; a handsome man, strong, young, and very honorable and courteous. He was sufficiently discreet in governing his country, though in certain matters he was at fault. This young lord was named Walter. I said he was at fault in some things because he gave no thought to what might happen to him in the future, but considered only his immediate pleasures, such as hawking and hunting constantly. He let almost all other responsibilities slide, and also—and that was worst of all—he would not take a wife, whatever might happen. This one fact so disturbed his people that one day they flocked in to see him and one of them, the most learned—or else the one from whom the lord would most readily accept his people's ideas, or perhaps he was the most able at explaining the point—spoke to the Marquis as you shall hear:

"Oh, noble Marquis, your humane attitude reassures us and gives us the boldness to tell you, as is often necessary, why we are troubled. In your courtesy, accept, lord, what, with sad heart, we tell you, and do not disdain to hear my voice. I have no more to do with this matter than anybody else here, but inasmuch as you, my dear lord, have always shown favor and grace to me, I have dared to request a brief audience with you to present our plea, for the decision you, my lord, judge best.

"Truly, lord, you and all your deeds have always pleased us so highly that we could not imagine how it would be possible for us to live in greater happiness, except for one thing, lord: that it might be your desire to become a married man. Then your people would attain the highest happiness. Bow your neck under that blessed yoke of sovereignty, not of slavery, which men call espousal or wedlock. And think, lord, in your wisdom, how rapidly our time passes in various ways. For though we sleep or wake or travel or ride, the time always flees; it will wait for no man. And though you are still in the flower of your young manhood, age creeps on steadily, as quiet as a stone, and death menaces every age and strikes in every rank, for no one escapes. As surely as we know that we will die, so we are uncertain of the day when death shall fall on us.

"So accept from us, who never yet disobeyed your command, our true intention, lord, and in a short time, if you will agree, we shall choose for you a wife born of the noblest and greatest family in all this land, so that, in our opinion, it will seem an honor to God and you. Deliver us from all our constant fears and, for God's sake, take a wife! For if it should happen—God forbid—that through your death your line should end and a stranger succeed to your heritage, oh, woe to us who live! Therefore, we beg you speedily to marry."

The meek prayer and the mournful faces of his people brought pity to the lord's heart. "My own dear people," he said, "you would press upon me a thing to which I never before gave a thought. I have rejoiced in my freedom, which is so seldom found in marriage. Where I was free, I must now be in servitude. Nevertheless, I see your true purpose, and I trust, as I have always done, in your good sense. Therefore, of my own free will I shall agree to marry as soon as I possibly can. But, as for your offer today, to choose a wife for me, I shall relieve you of the choice and ask you to withdraw that suggestion. For God knows that children are often different from their noble parents who preceded them; all nobility comes from God and is not from the strain of which the children are conceived and born. I trust in the nobility of God and therefore lay the question of my marriage and my well being and peace of mind before Him. He may do as He thinks best. Leave me alone to choose my wife—I shall bear that responsibility upon my back. But I ask you, and charge you upon your lives, to assure me that you shall honor whatever wife I select as long as she lives, by words and deeds, both here and everywhere, as if she were the daughter of an emperor. And, furthermore, this you must swear: that you will never grumble or complain about my choice, for, since I shall give up my liberty at your request, I will marry whomever my heart is set on, as I hope to prosper. Unless you will agree to such a procedure, I ask that you speak no more about this matter."

They swore and agreed to all his conditions with good will; no one there said him nay. Before leaving they asked that he do them the favor of setting a certain day for his wedding as soon as he possibly could, for the people were still somewhat fearful lest the Marquis would not take a wife. He set them a day which suited him on which he would without fail be married, and he said that he did all these things at their request. And they all thanked him with humble attention, kneeling obediently and reverently. In this fashion they fulfilled their purpose and returned home.

The Marquis at once commanded his officials to prepare for the feast, and to his trusted knights and squires he issued such orders as he wished to give them. They carried out his commands, each of them doing his best to make the feast memorable. THE FIRST PART ENDS.

THE SECOND PART BEGINS: Not far from that fine palace in which the Marquis made plans for his marriage, there stood a pleasantly situated village in which the poor folk of that district had their cattle and their lodgings. There they earned their living by their labor, after which the soil repaid them with abundance. Among these poor people there lived one man who was considered the poorest of them all; but yet the Lord God can sometimes send His blessing into an ox's little stall. The people of that village called this man Janicula. He had a daughter, pleasing enough to the eye, and this young girl was named Griselda. But, if one speaks of the beauty of virtuous acts, then she was among the fairest under the sun, though she was reared in poverty. No wanton desires ran through her heart; she drank more often from the well than from the barrel, and, in furtherance of her idea of virtuous conduct, she was accustomed to work and not to idle comfort. But although this girl was of a tender age, there was, nevertheless, a mature and steadfast heart within her virgin breast, and she respectfully and generously took care of her poor old father. In the fields, she watched over a few grazing sheep and was never idle until she slept. When she came home, she often brought roots or other herbs which she sliced and boiled for their dinner; thus, she had a hard bed, in no way soft. Yet she always sustained her father's good spirits with all the obedience and diligence a child can show to a revered father.

The Marquis had frequently cast his eye upon this poor creature, Griselda, as he accidentally passed in his hunting. And when it happened that he caught sight of her, he did not stare with a wanton leer of folly, but seriously pondered at length about her behavior, commending in his heart her womanhood and her virtue, which in disposition as well as in acts surpassed that of any person so young. Though the people took no great notice of her virtues, he carefully considered her excellence and decided that he would wed only her, if he ever should marry.

The day for the wedding arrived, but no one could say who the bride would be. Many people wondered about this unusual situation and said, when they were in private, "Will our lord still not forsake his vanity? Will he not marry? Alas, alas, if that is so! Why does he deceive himself and us in this way?"

Nevertheless, the Marquis had had made brooches and rings of gems, set with gold and azure, for Griselda, and he had had clothing and also all the other adornments which are suitable for a wedding prepared for her by taking the measurement of a girl the same size as Griselda. Nine o'clock of the morning on which the wedding was to be drew near, and all the palace was fittingly decorated with finery, both halls and bedrooms. You could see storehouses there stuffed with an abundance of the rarest edibles to be found as far as Italy reaches.

The royal Marquis, richly dressed, escorted by the lords and ladies who had been invited to the feast, and with the young knights of his retinue, went in this fashion straight to the village which I told you about, accompanied by the playing of many melodies. Griselda, God knows, was quite unaware that all this finery had been prepared for her. She went to fetch water from a well and returned home as quickly as possible, for she had heard talk of the Marquis being married on this day and was eager to see some of the ceremony if she could. She thought: I shall stand in our door with the other girls who are my friends and see the Marchioness; and, therefore, I shall try to finish the work which I am supposed to do at home as rapidly as possible. Then I can watch her at my leisure, if she passes this way going to the castle.

As she started to cross her threshold, the Marquis came forth and called to her. She immediately put down her water jug in an ox's stall beside the door, fell down on her knees, and remained there with a serious face until she had heard what the lord desired.

The thoughtful Marquis spoke very earnestly to the girl, "Where is your father, Griselda?" She replied respectfully and humbly, "Lord, he is right here." She went inside without further delay and led her father to the Marquis, who took the old man by the hand and said to him aside: "Janicula, I can no longer hide my heart's desire. If you will agree, no matter what happens, I shall take your daughter, before I leave, as my bride for the rest of her life. You love me, I am certain, and you were born my faithful subject. That pleases me, and I dare say it pleases you; therefore, tell me particularly your answer to my previous question: do you agree to take me for your son-in-law?"

This sudden question so surprised the old man that he turned red; he stood shivering and shaking all over and could scarcely say more than "Lord, my desire is your desire; I wish nothing against your will, for you are my very dear lord. Arrange this matter just as you wish."

"Still, I desire that you, she, and I hold a discussion in your bedroom; do you know why?" said the Marquis gently. "For I wish to ask her if she desires to be my wife and govern herself according to my wishes. And all this shall be done in your presence; I will not say anything out of your hearing."

While they were making their contract in the bedroom as you shall hear later, the people entered the house and marveled at the considerate and attentive way in which Griselda took care of her dear father. But Griselda could marvel openly, for never before had she seen such a sight. It is no wonder, though, that she was dazed to see so great a guest in that house. She was not accustomed to such guests and, consequently, she turned pale.

Soon, however, to accomplish his purpose, the Marquis spoke these words to this kind, true, faithful girl: "Griselda," he said, "you understand clearly that it will please your father and me that I marry you, and it is, I think, your desire also. But first I shall ask several questions: since it is to be done hastily, do you agree, or do you wish to consider further? I also ask whether you are prepared to submit willingly to whatever I may desire, and to agree that I shall be at liberty to cause you delight or pain, as I think best, without your grumbling about it, night or day? And also when I say 'yea,' will you not say 'nay,' either by word or by frowning? Swear to these things, and I shall announce our betrothal here."

Marveling at his words, and quivering with fright, Griselda answered: "Lord, I am undeserving and unworthy of the honor you do me; but your desire is mine also. So I hereby swear that I will never willingly disobey you in act or thought, under threat of death, though I would be loath to die."

"That is sufficient, my Griselda," he said, and he went out of the door with a very serious face. She followed him, and he spoke these words to the people: "This is my wife who stands here. I ask that all who love me will honor and love her; there is no more to be said."

In order that she would not come to his house with any of her old belongings, he commanded the ladies to undress her right there. These ladies were not eager to handle the clothes in which she was dressed. Nevertheless, they dressed this beautiful girl in new clothes from head to foot. They combed her hair which had been unattractively arranged, and with their small hands they placed a crown upon her head. Then they adorned her with many large and small jewels. Why should I make a long story of her finery? When she was so richly dressed, the people scarcely recognized her for her beauty.

The Marquis married her with a ring brought along for that purpose, then placed her upon a snow-white, gentle-gaited horse, and without longer delay conducted her to his palace, accompanied by the joyful people who led her and met her. In this fashion they spent the day in revelry until the sun began to sink. To hasten my story, I shall say that God shed his favor on the new Marchioness in such plenty that nobody could tell from her appearance that she was born and reared in poverty in a hut or an ox-stall; rather she seemed to have been raised in the palace of an emperor. She became so beloved and respected that the people who had known her from year to year since her birth scarcely remembered—though they would have sworn it—that she was the daughter of Janicula, whom I spoke of before, but imagined that she was another person. For, though she had always been possessed of many virtues, she increased in those excellent qualities which are rooted in the highest goodness. She was so discreet and eloquent, so kind and deserving of reverence, and so able to win the hearts of the people, that everyone who looked into her face loved her. The excellence of her name was proclaimed not only throughout the town of Saluzzo, but also in other neighboring districts; if one person spoke well of her, another said the same. Her reputation for great goodness spread abroad so widely that men and women, young and old, came to Saluzzo to look at her.

In this way, Walter—married lowly, nay, royally, with fortunate honor—lived comfortably at home in God's peace. To all appearances he had sufficient happiness. The people considered him that rare individual, a wise man, because he had been able to see that virtue is often hidden by low station. Through her natural intelligence, Griselda not only knew all the details of a housewife's work, but also, when the situation demanded, she would wisely manage the commonwealth. In all that land there was no rancor, strife, or sadness which she could not appease, and thus bring everybody to a sensible and peaceful agreement. When nobles or others of her country quarreled, when for the time being her husband was absent, she could bring them together. She possessed such wise and eloquent words and such impartial judgment that the people thought she was sent from heaven to save the innocent and to amend injustices.

Not long after the marriage, Griselda bore a daughter. Though they would have preferred a son, the Marquis and the people were happy. For, though her first-born was a girl, it was now evident that she was not barren, and it was possible for a boy to follow. THE SECOND PART ENDS.

THE THIRD PART BEGINS: It happened, as is very often the case, that before the baby had left its mother's breast the Marquis so longed in his heart to test his wife and to prove her steadfastness that he could not put this strange idea out of his heart. God knows, he planned to frighten her needlessly. Already he had tested her sufficiently and had never found her lacking. What was the need of continuing more and more to tempt her, even though some people endorse such methods as cunning strategy. As for me, I say it is wicked to test a wife unnecessarily and cause her anguish and fear.

But with that purpose the Marquis acted in this way: one night he came alone with a stern face and a troubled manner to where she lay, and said: "Griselda, the day that I took you from poverty and placed you in a high and noble station—I don't think you have forgotten it? I say, Griselda, your present high position, to which I elevated you, has not, I think, caused you to forget that I found you in abject poverty, in spite of any comfort you now enjoy. Pay close attention to every word I say; there is no one who can overhear us: You know well how you came here to this house; it was not long ago. And though you are dear and beloved to me, you are not so to my nobles. They say that it is a great shame for them to be subjects and servants to you who were born in a small village. And particularly since the birth of your daughter they have said these things unquestionably. Now, I desire to live my life at peace and in accord with them, as I have done before. I cannot be careless in this matter; therefore, I must act for the best with your daughter—not as I wish, but as my people desire. Yet, God knows, I hate to do it; in any case, I will not do it without your knowledge, but I hope that you assent to this plan. Exhibit now the patient acceptance which you promised and swore to me in your village on the day we were married."

When she had heard all this, she did not change by word, manner, or look; indeed, she seemed not to be troubled. She said: "Lord, all lies within your pleasure. My child and I are completely yours with willing obedience, and you can save or destroy that which belongs to you. Do as you like. May God save my soul, there is nothing that pleases you which can displease me. I want nothing, and I fear to lose nothing except you. This feeling is in my heart, and always shall be. Neither the passing of time nor death can erase it or sway my love in another direction."

The Marquis was happy at her answer, but he pretended not to be. He was quite sad in manner and appearance when he left the room. A few minutes after this, he secretly told all his intentions to a man and sent him to Griselda. This trusted man was a kind of sergeant whom he had often found trustworthy in important matters; such men can execute evil orders well. The lord knew that this man loved and feared him, and, when the sergeant understood his lord's wishes, he quietly crept into the bedroom.

"Madam," he said, "you must forgive me for doing what I am forced to do. You are so wise that you know very well that the commands of lords cannot be disobeyed. One may lament and bewail such commands, but he must carry them out. And so it is with me; there is no more to say. I have been commanded to take this child."

He spoke no further but roughly caught up the child and acted as if he would kill it before he left. Griselda had to allow and consent to all this; she sat as quiet and meek as a lamb and let the cruel sergeant do as he liked. This man's evil reputation was ominous, his face and his words were suspicious, and the time at which this deed was done was frightening. Alas, she thought he would kill the daughter that she so loved, right then and there. Nevertheless, she neither sighed nor wept, consenting to that which the Marquis desired. But at last she humbly spoke and meekly begged the

sergeant, as a noble gentleman, to allow her to kiss the child
before it died. Then, with a very sad face, she laid the child
upon her bosom, kissed it and soothed it, and then blessed it.
After this she said in her kind voice: "Farewell, my child!
I shall never see you. But since I have marked you with the
cross of that Father—blessed be He!—who died for us upon
the wooden cross, I consign your soul to Him, little one, for
tonight you shall die because of me."

I think it would have been hard for a nurse to watch this
pitiful sight. A mother in these circumstances might well
have cried "alas!" Nevertheless, Griselda was so steadfast that
she endured all adversity and meekly said to the sergeant,
"Here, take back your little girl. Go now, and carry out my
lord's command. But one thing I shall ask you for kindness'
sake: unless my lord forbids it, at least bury this little body
in some place where the beasts and birds cannot devour it."
He said not a word in agreement, but took the child and went
his way.

The sergeant returned to his lord and related briefly and
plainly, point by point, Griselda's words and her behavior.
Then he gave the lord his adored daughter. The lord's man-
ner had some pity in it, but he still held to his purpose, as
lords do when they wish to have their way. He told the
sergeant to wrap and cover the child softly and to place it
with the greatest care in a box or blanket; but, on pain of
having his head struck off, he must allow no one to know of
his actions—where he came from or where he went. The
sergeant was to take the child to Bologna, to the lord's be-
loved sister, at that time Countess of Panik, and to explain
the whole thing to her, asking that she accept the respon-
sibility of rearing the child in a manner fitting for one well
born. She was also to be requested to conceal the child's
identity from everyone, whatever happened. The sergeant
left and carried out his mission.

But let us return to the Marquis. He now busied himself
in determining whether or not he could tell from his wife's
manner or words that she was changed; but he found her still
the same, serious and kind. She was in every way as pleasant,

as humble, and as industrious in service and love for him as
she was accustomed to be. She never spoke of her daughter.
No outward sign of misfortune was to be seen in her, and she
never once mentioned her daughter's name in mirth or sad-
ness. THE THIRD PART ENDS.

THE FOURTH PART FOLLOWS: Four years passed in this fashion
before Griselda was pregnant again. But this time, as God
would have it, she gave birth, by Walter, to a son, a very
gay and pretty child. When the father was told of this, not
only he but all the country rejoiced and gave thanks and
praise to God for the child.

When the boy was two, and had been taken from its
nurse's breast, the Marquis one day felt again the desire to
test his wife, if he could. Oh, needlessly was she put to the
test! But married men know no moderation when they find a
patient wife.

"Wife," said the Marquis, "you have already heard that
my people are unhappy about our marriage; now, since my
son was born, it is worse than ever before. This grumbling
pains my heart and my spirit, for such bitter complaints
come to my ears that my tranquillity is practically destroyed.
People now say, 'When Walter dies, the blood of Janicula
shall succeed him and be our Lord, for we have no other.'
Such things are my people certainly saying; I must pay heed
to this unrest. For, in truth, even though they do not speak
openly in my presence, I fear such a charge. I wish to live
in peace, if possible. Therefore, I have fully determined to
deal secretly with this boy just as I did at night with his
sister. I give you the warning ahead of time so that you will
not suddenly be beside yourself with sorrow. Be patient, I
beg you."

"I have said and I always will say," she replied, "that I
do not desire and surely never will desire anything except

what you wish. It does not grieve me at all that my daughter, and soon my son, are killed—that is, if at your command. I have had nothing from my two children but first illness and then pain and sorrow. You are our lord; do as you like with your own possessions; ask no advice from me. For, just as I left all my clothing at home when I first came to you, so I left my desires and all my liberty and accepted your clothing. Therefore, I beg you, do what pleases you; I will obey your will. And, truly, if I had foreknowledge of your wishes before you told them to me, I would have done them diligently. But now that I know your intention and what you wish, I hold firmly and unswervingly to your decision. If I knew that my death would make you happy, I would gladly die to please you. Death cannot compare to your love."

When the Marquis saw the steadfastness of his wife, he cast down his eyes and marveled that she could patiently endure all of this. Though he went out with a troubled face, he felt great pleasure in his heart. The ugly sergeant took away Griselda's beautiful son in the same way, or worse, if possible, as he had her daughter. And still she was so patient that she showed no grief, but kissed her son and blessed him. She asked only this: that the sergeant, if he could, bury the tender and delicate body of the little boy to keep it from birds and beasts. But he would give her no promise, and went on his way, as if unmoved. However, he tenderly took the child to Bologna.

The Marquis marveled ever increasingly at Griselda's patience. If he had not known for certain before that she dearly loved her children, he would have thought that she endured his cruelty with a calm manner out of cunning, or malice, or hard-heartedness. But he knew very well that, next to him, she certainly loved her children best of all.

Now I should like to ask you women if these tests should not have been enough? What more could a harsh husband devise to test her faithfulness and her steadfastness in the face of his constant severity? But there are people of such a nature who when they get one idea cannot give it up; even if bound to a stake, they will not abandon their original plan.

In just that way, this Marquis fully intended to continue his testing of his wife.

He watched to see if in word or manner she was at all changed towards him, but he could never detect a difference. She was always the same in affection and appearance, and the older she grew, the more faithful she was in loving him—if that were possible—and the more assiduous. It seemed that the two of them had but one will, for whatever Walter wished, that was what she wanted; and, thank God, everything turned out for the best. She gave clear evidence that for nothing on earth should a wife desire anything for herself except what her husband wishes.

Ill reports about Walter spread far and wide. It was common talk that because he had married a poor woman, he had out of hard-heartedness wickedly murdered both his children in secret. It was no wonder, for no word came to the people's ear except that the children had been murdered. As a result, though his people had loved him well before, his bad reputation now made them hate him.

To be called a murderer is hateful; nevertheless, he would not give up his cruel purpose for anything. He determined to test his wife again. When his daughter was twelve years old, he sent a messenger to the court at Rome, which had been secretly told his real purpose, requesting such papal bulls to be prepared as would permit him to carry out his cruel purpose. He asked that the Pope should command him to marry another woman, if he so desired, in order to pacify his people. He requested, I say, that the Pope's bull be forged to show that he had permission, as if by the Pope's dispensation, to leave his first wife in order to stop the trouble and strife between him and his people. The papal bull, which was widely published, said exactly that. It is no wonder that the ignorant people took this at its face value.

When the news reached Griselda, I assure you, her heart was filled with grief, but she, this humble creature, always steadily patient, was prepared to endure all the adversity of Fortune, always obeying the desire and wishes of him to whom she had given herself, heart and all, as to what should be her earthly disposition.

But, to make the story brief, the Marquis wrote a special letter setting forth his purpose and sent it secretly to Bologna. He particularly requested the Earl of Panik, who had married his sister, to bring his two children home, openly and in dignified state. One thing he insisted upon: that the Earl tell no one, no matter who asked, the parentage of the children, but say that the girl was to marry the Marquis of Saluzzo in the near future.

The Earl did just as he was requested. On the appointed day he set out for Saluzzo, accompanied by many finely dressed lords, to lead the girl, and her young brother who rode beside her. This beautiful girl was prepared for her wedding, plentifully ornamented with fine jewels. Her brother, who was seven years old, was also dressed in a splendid fashion. And, thus, in great magnificence and with happy hearts, they rode along day by day on the journey to Saluzzo. THE FOURTH PART ENDS.

THE FIFTH PART FOLLOWS: Meanwhile, the Marquis, in accordance with his cruel practice and in order to test his wife to the very breaking point of her spirit, so that he might learn and be perfectly able to tell whether she was as steadfast as before, arrogantly announced this decision one day in public:

"Griselda, I have had pleasure enough, certainly, in having you as my wife, because of your goodness, honor, and obedience, not for your lineage or wealth. But now I realize, if I consider carefully, how very true it is that high position carries with it many sorts of grave responsibilities. I may not act like any plowman. My people cry out day by day and urge me to take another wife; even the Pope, to overcome their displeasure, consented to that which I plan. Bluntly, I must tell you this: my new wife is on her way here. Be strong in spirit and vacate her place immediately. Take back the dowry that you brought me; I agree to that, out of generosity. Return to your father's house. No one can remain prosperous always. I advise you to endure the blow of Fortune or chance with a steady heart."

In return, she answered patiently: "My lord, I know and always shall know that nobody can compare your magnificence and my poverty; there is no denying that. I never considered myself in any way worthy of being your wife, no; nor even your chambermaid. And, in this house, where you made me a lady—I take the Lord God as my witness, so surely may he gladden my soul—I never behaved as mistress or lady, but as a humble servant to your worship; and as long as I live I shall always serve you above every earthly creature. That you have for so long, in your goodness, kept me in nobility and honor, which I did not deserve, I thank you and God, whom I pray to reward you. There is no more to say. I shall gladly return to my father and live with him till the end of my life. I was reared there as a small child, and I shall lead my life there as a widow till I die, pure in body, heart, and spirit.

"For, since I gave my body first to you and have been your faithful wife, beyond any doubt, God forbid that the wife of such a lord shall take another man as husband, or mate. May God in his grace grant you happiness and prosperity with your new wife! I shall gladly yield her my place, in which I used to be happy. Since it pleases you, my lord, the one-time comfort of my heart, that I go, I shall leave whenever you like. But, as for your offer of whatever dowry I brought here, I clearly recall that I brought nothing better than ragged clothes which it would be difficult now for me to find. Oh, dear God! How gentle and kind you seemed by your speech and your appearance the day that we were married! But it is true—at least, I find it true, for my experience proves it—that old love is not like new love. But, indeed, lord, no matter what hardship I suffer, even death, I will never by word or deed repent that I gave you my heart with a firm purpose.

"My lord, you know that at my father's house you had my

poor clothes stripped from me and generously replaced by fine ones. I brought you nothing else, certainly, except faith and nakedness and virginity. Now I return your clothing, and your wedding ring, too, forever. The rest of your jewels, I assure you, will be found in your bedroom. I came naked from my father's house," she said, "and naked I must return. I would willingly follow all your wishes, but I hope it is not your plan that I leave your palace without even a smock. You could not be so unkind as to force me to exhibit this body, which bore your children, to the public by walking home naked. Therefore, I beg you, do not make me go down the road like a worm; remember, my own dear lord, I was your wife, though unworthy. In exchange for my virginity, which I brought to you but which I cannot take away with me, permit me to be given, as my reward, such a smock as it was my custom to wear, so that with it I can cover the body of your former wife. Now, I shall take my leave of you, my own lord, for fear of displeasing you."

"Keep the smock," he said, "which you now have on your back, and wear it when you leave." But he could scarcely speak these words, for pity and compassion. Then he rushed away, and she stripped off her outer clothes before the people. In her smock, barefooted and bareheaded, she turned towards her father's house.

The people followed her, weeping and steadily cursing Fortune as they walked. She, however, kept her eyes dry of tears and spoke no further word. Her father, who soon heard the news, cursed the day and time that nature had made a living creature of him. For, truly, this poor old man had always been suspicious of her marriage, and had thought from the beginning that when the lord had fully satisfied his physical desires it would appear to him a disgrace to his rank to have descended so low, with the result that he would discard her as soon as he could. The old father quickly went out to meet his daughter, for the noise of the people announced her coming. He covered her as well as possible with her old coat, weeping sorrowfully. But he could not put the coat about her, for the cloth was coarse and much older by many days than at her marriage.

In this way, this flower of wifely patience lived for a time with her father; and neither by speech nor appearance, in public or in private, did she show that a wrong had been done her. Neither did she appear to think back upon her former high position, judging from her manner. It is no wonder, for while she had held that high position her spirit had always been fully humble. She had had no tender mouth or delicate heart, nor pomp or royal ceremony; rather, she had been full of patient kindness, discreet and humble, always honorable, and forever meek and constant to her husband. People talk of Job, especially of his patience; clerics, for example, when they wish, can write very well about men; but for steadfastness, though clerics give little praise to women, there is no man who can be as patient or half so faithful as a woman—unless it happened lately. THE FIFTH PART ENDS.

THE SIXTH PART FOLLOWS: The Earl of Panik arrived from Bologna. The news of his coming spread among the people, great and small, and it came to the ears of all and sundry that he had brought a new Marchioness with him, in such pomp and splendor that the eyes of men in West Lombardy had never seen such finery. The Marquis, who had planned and knew all this, sent his messenger for poor, innocent Griselda before the Earl arrived. And she, with humble heart and happy face, not with angry thoughts in her mind, came at his command, fell on her knees before him, and greeted him reverently and discreetly.

"Griselda," he said, "it is my particular wish that this girl who shall marry me be received tomorrow as royally as possible in my house and also that everyone be treated in accordance with his rank, as nearly as I can arrange it, in the seating and in service and entertainment. I certainly do not have sufficient women to prepare the bedrooms as I wish them, and, therefore, I should like you to supervise all such arrangements. You know all my preferences of old. Though your clothing is poor and ill-looking, do your duty fully."

"Not only am I happy, lord," she replied, "to do your bidding, but I desire now, and always shall, to serve and to please you in my proper station without pretense. Never in happiness or hardship shall the spirit within my heart stop loving you best, with all my faithful endeavor." With these words she began to arrange the house, set the tables, and make the beds. She tried to do all that she could, begging the chambermaids to hurry, for God's sake, in their sweeping and dusting. And she, working harder than anyone else, arranged every bedroom, as well as the lord's hall.

About nine o'clock in the morning, the Earl, who had brought these two noble children with him, appeared. At this, the people ran to see the girl's clothing, so rich in appearance. Then the people said among themselves that Walter was no fool to wish to change wives, that it was for the best. For this girl was lovelier than Griselda, they all agreed, and far younger. More handsome and noble children would result because of her noble birth. Her brother was also so attractive that the people were pleased at the sight of him, and commended the Marquis' arrangements.

"Oh, fickle people! Changeable and always faithless, ever indiscreet and unstable as a weather vane! Always delighting in new rumors and chattering about that which isn't worth a coin, you constantly wax and wane like the moon. Your judgment is false, your constancy turns out badly. Anyone who puts his faith in you is a very great fool." So said the serious-minded inhabitants of that city when they observed how the people gazed up and down and were happy just at the novelty of having a new lady for their town. I shall make no further mention of this now; rather, I shall return to Griselda and tell about her steadfastness and industry.

Griselda occupied herself with everything that needed doing for the feast. She was not at all ashamed of her clothes, though they were crude and somewhat tattered. She went happily to the gate with the other folk to greet the Marchioness, and afterwards she returned to her work. She received Walter's guests so pleasantly and fittingly, each according to his rank, that no one could find fault; instead, they wondered continually who this woman might be, so poorly dressed but so tactful and courteous, and gave full praise to her wisdom. Meanwhile, she never ceased to commend the girl and her brother with all her heart and with the kindest intentions; no one could have praised them higher. But at last, when the nobles went to sit down to dinner, Walter called Griselda from her work into his hall.

"Griselda," he said, as if in jest, "how do you like my wife's appearance?"

"Very well, my lord," she replied. "For, in good faith, I never saw anyone lovelier than she. I pray God to send her happiness, and I hope that He will send you sufficient pleasure to the end of your life. One thing I beg you and also warn you about: do not torment this young girl as you did others, for she has been more tenderly reared and does not seem to me able to endure adversity as could a woman brought up in poverty."

When this stern Marquis observed her patience and her happy manner, devoid of all malice, even though he had so often tormented her, and when he saw how she was always as stable and constant as a wall, never failing in her innocence, he began to incline his heart to pity her wifely steadfastness.

"This is enough, my Griselda," he said. "Do not be afraid or ill-pleased any more. I have tested your faith and kindness in both poverty and high place, as well as any woman was ever tested. Now I know, dear wife, your steadfastness," and he took her in his arms and kissed her. She, marveling, paid no attention; she did not hear what he said to her. She acted as if she had just awakened, until she recovered from her amazement.

"Griselda," he said, "by God who died for us, you are my wife; I do not have nor have I ever had any other, may God save my soul! This is my daughter, whom you took to be my wife. The boy will positively be my heir, just as I have always planned. You certainly gave birth to him; I have kept him secretly at Bologna. Take them back, for now you cannot say that you have lost either of your two children. And to those people who spoke against me, I say firmly that I did these things not from malice or cruelty, but to test your woman-hood, and not to kill my children—God forbid!—but to keep them privately and quietly until I knew your resolution and all your qualities."

When Griselda heard this, she fell down in a faint for piteous joy. When she recovered, she called her two young children to her, took them in her arms, weeping piteously, and kissed them tenderly like a mother, her salt tears bathing their hair and faces. Oh, what a pitiful thing it was to see her fainting and to hear her humble voice! "Thank you, lord, God thank you," she said, "for saving my two dear children! Now I do not care if I die on the spot; since I am restored to your love and favor, it does not matter when I die! Oh, my dear, noble, young children! Your poor mother thought that you surely had been eaten by some cruel dogs or foul worms, but God in His mercy and your kind father have caused you to be tenderly guarded," and at that moment she suddenly fell to the ground.

In her swoon she clasped the two children so tightly in her embrace that it was with great effort and difficulty that they were extricated from her arms. Oh, many a tear ran down the piteous faces of those who stood near by; they could scarcely remain near her. Walter cheered her and banished her sorrow. She rose shyly from her trance, but every-one congratulated and made much of her until she recovered her usual manner. Walter strove so hard to please her that it was delightful to see their happiness now that they were re-united. The ladies, when they saw their opportunity, took her into the bedroom, stripped off her ragged clothing, and brought her back into the hall dressed in brightly shining cloth of gold, with a crown of many rich jewels upon her head. There she was fittingly honored.

In this fashion, this pitiful day had a joyous end, for every man and woman did his best to add to the mirth and revelry of that day until the stars appeared in the heavens. And everybody thought that this feast was more splendid and lavish than that with which her marriage was celebrated.

These two lived for many years in great happiness, peace, and agreement. Walter married his daughter richly to one of the finest lords in all Italy, and Griselda's father was kept in peace and quiet at the court until the soul left his body. The son succeeded to his inheritance in peace and accord after Walter's day, and he was also fortunate in marriage, though he put his wife to no great test.

The world is not so strong, there is no denying it, as it was in olden times; listen, therefore, to what my author says: This story was not told so that wives will follow Griselda's example in humility, for that would be intolerable even if they wanted to, but so that everyone, according to his station, will be steadfast in adversity as Griselda was. It was with this purpose that Petrarch wrote this story, which is set down in high style. Since one woman was so patient towards a mortal man, the more we should receive with patience all that God sends us, for it is reasonable that He should test those whom He created. However, He will not tempt anyone whom He had redeemed, as St. James will tell you if you read his epistle. Undoubtedly, God tests folk every day and causes us often to be beaten in various ways, for our own good, with the sharp lashes of adversity—not so that He may know our qualities, for surely He knew all our weaknesses before we were ever born. His arrangements are all for our profit; let us live then in virtuous patience.

Hear but one more word, ladies and gentlemen, before I stop. Nowadays it would be very hard to find two or three like Griselda in a whole town. For if they were put to such tests, their gold is so badly alloyed with brass that, though the coin appears to be good, it is more likely to break in two than bend. And so, because of my affection for the Wife of Bath—may God keep her and all her sex in supremacy; it would be a pity otherwise—with a lusty spirit, fresh and vigorous, I shall sing you a song which I think will please you.

God's bones, I'd rather my wife at home had heard this story just once than have a barrel of ale! That's a good story for that purpose. You people know what I'd like at home; but there's no use wishing for what can't be." HERE ENDS THE CLERIC OF OXFORD'S TALE.

THE MERCHANT

THE PROLOGUE OF THE MERCHANT'S TALE: "I know enough,"
said the Merchant, "about weeping and wailing, care and
other sorrow, both morning and evening; and so do many
others who are married. I believe that this is true, for I know
very well that it is that way with me. I have a wife, the worst
possible; for though the devil were married to her she would
outdo him, I'll swear. Why should I list for you all the details
of her great malice? She is a thorough shrew. There is a tre-
mendous difference between the unusual patience of Griselda
and my wife's incredible cruelty. How well off I'd be if I
were only free again! Never again would I be caught in such
a trap. We married men live in sorrow and care. Let anyone
who wants to do so try it, and he will find that what I say,
by St. Thomas of India, is true, of most men—I won't say
all. God forbid that it should happen so!

"Ah! good Sir Host, I have been married for two months;
really that's all. Yet I believe that a man who had been wife-
less all his life, even though people cut him to the heart,
could not in any way tell so much about grief as I could tell
here and now about my wife's cursedness!"

"Now," said our Host, "Merchant, as God may bless you,
since you know so much about this matter, I sincerely ask
you to tell us something about it."

"Gladly," he said, "but because of a troubled heart I shall
speak no more about my own misfortunes."

H ERE BEGINS THE MERCHANT'S TALE: Once upon a time there lived in Lombardy a worthy knight who had been born in Pavia and who lived there in great prosperity. He had been a single man for sixty years and had always satisfied his physical desires for women wherever he pleased, as these fools do that are secular. But when he had passed his sixtieth year, either because of holiness or dotage —I don't know which—this knight had such a great longing to be a married man that day and night he did all he could to ferret out a satisfactory wife. He prayed our Lord to grant that he might once experience the happy state which exists between a husband and his wife, and live under the holy vows with which God first bound man and woman. "No other life," he said, "is worth a bean; for marriage is so comforting and so pure that it is a paradise on earth." So said this old knight, who was so wise.

And, truly, as sure as God is King, it is a glorious act to take a wife, especially when a man is old and gray; then a wife is his prize treasure. He should then take a young, fair wife with whom he can have an heir and spend his days in joy and in comfort, while these bachelors sing "Alas!" whenever they are not fortunate in love—that's just childish vanity. Actually, it is very fitting that bachelors often experience pain and woe; they build on promiscuous ground, and they find promiscuity where they look for fidelity. They live like a bird or a beast: free and with no restraints; but a married man lives a happy and orderly life bound by the yoke of marriage. His heart may well be filled with joy and bliss, for who can be so obedient as a wife? Who is so faithful and also so attentive in caring for him, sick or well, as is his mate? She will not desert him in good times or bad; she never wearies of loving and serving him, even though he is bedridden, until he dies.

Yet some clerics, of whom Theophrastus is one, say that is not true. What does it matter if Theophrastus wishes to lie? He said: "Do not take a wife in an effort to save money by lessening your household expenses; a good servant is more diligent in saving your money than your own wife, who all her days will claim half as her share. And if you are sick, so help me God, your true friends or a good serving-boy will take better care of you than she who is just waiting, as she has done for a long time, for your property. And if you bring a wife into your home, you can very easily become a cuckold." This opinion and a hundred things worse were written by this man—God curse his bones! But don't pay any attention to all such vain talk; defy Theophrastus and listen to me.

A wife is truly a gift from God. All other kinds of gifts—lands, rents, pasture, common rights, and moveable property—are just gifts of Fortune which pass away like a shadow on a wall. But you can be sure—if I speak plainly—that a wife will last and remain in your house, perhaps even longer than you wish. Marriage is a truly great sacrament. I consider any man lost who has no wife; he lives helpless and completely desolate—I mean folk who are laymen. And here's why I am not talking idly: woman was created to be man's mate. High God, when He had created Adam and saw him all alone, belly naked, said then in His great goodness, "Now let us create a helpmate for this man, similar to him"; and then He created Eve. You can therefore see that it can be proved that the wife is the man's help and his comfort, his earthly paradise and his pleasure. She is so obedient and so virtuous that they are sure to live in harmony. They are as one body, and one body, as I see it, has only one heart in happiness or in misery.

A wife—ah, St. Mary, bless me! How can a man who has a wife have any troubles? Certainly, I can't say. No tongue can tell, no heart can feel, the happiness which exists between those two. If he is poor, she helps him work. She saves his money and wastes nothing at all. Anything which her husband wants pleases her well. Not once does she say, "No" when he says "Yes." "Do this," says he; "All ready, sir," says she. Oh blissful state of precious wedlock, you are so happy, so virtuous, and so commended and also approved, that every man who considers himself worth an onion ought to thank God all his days upon his bare knees for sending him a wife, or else he should pray God to send him a wife who will live as long as he. For then his life will be founded in truth; he cannot be deceived, I think, so long as he follows his wife's advice. Then he can carry his head high—a wife is so faithful and so wise in all things. Therefore, if you wish to follow the example of the wise, always accept the counsel of women.

Observe how Jacob, as the clerics tell us, bound the goat's skin about his neck on the good advice of his mother Rebecca, whereby he won his father's blessing. See how Judith, as the stories also relate, protected God's people by wise counsel and slew Holofernes while he slept. Note Abigail, who by good judgment saved her husband Nabel when he was to be killed, and remember Esther who delivered the people of God from trouble by good counsel also, and caused Mordecai to be promoted by Ahasuerus.

As Seneca says, there is nothing better than a humble wife. Endure your wife's tongue, as Cato urges. Let her command and you obey; and still she will courteously make you think you command. A wife is the guardian of your household economy; the sick man who has no wife to keep his house may well weep and bewail his state. I warn you: if you wish to be wise, love your wife dearly, as Christ loved His church. If you love yourself, you will love your wife. No man hates his own flesh; rather, he always cares for it tenderly. Therefore, I suggest that you cherish your wife or you will not prosper. Husband and wife—no matter what jokes people tell—are most secure in this world. They are so united that no harm can result, especially from the wife's side. For these reasons, January, the old man whom I spoke of before, gave thought in his old age to the full life and the virtuous peace which lie in honey-sweet marriage, and he sent one day for his friends to tell them his decision.

With a serious face he told them his story. "Friends," he said, "I am old and gray and almost, God knows, at the edge of my grave; I must to some extent consider my soul. I have foolishly wasted my physical powers; blessed be God, I will now amend that! Certainly, I will become a married man in all possible haste. Arrange my marriage quickly, I beg you, to some lovely young girl, for I cannot wait. For my part, I will search for one to whom I can be married at once. But, inasmuch as you are more numerous than I, you will be able to find such a girl more quickly than I can, and you can determine the most suitable match for me.

"But one thing, my dear friends, I warn you about: I will by no means accept an old wife. She must certainly not be over twenty. I very much like to have old fish and young flesh. A pike is better than a pickerel," he said, "tender veal is better than old beef. I want no woman of thirty; she is just bean-straw and fodder. And also, these old widows, God knows, are so cunning in the tricks of marriage, and know so well how to cause troubles when they want to, that I could never live peacefully with one of them. For attendance at many schools causes clerics to be subtle; and a woman who has had various husbands is half a cleric. But, on the other hand, one can surely guide a young thing, just as warm wax can be molded in the hands. Therefore, I tell you plainly and briefly, I want no old wife for this reason. For if I should have the misfortune to find that I could have no pleasure in my wife, then I would spend my time in adultery and go straight to hell when I die. I would have no children by her, though I would rather that hounds should eat me than to have my heritage fall in the hands of strangers; I say this to all of you. I am not in my dotage; I know why a man should marry.

"Furthermore, I know that many a man talks about marriage who knows no more about the reasons for taking a wife than my page does. If a man cannot lead a chaste life, he should piously marry to beget legitimate children in honor of God above, not from physical desire alone, or in order to avoid lechery and pay his debt of love regularly, or so that each of them could help the other in time of trouble, like brother and sister who thus live piously and chastely. But, by your leave, sirs, I am not like that, for, thank God, I can boast that I feel my body to be strong and able enough to do all that a man should do; I myself know best what I can do. Though I am gray, I am like a tree which blossoms before it bears fruit; and trees which bloom are never dead or dry. I feel gray nowhere but on top of my head; my heart and all my limbs are as green as laurel all year long. And now that you have heard my full purpose, I ask you to do as I say."

Various men told him different old stories about marriage. Some blamed it and some certainly praised it; but at last, to make the story brief, as arguments always arise among friends who dispute at length, so a quarrel broke out between January's two brothers; one of them was named Placebo, and the other was rightly called Justinus.

Placebo said: "Oh January, my brother, there was very little need, my dear lord, for you to ask advice from anyone here, except that you are so wise that you prudently did not wish to go against the words of Solomon. He said to every one of us: 'Do everything under advisement, and then you shall never be sorry.' But though Solomon said these words, my dear brother and my lord, I consider your own opinion the best, as I hope God will grant rest to my soul. Take my word for that, my brother, for I have been a courtier all my life, and God knows, though I am unworthy I have stood in very high place among lords of extremely high rank; yet I never had arguments with any of them. Actually, I never opposed them. I know very well that my lord knows more than I; whatever he says, I consider it sound and stable. I say the same or something very similar. Any counselor who serves a lord of high rank, and who dares presume or think that his opinion is better than his lord's, is a very great fool. No, lords are not fools, by my faith! You yourself have uttered such sound sentiment here today, so piously and well, that I agree and conform wholly with all your words and your decision.

By God, there is no man in all this town or in Italy who could have spoken better! Christ should consider Himself well served by your judgment. And truly, it is a sign of fine spirit for any man so advanced in years as you to take a young wife; by my father's soul, your heart hangs on a jolly peg! Now do just as you like in this matter; for in conclusion, I consider that best."

Justinus, who had sat quite still and listened, answered Placebo in this fashion: "Now, my brother, be patient, I beg you; since you have spoken, now listen to me. Seneca, among his other wise statements, says that a man should be well advised in deciding to whom he will give his lands or his belongings. And since I should be well advised in the giving of my property to someone else, I should consider even more carefully to whom I shall give my body permanently. I warn you: it is no child's play to take a wife without investigating. In my opinion, a man should inquire whether she is wise or sober or a drunkard or proud or perhaps a shrew, a nagger, or a spendthrift. Is she rich or poor, or is she man-crazy? Although it is certain that no one can find a creature in this world who is wholly perfect, neither man nor beast, such as he might desire, nevertheless, it should be sufficient for any wife to have more good traits than defects. But all this takes time to determine. God knows, I have wept many a tear in private since I married. Let whoever wants to do so praise a married man's life; surely I see in it only worry, expense, and duties, lacking all joy. And yet, God knows, my near neighbors, especially many of the women, say that I have the most steadfast wife and also the meekest who lives; but I know best where my own shoe pinches. You can, for my part, do as you please. Consider—you are no youngster—before you enter into marriage, particularly with a young and lovely wife. By Him who made water, earth, and air, even the youngest man in this whole group is busy enough trying to keep his wife for himself alone. Trust me, you won't be able to satisfy her for three full years, that is, completely. A wife demands many attentions. I beg you not to be disappointed."

"Well," said January, "have you finished? A straw for your

Seneca and for your proverbs! I care not a pan full of herbs for academic talk. Wiser men than you, as you have heard, agree with my plan. Placebo, what do you say?"

"I say it is truly a wicked man who hinders marriage," said Placebo.

With these words everyone immediately got up, agreeing fully that January should marry whenever he wished and whomever he pleased.

Wild imagining and curious thoughts began to fill January's soul from day to day in connection with his marriage. Many fair shapes and faces passed through his mind night after night, just as if someone took a brightly polished mirror, put it in the general market place, and then observed many figures pass by in his mirror. In the same way January began to think hard about the various girls who lived near him. He did not know which to prefer. For if one had great facial beauty, another was so respected by the people because of her seriousness and her kindness that she had their greatest praise. And some were rich, but had bad reputations. Nevertheless, half jokingly and half in earnest, he at last picked out one and dismissed all others from his heart. He chose her of his own initiative, for love is always blind and can see nothing. Then, when he went to bed, he saw in his mind and he felt in his heart her fresh beauty and her youth, her small waist, her long and slender arms, her wise judgment, her courtesy, her womanly manner, and her steadfastness. And when he had selected her, it seemed to him that he could not have made a wiser choice. For after he had himself arrived at a conclusion, he considered every other man too stupid to object in any way to his choice—this was his fancy. He sent a message to his friends and requested them to do him the pleasure of coming to him quickly; he wished to shorten their work, one and all. It was no longer necessary for them to travel around searching; he had decided on his choice.

Placebo came and, soon afterwards, his other friends. First of all, January asked a favor of all of them: that no one make any objections to the decision which he had reached, and which was pleasing to God, he said, and the true basis for his happiness. Then he said that there was a girl in the town, well known for her beauty though she was of low birth. Her youth and her beauty were enough for him. He said that he planned to marry this girl and lead his life in comfort and holiness. Then he thanked God that he could have her entirely, and that no one would share his bliss. He asked them to assist in this matter and to arrange things successfully for him. For then, he said, his spirit would be at rest.

"There is," he said, "nothing which disturbs me except one thing which pricks my conscience; I shall tell you all about it. I heard very long ago," he said, "that no man can have perfect bliss twice, that is on earth and also in heaven. For though he avoids the seven sins and also every branch of the forbidden tree, still there is such perfect felicity and so much comfort and joy in marriage that I am constantly afraid that I shall now in my old age lead such a happy and rare life without trouble and discord that I shall have my heaven here on earth. Since the true heaven is so dearly paid for in tribulation and great penance, how can I, who will live in that joy which all married men find with their wives, come into that bliss where the eternal Christ lives? That is my fear, and you, my two brothers, must settle this question for me, I beg you."

Justinus, who considered all these plans utter folly, at once made a mocking answer; and since he wished to cut this long discussion short, he cited no authorities, but said: "Sir, even with only the one difficulty you mentioned, God in His miraculous way and in His mercy may help you so much that, before you have your sacrament from Holy Church, you may lose your enthusiasm for the life of a married man, in which you say there is no trouble or discord. Otherwise, God forbid that He should not send a married man the grace to repent far more often than a single man! Therefore, sir—here is my best advice—don't despair; but bear in mind that this girl may be your purgatory! She may be an agent and a whip of God; if so, your soul will shoot up to heaven faster than an arrow out of a bow. I hope to God that you learn later that there is not and never shall be sufficient felicity in marriage

to interfere with your salvation, so long as you enjoy your
wife temperately and reasonably, and do not please her too
amorously, and also keep yourself from other sins. My tale is
over, for I am not too wise. Don't be frightened about this,
my dear brother; we shall manage to wade out of this diffi-
culty. The Wife of Bath, if you understood her, spoke very
briefly and well about marriage such as that you plan. Fare-
well, now; may God save you."

Then, after these words, Justinus and Placebo parted from
January and from each other. For once they saw that this
marriage must take place, they so arranged matters by subtle
and wise planning that the girl, whose name was May, would
marry January as quickly as she could. I think it would take
too long if I told you of every deed and bond of his prop-
erty with which she was endowed, or recounted all her fine
array. But, finally, the day arrived when both parties went to
the church to receive the holy sacrament. The priest with his
stole about his neck came forward and instructed her to be
like Sarah and Rebecca in wisdom and in faithfulness in mar-
riage; he said his usual prayers, told them to kneel, asked God
to bless them, and placed the stamp of the church's holy
approval upon this marriage.

In this fashion these two were ceremoniously married and
sat at the feast with other respected people upon a dais. The
palace was filled with joy and happiness, with music, and
with the daintiest food in all Italy. Music of a beauty sur-
passing that which was even made by Orpheus or Amphion of
Thebes was played before the new couple. With every course
the minstrels played loudly; Joab never trumpeted so well,
nor Theodamas so clearly when Thebes was in peril. Bacchus
kept every glass filled with wine, and Venus smiled upon ev-
eryone. For January had become her knight and would test
his strength in marriage as he had done in freedom. Then,
with her torch in hand, Venus danced about before the
bride and all the company. Truly, I dare say that Hymen, god
of marriage, never in his life saw a married man so merry.
Hold your peace, poet Martianus, who wrote for us of the
mirth and of the songs which the Muses sang at the merry

marriage of Philology and Mercury! Your pen and also your tongue would have been incapable of describing this wedding. When tender youth has wedded stooping age, there is such mirth that it defies description. Try it yourself, then you will know whether or not I am lying about this matter.

May sat at the feast with so radiant a face that to look at her was enchanting. Queen Esther never gazed with eyes so meek upon Ahasuerus. I cannot fully describe May's beauty to you, but this much I can tell about it: she was like the bright May morning, filled with beauty and delight.

January was ravished into a trance each time he looked at her face, and in his heart he began to plan how he would crush her in his arms that night, tighter than Paris ever held Helen. Nevertheless, he had great fears that he would have to offend her that night, and he thought: "Alas! Oh, tender creature, I hope to God you can sustain all my sharp, keen passion! I am afraid you won't be able to endure it; but God forbid that I should make love with all my strength! I wish to God that it were night and that the night would last forevermore. I wish that all these people would go home." Finally, he did all he could, within the bounds of good manners, to hasten the guests subtly from the table.

The proper time for leaving the table came, and then the guests drank, danced, and cast spices all around the house; everyone was full of joy and happiness—except one squire named Damian, who had served for a long time as carver for January. He was so enamored of his lady May that he was almost crazy with longing. He almost fainted and died where he stood, so sharply had Venus hurt him with her torch which she bore in her hand as she danced; and he went quickly to bed. I shall speak no more of him at this time, but leave him there weeping and complaining, until young May takes pity on his pain.

Oh, perilous fire which starts in the bedstraw! Oh, enemy to the family you serve! Oh, treacherous servant, false in loyalty to the household; you are like a sly, faithless adder in the bosom. God shield us from getting to know you! Oh, January, drunk with the joy of marriage, observe how your

Damian, your own squire and your born servant, intends to do you harm. God grant that you discover this foe within your home! For in all the world no pestilence is worse than having a household enemy always in your presence.

The sun had run its daily arc; no longer could it remain above the horizon in that latitude. Night, with its dark, coarse cloak began to overspread the whole hemisphere. Therefore, the gay guests parted from January with thanks on every side. They merrily rode home to their houses, where they did whatever they wished until they decided it was time to go to bed.

Right away the impulsive January wished to go to bed; he did not want to wait any longer. He drank hypocras, claret, and hot spicy drinks to increase his amatory powers; and he took many very rare aphrodisiacs, such as that cursed monk, Don Constantine, listed in his book *De Coitu;* he took every one of them. Then to his closest friends he said: "For God's sake, clear this house as soon as politeness permits." And they did just as he asked. People drank, and soon drew the curtains. The bride was led to the bed as still as stone, and, when the priest had blessed the bed, everyone left the bedroom. Then January firmly embraced his young May, his paradise, his mate. He soothed her and kissed her many times. He rubbed her tender face all over with the thick bristles of his prickly beard, like the skin of a dogfish, sharp as a brier—for he was recently shaved this way—and he said, "Alas! I must violate you and deeply offend you, my spouse, before my passion is abated; nevertheless, consider this," he said. "There is no workman, whoever he is, that can work both hastily and well. This will be done in perfect leisure. It doesn't matter how long we play; we two are coupled in true wedlock. And blessed be the yoke which binds us, for in our acts we can do no sin. A man can do no sin with his own bride, nor harm himself with his own knife. Thus we have a legal right to enjoy ourselves."

In this manner he worked away until the day began to dawn; and then he took some bread dipped in fine claret, sat upright in bed, and began to sing very loud and clear. He kissed his wife and frolicked merrily. He was exactly like a young colt, and as full of pranks and chatter as a magpie. The loose skin about his neck trembled as he sang, so vigorously did he chant and croak. But God knows what May thought in her heart when she saw him sitting there in his nightcap, with his skinny neck exposed. She didn't consider his love-making worth a bean.

Then he said to her, "Now that day has dawned, I shall take my rest; I can stay awake no longer." And he put his head on the pillow and slept until nine; then when he saw the time, he rose. But young May stayed in her room until the fourth morning, as is the custom among the best wives, for every worker must have some rest or else he cannot last long—that is, every living creature: fish, bird, beast, or man.

Now I shall speak of woebegone Damian, who languished for love, as you shall hear. Therefore, I speak to him in this way; I say: "Oh, poor Damian, alas! Answer my question about this matter; how do you expect to tell your trouble to your young lady, May? She will always deny you. Also, if you tell her she will betray you. God help you; that is the best that I can say."

Sick Damian so burned with Venus' fire that his passion threatened to overcome him. He, therefore, was willing to risk his life. He could no longer endure this situation, but secretly borrowed a pen and poured out his sorrow in a letter, in the form of a love-poem to his fair young lady May. Then he put the letter into a silken purse which hung from his shirt, and laid it next to his heart.

The moon, which had been in the second degree of Taurus on the day of the marriage of January and young May, had now glided into Cancer; during this time May had remained in her bedroom, as is customary among all the nobility. A bride should not eat in the main hall until four days, or at least three, have passed; then let her go feast. When high Mass on the fourth day was over, January sat in the main hall with May, who was fresh as a bright day in summer. And it so happened that the thoughts of this good man turned to Damian.

He said, "St. Mary! How is it possible that Damian neglects me? Is he always sick, or what has happened?"

His squires, who stood near him, excused Damian because sickness kept him from performing his usual duties, from which no other cause could keep him.

"That grieves me," said January; "he is a courteous squire, I'll swear! It would be a great harm and pity for him to die. He is as wise, discreet, and as dependable as any man of his rank whom I know; he is manly and serviceable, besides, and capable of becoming prosperous. After dinner, as soon as possible, I shall visit him myself, and May also, to make him as comfortable as possible."

These words caused everyone to bless January for the generosity and the courtesy which led him to comfort his squire in sickness, for it was a kind act.

"Madam," said January, "after dinner be sure, when you retire from this hall to your room, that you and all your women go to visit Damian. Cheer him up—he is a gentleman. And tell him that I shall visit him as soon as I have rested a bit. Now make haste, for I shall be waiting for you to take a nap by my side." Then he called a squire who served as major-domo of the house and gave him certain instructions.

Young May went at once with all her women to visit Damian. Then she sat down beside his bed and comforted him as best she could. Damian, when he saw his opportunity, put the purse containing the letter telling of his desire into her hand. He made no sign, except that he sighed deeply and bitterly, and whispered these words to her: "Mercy! Do not give me away, for I shall be killed if this is known." She hid the purse in her bosom and went away. That's all I shall tell you.

She went in to January, who sat very quietly on the side of his bed. He embraced her, kissed her frequently, and at once lay down to sleep. She pretended that she had to go—you know where everyone must go. And when she had read the letter, she tore it all to shreds and dropped it quietly down the privy.

Now, who is in a quandary but young May? She lay down beside old January, who slept until his cough awakened him. At once he requested her to take off her clothes; he said that he wished to have some fun with her and that the clothes got in his way. She obeyed, whether she wanted to or not. For fear that overnice people will be angry with me, I dare not tell you what he did, or whether she thought it heaven or hell. But I leave them there to do as they wish until the bell rang for evensong, at which they had to rise.

Whether because of destiny or chance, influence or nature, or the position in which the stars stood in the heavens, I cannot say, but that time was a fortunate one for a letter concerning Venus' work to be presented to any woman, in order to win her love—for all things have a suitable time, as the clerics say. Let great God above, who knows that no act is without cause, judge in this, for I shall hold my peace. The truth is that on that day young May was so struck with pity for the sick Damian that she could not put out of her heart the desire to comfort him.

"Certainly," she thought, "I do not care who will not like what I do, for I will assure Damian that I shall love him above every other creature, though he owns no more than his shirt." See how quickly pity touches a gentle heart!

In this matter you can see what superior kindness there is in women, when they think things over carefully. There is some tyrant—perhaps there are many—with a heart as hard as any stone, who would have allowed Damian to die in his bed before she granted him her favor; and then she would have rejoiced in her cruel pride and cared nothing for having been a murderer.

Gentle May, filled with pity, wrote him a letter in her own hand, in which she granted him her full favor. Nothing was lacking, except the day and place where she might satisfy his desire, and that would be exactly as he arranged it. One day, when she saw her opportunity, she went to visit Damian, and secretly she thrust her letter under his pillow; let him read it if he wished. She took him by the hand and squeezed it hard, so secretly that no one noticed it, and she urged him to

get well. Then she went back to January, when he sent for
her.

The next morning Damian got up; his sickness and his sor-
row were completely gone. He combed his hair, preened and
dressed himself, and did everything which would please and
suit his lady. Then he went in to January as humbly as ever a
dog came for a bone. He was so pleasant to everyone—for
pretense is everything, if you can manage it—that all were
eager to speak well of him. And he stood perfectly in his
lady's favor. Thus, I shall leave Damian accomplishing his
purpose and proceed with my tale.

Some clerics hold that felicity rests in physical pleasures,
and, for that reason, it is certain that this noble January did
all that he could honestly do as a knight to live in complete
pleasure. His house and his dress were as suitable to his sta-
tion as a king's. Among other fitting acts, he built a garden
with a stone wall; I know of no garden so lovely anywhere.
For, without doubt, I truly think that even the man who
wrote the *Romance of the Rose* could not describe the beauty
of this garden. Neither would Priapus, though he is god of
gardens, be able to describe the beauty of the garden and of
the well which stood under a green laurel tree. Many times,
people say, Pluto and his Queen, Proserpina, with all her
fairies, played, sang, and danced around this well.

This noble knight, this aged January, found such joy in
walking and playing in his garden that he would allow no
one else to have a key to it. He always carried the small sil-
ver key to the wicket gate, with which he unlocked it when-
ever he desired. And he and his wife, May, would go alone
to the garden when he wished to make love to her in sum-
mer; he could easily do things in the garden which he could
not accomplish in bed. In this manner, January and fresh
May passed many days merrily. But worldly pleasures can-
not continue forever, for January or for anyone else.

Oh, sudden change! Oh, fickle Fortune! You, like the
treacherous scorpion, flatter with your head as you prepare
to sting. Your tail, filled with poison, brings death. Oh, brittle
joy! Oh, strange, sweet poison! Oh, monster, who can so

subtly gild your gifts with the aspect of steadfastness that you deceive both great and small! Why did you deceive January, whom you had received as your true friend? And now you have taken from him the sight of both eyes, leaving him so sorrowful that he wished to die.

Alas! The noble, generous January, in the midst of his pleasure and his prosperity, suddenly went blind. He wept and wailed piteously. And the fire of jealousy so burned in his heart, because he feared that his wife might now be unfaithful to him, that he wished sincerely for someone to kill both him and her. For he hoped that May, after his death or during the rest of his life, would not be loved or married by another, but that she would always live as a widow in black clothes, as solitary as a turtledove which has lost its mate. But at last, after a month or two, to tell the truth, his sorrow grew less. For when he realized that he could not do otherwise, he accepted his blindness patiently, except that he certainly could not avoid becoming increasingly jealous. So ridiculous was his jealousy that he would not allow May to walk or ride anywhere, even to a neighbor's house or about their own home, without constantly having his hand on her. As a result of this, young May wept often; she loved Damian so warmly that she must either satisfy her desire for him or soon die. She expected her heart to break.

On the other hand, Damian became the saddest man there ever was, for neither by day or night could he speak a word to young May of what he really felt, or of any such thing, unless it was heard by January, who always had his hand upon her. Nevertheless, by writing back and forth and by secret signs, Damian knew how she felt, and she also knew what he wanted.

Oh, January, how could it profit you even if you were to see as far as the ships can sail? For it is just as well for a man to be deceived when blind as when he can see. Consider Argus, who had a hundred eyes: in spite of all his peeking and prying, he was still deceived, and so are many others, God knows, who are so sure that it is not so. But to pass over that fact is a pleasure; I shall say no more.

This young May, of whom I have spoken for so long, made an impression in warm wax of the little key to the garden gate which January carried and with which he so often entered the garden. Then Damian, who understood her purpose fully, secretly made a similar key from the wax impression. There is no more to tell, but soon a marvel concerning this key will occur, which you shall hear, if you will wait.

Oh, noble Ovid, you truly say, God knows, that there is no trick so long and painful but what Love will somehow discover it. People can see this in the story of Pyramus and Thisbe: though they were kept apart for a long time, they came together by whispering through a wall, a trick which no one could have discovered.

But back to my story. Before eight days in June had passed, it happened that January, egged on by his wife, developed so great a desire to play in his garden alone with her that he said to May one morning: "Arise, my wife, my love, my noble lady! The voice of the turtle is heard, my sweet dove. The winter with all its damp rains has passed. Come out now, with your eyes like a dove! Your breasts are far fairer than wine! The garden is all around enclosed. Come out, my fair spouse! Surely, you have wounded my heart! Oh, I have known of no fault in you all my life; come out, let us go play. I chose you for my wife and my comfort."

He spoke just such stupid words. She made a sign to Damian that he should enter the garden first with his key. Then Damian opened the gate and slipped in, so slyly that no one saw or heard, and he sat quietly beneath a bush.

January, blind as a stone and holding May by the hand, but without other company, entered his budding garden and quickly slammed the gate. "Now, wife," he said, "you only, the creature whom I love best, are here with me. By the Lord who sits in heaven above, I had rather die by a knife thrust than offend you, my true dear wife! For God's sake, think how I chose you: not from greed surely, but only because of the love I had for you. And though I am old and have lost my sight, be true to me; I shall tell you why. There are three things that you shall certainly gain as a result: first,

love of Christ; then, honor to yourself; and all my lands and
buildings. I give them to you; draw up whatever legal papers
you wish. This shall be done before the sun sets tomorrow,
as I hope kind God will save my soul. I beg you first to kiss
me as a seal of the agreement, and don't blame me if I am
jealous. You are so deeply imprinted in my thoughts that,
when I think of your beauty and my advanced age, I cer-
tainly cannot bear to be out of your company, because of
my love for you, even though I should die for it. That is true;
now kiss me, wife, and let's stroll about."

Young May, having heard this speech, first began to weep
and then unctuously answered: "I have a soul to guard as
well as you," she said, "and also my honor and the tender
flower of my wifehood, of which I assured you when the
priest united my body to yours. Therefore, with your permis-
sion I shall answer you in the following fashion, my dear
lord: I pray God that I will not fail to die as foul a death as
is possible for a woman if I ever bring shame to my family
or injure my good reputation by being false. But if I commit
such a fault, have me stripped, put into a sack, and drowned
in the nearest river. I am a gentlewoman, not a wench. Why
do you speak of these matters? Men are always unfaithful,
yet they continually blame women for that fault. You men
know of nothing else to do, I think, but to chide us for
infidelity."

As she spoke, she saw Damian sitting under the bush. Then
she began to cough, and made signs with her finger for him
to climb a tree which was loaded with fruit. Up he went,
for he understood all her purpose and every sign that she had
made far better than January, her own husband. She had
explained her plan in a letter and everything that he should
do. So now I leave him sitting in the pear tree, while January
and May stroll gaily through the garden.

The day was bright and the skies blue; Phoebus had sent
down his golden rays to gladden every flower with his
warmth. He was at that time, I think, in Gemini, a little be-
fore his declination in Cancer, which is the exaltation of Jove.
And so it happened on that bright morning that there were

on the farther side of the garden Pluto, King of Fairyland, and many ladies in the retinue of his wife, Queen Proserpina, whom he stole from Etna while she gathered flowers in the meadow—you can read the story in Claudian of how he came for her in his horrible chariot.

Then the King of Fairyland sat down on a fresh green bank of turf and at once said to his Queen: "My wife," he said, "no one can deny that experience proves that every day women betray men. I can tell a million remarkable tales of the infidelity and unfaithfulness of women. Oh, Solomon, wise, and richest of the rich, filled with prudence and with earthly glory, your words are worth remembering for every clever and reasonable man. Speaking of people characterized by true excellence, he said: 'Among a thousand men I found one; but I found none among all women.' So said a king who understood your wickedness.

"And I think Jesus, son of Sirach, speaks of you infrequently with respect. May wildfire and a corrupting pestilence fall upon your bodies tonight! Don't you see this honorable knight? Alas, because he is old and blind his own servant will make him a cuckold. Look where he sits, that lecher, in the tree! Now I, in my majesty, will grant this worthy, old, blind knight the return of his vision at the moment that his wife tries to betray him. Then he will understand all her adultery, to her shame and that of many others."

"Shall you?" said Proserpina. "Do you wish to do that? Now, by the soul of my mother's father, I swear that I shall furnish her and, for her sake, all other women after her with a satisfactory answer, so that even though they are caught in any sinful act they shall be able to excuse themselves with a bold face and bear down their accusers. Not one of them shall die for lack of an answer. Even though a man sees a thing with his own eyes, so shall we women pretend the opposite, weep and swear, and subtly nag, that you men will be as ignorant as geese.

"What do I care for your authorities? I know very well that this Jew, this Solomon, found many of us women fools. But though he found no good woman, yet many another man has found faithful, good, and virtuous women. Witness those women who dwell in Christ's house; they proved their constancy with martyrdom. The Roman histories also mention many a true, faithful wife. But, sir—don't be angry—although he said that he found no good woman, I beg you to interpret his meaning broadly; he meant that no one is sovereignly excellent except God, who sits in Trinity. And, by the one true God, why do you make so much of Solomon? What though he built a temple, God's house? What though he was rich and glorious? He also built a temple to false gods. How could he do anything more forbidden? By God, whitewash his name as you will, he was a lecher and an idolator, and in his old age he forsook the true God. Then, if God had not, as the Book says, spared him for his father's sake, he would have lost his kingdom earlier than he did. I care nothing, not even a butterfly, for all the dishonor you men write about women! I am a woman; I must needs speak out, or else swell until my heart bursts. For, since he called us chatterboxes, as I hope always to keep my hair intact, I will not for the sake of courtesy refrain from speaking harm of the man who wishes to dishonor us."

"Madam," said Pluto, "don't be angry any longer. I give up! But since I swore my oath that I would give this man back his sight, I will keep my word; I give you fair warning. I am a king; it would not be fitting for me to lie."

"And I," said Proserpina, "am Queen of Fairyland! I swear that she shall have an answer. Let's not discuss it further, for, truly, I don't wish to oppose you any longer."

Now let us turn once more to January, who sings in the garden with his beautiful May more happily than a jay bird: "You I love best and ever shall, and no other." He wandered about the garden until he came to the pear tree in which Damian gaily sat, high up among the green leaves.

Young May, the bright and shining one, began to sigh, and said, "Alas, my side! Now sir," she said, "whatever happens, I must have some of these pears which I see, or I shall die; I crave so strongly to eat some small green pears. Help me, for love of Her who is Queen of Heaven! I tell you plainly that a woman in my delicate condition can have so great an appetite for fruit that she may die unless she eats some."

"Alas," he said, "that I have no servant here who could climb the tree! Alas, alas," he said, "that I am blind!"

"It doesn't matter," she said. "But will you, for God's sake, encircle the tree trunk with your arms, for I know that you distrust me? Then I can easily climb up by putting my foot on your back," she said.

"Surely," he said, "I shall not fail to do that. I only wish that I could help you with my heart's blood." He leaned down; then she stood on his back, caught a limb, and up she went—ladies, I beg you, don't be angry; I cannot flatter; I am a crude man. Damian immediately pulled up her dress and went to work.

When Pluto saw this great wrong, he restored January's eyesight, so that he could see as well as ever. Never was a man so happy about anything as January when he found that he could see again. At once he thought about his wife, and raised his eyes up into the tree. There he saw Damian using his wife in a way which cannot be described, if I wish to speak politely. Then January roared and screamed like a mother whose child has died: "Help, help, alas!" he said. "Oh, harsh, bold woman, what are you doing?"

May answered: "Sir, what ails you? Have patience and be reasonable! I have helped you regain your sight. Upon peril of my soul, I shall not lie; it was explained to me that nothing would help you regain your sight so much as for me to struggle with a man in a tree. God knows, I did it with very good intentions."

"Struggle!" he cried. "It certainly went in all the way! May God send a shameful death to both of you! He made love with you; I saw it with my own eyes, or else may I be hanged by the neck!"

"Then," she said, "my cure hasn't worked properly; for if you could see well again, you would not say such things to me. You are able to catch glimpses, but not to see perfectly."

"I can see as well as ever with both my eyes, thank God,"

he said, "and, on my word, it seemed to me that he did that to you."

"You are bewildered, good sir, bewildered," she said. "Is this all the thanks I get for restoring your sight? Alas," she said, "that I was ever so kind!"

"Now, madam," he said, "forget all this. Come on down, my love, and if I have spoken amiss, so help me God, I am sorry. But, by my father's soul, I thought that I saw Damian lie with you, and that your dress was up to your breast."

"Yes, sir," she said, "you can think what you like. But, sir, when a man awakes from sleep, he cannot immediately perceive and see things clearly until he is fully accustomed to the light. So it is with a man who has for a long time been blind. He cannot see as well when his sight first returns as a man who has been seeing for a day or two. You may see numerous deceptive sights, until your eyes become settled. Be careful, I beg you, for, by the King of Heaven, many a man thinks he sees a certain thing which is in reality altogether different. A man who does not see clearly misjudges." And with these words, she came down from the tree.

Who was now happy but January? He kissed her and embraced her many times, and he gently stroked her body and led her home to his palace.

Now, good men, I beg you to be happy. Thus ends my tale of January. May God and his mother St. Mary bless us all!
HERE ENDS THE MERCHANT'S TALE OF JANUARY.

꽃

EPILOGUE TO THE MERCHANT'S TALE: "Aye, God's mercy!" our Host then said. "I hope God will deliver me from such a wife! See what tricks and subtleties there are in women! For they are always as busy as bees to deceive us poor men, and they always turn away from the truth; the Merchant's tale proves that well. But, without doubt, I have a wife as true as steel, although she is poor. But in talking, she is a veritable shrew, and, in addition, she has many other vices. Still, it doesn't matter! Let's forget all such things. But you know what? To tell the truth, I regret bitterly that I am tied to her. For, if I should count off each of her vices I would certainly be too foolish. Do you know why? It would be reported to her by someone in this group—no need to say which one; women know how to do such business. Also, I don't have enough brains to describe them all; therefore, my story is over."

THE SQUIRE

THE SQUIRE'S PROLOGUE: "Squire, move nearer, if you care to do so," said the Host, "and tell us some love story; for, surely, you know as much about such matters as any man."

"No, sir," replied the Squire. "But I shall gladly tell a story as best I can, for I do not want to rebel against your desire; I shall tell a tale. Excuse me if I speak amiss; my intention is good. Listen, here is my tale."

HERE BEGINS THE SQUIRE'S TALE: At Tsarev, in the land of Tartary, there lived a king who made war on Russia, as a result of which many a brave man died. This noble King was named Cambiuskan, and he was so famous in his day that there was nowhere in any land a lord so outstanding in all ways. He lacked no kingly trait, and he kept the faith that he had sworn in that religion into which he had been born. Also, he was brave, discreet, rich, merciful and just without partiality, true to his word, gracious, honorable, and steadfast to the core, young, vigorous, strong, and as desirous of military glory as any squire in his whole court. He was a handsome and fortunate person, and he always maintained his kingly station so well that nowhere was there another like him.

This noble King, Cambiuskan of Tartary, had two sons by his wife Elpheta, of whom the elder was called Algarsyf and the younger one, Cambalo. He also had a daughter younger still, whose name was Canace. But I have neither the words nor the skill to tell you of all her beauty; I dare not try so difficult a task. My English is inadequate. It would take an excellent rhetorician, who knew his colorful figures of speech, to describe her adequately. I am not that; I must speak as best I can.

And so it happened that when Cambiuskan had ruled for twenty years, he had his birthday feast announced throughout his city, Tsarev, on March fifteenth, as was his custom, I think, each year. Phoebus, the sun, shone clear and bright, for he was near his exaltation in Mars and in his house in Aries, the hot, choleric sign of the zodiac. The weather was pleasant and invigorating, and the birds, because of the sunshine and the budding season, loudly sang their love songs. They thought themselves well protected against the bitter cold sword of winter.

Cambiuskan, whom I was telling you about, sat high on the dais in his palace. He wore his royal robes and crown, and held his feast, the richest and most impressive in all the world. If I told you about all the sights there, it would take up many a summer's day. But there is no need to explain in detail every course served; I shall not tell of their rare broths, their swans, or their young herons. Anyway, in that land, so ancient knights tell us, there are some meats which are considered excellent but which are not thought much of in our country; no one man can report everything. I shall not delay you, for it is already nine in the morning; and there would be no profit, just waste of time. Therefore, I shall return to my tale.

It happened after the third course, while the King sat thus in splendor, listening to his minstrels standing beside the table play their delightful songs, that a knight upon a brass horse suddenly entered the hall door. In his hand he carried a large glass mirror; he wore a gold ring upon his thumb, and a naked sword hung by his side. He rode up to the head table. Not a word was spoken in the whole hall, so marvelous was this knight; young and old watched him attentively. The strange knight, who had entered so suddenly, was completely and richly armed except for his head. He saluted the King, the Queen, and all the lords in the order in which they sat in the hall. His speech and behavior showed such high respect and courtesy that even Gawain, with his fine old manners, had he returned from fairyland, could not have found a single fault. Then, standing before the head table, the knight spoke his message in a manly voice, according to the form customary in his language and without the slightest flaw in word or syllable. And in order to make his tale more moving, he fitted his manner to his words, as is taught to those who study the art of speaking. Though I cannot reproduce his manner, nor reach to so high a style, yet I shall state that, as to the main point, all that he said amounted to this, if I can remember it:

"My liege lord, the King of Arabia and India," he said, "salutes you as sincerely as possible on this festive occasion. In honor of your birthday, he sends by me, who stands ready at your command, this brass steed. This steed, in the course of one natural day—that is, twenty-four hours—can very easily and comfortably carry you wherever you wish to go, in drought or rain, without injury, through fair or foul. Or, if you wish to fly as high in the air as an eagle when it soars, this same horse will always take you without harm to your destination, no matter whether you are awake or asleep on his back. And he will come back whenever you turn the proper pin. The man who made this horse understood many contrivances; he observed many a constellation before he completed this task, and he knew a magic seal and bond.

"This mirror, too, which I hold in my hand has such power that you can see in it just when misfortune will occur to you or your realm, and exactly who is your friend or foe. More than all this, if any fair lady has set her heart on a man who is false, she can clearly see all his treachery, his new mistress, and all his craftiness in this mirror; nothing can be hidden. Thus, as a protection in this amorous summer season, my sovereign has sent this mirror and this ring that you see to Lady Canace, your excellent daughter. The power of the ring, if you care to hear it, is this: if she desires to wear it on her thumb, or carry it in her purse, there is no bird flying in the heavens whose voice and meaning she will not clearly understand and be able to answer in his own language. And she will know the power of every herb that grows from a root and whom it will heal, no matter how deep and wide the wounds.

"This naked sword hanging by my side has such power that it will bite through the armor of whatever man you strike with it, no matter if it is as thick as gnarled oak. And any man wounded by a stroke of this sword will never be healed until you decide out of kindness to strike him with the flat of the sword on the spot where he is wounded; that is to say, you can strike him on the wound with the flat of the sword and it will close. All this is true, without exaggeration. The sword will not fail in your hands."

When the knight had given his message he rode out of the hall and dismounted. His horse, shining as brightly as the sun, stood in the courtyard, as still as a stone. The knight was led to his room, his armor was removed, and then he was seated at the table. The presents—that is, the sword and mirror—were ceremoniously borne by appointed officials to the high tower, and the ring was duly taken to Canace, where she sat at the table. But, in all truth, the brass horse could not be removed; he stood as if he were glued to the ground. No one could draw him away with any windlass or contrivance; and do you know why? Because no one knew the secret. And therefore they left him on the spot until the knight taught them the way to remove him, as you will hear later.

A great crowd swarmed back and forth to stare at the horse as he stood there. For he was as tall, broad, long, and well and strongly built as a Lombard horse; and at the same time as excellent in quality and as quick of eye as an Apulian horse. And certainly, from head to tail, neither nature nor art could have in any way improved upon him, as everyone agreed. But the thing everyone marveled at most was how a horse made of brass could move. The people thought he was from fairyland. Various ones judged differently; there were as many opinions as there were heads. The people buzzed like a swarm of bees and made up imaginary explanations, retelling old poetic fancies. They said he was like Pegasus, the horse that had wings for flying; or else it was the horse of Sinon the Greek, which brought Troy to destruction, as one can read in the old histories. "My heart," said one man, "is afraid from now on; I think some men-at-arms are inside who plan to conquer this city. It would be good to find out about such a possibility." Another whispered to his friend: "He lies, for it is rather an illusion created by some magic, as jugglers do at these great feasts." In this way they quarreled and discussed various fears, as ignorant people usually do about things which are made more subtly than their understanding can comprehend; they are always willing to suppose the worst.

Some of them marveled at the mirror, which had been carried up to the main tower. How could one see such things in it? Another answered, saying that it might easily be constructed in a natural way, by arrangements of angles and crafty reflections, and that there was such a mirror in Rome. They spoke of Alhazen, Witelo, and Aristotle, who in their times wrote about strange mirrors and perspective glasses, as everyone who has heard of their books knows.

Other people marveled at the sword which could pierce anything. And they talked about King Telephus and about the marvelous spear of Achilles, with which he could both heal and harm, just as could be done with this sword which you have just heard about, yourselves. They spoke of various ways of tempering metal, of acids to be used and of how and when it should be hardened—things unknown, at least to me.

Then they discussed Canace's ring and said that they had never heard of anyone who had such a remarkable example of the craft of ringmaking, except Moses and King Solomon, who had reputations for great skill in that art. Thus the people talked, standing at a distance. But, nevertheless, some said, it is miraculous to make glass from fern-ashes when glass is not like fern-ashes; but, since that skill has been known so long, people have stopped talking and marveling about it. Some people wonder greatly about the cause of thunder, the ebb and flood of the tides, gossamer, mist, and everything else, until the causes are known. So these people chattered, gave opinions and explanations until the King rose from the table.

When, about two hours after noon, Cambiuskan, the Tartar King, rose from the table at which he proudly sat, Phoebus had left the angle of the meridian, and the royal beast, noble Leo, with his star Aldiran, was still ascending. Minstrels went before the King, playing loudly until the reception chamber was reached, where they played so well on various instruments that it was heavenly to hear. Then the joyous children of Venus danced, as their lady sat high in Pisces and looked down on them with a friendly eye.

The noble King took his place upon the throne. The foreign knight was soon brought to him, and joined in the dance with Canace. There was such revelry and fun as a dull man cannot imagine. Anyone who describes such entertainment must surely understand love and its ritual, and be a festive man, fresh as May. Who could tell of such rare dances, such beaming faces, such sly glances and dissimulating for fear of jealous men's noticing? No man but Lancelot, and he is dead. Therefore, I pass over all this gaiety. I shall say no more, but leave them at their fun, until the supper is ready.

Amid all this music, the steward ordered the spices to be brought forth, and also the wine. The ushers and squires ran out; soon the spices and wine appeared. The people ate and drank, and after that they went to the temple, as was fitting. When the service was over, they had supper, still by daylight. What need to tell you about all the arrangements? Everyone knows very well that there is plenty for everybody, great and small, at a king's feast, and more dainties than I know about. After supper the noble King went to see the brass horse, with all his lords and ladies following him.

There was never such marveling about a horse since the great siege of Troy, where, too, people speculated about a horse. Finally, the King asked the knight about the power and strength of this horse, and requested him to tell what supervision it required. When the knight placed his hand on the reins, the horse at once began to dance and jig. The knight said, "Sire, there is nothing to explain, except that when you wish to ride to any destination you must turn a pin which is to be found in his ear; I shall tell you about that privately. Also, you must tell him what place or what country you wish to visit. And when you reach the place where you want to stop, tell him to descend and turn another pin—for in this lies the secret of the whole contrivance—and he will descend as you wish and wait there quietly for you. Though all the world should swear otherwise, he cannot be drawn or carried from that spot. Or, if you wish to tell him to go away, turn this pin; and he will vanish immediately out of sight of everyone, and return whenever you wish to call him again, day or night, in a way which I shall explain to you very soon in private. Ride when you wish; that is all that needs to be done."

When the knight had explained matters and the brave and noble King had fully understood the nature and all the workings of this horse, the King returned to the revelry. The bridle was carried to the tower and placed among his most precious jewels. The horse vanished from their sight—I don't know how. You will get no more from me, for I shall leave Cambiuskan and his lords feasting in pleasure and gaiety until almost daybreak. THE FIRST PART ENDS.

THE SECOND PART FOLLOWS: Sleep, the nurse of digestion, blinked at the revelers and instructed them to remember that excessive drinking and exercise make rest necessary. With a yawning mouth he kissed each of them and said it was time to lie down, for blood was dominant. "Cherish blood, nature's friend," said he. Yawning, they thanked him by twos and threes, and everyone made ready for bed as Sleep demanded; they considered it best. I shall not tell you now about their dreams; their heads were filled with the fumes of wine, which bring dreams of no consequence. They slept until fully nine o'clock, almost everybody except Canace. She was temperate, as women usually are; for she had taken leave of her father to go to bed soon after nightfall. She did not wish to seem pale or in poor spirits the next morning. After she had her first few hours' sleep, she awoke and found such pleasure at the thought of her strange ring and her mirror that she changed color twenty times. And in her sleep, because of the impression her mirror left, she had had a vision. Therefore, before sunrise, she called her governess to her and said that she wished to get up. This old woman was one of those who wished to be thought very wise. She at once inquired, "Madam, where will you go this early? Everyone is still in bed."

"I wish," said Canace, "to get up and walk around, for I cannot sleep any longer."

Her governess summoned a great crowd of women—ten or twelve—who at once got up. Young Canace herself arose, as ruddy and bright as the young sun when it has climbed four degrees in the Ram—it was no higher when she had finished dressing. Then she walked out at a leisurely pace, properly dressed for the sweet season, to take the air and roam around with five or six of her retinue. She went into a path in the park. The mist which rose from the earth made the sun seem ruddy and broad, but the season and the morning were so fine that everyone was lighthearted. Canace heard the birds singing and at once understood the full meaning of their song and knew what was in their minds.

If the point for which a tale is told is put off until the desire of those who have faithfully listened is dulled, the enjoyment becomes progressively less in proportion to the teller's long-windedness. For that reason, it seems to me that I should get to the point and quickly put an end to Canace's walking.

As Canace was enjoying her stroll, there was a falcon sitting in a tree, dry and white as chalk, high over her head. The falcon began to cry in a piteous voice that made the whole wood resound. She had beaten herself so mercilessly with both her wings that the red blood ran down the length of the tree in which she sat. And, continually, she cried and screamed and so tore herself with her beak that there is no tiger or other cruel beast dwelling in the woods or forest which would not have wept, if he could, out of sorrow for her, she shrieked so loud. If I could adequately describe a falcon, there would be no man alive who had ever heard of another of equal beauty, in plumage, in nobility of form, and in every other respect. She seemed a hawking-falcon from a foreign land, and, every now and then, she fainted from loss of blood, until she almost fell from the tree.

Canace, the beautiful daughter of a sovereign, who wore on her finger the strange ring through which she could understand the speech of any bird and answer in its own language, understood what this falcon said and almost died of pity. Hastily, she went to the tree, looked up pityingly at this falcon, held out the skirt of her gown, for she knew very well that the falcon must fall from the limb when it next fainted from loss of blood. She stood a long while watching her and then at last spoke to the bird, as you will now hear:

"What is the cause, if it may be told, of your suffering these furious pains of hell? Is your grief from death or from loss of love? For I think that these are the two causes which most grieve a gentle heart; there is no need to speak of other troubles. You are avenging yourself upon yourself, and that proves clearly that either love or fear must be the cause of your cruelty, since I see that no one is hunting you. For the love of God, spare yourself, or how can anything be of help to you? In neither east nor west have I ever seen a bird or beast before now who treated himself so cruelly. Truly you are killing me with your sorrow, I have such compassion for you. For God's love, come down from that tree. And, as surely as I am the true daughter of a king, if I know the real cause of your troubles and it lies within my power to do so, I will amend it before nightfall, so help me great God of nature! I shall find plenty of herbs to heal your wounds quickly."

Then the falcon, shrieking even more piteously than before, fell to the ground, and lay there unconscious, still as a stone. Canace took her in her lap until the bird began to recover from the fainting. After she had revived, she began to speak in her bird's language: "That pity rises soon in a gentle heart, feeling its own likeness in sharp pain, is proved each day, as anyone can see, by deeds as well as by texts; for a gentle heart knows gentle acts. I see well, my fair Canace, that you have compassion for my suffering, out of the true womanly kindness which Nature has put among your qualities. While I have time, before I go, I shall explain my trouble to you, not in the hope of improving my situation, but to obey your kind request, and to warn others by my example, as the lion is warned by the example of a punished dog."

And steadily, while the falcon told of her grief, Canace wept as if she would turn to water, until the falcon bade her be quiet and, sighing, told her story.

"Where I was born—ah, that cruel day—on a rock of gray marble, I was cared for so tenderly that nothing went wrong for me; I did not know what hardship was until I could fly far up into the sky. There lived near me a falcon who seemed the well of all courtesy. Though he was full of treachery and falseness, it was so hidden under humility, the colors of truth, gaiety, and industrious service, that no one could have guessed that it was all pretense, so deeply had he dyed his colors. Just as a serpent hides himself under flowers until he sees his opportunity to bite, so this god of love, this hypocrite, performed his duties and courtesies and attentions with all the appearance of the delicacy pertaining to love. As with a tomb, all is pretty above but beneath is the corpse, as you know; so it was with this hypocrite, both hot and cold. And in this way he carried out his purpose; except for the devil, no one knew what he meant. He wept and wailed for such a long time, and he pretended to pay court to me for so many years, that my heart, too pitying and simple, all innocent of his consummate malice, afraid that, as it seemed to me, he might die, granted my love to him, upon receiving his oaths and assurances. The one condition was that my honor and reputation would always be preserved, both privately and openly; that is to say, because of his good qualities I gave him all my heart and thoughts—on no other terms, God and he know—and accepted his heart forever in exchange.

"But it was truly said long ago: 'An honest man and a thief do not think alike.' When he saw that the matter had progressed so far that I had fully granted him my love, as I just explained, and had freely given him my true heart, he swore that his heart was mine. At once this tiger, full of duplicity, fell on his knees with such devout humility, with such high respect, and, judging from his manner, so like a gentle lover in his bearing, so ravished, it seemed, with happiness, that neither Jason nor Paris of Troy—Jason? certainly not, nor any other man since Lamech, who was the first to have two loves, so ancient writers say—nor any other man since the world began, could ever, by one twenty-thousandth, have imitated the sophistry of his artfulness. They couldn't approach him in double-dealing; they weren't worthy of unbuckling his shoe. Never could a man give thanks as he did to me! His manner was heavenly for any woman to behold, no matter how wise, so well did he preen and comb his words and himself. And I loved him so for his attentions and for the truth I thought was in his heart, that if I knew of even the smallest thing which inconvenienced him, it seemed that I felt death twist my heart. And, briefly, this matter went along so far that my will became only the instrument of his will; that is to say, my will obeyed his will in all things reasonable, guarding only the bounds of my honor. I never had anything so dear as or dearer than he, God knows; and I never will.

"This lasted longer than a year or two, and I thought only good of him. But things were such that at last Fortune decreed that he must leave the place where I was. There is no question of my woe; I cannot describe it. For I can tell you one thing assuredly: as a result, I know what the pain of death is. I felt such grief that he could not believe it. So, one day he took his leave of me so sorrowfully that I truly believed that he felt pain equal to mine, when I heard him speak and observed his face. Indeed, I thought that he was faithful and also that he would return in a short time, to tell the truth. And it seemed so reasonable that he had to leave in order to maintain his honor, as it often happens, that I made a virtue of necessity and took it well, since it could not be helped. As best I could, I hid my sorrow from him, took him by the hand, and, with St. John as my witness, told him, 'You see, I am all yours; be to me as I have been and will be to you.'

"There is no need to repeat his answer; who can speak better and act worse than he? When he has talked well, he has finished; that is as far as he goes. I have heard it said: 'She who eats with a fiend should have a long spoon.' At last, he had to leave, and he flew until he reached his destination. When the time came for him to rest, I am sure that he remembered the saying, 'everything, returning to its nature, becomes happy'; I think people say that. Men by their very nature love newfangled things, as do birds kept in a cage. For, though you care for a bird day and night, and strew his cage well, making it as silk, and give him sugar, honey, bread, and milk to eat, as soon as the cage door is opened he will overturn the cup with his feet and fly to the woods to eat worms. So newfangled are birds about their food, and so naturally do they love novelty, that no nobility of blood binds them.

"So it was with this falcon, alas! Though he was of noble birth, bold and gay, handsome, humble, and generous, he once saw a kite fly by, and suddenly he loved the kite so much that all his love for me was completely gone. And in this way he broke his faith. So the kite now has my lover in her service, and I am lost without remedy!" With these words the falcon began to wail and fainted again on Canace's bosom.

Canace and all her women made great lamentation over the falcon's betrayal. They did not know how they could cheer her up, but Canace took the bird home in her gown and gently wrapped bandages around the places where she had wounded herself with her beak. Now Canace could do nothing but dig herbs from the ground and make new salves out of the delicately colored, precious herbs to heal the bird. From dawn to dark, Canace busied herself and did all she could. By the head of her bed she made a cage and covered it with blue velvet, as a sign of woman's fidelity. The cage was painted green on the outside, with pictures of all the unfaithful birds: wrens, falcons, and owls. Just for spite, magpies were painted nearby to scold them.

Now I shall leave Canace taking care of her falcon; I shall say no more about her ring until it is necessary to explain how the falcon won back her repentant lover, as the story tells us, through the mediation of Cambalo, the king's son, whom I told you about. But now I shall continue my story with talk of adventures and battles; never before were such miracles heard of.

First, I shall tell you about Cambiuskan, who in his day conquered many cities. And then I shall speak of Algarsyf and how he won Theodora as his wife, for whom he would often have been in great danger, if he had not been aided by the brass horse. After that, I shall speak of Cambalo, who fought in the lists against two brothers for the sake of Canace before he could win her. And I shall now begin where I left off. THE SECOND PART ENDS.

꧁

THE THIRD PART BEGINS: Apollo whirled his chariot on high until he reached the house of the cunning God Mercury——

[*Chaucer left the Squire's story unfinished.*]

HERE FOLLOW THE WORDS OF THE FRANKLIN TO THE SQUIRE, AND THE WORDS OF THE HOST TO THE FRANKLIN: "In faith, Squire, you have acquitted yourself admirably and like a gentleman. I think highly of your intelligence," said the Franklin, "considering your youth. You speak so touchingly I commend you. According to my judgment, there's no one here who will be your equal in eloquence, if you live. God give you good luck and send you continued strength! For I thoroughly enjoy your speech. I have a son, and, by the Trinity, I would rather have him a man of such discretion as you than land worth twenty pounds' rent a year, if it were to fall into my hands this minute! To the devil with possessions, if a man is capable! I have scolded my son, and will again, because he won't pay attention to education; it is his habit to play at dice and to spend and lose all he owns. He had rather talk with a page from court than with any educated man from whom he might properly learn courtesy."

"A straw for your courtesy!" said our Host. "How now, Franklin; by God, sir, you know very well that each of you must tell a tale or two at least, or else break his promise."

"I know that quite well, sir," said the Franklin. "I beg you, do not hold me in contempt for speaking a word or two with this man."

"Tell your tale without more talk."

"Gladly, Sir Host," he said. "I shall obey your command; now listen to what I say. I won't intentionally cross you in any respect. I pray God that my tale will please you; then shall I know very well that it was good enough."

THE FRANKLIN

THE PROLOGUE OF THE FRANKLIN'S TALE: The worthy old Bretons in their time made rhymed tales in their earliest Breton language about all kinds of adventures. They sang these tales to the accompaniment of their instruments, or else read them for their pleasure, and I remember one of them which I shall gladly tell as best I can.

But, friends, since I am an ignorant person, I beg you, right here at the start, to forgive my crude speech. I never learned rhetoric, to tell you the truth; whatever I say must be blunt and plain. I never slept on Mount Parnassus, or studied Marcus Tullius Cicero. The only colors that I know about are such as grow in the meadows, or those used for dyeing or painting. Rhetorical colors are strange to me; I have no feeling for such matters. But, if you care to, you shall hear my tale.

HERE BEGINS THE FRANKLIN'S TALE: In Armorica, which is called Brittany, there was a knight who loved a lady and took pains to serve her in the finest fashion; he performed many a task and many a large undertaking for her before he won her. For she was one of the fairest women under the sun, and came from such a noble family that this knight scarcely dared to tell her about his woe, his pain, and his distress. But, finally, impressed by his worth, and especially by his meek obedience, she took such pity on his suffering that she secretly agreed to take him as her husband and her lord—such lordship, at least, as husbands have over their wives. And in order that they might live the more happily, he swore to her of his own free will as a knight that never, day or night, in all his life would he assume any sovereignty over her against her will, or show any jealousy, but would obey her and follow her decisions in all things, as any lover should do towards his lady. He made only one exception; he would claim the semblance of sovereignty for the sake of the dignity of his position.

She thanked him and said, with great humility: "Sir, since out of courtesy you offer me so free a rein, God forbid that there should ever be war or strife between us two as a result of my faults. Sir, I will be your humble, true wife; you now have my promise for that, until my heart shall burst." In this way they were both in peaceful agreement.

One thing, ladies and gentlemen, I may safely say: friends must be considerate of each other if they wish to remain long in companionship. Love will not be held by mastery. When mastery comes, the god of Love at once beats his wings, and farewell—he is gone! Love is a thing as free as any spirit. Women naturally desire liberty, and not to be treated as slaves; and so do men, if I tell the truth. Consider the man who is most patient in love; certainly he has a great advantage. Patience is surely a great virtue, for it overcomes things, as the clerics say, which could not be overcome by discipline. People should not nag or scold with every word. Learn to suffer, or else, as I may prosper, you shall learn it whether you want to or not. For, certainly, there is no one in this world who does not at some time do or say something amiss. Wrath, sickness, the stars, wine, woe, or change in temperament very often cause people to act or speak amiss. A man cannot be revenged for every wrong. Every person who understands behavior knows there must be moderation according to the occasion. And, therefore, this wise, brave knight promised his wife forbearance, in order to live in agreement; and she, equally wisely, swore to him that he would never find her at fault.

Here people may see a humble, wise agreement; she has gained a servant and a lord: a servant in love and a lord in marriage. He, consequently, found himself in lordship and in bondage. Bondage? No, rather in lordship, for he had both his lady and his love—his lady, certainly, but also a wife who agreed to follow the laws of love. And when he had accomplished this happy state, he went home with his wife to his own country; his house was not far from Penmarch, and he lived there in joy and comfort. Who except one who has been married can tell about the joy, the comfort, and the bliss that there is between a husband and his wife? This happy state lasted more than a year, until this knight whom I am talking about—Arveragus of Kayrrud—prepared to go to live a year or two in England, which was also called Britain, to seek honor and glory in arms, for he loved such activity. And he stayed there two years, so the book says.

Now I shall leave Arveragus, and turn to his lady Dorigen, who loved her husband as her life. She wept and became ill because of his absence, as all noble wives do when it pleases them. She mourned, could not sleep, wailed, fasted, and lamented. She missed her husband so keenly that she cared nothing for all this wide world. Her friends, who knew her heavy thoughts, did their best to comfort her. They lectured her, repeating day and night that she was killing herself for no good cause, and they diligently did everything they possibly could to cheer her up.

In time, as all of you know, men may by continued chipping carve some figure in stone. Dorigen's friends comforted her so persistently that at last, through hope and reason, their consolation had some effect. Her great sorrow began to decrease; she could not have continued forever in such a state. Also, in the midst of her sorrow, Arveragus had sent her some letters saying that he was well and would soon return; otherwise, she would have died of grief. Her friends observed that she became more cheerful, and on their knees they begged her, for God's sake, to go on trips with them in order to drive away her black melancholy. Finally, she agreed to do this, for she saw that it was for the best.

Now her castle stood close to the sea, and often for pleasure she walked with her friends on the high shore, from which she saw many a ship and barge sailing their courses, headed where they pleased. But at this sight her woe increased, for she often said to herself: "Alas, is there no ship of all these I see which will bring my lord home to cure my heart of its bitter hurt?" At other times she would sit and think, casting her eyes downward from the cliff's edge. But when she saw the terrible black rocks below, her heart would quake so much from pure fear that she could not stand on her feet. She would sit down upon the grass and look pitifully out to sea, saying with deep sighs:

"Eternal God, who through Thy providence guides the world by sure government, men say that Thou makest nothing in vain. But, Lord, why didst Thou, so wise and perfect and stable a God, make something as unreasonable as these terrible, fiendish, black rocks, which seem rather a foul confusion than Thy fair creation? For neither man, nor bird, nor beast, east, west, south, or north, is helped by these rocks; to my mind, they do not do good but harm. Dost Thou not see, Lord, how mankind is destroyed by them? Man is so fair a part of Thy work that Thou madest him in Thy image, and yet such rocks have destroyed a hundred thousand people, though I can't recall them all. At first it seemed that Thou hadst great charity towards mankind; how is it then that Thou allowest destruction of men through such things, things which do no good, but always injury? I know very well that the clerics will say whatever they wish, with arguments that all is for the best, though I can't understand the logic. But I pray the same God who made the wind blow to protect my husband: that is my conclusion. I leave all debate to the clerics. But would God all these black rocks were sunk into hell, for his sake! These rocks kill my heart with fright."

This is how she would speak, with many a pitiful tear. Her friends saw that it was no pleasure to roam by the sea—

rather, discomfort—and they planned to entertain her some-where else. They took her to rivers and springs and to other pleasant spots; they danced and played chess and back-gammon.

One day, early in the morning, they went into a nearby garden, where they had made preparation of food and drink, to spend the day at play; this was on the morning of the sixth of May. The gentle May rains had painted this garden full of leaves and flowers, and it had been so intricately decorated by the skill of man's hand that it was a veritable paradise—the finest garden anywhere. The scent of the flowers and the fine view would have made any heart light that was ever born, unless it were distressed by too great sickness and sor-row, the garden was so full of delight and beauty. After din-ner they began to dance and sing, everyone except Dorigen, who constantly mourned and lamented because she could not see her husband and lover dancing. Nevertheless, it was necessary for her to remain there a while and with a cheerful appearance to put aside her sorrow.

In the dance, among other men, there was a squire who danced in front of Dorigen and who was gayer and more finely dressed, in my judgment, than is the month of May. He sang and danced better than anyone since the world be-gan. Besides, he was, if one is to describe him, one of the handsomest men alive, and young, strong, capable, rich, wise, well liked, and respected. And briefly, if I tell the truth, this lusty squire, servant of Venus, who was named Aurelius, had loved Dorigen better than anyone else, though, as his luck would have it, without her knowing it, for more than two years. He had never dared to tell her about his woe, but had suffered in silence. He had despaired; he had not dared to say anything, except that in his songs he sometimes had hinted at his sorrow in a general lament. He had said that he loved but was not loved in return. Of such material he had made many songs of various sorts—lays, complaints, rondels, ballads—tell-ing how he did not dare mention his sorrow, but languished as a Fury does in hell, and how he must die as Echo did for Narcissus, not daring to tell her woe. In other ways than this that I am telling you about he had been afraid to indicate his trouble to her; except that occasionally at dances, where young folk greet each other, he had perhaps gazed into her eyes as a man who asks for kindness. But she knew nothing of his intention. Nevertheless, it happened before they left the garden that they got to talking, because he was her neighbor and a man of principle and honor whom she had known for a long time. Then, little by little, Aurelius approached his chief concern, and, when he saw his chance, he said:

"Madam, by God who made this world, if I thought it would have made you happy, I wish that I had gone overseas, never to return, on the same day that Arveragus left. For I know very well that my devotion to you is in vain; my only reward will be a broken heart. Madam, take pity on my heartsickness, for you can slay or save me with a word. Would God I were buried here at your feet! I have not the time now to say more. Take pity, sweet one, or you will cause me to die!"

She looked at Aurelius. "Is this your desire?" she said. "Is this true? Never before did I know what you felt. But, Aurelius, now that I know your intention, by the same God who gave me soul and breath, I will never be an unfaithful wife in word or deed as long as I have my senses. I will always belong to the man to whom I am married. Take this as my final answer."

But then she said playfully: "Aurelius, by God above, I would like to agree to be your love, because I see you complain so piteously. Look, on the day that you remove all the rocks from along the coast of Brittany, stone by stone, so that they no longer hinder the passage of ships and boats—I say, when you have made the coast so clear of rocks that there is no stone to be seen—then I will love you best of all men; you have here my promise, as far as is in my power."

"Is there no more kindness than this in you?" he asked.

"No, by the Lord that made me!" she said. "For I know very well that it shall never happen. Put such foolishness out of your mind. What estimation of himself can a man have who loves another man's wife, knowing that she gives herself to her husband whenever he wishes?"

Aurelius sighed deeply; he was sad when he heard this, and with a sorrowful heart he answered, "Madam, this is impossible! May I die a sudden, horrible death." And with those words he at once turned away.

Then many of her other friends came to her, and they wandered up and down the paths, knowing nothing of what had happened. New revelry was soon started, which lasted until the shining sun began to fade, for the horizon had taken away its light—that is to say, night fell. They all went home in joy and comfort except one—wretched Aurelius, alas! He went home with a sorrowful heart; he saw that he could not avoid death, and he thought he felt his heart turn cold. He raised his hands to heaven and fell down upon his bare knees. In his ravings he said his prayers, for he actually went out of his mind with grief. He did not know what he said, but with piteous heart he began to plead to the gods, first of all to the sun.

"Apollo," he said, "god and governor of every plant, herb, tree, and flower, who gives to each its time and season as your dwelling changes from low to high, according to latitude —lord Phoebus, cast your merciful eye on wretched Aurelius, who is as good as lost. For, lord, my lady has sworn my death, though I am guiltless; out of your kindness, take pity on my dying heart. I know well, lord Phoebus, that, if you desire, you can help me more than anyone except my lady. Now give me leave to describe in what way I can be helped.

"Your blessed sister, Lucina the shining, is chief goddess and queen of the sea (although Neptune is god of the sea, she is empress over him). You know very well, lord, that, just as it is her wish to be kindled and lighted by your fire, because of which she faithfully follows you, in the same way the sea naturally desires to follow her, for she is goddess both of the sea and the rivers, great and small. Therefore, lord Phoebus, here is my request—do this miracle, or my heart will burst—that at the next high tide, she being in opposition when you are in Leo, you will beg her to bring so great a flood that at least five fathoms will overflow the highest rock in Armorican Brittany; and let this flood last for two years. Surely, then I can say to my lady: 'Keep your promise; the rocks are gone.'

"Lord Phoebus, perform this miracle for me. Beg Lucina to go no faster in her course than you; I say again, ask your sister not to travel faster than you during these two years. Then she will always be at the full, and the spring flood will last both night and day. Ask her, unless she agrees to give me my dear lady in this manner, to sink every rock down into her own dark, underground region where Pluto lives, or I shall never win my lady. Barefoot, I will visit your temple in Delphi. Lord Phoebus, see the tears on my cheek and have compassion on my pain."

With these words Aurelius fell down in a swoon and lay in a trance for a long time. His brother, who knew of his troubles, picked him up and carried him to bed. I shall let this woeful man lie in despair and torment; let him choose, for all of me, whether he will live or die.

Arveragus had come home, along with other worthy men, in good health and with great honor, the flower of chivalry. Oh, now, Dorigen, you are happy! You have your lusty husband in your arms—the young knight, the brave warrior, who loves you as the life of his heart. He had no wish to be suspicious of any man having spoken to her of love while he was away. He had no doubt of that, and gave no thought to such matters. He danced, jousted, and made merry with her. Let them live in this joy and bliss; I shall speak of sick Aurelius.

For more than two years wretched Aurelius lay in sickness and furious torment, before he could set foot on the ground. During this period he had no comforter except his brother, who was a cleric. This brother knew well all the history of the trouble; Aurelius had certainly not dared to say a word to any other person. He kept the secret more closely than did Pamphilus his love for Galatea. Outwardly, he seemed unhurt, but the sharp arrow of his grief remained within his heart, and you know very well that, in surgery, curing a wound which heals only on the outside is risky unless the arrow can be reached and withdrawn. The brother wept and wailed in secret, until at last he recalled the time when he had been a student at Orleans in France, where the young clerics, greedy to read of curious arts, sought in every nook and cranny to learn particular sciences. He remembered that one day, while studying at Orleans, he had seen a book on natural magic which a friend, who was then a bachelor of law, had covertly left upon his desk, although he was there to study other matters. This book dealt extensively with the operations concerning the twenty-eight mansions of the moon, and with other such foolishness which, nowadays, is not worth a fly—for the faith of Holy Church, which is in our Creed, does not permit such illusions to trouble us. When he remembered this book, his heart at once began to dance with joy, and he said to himself:

"My brother shall be cured rapidly, for I am sure there are methods whereby men create illusions such as these tricky magicians bring about. Often at banquets I have heard it said that magicians have made both water and a boat come into a large hall, with the boat rowing up and down the room. Sometimes a terrible lion has seemed to appear; sometimes flowers grow as in a meadow; sometimes a vine with red and white grapes; sometimes a limestone castle. And, yet, everything disappears as soon as the magician desires; so it seemed to everyone present.

"Now, I believe that if I could find some old colleague at Orleans who had fresh in his mind the mansions of the moon, or natural magic of an even higher order, that man could cause my brother to win his lady. For a cleric can produce an illusion whereby it will seem to men's eyes that all the black rocks of Brittany have disappeared, and that ships come and go right up to the shore. Such an illusion can continue a week or two. Then my brother would be cured of his woe; she would have to keep her promise, or else he could at least shame her."

Why should I make a longer tale of this? The cleric came to his brother's bed and gave him such encouragement to start for Orleans that Aurelius jumped up at once and went on his way with his brother, hoping to be cured of his trouble. When they approached within a quarter-mile of that city, they met a young cleric traveling alone who greeted them pleasantly in Latin and then said a remarkable thing: "I know," he said, "the cause of your coming." And before they went a foot farther, he told them their whole purpose. Aurelius' brother asked this Breton cleric about friends he had known in the old days. The cleric answered that they were all dead, at which news Aurelius' brother wept bitterly.

Aurelius dismounted at once and went home with this magician, who was extremely hospitable. There was all the food that anyone could desire. Aurelius had never before seen such a well-appointed house in his life. Before supper the cleric showed him forests, parks full of wild deer, and bucks with tall horns, the largest imaginable. He saw a hundred of these bucks killed by hounds, some bleeding from deep arrow wounds. After the wild deer had disappeared, he saw falconers upon a fair river, killing a heron with their hawks. Then he saw knights jousting on a plain; and after this the cleric, to make him happy, showed him Dorigen, who seemed to be dancing with him. And when this master magician, who had caused these visions, saw that it was the proper time, he clapped his two hands, and farewell—the dance was completely gone! Yet they had not moved from the house. They had seen all these marvelous sights, sitting still, in the cleric's study, where his books were, and no one was there but the three of them.

The magician called his squire to him and said, "Is our supper ready? It's almost an hour, I am sure, since I told you to prepare our supper, and these worthy men came with me into my study where my books are."

"Sir," said the squire, "everything is ready, whenever it pleases you, even if you want to eat it right now."

"It is best, then, that we eat now," said the magician. "All people in love must have their sleep sometime."

After supper they began to discuss what the magician's fee should be for removing all the rocks of Brittany, and also those from the Gironde to the mouth of the Seine. He made difficulties, and swore, so help him God, that he would not take less than a thousand pounds, and he would not do it willingly even for that figure.

Aurelius, with a happy heart, at once answered: "To the devil with a thousand pounds! I would give this whole world, which men say is round, if I were lord of it. This bargain is driven; we are agreed. You shall be fully paid, I promise you. But look now, don't keep us here, because of negligence or laziness, any longer than tomorrow."

"No," said the cleric, "you have my word on that."

Aurelius went to bed soon after this and slept well almost all night. Because of this work and his hope of happiness, his sad heart had respite from sorrow. At daybreak the next day, Aurelius and the magician took the shortest road to Brittany, and on a cold, frosty day in December, as the old books state, they arrived at their destination.

As time passed, Phoebus, who had shone in Cancer with bright rays like burnished gold, turned coppery; and now he descended into Capricorn, where his rays grew very pale. The bitter frosts, with sleet and rain, have destroyed the growing things in every garden. Janus sits by the fire, with a double beard, drinking wine from his oxhorn. Boar's meat stands before him, and every sturdy man shouts, "Merry Christmas!"

Aurelius did all he could to make the magician happy and comfortable, and begged him to work diligently toward putting an end to his troubles, or else he would slit his own throat with a sword. The skillful cleric took such pity on the poor sufferer that he worked night and day, doing all that was possible to arrive quickly at the results of his astrological computations; that is to say, to bring about an illusion by some juggling appearance—I do not know the terms of astrology—so that Dorigen and everyone would think and say that the rocks had either gone away from Brittany or else that they had sunk underground. At last he arrived at the proper time to work his tricks and magic in that cursed superstitious manner. He brought out his astronomical tables from Toledo, carefully corrected. He lacked nothing—neither his tables for short periods of years nor those for longer periods; nor his roots or other mathematical gear, such as his centers, his quantities, and his tables of proportions for all sorts of equations. And in his computations, he knew very well how far the star Alnath was pushed into the eighth sphere from the true equinoctial point, the fixed Aries, which is considered to be in the ninth sphere. He calculated all these things very expertly. When he had found his first mansion of the moon, he knew the rest by proportion. And he understood the rising of the moon very well: in which planet's face and term, and everything else. He was quite sure that the moon's mansion was favorable for his operation, and he knew all the other details to be observed in order to produce such illusions and evil tricks as the heathen people practiced in those days. Therefore, he waited no longer, but, as a result of his magic, it seemed for a week or two that all the rocks had disappeared.

Aurelius, who was still in despair as to whether or not he would have his lady, waited night and day for the miracle. When he saw that there was no doubt that every one of the rocks was actually gone, he immediately fell at the cleric's feet and said: "I, the woeful wretch, Aurelius, thank you, lord, and my lady Venus, who helped me in my bitter trouble." And he went straight to the temple, where he knew he would find his lady. When he saw his chance, with fearful heart and humble manner he greeted his dear sovereign lady.

"My own lady," he said, "whom I most fear and love as best I know how and least wish to displease of all the world, if it were not that I have such a longing for you that I may soon die right here at your feet, I would not tell you how I suffer. But certainly, I must either tell you or die. Though guiltless, I am dying with longing for you. Even if you have no pity for my death, think carefully before you break your promise. Repent, by that God on high, before you kill me because I love you. For, madam, you well know what you promised—not that I wish to demand anything of you; only your charity—but there in the garden, on that very spot, you remember what you promised me. Upon my hand you gave your promise to love me best—God knows you said so, though I am most unworthy. Madam, I say this more for the sake of your honor than to keep my heart from breaking now. I have done as you commanded me; if you care to do so, you may go look. Do as you like; bear your promise in mind, for on that spot you shall find me, dead or alive. You have the power to make me live or die—but I know very well that the rocks are gone."

He left, and she stood there dazed, with not a drop of blood left in her face. She had never expected to be trapped in this way. "Alas," she said, "that this tragedy has happened! For I never thought that there was any chance that such a freak or miracle would come to pass. It is against the laws of nature."

Then she went home, a sorrowful creature, hardly able to walk for fear. She wept, wailed, and fainted for a day or two —it was pitiful to see. But she told no one the reason, for Arveragus was out of town. She spoke only to herself, with pale face and sorrowful manner, lamenting as you shall hear.

"Alas," she said, "I complain to you, Fortune; you have caught me unawares in your chain. I see no escape or help except death or dishonor. I must choose between the two. But of the two, I had rather lose my life than to have the shame of giving my body to Aurelius, and thus to know myself unfaithful and without a good reputation; at least by death I can escape. Haven't many admirable wives and maidens before me killed themselves, alas, rather than be guilty of bodily sin?

"Yes, indeed; see, there are stories which bear witness to it: when Phidon was killed by the thirty cursed tyrants at a banquet in Athens, they, out of spite, had his daughters arrested and led before them completely naked, to satisfy their lusts. And they made these daughters dance in their father's blood upon the pavement—God send them bad luck! Because of this, these woeful maidens, full of fear, rather than lose their virginity, secretly leaped into a well and drowned themselves, as the books recount.

"The Messenians sent for fifty maidens from Lacedaemonia upon whom to satisfy their lusts. But there was not one of that fifty who was not killed, choosing with good intent to die rather than to agree to have her virginity violated. Then why should I be in fear of death? Look, also: the tyrant Aristoclides loved a maiden named Stymphalis. When her father was killed one night, she went immediately into the temple of Diana, clasped the image of Diana in her two hands, and would not let it go. No one could pull her hands away until she was killed right there in the temple.

"Now, since these maidens had such hatred of being dishonored by men's foul lusts, surely a wife should prefer suicide to dishonor, it seems to me. What shall I say about Hasdrubal's wife, who killed herself at Carthage? For when she saw the Romans conquer the town, she jumped into the fire with all her children, preferring to die rather than to suffer disgrace from any Roman soldier. Didn't Lucrece kill herself at Rome, alas! When she was raped by Tarquin, it seemed to her shameful to live after she had lost her reputation. The seven maidens of Miletus also killed themselves, out of pure fear and sorrow, rather than have the Gauls ravish them. I could tell more than a thousand stories, I suppose, concerning this subject. When Abradates was slain, his beloved wife killed herself and let her blood run into her husband's deep, wide wounds saying, 'My body, at the least, no man shall defile, if I can avoid it.'

"Why should I recite more examples here, since so many women have killed themselves rather than be dishonored? I shall conclude that it is better for me to kill myself than to be defiled in this way. I will be true to Arveragus, or kill myself in some way, as Demotion's dear daughter did to avoid dishonor. Oh, Scedasus, it is indeed a pity to read how your daughters died, alas, who killed themselves for just such a reason. It was as great a pity, or indeed greater, that the Theban maiden killed herself to escape Nicanor because of the same trouble. Another Theban maiden died in the same fashion because of a Macedonian who violated her; she redeemed the loss of her virginity by death. What shall I say about the wife of Nicerates, who committed suicide in the same situation? How true, also, was Alcibiades' sweetheart, who chose to die rather than to allow his body to lie unburied. Remember what sort of wife Alcestis was, and read what Homer says of the good Penelope. All Greece knew about her chastity. By my faith, it is written about Laodamia that when Protesilaus was killed at Troy she would not live a day longer. I can say the same about noble Portia; she could not live without Brutus, to whom she had given her whole heart. The perfect wifehood of Artemisia is honored all through heathendom. Oh, Queen Teuta! your wifely chastity will serve as a model for all wives. I say the same thing about Bilia, about Rhodogone, and about Valeria."

Dorigen reasoned this way for a day or two, steadily determined that she would die. Nevertheless, Arveragus, the worthy knight, came home on the third evening and asked why she wept so sorely, at which she began to weep harder than ever. "Alas," she said, "that I was ever born! I have said such-and-such, and I have promised such-and-such"—and she told him everything, just as you have heard it; there is no need for me to repeat it. This husband, with a cheerful manner and in a friendly fashion, answered as I shall tell you: "Is there anything else, Dorigen, except this?"

"No, no," she said. "God help me, certainly not! This is already too much, even if it is God's will."

"Well, wife," he said, "what's done is done. Perhaps things may turn out well yet. You shall keep your promise, by my faith! So surely may kind God have mercy on me, I had rather be stabbed because of my very love for you than see you fail to keep a promise. A promise is the highest thing that one can hold to"—but with that word he burst into tears and said, "I forbid you, upon pain of death, ever to tell anyone about this adventure, as long as you live or breathe—I will endure my sorrow as best I can—and I forbid you to look so melancholy that people shall suspect or guess ill of you."

At once he called a squire and a maid. "Go out immediately with Dorigen," he said, "and conduct her to such-and-such a place." They left and proceeded on their way, but they did not know why she went there. He would not tell his intention to anyone.

Perhaps many of you would think Arveragus a stupid man, certainly, to put his wife in jeopardy in this way. Listen to the rest of the tale before you exclaim over her; she may have better fortune than you suspect. And when you have heard the whole tale, judge it.

The squire, Aurelius, who was so much in love with Dorigen, happened by chance to meet her in the center of town, right in the busiest street, as she hurried on her way to the garden, in accordance with her promise. He was going to the garden also, for he had watched closely to see when she would leave her house to go anywhere. But now they met, by chance or by luck, and he saluted her eagerly and asked where she was going. She answered, half-crazily, "To the garden, as my husband instructed, to keep my promise, alas!"

Aurelius began to wonder about this situation. In his heart he felt great pity for her and her troubles, and also for Arveragus, the worthy knight, who had instructed her to hold to all that she had promised, so unwilling was he to see his wife break faith. Because Aurelius felt such great pity in his heart, he began to consider all sides of the question. He decided that he would rather have his desire for Dorigen remain unsatisfied than to carry out so very churlish a deed, against all generosity and courtesy. Therefore, in a few words, he said:

"Madam, tell your lord Arveragus that because I see his courtesy to you is so great that he would rather endure shame (and that would be a pity) than have you break your promise to me—and also because I observe your great distress—I prefer to suffer eternal sorrow rather than come between you two. I therefore release you, madam, and return into your hands every promise and every pledge which you made me since the time that you were born. I swear that I will never reproach you for any promise, and now I take my leave of the truest and best woman I have ever known in all my life.

Let every wife be careful of her promises! Remember Dorigen, at least. Thus can a squire, it is certain, do a courteous deed as well as a knight."

Upon her bare knees she thanked him, and then went home to her husband. She told him everything, as you have heard me tell it; and you can be sure that he was so overjoyed that it is impossible for me to write about it. Why should I speak any longer about this matter? Arveragus and his wife, Dorigen, led their lives in perfect happiness. There was never again any difficulty between them. He cherished her as though she were a queen, and she was always faithful to him. You shall get no more from me about these two people.

Aurelius, who had forfeited all his expenses, cursed the time that he was born. "Alas," he said, "why did I promise a thousand pounds of pure gold to this philosopher? What shall I do? I can only see that I am doomed. I shall have to sell my inheritance and become a beggar. I cannot live here any longer and shame all my relatives in this district, unless the philosopher lets me off more lightly. But, nevertheless, I shall try to pay him in installments, year by year, and thank him for his great kindness. I will keep my promise; I will not lie."

With a sad heart he took from his safe about five hundred pounds of gold, which he gave to the philosopher, begging him in the name of courtesy to agree to payment of the remainder in installments. He said: "Master, I can boast that I never yet broke my word. Truly, my debt to you shall be paid, even if I have to go begging in a ragged coat. If you will agree to give me two or three years' delay, with security, all will go well with me; otherwise, I will have to sell my inheritance; there is no more to say."

The philosopher gravely answered, after hearing Aurelius' words, "Have I not kept faith with you?"

"Certainly you have, to the letter," said Aurelius.

"Have you not had your lady as you wished?" asked the philosopher.

"No, no," said Aurelius, and he sighed sadly.

"Why was that? Tell me if you can," said the philosopher.

Aurelius at once told him everything, as you have heard

before; there is no need to repeat it. He said, "Arveragus, because of courtesy, would rather have died of sorrow and distress than see his wife break her promise." He recounted also the grief of Dorigen: how unwilling she was to be an unfaithful wife, how she would rather have killed herself, and how she had made her promise innocently, in that she had never before heard of such magic. "That made me feel such pity for her that I sent her back to her husband as freely as he had sent her to me. That is all; there is no more to tell."

The philosopher answered, "Dear friend, each of you dealt courteously with the other. You are a squire and he is a knight, but may all-powerful blessed God forbid that a cleric may not do as courteous a deed as any of you! Sir, I release you from your debt of a thousand pounds; now it is as if you had just come out of the ground and had never known me before. For I will not take a penny from you, sir, for all my skill and my labor. You have paid well for my living expenses. That is enough: farewell; good-by!" And he mounted his horse and went on his way.

Ladies and gentlemen, there is one question I would like to ask now: which one of these people seems to you the most generous? Tell me before you go any farther. I know nothing more; my tale is at an end. HERE ENDS THE FRANKLIN'S TALE.

HERE FOLLOWS THE PHYSICIAN'S TALE: Once there was a knight, as Livy tells us, named Virginius, very honorable and worthy, with many friends, and very wealthy. This knight and his wife had one daughter, but no other children, during their lives. This girl surpassed all others in exceptional beauty, for Nature, with sovereign care, had endowed her with supreme excellence, as if to say: "See, I, Nature, can create and adorn a creature thus when I so desire. Who can counterfeit my work? Not Pygmalion, even if he forged and beat, or engraved, or painted forever. And I dare say that Appelles and Zeuxis would also work in vain at their engraving, painting, forging, or beating, if they presumed to counterfeit my work. For He who is the Chief Creator has made me his Vicar General, to form and paint earthly creatures just as I wish, and everything under the waxing and waning moon is in my care. And in my own work I do not need to ask anyone's advice; my Lord and I are in complete agreement. I created this girl out of worship for my Lord, just as I do with all my other creatures, whatever their complexions or figures." It seems to me that Nature would speak in this fashion.

This girl in whom Nature took such delight was fourteen

years old. Just as Nature can paint a lily white or a rose red, so she had painted the lovely body of this noble girl before birth, wherever such colors were appropriate, while Phoebus had dyed her long hair so that it resembled his burnished sunbeams. And if her beauty was extraordinary, a thousand times more so was her virtue. In her there was lacking no quality which deserves praise for discretion. She was chaste in spirit as well as in body, and she grew into a virgin, humble, abstinent, temperate, patient, and moderate both in manner and dress. She was always discreet in answering; though I'll venture that she was as wise as Pallas, and her eloquence was always womanly and plain, she used no counterfeit terms to appear wise, but spoke in accordance with her station, and all her words, great and small, were proper and courteous. She was modest with a maiden's modesty, constant in affection, and always industrious to avoid idleness. Bacchus had no power at all over her mouth; wine given to the young increases Venus' influence, just as when people feed a fire with oil or grease. Because of her natural purity, she frequently pretended to be ill in order to avoid company where there was likely to be talk of folly, as is the case at feasts, revels, and dances, which are the occasions for wantonness. Such things make children become ripe and bold too early, as anyone can see—a thing that has always been very dangerous. For a girl learns about boldness all too soon, when she becomes a woman.

You governesses, who in your old age have supervision over the daughters of lords, do not take offense at my words. Remember, you are placed in charge of the daughters of lords for one of only two reasons: either because you have retained your virtue, or else because you have fallen into such frailty that you are very familiar with the old dance and have decided to give up such misconduct forever. Therefore, for the sake of Christ, be sure that you are not lax in teaching virtue to your charges. A man who has stolen venison, but has given up all his evil ways and his old trade, can guard a forest better than any other man. Now guard your charges well, for you can do it if you want to. See that you do not countenance any kind of vice, or you will be damned for your wicked intentions; for whoever does so is surely a traitor. And take heed of what I say: of all betrayals the most evil occurs when a man betrays an innocent.

You fathers and you mothers, also; whether you have one child or more, their supervision is your full responsibility while they are under your control. Beware that they do not perish because of the poor example you set them or because of your negligence in scolding them; for I dare say that if they die you shall pay dearly for it. Under a soft and negligent shepherd, many a sheep and lamb have been devoured by the wolf. Let this one example suffice for the present, for I must turn again to my story.

This girl, who is the subject of this tale, so conducted herself that she needed no governess; for she was so prudent and generous that in her manner of living all girls could read, as in a book, every good word or deed which befits a virtuous maiden. As a result, the fame of both her beauty and her excellence spread far and wide. Everyone who admired virtue in that land, except Envy, who regrets anyone else's prosperity and rejoices in his woes and misfortunes (so St. Augustine describes it), sang her praises.

One day this girl went to a temple in the town with her dear mother, as is the custom for young girls. Now there was then a judge in this town who was governor of that region. And it so happened that this judge cast his eyes upon the girl, appraising her rapidly as she passed by where he stood. At once his heart and his feelings changed, he was so taken by her beauty, and he said quietly to himself, "This girl must be mine, in spite of any man!"

At once the devil ran into his heart and taught him quickly that he could win the girl to his purpose by trickery. For, truly, it seemed to the judge that he would be unable to accomplish his purpose either by force or bribery, for she had many powerful friends, and also she was confirmed in such steadfast righteousness that he knew he could never persuade her to bodily sin. Therefore, after great deliberation, he sent for a fellow in town whom he knew to be cunning and bold.

The judge told his tale to this fellow secretly, and made him swear to tell no one, under the penalty of losing his head. When the wicked plan was agreed to, the judge was happy and treated the fellow generously, giving him many precious and expensive gifts.

When the conspiracy had been planned point by point, to the end that the judge's lust should be subtly satisfied, as you shall soon hear fully, the fellow, who was named Claudius, went home. The false judge, whose name was Appius (that was his name, for this is no fable; rather, it is widely known as a recognized historical fact; the moral of it is true beyond doubt)—this false judge bestirred himself to hasten his pleasure as much as possible. So, it happened one day soon afterwards, so the story says, that this false judge was sitting in his court, as was his custom, giving his decision on various cases.

The wicked fellow came rushing in and said: "Lord, if it be your will, give me justice in this pitiful complaint which I make against Virginius; and if he says it is not so, I will prove by reliable witnesses that what my bill of complaint sets forth is true."

"In the absence of Virginius," the judge answered, "I cannot give a definite decision on this matter. Have him called, and I shall gladly hear the case. You shall have only justice here; no partiality."

Virginius came to learn why the judge wanted him, and the cursed complaint was immediately read. Its contents were as you shall hear: "To you, my dear lord Appius, your poor servant Claudius wishes to show how a knight named Virginius, against the law, against all equity, and directly against my wishes, holds my servant, who is my rightful slave, and who was stolen from my house one night when she was very young. I will prove this by witnesses, lord, so that you will have no doubts. She is not his daughter, no matter what he says. Therefore, I pray you, my lord judge, give back my servant to me, if that is your will." See, this was the complete text of the complaint.

Virginius began to stare at the fellow before he had even

finished his complaint. He would have contested the case as a knight should, showing by many witnesses that everything claimed by his opponent was false, but the accursed judge would not wait at all, or hear a single word from Virginius. He immediately handed down his decision, saying, "I now decree that this fellow shall have his servant; you shall no longer keep her in your house. Go bring her here and put her into our keeping. This fellow shall have his servant; that is my judgment."

When the worthy knight, Virginius, had been ordered by the decision of the judge, Appius, to give up his dear daughter to the judge to live in lechery, he went home, sat down in his hall, and immediately sent for his beloved daughter. Then, with a face as deathlike as cold ashes, he gazed upon her humble face. A father's pity struck through his heart, but he would not swerve from his purpose.

"Daughter," he said, "Virginia to call you by name, there are two ways that you may take; death or dishonor. Alas, that I was born! For never have you deserved to die by knife or sword. Oh, dear daughter, beloved of my life, in whose raising I have taken such pleasure that you were never out of my thoughts! Oh, daughter, who are my final joy in life, and my final woe; oh, gem of chastity, take your death in patience, for that is my decision. For love and not for hate, you must die; my poor hand must cut off your head. Alas, that ever Appius saw you! His false judgment today was because of that"—and he told her the whole story, as you heard it before; there is no need to repeat it.

"Oh, mercy, dear father!" the girl said, and with these words put both arms around his neck, as was her custom. The tears rushed from her eyes, and she said: "Good father, must I die? Is there no mercy? Is there no remedy?"

"No, verily, my dear daughter," he said.

"Then give me time, dear father," she said, "to lament my death a little while. For indeed, Jeptha gave his daughter time to lament before he killed her, alas! And, God knows, her sin was only that she was the first to run to meet her father and welcome him fittingly." With these words she immediately fainted. When she had recovered, she rose and said to her father: "God be thanked that I shall die a virgin! Kill me before I am dishonored. Do your will with your child, in God's name!"

After these words she begged many times that he would smite gently with his sword; then she fell down in a swoon. Her father, with a very sorrowful heart and spirit, cut off her head. He grasped it by the hair and took it to the judge, who still sat in judgment in the court. When the judge saw the head, so the story says, he commanded that Virginius be taken and hanged at once. But, immediately, a thousand people burst in to save the knight, out of pity, for the wicked treachery was known. Because of the manner of the fellow's complaint, the people had quickly suspected that Appius had conspired in this case, for they knew very well that he was lecherous. Therefore, they took him into custody and cast him into prison, where he killed himself. And Claudius, who was Appius' servant, was condemned to be hanged from a tree, but Virginius, out of pity, begged that he be exiled instead, for he had truly been misguided. The others who were involved in this wickedness, great and small, were hanged.

From this story, you can see how sin is repaid. Beware, for no one knows what man of any rank God will smite, or in what way the worm of conscience will show the terror of a wicked life, even though it is kept so secret that no one knows of it but him and God. For no matter whether he is an ignorant man or a learned man, he does not know how soon he shall be brought to fear. Therefore, I advise you to accept this counsel: forsake sin, before sin destroys you. HERE ENDS THE PHYSICIAN'S TALE.

THE PARDONER

THE WORDS OF THE HOST TO THE PHYSICIAN AND THE PAR-
DONER: Our Host started swearing as if he were crazy. "Help!
By Christ's nails and blood," he said, "that was a false fel-
low and a false judge. May such judges and their witnesses
find deaths as shameful as the heart can imagine! All the
same, this poor virgin was killed, alas! She paid too dearly for
her beauty! Therefore, I always say that you can see that gifts
of Fortune and of Nature are the cause of death for many a
creature. Her beauty was the death of her, I dare say. Alas,
she was slain so piteously! From both these gifts I spoke of
just now, people very often get more harm than profit.

"But truly, my own dear master, that was a sad tale to
hear—nevertheless, let it pass, it doesn't matter. I pray God to
save your noble body, and also your urinals and chamber-
pots, your syrups and medicines, and also every box full of
your remedies; God and our Lady St. Mary bless them! As I
hope to prosper, you are a proper man, and like a prelate, by
St. Ronyan! Didn't I say that well? I can't say the medical
terms, but I do know that your story has so pierced my heart
that I have almost caught a bad pain. By God's bones, unless
I have some medicine or a draught of moist and malty ale, or
else hear a merry story at once, my heart will break with pity
for this poor maiden. You fine friend, you Pardoner," said he,
"tell us some gay stories or jokes immediately."

"It shall be done," said the Pardoner, "by St. Ronyan! But

first," he said, "I must have a drink and eat a cake here at this alehouse."

But at once the gentlefolk objected. "No, don't let him tell us any ribaldry! Tell us some moral thing so that we can be instructed, and then we shall be glad to listen."

"I agree, certainly," said the Pardoner. "But I must think up some honest piece while I drink."

HERE FOLLOWS THE PROLOGUE OF THE PARDONER'S TALE: *Radix malorum est cupiditas.* "Ladies and gentlemen," he said, "when I preach in churches, I strive to have a haughty speech and ring out the words as round as a bell; for I know all that I say by heart. My text is always the same, and ever has been—Greed is the root of all evil.

"In the beginning I announce where I come from, and then I show my papal bulls, one and all. First I show our bishop's seal on my license to protect myself, so that no one, priest or cleric, will be so bold as to interrupt me as I do Christ's holy work. And after that I tell my tales. I show bulls of popes, cardinals, patriarchs, and bishops, and I speak a few words in Latin to flavor my preaching and to stir the congregation to devotion. Then I show my long glass cases, crammed full of rags and bones—they are relics, everybody thinks. Then I have a shoulder bone from a holy Jew's sheep set in metal. 'Good men,' I say, 'pay attention to my words: if this bone is dipped into any well, and if a cow, or calf, or sheep, or ox is swollen from eating a worm or from being stung by an insect, take some water from that well and wash his tongue; he will at once be cured. Furthermore, any sheep which takes a drink from that well will be cured of pox and scabs and of every other sore. Take heed of what I say: if the farmer who owns the livestock will take a drink from this well every week, after fasting, before the cock crows, just as this holy Jew taught our ancestors, his livestock and his goods will multiply. And, sirs, it also cures jealousy; for even if a man is in a jealous rage, let him make his soup with this water and he shall nevermore distrust his wife, though he knows it to be true that she has been so unfaithful as to have had two or three priests.

" 'Here is a mitten which you can also look at. The man who puts his hand into this mitten will see his grain multiply, after he has sown it, no matter whether it is oats or wheat, if he contributes pennies or else groats.

" 'Good men and women, I warn you about one thing: if there is any man now in this church who has done a horrible sin and who is afraid and ashamed to be shriven of it, or any woman old or young who has made her husband a cuckold—such folk shall have no power or grace to make an offering to my relics in this church. But if whoever finds himself free from such fault will come up and make an offering in the name of God, I shall absolve him by the authority which was granted to me by papal bull.'

"By this trick I have gained a hundred marks year after year since I became a pardoner. I stand in my pulpit like a cleric and, when the ignorant people have taken their seats, I preach as you have just heard and tell a hundred other false tales. Then I take pains to stretch my neck out and nod east and west over the congregation, like a dove sitting on a barn. My hands and tongue go so fast that it is a joy to see me at work. All my preaching is about avarice and similar sins, in order to make the people generous in contributing their pennies, especially to me. For my purpose is nothing but profit, and not at all the correction of sin. I don't care if their souls go wandering when they are buried! Certainly, many a sermon grows out of an evil purpose: sometimes to please and flatter folk, to get advancement by hypocrisy, and sometimes for vanity and sometimes for hatred. For when I am afraid to quarrel in other ways, then I sting a fellow so sharply with my tongue in preaching that he can't escape being falsely defamed, if he has been rude to my brethren or to me. Even though I don't call him by name, everyone knows by signs and other circumstances who it is I mean. Thus I get even

with folk who mistreat us; in this fashion I spit out my venom
in the guise of holiness, to appear holy and true.

"But I shall explain my purpose briefly. I preach for nothing but avarice; therefore, my theme is now and always was:
Radix malorum est cupiditas. In this way I am able to preach
against the same vice which I practice: avarice. Yet, though I
am guilty of that sin myself, I can still make other folk turn
away from it and bitterly repent. But that's not my main purpose; I preach only for avarice. That ought to be enough
about this subject.

"Then I tell them many samples of old stories about ancient
times. For ignorant people love old stories; they can easily
remember and repeat such things. Why, do you think that I
would willingly live in poverty as long as I can preach and
win gold and silver by my teaching? No, no, I never really
considered that! For I will preach and beg in various countries, but I will do no labor with my hands, or live by making baskets to keep from being an idle beggar. I will not copy
any one of the apostles; I will have money, wool, cheese, and
wheat, even though it's given to me by the poorest page or
widow in a village, whose children will consequently starve.
No, I'll drink liquor from the vine and have a jolly wench in
every town. But listen, ladies and gentlemen, in conclusion:
your desire is that I tell a story. Now that I have drunk a
draught of malty ale, I hope, by God, that I can tell you
something which you will like reasonably well. For, though I
am a very vicious man myself, I can tell you a moral tale
which I am accustomed to preach when I am working. Now
hold your peace! I shall begin my tale."

HERE BEGINS THE PARDONER'S TALE: Once upon a time in Flanders there was a group of young people much given to dissipation, such as riotous living, gambling, and frequenting brothels and taverns, where they danced and played dice both night and day, to the music of harps, lutes, and guitars, and also ate and drank beyond their capacities. In this way they wickedly performed the devil's work within these devil's temples through abominable excesses. Their oaths were so great and so damnable that it was terrifying to hear them swear. They tore apart the body of our blessed Lord—it seemed to them that the Jews had not tortured him enough—and each of them laughed at the others' sins. And then small and shapely dancing girls would enter, and young girls selling fruit, singers with harps, bawds, and cake-sellers—all the confirmed agents of the devil —to kindle and blow the fire of lust that goes hand in hand with gluttony.

I take Holy Writ as my witness that licentiousness results from wine and drunkenness. Look how drunken Lot, against the laws of nature, slept with his two daughters without knowing it; he was so drunk that he did not know what he was doing. Herod, as anyone who reads the stories knows, when he was full of wine at his own feast, gave the order right at his own table for innocent John the Baptist to be slain. Seneca was without doubt correct when he said that he could see no difference between a man who is out of his mind and a man who is drunk, except that insanity, when it occurs in an ill-tempered man, lasts longer than drunkenness.

Oh, gluttony, filled with wickedness! Oh, first cause of our

290

ruin! Oh, origin of our damnation, until Christ redeemed us with His blood! To come to the point, see how dearly this cursed wickedness was paid for! All this world was corrupted by gluttony. Our father Adam and also his wife were driven from Paradise to labor and suffer because of that sin. There is no doubt about that, for as long as Adam fasted he was in Paradise, so I read, but when he ate of the forbidden fruit on the tree, he was at once cast out into trouble and pain. Oh, gluttony, well should we complain of you! Oh, if a man only knew how many illnesses follow excess and gluttony, he would be more moderate in his diet at the table. Alas, the short throat and the tender mouth; they cause men—east, west, south, and north—to labor hard in earth, air, and water to provide a glutton with his rare food and drink! Oh, Paul, you treated this subject well: "Meat for the belly and the belly for meat; God shall destroy both." So says Paul. Alas, it is an ugly thing, by my faith, to say these words, but uglier is the deed, when a man so drinks of the white and red wines that he makes a privy of his throat through such wicked excess.

The Apostle, weeping, says movingly: "There are many of those people about whom I told you—I say it now weeping, with a piteous voice: they are enemies of the cross of Christ; their end is death; the belly is their God!" Oh, stomach! Oh, belly! Oh, stinking gut. filled with dung and corruption! From either end of you, foul noises come forth. How great is the labor and cost to feed you! How these cooks stamp and strain and grind to turn substance into accident in order to satisfy your gluttonous appetite! They knock the marrow out of the hard bones, for they throw away nothing which will slide softly and sweetly down the gullet. The glutton's sauce is made tasty by spices of leaves, bark, and roots, to give him still a keener appetite. But, truly, the man who makes a habit of such delicacies is dead even while he lives in those vices.

Wine is a lecherous thing, and drunkenness is full of strife and wretchedness. Oh, drunken man, your face is distorted, your breath is sour, you are a foul thing to embrace, and a sound seems to come from your drunken nose as if you kept repeating "Samson, Samson!" And yet, God knows, Samson never drank wine. You fall down like a stuck pig; your tongue is lost, and all your self-respect. For drunkenness is the true tomb of a man's wit and discretion. That man who is dominated by drink cannot keep a secret; that is sure. Therefore, hold yourself aloof from the white and the red, and especially from the white wine of Lepe, which is sold in Fish Street or in Cheapside. This Spanish wine is secretly blended with other wines in stock, and from it rise fumes so powerful that a man who takes three drinks, though he believes himself at home in Cheapside, finds he is in Spain at the town of Lepe—not at La Rochelle or Bordeaux. And then he will say, "Samson, Samson!"

But listen to one word, ladies and gentlemen, I beg you. All the great deeds and victories in the Old Testament, I swear, were accomplished through the true and omnipotent God by abstinence and prayer. Read the Bible, and you will learn this. Look at Attila, the great conqueror; he died shamefully and dishonorably in his sleep, bleeding steadily from the nose because of drunkenness. A military leader should live soberly. And more important still, consider very carefully what God commanded Lemuel—I mean Lemuel, not Samuel; read the Bible and see what is expressly stated about giving wine to those charged with the dispensation of justice. No more of this matter, for that much should suffice.

Now that I have spoken of gluttony, I shall next forbid your gambling. Gambling is the true mother of lies, deceit, cursed perjury, blasphemy of Christ, and manslaughter, and also a waste of time and money. Furthermore, it is a reproof and a dishonor to be considered a common gambler. And, always, the higher the rank of the gambler, the more despicable is he considered. If a prince gambles, his governing and policy are held in low repute by general opinion. Stilbon, who was a wise ambassador, was sent from Sparta to Corinth, in great pomp, to make an alliance. And when he arrived, it happened by chance that he found all the highest officials of that land gambling. Therefore, as soon as possible, he stole home to his country, and said, "I will not lose my reputation there and so lay myself open to defamation as to ally you with gamblers. Send other wise ambassadors, for I swear that I had rather die than make an alliance for you with gamblers. For you who are so glorious in honor shall not be allied with gamblers by my efforts or treaties." So said this wise philosopher.

Observe also that the King of Parthia, as the book tells us, scornfully sent a pair of golden dice to King Demetrius because he was so accustomed to gamble; his glory or renown was utterly without value for him. Lords can find other kinds of games honest enough to pass the time.

I shall now speak a word or two in the manner of the old books about great and small oaths. Violent swearing is an abominable thing, and false swearing is even more to be reproved. The high God forbade all swearing—witness Matthew; but holy Jeremiah says this particularly about swearing: "You shall swear true oaths and not lie; swear discreetly and also righteously." But idle swearing is a sin. Observe that in the first table of the high God's illustrious commandments, the second of His commandments is: "Take not my name amiss or in vain." You see, He forbade such swearing ahead of homicide or many other cursed sins; I say it stands in that order. Be sure of this fact if you understand His commandments; that is the second commandment. Later I shall show you clearly that vengeance shall not leave the house of the man who is too outrageous in his swearing. "By God's precious heart," and "by His nails," and "by the blood of Christ that is at Hailes, seven is my number and yours is five and three!" "By God's arms, if you cheat, I will run this dagger through your heart!"—such is the fruit which comes from the two bitchy bones: swearing, anger, falsehood, homicide. Now, for the love of Christ who died for us, give up your oaths, both large and small. But now, sirs, I shall tell my tale.

These three rioters of whom I tell were seated in a tavern drinking, long before any bell rang for nine o'clock. And as they drank, they heard a bell toll before a corpse which was being carried to its grave. One of them called to his servant: "Boy, hurry and ask at once whose corpse it was that just passed by. And see that you get his name straight."

"Sir," replied the boy, "that's not at all necessary. I was told that two hours before you arrived. He was, by God, an old crony of yours, and last night he was suddenly killed as he sat straight up on his bench completely drunk. A stealthy thief, whom men call Death, who kills all the people in this country, came and cut his heart in two with a spear, and went away without a word. During this plague, he has slain a thousand. And, master, before you go into his presence, it seems to me that it will be necessary for you to be wary of such an opponent. Always be ready to meet him; my mother taught me that. I'll say no more."

"By St. Mary," said the tavern-keeper, "the boy speaks true, for this year Death has slain the men, women, children, laborers, and servants in a large village over a mile from here. I think he must live there. It would make great sense to be warned before he did you any harm."

"Yes, by God's arms!" said this rioter. "Is it so dangerous to meet him? I shall seek him out by roads and paths, I swear by God's worthy bones! Listen, friends, we three are of one mind; let's each of us give his hand to the other two, and each of us will become the other's brother. Then we shall slay this false traitor Death. He who has slain so many shall himself be slain, by God's worthiness, before night!"

These three pledged their faith together, each to live and die for the other two, as though they had been born brothers. And they jumped up in a drunken rage and went out towards the village which the tavern-keeper had told them about. And they swore many a horrible oath, completely tearing Christ's blessed body apart—Death shall be slain, if they can catch him!

When they had gone not quite half a mile, just as they were about to cross a fence, they met a poor old man. This old man greeted them very humbly and said, "Now, lords, God save you!"

The proudest of these three rioters replied, "Hey, bad luck to you, fellow! Why are you all covered up except for your face? Why have you lived so long and grown so old?"

The old man stared into his face and said: "Because I cannot find a man in any city or any village, though I walked to India, who wishes to change his youth for my age. And, therefore, I must continue to have my age for as long a time as it is God's will. Alas, not even Death will take my life. And so I walk about like a restless prisoner and knock both early and late with my stick upon the earth, which is my mother's door, saying, 'Dear mother, let me in; look how I shrink, flesh, skin, and blood! Alas, when shall my bones find rest? Mother, I will trade my strongbox, which for so long has been in my bedroom, for a hair shirt to wrap myself in!' Yet she will not do me that favor, and my face is therefore pale and wrinkled.

"But, sirs, it is discourteous of you to speak rudely to an old man, unless he does or says something wrong. You can read for yourselves in Holy Writ: 'You should rise before an old white-haired man.' Therefore, I shall give you some advice: do no harm now to an old man, any more than you would like people to do to you when you are old, if you live that long. And may God be with you, wherever you walk or ride! I must go where I have to go."

"No, old one, by God, you shall not go," the second gambler said at once. "You won't get off so lightly, by St. John! Just now you spoke of that same traitor Death, who kills all our friends in this country. Take my word, you are his spy; so tell where he is or you shall regret it, by God and by the holy sacrament! For, truly, you are in his plot to slay us young folk, you false thief!"

"Now, sirs," the old man answered, "if you are so eager to find Death, turn up this crooked path; for I left him in that wood, by my faith, under a tree. He will stay there; he won't conceal himself because of your boasting. You see that oak? You shall find him right there. May God, who redeemed mankind, save you and amend you!"

The old man spoke thus, and all the rioters ran until they reached the oak tree. And there they found what seemed to them almost eight bushels of fine round florins of coined gold. Then they looked for Death no longer. Each of them was so happy at the sight of the bright, shining florins that they sat down by this precious hoard. The worst of them spoke the first word.

"Brothers," he said, "listen to what I say. I have a great deal of sense, even though I joke and scoff. Fortune has given us this treasure so that we can live our lives in mirth and gaiety, and we shall spend it as easily as it came. Aye, God's precious worth! Who would have thought we should have such luck today? If we could only carry this gold from here home to my house or to yours—you realize, of course, that all this gold is ours—then we would have the highest happiness. Yet we really cannot do it by daylight. People would say that we were obviously highwaymen and would have us hanged because of our own treasure. This money must be transported by night, as carefully and quietly as possible. Therefore, I suggest that we draw straws among us and see where the cut falls. The one who draws the cut must willingly run into town as quickly as possible, and secretly bring bread and wine for us. Meanwhile, two of us will guard the treasure diligently, and, if he doesn't take too long, we shall be able at nightfall to carry the money wherever we agree is best."

He held the straws in his fist, and told the others to draw to see where the cut would fall. It fell to the youngest of the three, and he at once set out for town. But, as soon as he had left, one of the other two spoke to the second: "You know very well that you are my sworn brother; I shall now tell you something to your advantage. You see that our companion is gone, and this great heap of gold, which is to be divided among the three of us, is still here. But if I could so arrange matters that the gold would be divided between us two alone, would I not have done you a friendly turn?"

The second answered: "I don't see how that can be; he knows very well that the gold was left with the two of us. What shall we do? What shall we say to him?"

"Shall it be a secret?" asked the first scoundrel. "If so, I'll tell you in a few words what we can do to accomplish this."

"I agree not to betray you," said the second, "upon my word."

"Now," said the first, "you know that we are two, and the

two of us are stronger than one. When he returns and sits down, you get up at once as if to tussle with him, and I will run him through the sides while you scuffle with him as if in sport, and you be sure to stab him with your dagger also. Then, all this gold, my dear friend, can be divided between you and me. Both of us will be able to fulfill all our desires and to play dice whenever we like." Thus these two scoundrels agreed to murder the third, as you have heard me say.

The youngest, who went into town, kept turning over in his mind the beauty of the bright new florins. "Oh, Lord!" he said, "if it only were possible for me to have all this treasure for myself alone, no man living under God's throne would live so merrily as I!"

And at last the devil, our enemy, put into his mind the idea of buying poison with which he could kill his two companions. For the fiend found his way of life such that he wished to bring him into trouble. The fellow's clear purpose was to kill both the others and never to repent. He went on into town, without any more loitering, to the shop of an apothecary, whom he begged to sell him some poison to kill his rats; there was a polecat in his yard, also, he said, which had killed his capons, and he was eager to get revenge, if possible, upon vermin which harassed him at night.

The apothecary answered, "You shall have such a mixture, God save my soul, that no creature in all this world who eats or drinks of it, even the equivalent of a grain of wheat, shall fail to die at once. Yes, he shall die in less time than it takes you to walk a mile, this poison is so strong and violent."

This wicked man grabbed up the box of poison and ran quickly to a man in the next street from whom he borrowed three large bottles. He poured his poison into two; the third he kept clean for his own drink; for he planned to work hard all night transporting the gold from its place. When this rioter—bad luck to him!—had filled his three large bottles with wine, he returned to his companions.

What need is there to make a longer sermon of this? They quickly killed him just as they had already planned, and, when that was done, one said, "Now let's sit and drink and make merry. Afterwards we'll bury his body." It happened that with these words he took up a bottle in which there was poison, and drank, giving his friend a drink from the same bottle. As a result, both immediately died.

Truly, I doubt that Avicenna ever wrote a treatise or chapter in which there were more amazing symptoms of poisoning than these two wretches evidenced before they died. That was the end of these two murderers, as well as of the false poisoner.

Oh, cursed sin of all evil! Oh, treacherous murder, oh, wickedness! Oh, gluttony, luxury, and gambling! You blasphemer of Christ with vulgarity and large oaths, born of habit and pride! Alas, mankind, how can it be that you are so false and so unkind to your Creator, who made you and redeemed you with His precious heart's blood?

Now, good men, may God forgive you your trespasses and keep you from the sin of avarice! My holy pardon can cure you all, so long as you offer nobles, or silver pennies, or else silver brooches, spoons, or rings. Bow your head before this holy document! Come on up, you wives, offer some of your wool! I will at once enter your names here on my roll, and you shall go into the bliss of heaven. I absolve you by my great power—you who will offer—as clean and as white as you were born.—And there, ladies and gentlemen, that's the way I preach. And may Jesus Christ, who is our soul's physician, grant that you receive His pardon, for that is the best; I will not deceive you.

But, sirs, I forgot one word in my tale: I have relics and pardons in my bag, as fine as any man's in England, which were given to me by the Pope's own hand. If any of you wish, out of piety, to make an offering and to receive my absolution, come up at once, kneel down here, and humbly receive my pardon. Or else you can accept pardon as you travel, fresh and new at the end of every mile, just so you make another offering each time of nobles or pennies which are good and genuine. It is an honor to everyone here that you have available a pardoner with sufficient power to absolve you as you ride through the country, in case of accidents which might happen. Perhaps one or two of you will fall off your horses and break your necks. See what security it is to all of you that I happen to be in your group and can absolve you, both high and low, when the soul passes from the body. I suggest that our Host, here, shall be first; for he is most enveloped in sin. Come on, Sir Host, make the first offering right now, and you can kiss each one of the relics. Yes, for just a groat! Unbuckle your purse at once.

"No, no!" said the Host. "Then I would be under Christ's curse! Stop this, it won't do, as I hope to prosper! You would make me kiss your old breeches, and swear they were the relic of a saint, though they were foully stained by your bottom! But, by the cross that St. Helen found, I wish I had your testicles in my hand instead of relics or holy objects. Cut them off; I'll help you carry them. They shall be enshrined in hog's dung!"

The Pardoner answered not a word; he was so angry he would not say anything.

"Now," said our Host, "I will joke no longer with you or with any other angry man."

But at once the worthy Knight, when he saw everybody laughing, said, "No more of this; that's enough! Sir Pardoner, cheer up and be merry; and you, Sir Host, who are so dear to me, I beg you to kiss the Pardoner. And Pardoner, I pray you, come near. Let's laugh and play as we did before."

At once they kissed and rode ahead on their way. HERE ENDS THE PARDONER'S TALE.

THE SECOND NUN

THE PROLOGUE OF THE SECOND NUN'S TALE: We certainly should do everything within our power to avoid the minister and nurse of vices, which in English is called idleness, and which is the porter at the gate of voluptuousness, and to overcome her through her opposite, that is, lawful industry, lest the devil capture us through idleness. For he continually watches to ensnare us with his thousand sly cords. When he sees a man idle, he can so easily catch him in his net that, until a man is actually seized by the coat, he does not realize that he is in the devil's grip. We ought indeed to work hard and withstand idleness.

Even if people were never afraid of dying, still there is no doubt they can plainly see, by reason, that idleness is rotten sloth, from which no good or profit ever comes. They can see that sloth holds idleness on a leash, allowing her only to sleep, to eat, to drink, and to devour all that others get by labor. And in order to keep us from such idleness, the cause of such great confusion, I have here done my faithful best to translate correctly from the Legend thy glorious life and martyrdom, thou with thy garland wrought of rose and lily— I mean thee, St. Cecilia, virgin and martyr.

THE INVOCATION TO MARY: At my beginning I call first upon Thee, the flower of all virgins, of whom Bernard liked so well to write. Thou comforter of us wretches, help me to write of the death of one of Thy maidens, who through her merit won eternal life and victory over the devil, as men may read hereafter in her story. Thou Maid and Mother, daughter of Thy Son, Thou well of mercy, the cure of sinful souls, in whom God in His goodness chose to dwell, Thou humble one, high over every other creature, Thou didst so far ennoble our natures that the Maker of mankind had no hesitation in clothing and wrapping His Son in flesh and blood. The eternal Love and Peace, Who is Lord and Guide of the three-fold compass, and Whom earth and sea and heaven praise unceasingly, assumed man's form within the blessed cloister of Thy body; and Thou, spotless Virgin, bore of Thy body the Creator of every creature, and yet remained a virgin. In Thee magnificence is united with mercy, goodness, and with such pity that Thou, who art the sun of excellence, not only helpest those who pray to Thee, but often, in Thy kindness, most graciously goest before those who beseech Thy aid and art their life's physician.

Now help me, a wretched exile in this desert of gall, Thou meek and blessed fair Maid. Remember the Canaanite woman, who said that whelps eat some of the crumbs which fall from their masters' table; and though I, unworthy son of Eve, am sinful, accept my faith. For, since faith is dead without good works, then give me ability and time for sufficient work to escape that darkest place of all! Oh, Thou, so fair and full of grace, be my advocate in that highest of places, where "hosanna" is sung unceasingly. Thou Mother of Christ, dear daughter of Anne! Illumine with Thy light my imprisoned soul, which is troubled by the contagion of my body and also by the weight of earthly desire and false affection. Oh, Haven of refuge, oh, Salvation of those in sorrow and in distress, help me now, for I turn to my work.

I pray you who read this which I write to forgive me for making no effort to write this story skillfully. For I have taken both the words and the moral from him who wrote the story in reverence of the saint. Follow her legend and, I beg you, correct my work.

✳✳✳

THE INTERPRETATION OF THE NAME CECILIA PROPOSED BY BROTHER JACOB VORAIGNE IN THE "LEGEND": First, I wish to explain to you the name of St. Cecilia, just as anyone can find it in her story. In English it is equivalent to "lily of heaven"; "lily" was her name because of the pure chasteness of her virginity, or because she had the whiteness of honor, the greenness of conscience, and the sweet scent of good reputation. Or Cecilia is equivalent to "the way for the blind," for through good teaching she was an example for all; or else Cecilia, so I find it written, is a compound of "heaven" and "Leah" where "heaven" refers figuratively to her meditation upon holiness, and "Leah" to her constant industry.

Cecilia may also be taken as "lack of blindness," referring to the great light of her wisdom and to her clear features. Or, perhaps, the name of this bright maid comes from "heaven" and "leos," in which case one might justly call her the "heaven of people," the example of all good and wise works, for in English "leos" means "people." And just as men can see the sun, moon, and stars everywhere in heaven, so men can spiritually see in this noble maid the magnanimity of faith, the clarity of wisdom, and various shiningly excellent works. And, just as heaven is swift, and round, and burning, according to the philosophers, so the fair, pure Cecilia was always most swift and busy in good works, round and perfect by perseverance in good, and burning steadily in bright charity. Now I have explained to you what she was named.

HERE BEGINS THE SECOND NUN'S TALE OF THE LIFE OF ST. CECILIA: The shining maiden Cecilia, her biography states, came of a noble Roman family, and from her cradle she was reared in the Christian faith and kept Christ's gospel in her mind. I find it written that she never ceased to pray, and to love and fear God, begging Him to protect her virginity. And this girl was to be married to a very young man, who was named Valerian. When the day for her wedding arrived, she, very devout and humble in spirit, had put a hair shirt next to her body under her well-fitting robe of gold. Then, while the organ played, she sang in her heart to God alone, "Oh, Lord, keep my soul and my body spotless, lest they be doomed." And, for love of Him who died on the cross, she fasted every second or third day, always praying diligently in her devotions.

The night came when she must go to bed with her husband, as is usual, and she soon said to him in private: "Oh, sweet and well-beloved husband dear, there is a secret which I should gladly tell you, if you wish to hear it, and if you will swear that you shall not disclose it."

Valerian at once swore to her that he would on no condition, no matter what might happen, ever give away the secret. Then at last she said to him: "I have an angel who loves me with so great a love that he is always ready to protect my body, whether I am asleep or awake. And surely, if he sees that you touch me or love me physically, he will kill you at once, even as you act, and you will die in your youth. But if you govern me with a spiritual love, he will love you as he does me for your purity, and show you his joy and brightness."

303

Valerian, chastened as God desired, replied: "If I am to trust you, let me see this angel and examine him, and if he is a true angel, then I shall do as you have requested. But if you love another man, then truly I will slay you both with this sword."

Cecilia at once answered, "If you so desire you shall see the angel by believing in Christ and by being baptized. Go to the Appian Way," she said, "which is only three miles from this town, and say to the poor folk that live there that which I shall now tell you. Tell them that I, Cecilia, sent you to them to be shown the good, aged Urban, for secret needs and for a good purpose. And when you see St. Urban, tell him the words which I told you. Then, when he has purged you of sin, you shall see the angel before you leave."

Valerian went to the place and, just as he had been instructed by Cecilia, he soon found this holy, aged Urban, lurking among the graves of the saints. Without waiting, Valerian at once repeated his message, and when he had finished Urban raised his hands in joy. The tears fell from his eyes. "Oh, Jesus Christ, almighty Lord," he said, "Sower of pure counsel, Shepherd of us all, take unto Thee the fruit of that seed of chastity which Thou hast sowed in Cecilia! Lo, thine own servant, Cecilia, serves Thee constantly, like a busy bee, without guile. For the very husband whom she just married when he was like a fierce lion she has sent here to Thee, as meek as any lamb!" And, at once upon these words, an old man dressed in clear white clothes appeared, holding a book with golden letters in his hand, and stood in front of Valerian.

Valerian fell down as if dead from fear when he saw him, but the old man lifted him up and began to read these words from his book: "One Lord, one faith, one single God, one Christendom, and one Father of all, above all and over all everywhere." All these words were written in gold. When this had been read the old man asked, "Do you believe this or not? Say yes or no."

"I believe all this," replied Valerian, "for no one under heaven can imagine a truer thing than this, I dare state."

Then the old man vanished—Valerian did not know where—and Pope Urban christened him on the spot.

Valerian went home and found Cecilia standing in his room with an angel. The angel had two crowns of lilies and roses in his hand. And, as I understand it, he gave one first to Cecilia and then the other to her husband, Valerian. The angel said: "Always guard these crowns well, with pure bodies and with spotless thoughts. I have brought them to you from Paradise, and they shall never wither or lose their sweet scent, believe me; and no one shall ever see them unless he is chaste and hates villainy. Now you, Valerian, since you accepted good counsel so quickly, ask whatever you like and your request shall be granted."

"I have a brother," Valerian answered, "and there is no man in this world I love so much. I pray you that my brother may have grace to know the truth as I now know it."

"Your request pleases God," the angel said, "and both of you shall come to His blessed feast with the palm of martyrdom."

At these words, Tiburtius, Valerian's brother, entered, and when he perceived the sweet perfume which the roses and lilies sent into his heart, he was greatly puzzled and said: "I wonder where the sweet scent of roses and lilies which I smell now comes from at this time of year. For the scent could not strike me more deeply if I held the flowers in my two hands. This sweet smell which I perceive in my heart has changed me into a different person."

Valerian said: "We have two crowns, snow white and rose red, which shine clearly but which your eyes lack the power to see. And as you now smell them because of my prayers, so you shall see them, dear brother, if you will have faith and recognize without hesitancy the only truth."

Tiburtius answered, "Are you actually saying these things to me, or do I hear them in a dream?"

"Up until now, dear brother," said Valerian, "you and I have certainly only dreamt. But now for the first time our dwelling is in truth."

"How do you know this," asked Tiburtius, "and from what facts?"

"I shall show you," replied Valerian. "The angel of God has taught me that truth which you shall see if you will renounce the idols and be pure—otherwise, not."

St. Ambrose, the noble, beloved teacher treats this miracle of the two crowns in his preface. He solemnly commends it and speaks in this fashion: "St. Cecilia, in order to receive the palm of martyrdom, was filled with the gift of God and turned from the world and her marriage-bed; witness the confession of faith by Valerian and Tiburtius, to whom God in His generosity granted two crowns of sweet-scented flowers, which He caused His angel to bring to them. The maiden led these men to heavenly bliss. The world has certainly learned the worth of chaste devotion to love."

Then Cecilia showed Tiburtius plainly and openly that all idols are only vain things, for they are dumb and also deaf, and she charged him to give up his idols. Tiburtius then said, "Whoever does not believe this is a beast, if I shall not lie."

Cecilia, hearing this, kissed his breast, and was very glad that he could see the truth. "On this day I take you as my ally," said this beloved, blessed, fair maiden; and then she continued as you may hear. "See, just as the love of Christ made me your brother's wife," she said, "so I at once accept you here for my ally, since you will despise your idols. Now go with your brother; be baptized and purify yourself so that you can behold the face of the angel of whom your brother told you."

Tiburtius answered, saying, "Dear brother, first tell me where I am to go and to what man."

"To whom?" said Valerian. "Come along without fear; I shall lead you to Pope Urban."

"To Urban, brother Valerian?" asked Tiburtius. "Are you going to lead me there? That seems a marvelous thing to me. You don't mean that Urban," he continued, "who has been condemned to death so often, who lives perpetually in one hiding place and another, and does not once dare stick his head out? If he were discovered, or if men could spy him out, they would burn him in such a red fire!—and us also, to keep him company. It may be that we shall be burned in this world while we seek the Divinity hidden secretly in heaven!"

Cecilia boldly answered him: "Men might sensibly and reasonably fear to lose this life, my own dear brother, if this were the only life and there were no other. But there is a better life in another place, which can never be lost, be sure, and which God's Son in His grace has described for us. The Son of the Father created all things, and all that are created with reasonable intelligence the Spirit, which proceeds from the Father, has given souls; have no doubt of that. The Son of God, by word and miracle while He inhabited the earth, declared that there is another life in which men may live."

Tiburtius then answered, "Oh, dear sister, didn't you say earlier that there is only one God, the Lord in truth? But how can you now bear witness to three?"

"I shall explain that before I stop," she said. "Just as a man has three faculties: memory, imagination, and also reason, so in one divine Being three persons can easily be united." Then she began to preach earnestly to him about Christ's coming, and to teach him about His suffering and about many other points concerning His passion, and to explain how the Son of God was placed in this world to bring full remission to mankind, which was bound in sin and cold cares. She made all these things clear to Tiburtius. And afterwards, with firm purpose, he accompanied Valerian to see Pope Urban, who thanked God, christened him with a glad and light heart, and there made him a knight of God, perfect in his knowledge. After this, Tiburtius had such grace that he saw the angel of God in reality every day. And every request that he made to God, of whatever nature, was quickly granted.

It would be very hard to relate in order the many miracles Jesus performed for these three people. But finally—to make the story short—the officers of the law in Rome sought them out and conducted them before Almachius, the prefect, who questioned them, learned their point of view, and sent them to the idol of Jupiter, commanding, "Whoever will not sacrifice, strike off his head. That is my decision." Immediately, one Maximus, the assistant and clerk of the prefect, took these three martyrs I am telling you about into custody. And when he led these saints away, he wept because of the pity he felt.

When Maximus had heard their story, he got permission from the executioners to take them directly to his house, and before nightfall, by their preaching, they had converted the executioners, Maximus, and every one of his family from the false faith to a belief in the one God. When night fell, Cecilia brought priests who christened them all together. And later, at daybreak, she told them gravely, "Now, Christ's own beloved, dear knights, cast aside all the works of darkness and protect yourselves with the armor of light. You have indeed fought a great battle; your course is finished; you have preserved your faith. Accept the unfailing crown of life; the righteous Judge whom you have served will give it to you who have deserved it."

But when these happenings which I have related were over, the officers led the Christians forth to perform the ordered sacrifice; yet when they reached the appointed spot—to come quickly to the conclusion—they refused to burn incense or make sacrifice, but kneeled down with humbled hearts and steadfast devotion. Valerian and Tiburtius had their heads cut off there, and their souls went up to the King of Grace.

Maximus, who saw this happen, at once told with piteous tears how he had seen their souls rising to heaven, accompanied by bright, shining angels; and at his words many people were converted. Because of this, Almachius had him beaten so harshly with a leaden whip that he died. Cecilia took him up at once and gently buried him beside Valerian and Tiburtius in their burial place under the tombstone. After this, Almachius at once commanded his agents to lead Cecilia to make sacrifice and burn incense publicly to Jupiter in his presence. But they, converted by her wise teaching, wept bitterly, placed full faith in her words, and kept repeating,

"Christ, Son of God, without inequality, is the true God, who has so good a servant to follow Him—we truly believe this. We declare this with one voice, though we die for it!"

Almachius heard of these doings and ordered Cecilia to be brought to him so that he might see her. Then, first of all, this was his question: "What sort of woman are you?" he said.

"I am a gentlewoman by birth," she replied.

"Though it grieve you," he said, "I now ask you about your religion and your faith."

"You have begun your questioning foolishly," she replied, "to wish two answers for one question; you questioned stupidly."

Almachius answered that remark by saying, "Where do you find the courage to reply so rudely?"

"Where? In my conscience and unassumed good faith," she replied to his question.

"Don't you take any heed of my power?" inquired Almachius.

To him she replied: "Your power is to be feared very little, for the power of every mortal man is like nothing but a bladder full of wind: when it is blown up, all its swelling may be deflated with the point of a needle."

"You began in the wrong," he said, "and you still continue that way. Don't you know that our mighty, noble princes have commanded and passed an ordinance that every Christian shall be punished unless he renounces his Christianity, but that he shall go free if he will renounce it?"

"Your princes err as your nobles do," Cecilia then replied. "By an insane judgment, you prove us guilty, and it is not true. You know we are innocent, but because we do reverence to Christ and call ourselves Christians, you put the blame on us for a crime. But we know that there is such virtue in the name 'Christian' that we cannot renounce it."

Almachius answered, "Choose one of these two things: make a sacrifice or renounce Christianity, for in that way you can now escape."

At this, the holy blessed maiden began to laugh, and said

to the judge, "Oh, judge, confused in your ignorance, would you have me renounce innocence and become a wicked person? Look, this judge dissembles in public! He stares and raves in announcing his judgment!"

Almachius then said, "Foolish wretch, don't you realize how far my power stretches? Haven't our mighty princes given me both the power, yes, and the authority to make people either die or live? Why then do you speak so haughtily to me?"

"I speak only steadfastly," she said, "not proudly. For I declare in our defense that we hate the deadly sin of pride. And if you are not afraid to hear the truth, then I shall openly and clearly show you that you have lied greatly here. You said that your princes have given you the power both to kill people and to make them live; but you, who can only take away life, have no other power or authority. You can say only that your princes have made you a minister of death; but if you claim more you lie, for your power is helpless."

"Put aside your boldness and make sacrifice to our gods before you leave!" said Almachius. "I do not care what wrong you attribute to me, for I can endure it like a philosopher. But I cannot endure what you say here against our gods."

Cecilia answered: "Oh, foolish creature! Since you have been speaking you have said nothing which did not show me your folly and the fact that you are in every way an ignorant officer and a vain judge. There is nothing which meets your eyes to which you are not blind, for that which we all see to be stone, as anyone can tell—you call that same stone a god. I advise you, since you cannot see with your blind eyes, to place your hand upon it and to taste it, and you shall find it to be stone. It is a shame that the people shall so mock you and laugh at your folly. For men everywhere know above everything else that almighty God is in His high heavens, and these idols, as you can well observe, are not able to profit you or themselves, for they are actually not worth a mite."

She said these and other such words, and he grew angry

and ordered men to lead her home to her house. "Burn her entirely in a bath of red flames," he commanded. And as he commanded, so it was done; for they locked her tight in a bath, and day and night kept up a huge fire beneath it. In spite of the fire and the heat of the bath, she sat through the long night and also a day cool and unpained; the heat did not make her sweat a drop. But in that bath she was forced to give up her life, for Almachius, with wicked purpose, sent his emissary to slay her there. He smote her three times on the neck, this executioner, but by no means was he able to sever her neck. And since there was at that time an ordinance forbidding any man so to torment a person as to strike a fourth time, lightly or heavily, the executioner did not dare try it, but left her lying half dead, with her neck cut, and went his way.

The Christian people who were with her stopped the flow of blood with sheets. She lived for three days in this torment and never ceased to teach the faith to those whom she had converted. She preached to them, gave them her belongings and possessions, and committed them to the care of Pope Urban, saying, "I asked the Heavenly King to give me only three days' respite so that I might commend these souls to you before I depart, and, indeed, that I might have a permanent church made here of my house."

St. Urban, with his deacons, secretly fetched the body by night and buried it with honor among the other saints. Her house was named the Church of St. Cecilia. St. Urban hallowed it, as he was well fitted to do. In that church to this day men do fitting service to Christ and to His saint. HERE ENDS THE SECOND NUN'S TALE.

THE CANON'S YEOMAN

THE PROLOGUE OF THE CANON'S YEOMAN'S TALE: Before we had ridden even five miles, after the life of St. Cecilia had been finished, a man dressed in black clothes with a white surplice underneath overtook us at Boughton-under-Blean. His aged horse, which was a dappled gray, was sweating so much that it was a marvel to behold. It seemed as if the man had spurred on at top speed for fully three miles. Also the horse on which his yeoman rode was sweating so hard that it could scarcely walk. The foam lay thick about its collar; in fact, it was so foam-flecked all over that it looked like a magpie. A bag lay doubled over on its crupper; but the yeoman seemed to be traveling light.

The worthy man rode in lightweight clothes suitable for summer, and I began to wonder in my heart what he was, until I observed how his hood was sewn to his cloak, from which, after long deliberation, I judged him to be some sort of canon. His hat hung down his back by a string, for he had ridden faster than a walk or trot: he had steadily spurred ahead as though he were crazy. He had a large burdock leaf under his hood against the sweat and to keep the sun off his head. But what a joy to see him sweat! His forehead dripped like a still full of plaintain leaves and nettles.

When this man caught up with us, he began to shout: "God save this jolly company! I have spurred fast on account of you," he said, "because I wished to overtake you in order to ride with such a merry group."

His yeoman was also full of courtesy and said: "Sirs, this morning I saw you ride away from your inn and warned my lord and master here, who is so eager to accompany you for his pleasure; he loves dalliance."

"Friend, may God give you good luck for that warning!" said our Host then, "for certainly it would seem that your master is wise, if I am any judge. He is quite gay also, I'll swear. Can he tell any kind of merry tale or two with which to gladden this company?"

"Who, sir? My master? Yes, yes, without a doubt, he knows more than enough of mirth and also of jollity; also, sir, believe me, if you knew him as well as I do, you would marvel how cleverly and well he can work in various ways. He has taken upon himself many a great enterprise which would be very difficult for anyone here to carry out, unless they learned it from him. Unostentatiously as he rides among you, if you got to know him, it would be to your advantage. You would not give up his acquaintance for a great deal of money; I will bet all I own on that. He is a man of great discretion; I warn you well, he is an outstanding man."

"Well," said our Host, "I beg you to tell me this, then: is he a cleric, or not? What is he?"

"No, he's greater than a cleric, certainly," said this yeoman, "and in a few words, Host, I shall tell you something about his cleverness. I say that my master has such subtlety—but you can't learn all his cunning from me, though I do help him somewhat in his work—that he could turn all this ground on which we are riding, from here to Canterbury, completely upside down and pave it all with silver and gold."

When the yeoman had made this statement, our Host exclaimed, "Bless you! It seems to me a marvelously astonishing thing that, though your master is of such high wisdom that men should hold him in reverence, he still pays so little attention to his own dignity. As I hope to prosper, his coat is really not worth a mite, for such a man! It's all dirty, and ragged, too. Why is he so sloppy, I ask you, when he surely can afford to buy better clothes, if he can do all you claim? Tell me that, I beseech you."

"Why?" inquired this yeoman. "Why do you ask me? So help me God, he shall never prosper! (But I will not make public what I say, and therefore, I beg you, keep it secret.) Indeed, he is too wise, I believe. That which is overdone will not come out right—so the clerics say; it is a fault. Therefore, in that respect I consider him stupid and foolish. For when a man has too great a wit, it very often happens that he misuses his abilities. So my master often does, and that grieves me sorely; may God amend it! I can tell you no more."

"That doesn't matter, good yeoman," said our Host. "But since you understand your master's cunning, tell us how he fares, since he is so crafty and sly, I sincerely beg you. Where do you live, if it can be told?"

"In the outskirts of a town," he said. "We lurk in corners and blind alleys where robbers and thieves instinctively huddle secretly and fearfully together, like men afraid to show themselves. So it is with us, if I tell the truth."

"Now," said our Host, "let me ask you something else. Why is your face so discolored?"

"St. Peter!" he replied. "Bad luck to it! I am so accustomed to blowing the fire that it has changed my complexion, I think. I'm not used to primping in a mirror, but to slaving hard and studying transmutation of metals. We continually flounder around and pore over the fire; but in spite of all our efforts, we fail in our desire, for it always turns out wrong. We delude many people and borrow gold—be it a pound or two, or ten or twelve, or many times more—and we make them think that at least we can make two pounds from one. Yet it is false; but we always have great hope of success, and we continue to grope for it. But that science is so far ahead of us that we cannot overtake it, although we swear to do so, because it slips away so fast. In the end, it will make us beggars."

While the yeoman was talking this way, the canon approached him and heard everything he was saying, for the canon was always suspicious of people's conversation. Truly, as Cato says, a man who is guilty is convinced everyone talks about him. That is why the canon drew near to listen to everything his yeoman said. Then he said to his yeoman, "Hold your peace and speak not another word, for, if you do, you shall pay for it dearly. You slander me here in this company, and also you reveal what you should hide."

"Tell on," our Host said, "whatever happens. Don't you care a mite about his threats!"

"In faith," said the yeoman, "I don't care much any longer."

And when the canon saw that he could not have his way and that his yeoman would tell his secrets, he fled away in grief and shame.

"Ah!" said the yeoman. "Now we'll have some fun. I'll soon tell all I know, since he has gone—the foul fiend strike him! For I promise you that hereafter never will I have anything to do with him, for penny or for pound. May the man who first brought me into this game have dishonor and sorrow before he dies! For, by my faith, this is serious work for me; I know that very well, no matter what anyone says. And still, in spite of all my pain, grief, sorrow, labor, and hard luck, I could never manage to leave it. Now I wish to God I had enough wit to tell all the details of that art! Nevertheless, I'll tell you something of it. Since my master has gone, I'll hold nothing back. Such things as I know I'll tell fully. HERE ENDS THE PROLOGUE OF THE CANON'S YEOMAN'S TALE.

HERE BEGINS THE CANON'S YEOMAN'S TALE. PART ONE: For seven years I have lived with this canon, and for all his wisdom I'm no better off; I have lost all I owned, as a result, and, God knows, so have many others. Where I was once accustomed to bright and gay clothes and other finery, now I must wear a stocking on my head. And where my complexion was once fair and ruddy, now it

is pale and leaden—whoever practices this art shall sorely
regret it! And in spite of my labors, the wool was pulled
over my eyes. See the advantages of transmuting metals!
That slippery science has made me so bare that I own nothing
wherever I turn. And, as a result, I am so far in debt, truly,
for gold that I have borrowed that I can never live long
enough to repay it. Let every man be warned by me for
evermore! Whatever sort of man takes up this science, I
consider his prosperity over, if he continue with it. For, so
help me God, he shall not profit thereby, but shall empty his
purse and dull his wits. And when through his madness and
folly he has lost his own goods in this hazardous business,
then he incites other folk to it, so that they will lose their
goods, as he has done. For to malicious people it is a joy and
a comfort to see their fellow men in trouble and misfortune.
I learned that once from a cleric. But that's not important;
I'll tell about our work.

When we are in the place where we practice our elvish
craft, our terms are so strange and scholarly that we seem
wonderfully wise. I blow the fire until my heart grows faint.
Why should I tell the exact proportions of the ingredients we
work with—such as perhaps five or six ounces of silver, or
some other amount—and busy myself with telling you about
the names of arsenic trisulphide, burnt bones, and iron flakes
which are ground into fine powder; or how everything is
placed into an earthen pot—salt and pepper having been put
in before the powders which I told you about—and covered
well with a glass plate; or many other details of the process;
or of the sealing of the pot and glasses so that air cannot pos-
sibly escape; or of the slow and fast fires which were built;
or of the troubles and woes we have with our sublimation of
matter, and with our amalgamation and calcination of quick-
silver, called crude mercury? For in spite of all our tricks,
we cannot succeed. Neither our arsenic trisulphide, or sub-
limated mercury, our fused lead monoxide ground on por-
phyry—a definite number of ounces of each of these—nor any-
thing else helps us; our work is in vain. Nor does our ascen-
sion of vapors or our settled solid matter aid our process in

any way, for all our work and worry is lost, and all the money which we invested—the devil take it—is lost, too.

There are also many other details pertaining to our craft. Though I cannot name them in order, since I'm an ignorant man, nevertheless I shall name them as they come to my mind, even if I cannot put them in their proper categories. Such things as Armenian red clay, verdigris, borax, various vessels made of earth and glass, our urinals and our vessels for distilling by descent, vials, crucibles, vessels for sublimation, flasks, alembics, and many such things which cost quite a sum. No need to go over all of them—reddening waters and bull's gall, arsenic, sal ammoniac, and brimstone; and I could tell about many an herb, such as agrimony, valerian, moonwort, and others, if I cared to linger over them. I could tell about our lamps burning night and day to accomplish our aim, if possible; about our furnace for calcination and the albification of water; about unslaked lime, chalk, egg-white, various powders, ashes, dung, urine, clay, wax-sealed bags, saltpeter, vitriol, and various fires made of coal and wood; of salt, of tartar, alkali, prepared salt, and matter burnt and coagulated; of clay made of horse's or human hair, oil of tartar, alum glass, yeast, unfermented beer, crude tartar, disulphide of arsenic, and other absorbent matter; of our compounding matters, our citronation of silver, our cementing and fermenting, our molds, assaying vessels, and many other things.

I shall tell you, just as it was taught to me, about the four vapors and the seven bodies, in the order that I have often heard my master name them. The first vapor is called quicksilver, the second arsenic trisulphide, the third, of course, is sal ammoniac, and the fourth brimstone. Now the seven bodies—see, here they are: Sol is gold, and Luna, we are agreed, is silver, Mars iron, Mercury we call quicksilver, Saturn lead, Jupiter is tin, and Venus copper, by the soul of my father!

Whoever practices this accursed craft shall not have enough money for his needs, for he shall lose everything that he invests in it; I have no doubt about that. Whoever wishes to advertise his folly, let him come forth and learn transmuting metals; and let every man who has anything in his strongbox appear and become a philosopher. Perhaps that skill is quite easy to learn? No, no, God knows. Though he be monk, friar, priest, canon, or anything else, and though he sit with his book day and night learning this strange and foolish lore, all will be in vain, and much worse, by God! To teach an ignorant man this subtlety—fie, don't talk of it, for it's impossible. And whether he has book learning or not, in the end he shall find it just the same. For in either case, by my salvation, the results of transmuting metals are the same when they are all finished; that is to say, both fail.

But I forgot to mention corrosive waters, metal filings, softening of bodies and also their hardening, oils, ablutions, and fusible metal—to tell everything would surpass any Bible, anywhere; therefore, it seems best for me to stop reciting all these names. For I think I have told you enough to raise a devil, no matter how savage he looks.

Oh, no! Wait. We all search hard for the philosopher's stone, called elixir, for if we had it we would be secure enough. But I vow to God in heaven, in spite of all our cunning and all our tricks, when we are all finished it shall not have appeared for us. We spend a great deal of money on account of it, which almost drives us crazy with regret, but always the high hope creeps into our hearts that no matter how we suffer we will finally be rewarded with success. Such supposing and hoping bring hard and sharp results; I warn you, it will never be found. Their trust in future success has made men part with all they ever owned. Yet people can never get enough of that business; it is bittersweet for them, it seems—if they had nothing but one sheet in which to wrap themselves at night and a poor coat to walk in during the day, they would sell both and spend the money on this game. They cannot stop until there is nothing left. And ever after, wherever they go, men will know them by the smell of brimstone. They stink for all the world like a goat; their smell is so rammish and so strong that though a man is a mile away from them he will be infected by it, believe me. Thus, if they care to, people can recognize these folk by their smell and by their threadbare clothes. And if somebody asks them privately why they are so poorly clothed, at once they whisper in his ear and say that if they were recognized they would be killed because of their science. See, that's how these folks betray the innocent!

Pass over all that; I shall get to my story. Before the pot is placed on the fire, my master, and he only, treats the metals with specified amounts of other ingredients—now that he's gone, I'm not afraid to speak openly—for, as everyone says, he is cunning at such work. At least, I know very well he has that reputation, though he often runs into trouble. And do you know why? Many times it happens that the pot breaks to pieces, and, farewell, all is lost! These metals are so violent that our walls can't resist them unless made of lime and stone. They are very piercing, and they go through the wall. Some of them bury themselves in the earth—sometimes we've lost many pounds that way—and some are scattered all over the floor, and some shoot up to the roof. Without doubt, though the devil never shows himself in our sight, I'll swear he's with us, that old scoundrel! In Hell, where he is lord and master, there is no greater trouble, or more rancor or anger. When our pot breaks, as I have explained, everyone scolds and considers himself cheated. One man says it was because of the way the fire was laid; another says no, the fire wasn't properly blown—that's when I'm frightened, for that's my job. A third says, "A straw for that! You are ignorant and stupid. The metal was not properly tempered." "No," says the fourth. "Stop and listen to me. It's because our fire was not made of beech; that's the reason and nothing else, as I hope to thrive!" I can never tell what the cause was, but I know very well that there are great arguments among us.

"Well," my master says, "there's no more to be done. Another time I'll beware of these dangers. I'm quite sure the pot was cracked. Be that as it may, don't be discouraged. Sweep the floor quickly, as usual, pluck up your spirits, and be gay and cheerful." The trash is swept into a heap, canvas is spread on the floor, and all the rubbish thrown into a sieve and sifted and picked over many times.

"By God," says one man, "some of our metal is still left, though we have not recovered all of it. Though our plan miscarried this time, next time it may work excellently. We must put up our money for this enterprise. By God, a merchant, believe me, can't always be prosperous. One time his goods are drowned in the sea, but another time they come safely to land."

"Peace!" my lord shouts. "The next time I will manage to bring our work to an entirely different result; and if I don't, sirs, let me have all the blame. There was a mistake somewhere, I know."

Another man says that the fire was too hot—but, hot or cold, I dare say this: we always end without success. We fail to get what we want, and we are constantly raving in our madness. When we all meet together, every man seems a Solomon. But all that glistens is not gold, as I've heard it said; nor is every apple good which looks good, no matter what men boast or claim. See, that's just the way it is among us: the man who seems wisest, by Jesus, is the greatest fool, when it comes to the test. And the one who seems most honest is a thief. You'll believe that before I leave you, by the time I have reached the end of my tale. THE FIRST PART ENDS.

THE SECOND PART FOLLOWS: There is among us a religious man, a canon, who would poison a whole town, though it were as great as Nineveh, Rome, Alexandria, or Troy, and three more besides. No man, I think, though he lived a thousand years, could write down his tricks and infinite falseness; there is not his equal for falsehood in the whole world. For when he does business with anyone, he so winds himself up in cunning terms and speaks his words in such a sly manner, that unless the person is as much a devil as he, the canon soon makes a fool of him. Many a man has this canon deceived up to now, and he will deceive many more if he continues to live for a while. And yet men walk and ride many miles to seek him and make his acquaintance, not knowing about his dishonesty. Now, if you care to listen to me, I'll tell you about it.

But, honorable religious canons, don't think that I am slandering your order, even though my tale is about a canon. In every order, surely, there is a scoundrel, and God forbid that the whole group should be blamed for one man's folly. To slander you is not at all my intention; I mean only to correct what is amiss. This tale is not told just for you, but for other people also. You are well aware that among Christ's twelve apostles there was no traitor except Judas. Why, then, should all the other innocent ones be blamed? I make the same point concerning you, with this exception, if you will listen to me: if there is a Judas in your house, remove him at once, I advise you, if you have any fear of shame or dishonor. And, I beg you, don't be displeased, but listen to what I shall say in this story.

In London there was a priest who lived there for many years by singing annual masses for the dead, and who was so pleasant and helpful to the housewife where he boarded that she would not allow him to pay anything for board or clothing, no matter how splendidly he dressed. And he had plenty of spending money. But all that doesn't matter; I'll now proceed to tell my tale about the canon who brought this priest to confusion.

One day this false canon came to the room where the priest slept, begging him for the loan of a certain amount of gold, which he would pay back. He said: "Lend me a mark for only three days, and on the third day I'll repay you. And if you find me unreliable, have me hanged by the neck the next time."

The priest immediately gave him a mark, and this canon thanked him many times, took his leave, and went on his way. Then on the third day he brought the money and gave it back to the priest, at which the latter was very happy and pleased. "Certainly," he said, "I don't mind at all lending a man a noble, or two or three, or anything else I may own, when he is so dependable that he doesn't under any condition forget the appointed day. I can never say no to such a man."

"What!" said this canon, "Did you think I'd be untrustworthy? No, that would be a new thing for me. A promise is a thing which I will always respect until the day I creep into my grave, God forbid otherwise. You can be as sure of that as of your Creed. I thank God, and I don't mind saying it, that there was never a man who failed to have repayment of gold or silver which he lent me, and that never in my heart have I intended to be dishonest. And, sir," he said, "since you have been so good to me and have shown me so much courtesy, to repay your kindness to some extent I shall show you some of my secrets and, if you wish to learn it, I shall teach you the complete method by which I work in philosophy. Pay close attention, and with your own eyes you shall see me perform a master stroke before I go."

"Yes," said the priest, "yes, sir; will you do that? By Mary, I sincerely beg you to do so."

"At your command, sir, truly," said the canon. "God forbid otherwise!"

See how this thief could offer his services! It is very true that such proffered service stinks, just as old wise men say. And I shall soon verify it by the example of this canon, root of all treachery, who constantly takes delight and joy—such devilish thoughts are engraved upon his heart—in how many of Christ's people he can lead into mischief. May God save us from his false dissimulation!

The priest did not realize at all with whom he dealt, nor did he sense his coming harm. Oh, poor priest! Oh, poor innocent! You shall soon be tricked by greed! Oh, unlucky one, your conceit is quite blind; in no way are you aware of the deceit which this fox has planned for you! You cannot escape his wily tricks. Therefore—to get to the conclusion, which concerns your undoing, unhappy man—I shall hasten to tell about your stupidity and folly, and also about the wickedness of that other wretch, as far as my ability permits.

You think this canon was my master? Sir Host, in good faith and by the Queen of Heaven, it was not he but another canon who knows a hundred times more subtlety. He has betrayed folk many times; it bores me to repeat all his wickedness. My cheeks turn red with shame every time I talk about it. At least, they begin to glow, for I realize I have no redness in my face—the various vapors of metals which I told you about have consumed and wasted all my color. Now take heed of the cursedness of this canon!

"Sir," he said to the priest, "send your man for quicksilver; let us have it at once, and have him bring two or three ounces. Then, as soon as he returns, you shall see a miraculous thing which you never saw before."

"Sir," said the priest, "it shall certainly be done."

He ordered his servant to fetch this thing, and the latter was ready at his bidding. He went out and soon returned with the quicksilver, and—to get to the point—gave the three ounces to the canon, who put them down carefully and told the servant to bring coals so that he could start his work at once. The coals were immediately brought, and the canon took a crucible from inside his robe and showed it to the priest.

"Hold this instrument which you see in your hand," he said. "Put an ounce of quicksilver in it yourself, and with that you begin, in the name of Christ, to become a philosopher. There are very few to whom I would offer to show this much of my science. For you will now actually see that I shall transmute this quicksilver right before your eyes, without lying, and make it into as good and fine silver as any that is in your purse, or mine, or elsewhere. And I shall make it malleable; otherwise, consider me false and unfit ever to appear in public. I have here a powder which cost me dear and which will accomplish all this, for it is the root of all my skill which I shall show you. Send your man away, but have him wait nearby; and shut the door, so that no one can spy upon us while we are about our private business and while we work on our philosophy."

Everything which he commanded was carried out. The

servant at once went out, his master shut the door, and they speedily turned to their work. The priest, at the bidding of this cursed canon, set the vessel on the fire and blew the fire, working very busily. And the canon threw a powder into the crucible to deceive this priest. I don't know what it was made of, but whether it was chalk, or glass, or something else, it wasn't worth a fly. Then the canon told him to hasten and bed the coals above the crucible. "For as a token of my love for you," the canon said, "your own two hands shall perform all things which shall be done here."

"Thank you," said the priest, very happy, and he arranged the coals as the canon directed. Then while he was busy, this devilish wretch, this false canon—the foul fiend take him!— pulled an imitation coal, made of beechwood, in which a hole had been craftily drilled, from inside his robe. Into this hole an ounce of silver filings had been placed, and the opening sealed tight with wax to keep the filings in. You understand that this contrivance was not prepared on the spot, but had been arranged earlier. Later I shall tell about some other things which the canon had brought with him. He had planned before he came to deceive the priest, and so he did before they parted; he couldn't stop until he had skinned him. It bores me to talk about him. I'd like to avenge myself for his falsehood, if I knew how. But he is now here now there; he's so slippery, he stops nowhere for long.

But take heed now, sirs, for the love of God! The canon took his coal, which I told you about, and hid it in his hand. And while the priest busily arranged the coals, as I told you, the canon said: "Friend, you're doing wrong; this is not arranged as it should be, but I'll soon mend it. Now let me meddle with it a bit, for I pity you, by St. Giles! You are very hot; I can see how you sweat. Here, take a cloth and wipe off the water."

And while the priest wiped his face, the canon took his imitation coal—bad luck to him—and laid it among the coals on top, over the middle of the crucible and then blew hard until the coals burned fast. "Now give us a drink," he said.

"All will soon be well, I'll swear it. Sit down and let's make merry."

When the canon's beechwood coal had burned, all the filings fell down from the hole into the crucible, as it stands to reason they had to do, considering where the coal had been placed. But the priest knew nothing of this, alas! He thought all the coals were exactly the same, for he understood nothing about that trick.

When the alchemist saw his opportunity, he said, "Get up, Sir Priest, and stand by me. Since I am sure that you don't have a mold, go out and get us a chalkstone; I'll make it into the same shape as a mold, if possible. And also bring with you a dish or a pan full of water, and then you'll see how well our business will thrive and prosper. Yet, in order that you will not have any suspicion or doubt about me in your absence, I shall not be out of your sight; I'll go with you and return with you."

To be brief—they opened and shut the door of the room and went on their errand, taking the key with them and returning without any delay. Why should I waste all day talking? The canon took the chalkstone and shaped it in the form of a mold, as I shall explain to you. I say, he took from his own sleeve a sheet of silver which weighed only an ounce —may he find ill luck! Now notice his accursed trick! He shaped a mold from the length and breadth of this sheet of silver, so slyly that without doubt the priest saw nothing, and he hid it again in his sleeve. Then he picked up his materials from the fire, merrily put them into the mold, and threw it into the pan of water when he was ready. At once he told the priest: "Put your hand into the water and grope around; see what is there. You'll find silver there, I hope. What the devil in hell else can it be? A shaving of silver is silver, by God!"

He put in his hand and picked up the sheet of fine silver, and the priest was thrilled in every vein when he saw the result. "Sir Canon, may you have God's blessing and that of His Mother also and the saints, all of them," he said. "And may I have their curse if I am not your man in every way possible, if you will vouchsafe to teach me this noble craft and skill!"

The canon said: "I shall make yet a second test, so that you can pay close attention and become expert in this; then some other day when you need silver, you can try this discipline and this subtle science without me. Get another ounce of quicksilver," he said, "without further discussion, and do with it as you did before with the other ounce, which is now silver."

The priest busied himself about every detail which the canon, that cursed man, told him to do, and he blew hard on the fire to arrive at his desired effect. Meanwhile, the canon was fully prepared to deceive the priest a second time. For show, he held in his hand a hollow stick—take heed and beware!—in the end of which one ounce, no more, of silver filings had been put, as was the case before with his imitation coal; and the opening had been well sealed with wax to keep in every bit of the filings. While the priest was busy, the canon, carrying the stick, approached him quickly and threw in the powder as he had before—I pray God that the devil will beat him out of his skin for his falsehood! For he was always false in his thoughts and acts. Then he stirred the coals above the crucible with his stick, which was arranged with this false contrivance, until the wax began to melt because of the heat, as everyone knows must happen, unless he is a fool. Then all that was inside the stick ran out and fell quickly into the crucible.

Now, good sirs, what better can you hope for than well enough? When the priest, thinking everything was honest, was thus deceived again, he was actually so happy that I can in no way describe his merriment and glee. And once again he offered himself and his possessions to the canon.

"Yes," the canon said, "though I am poor, you will find me skillful. I warn you, there is still more to come. Is there any copper here?"

"Yes, sir," said the priest, "I believe there is."

"Otherwise go buy some," commanded the canon, "as quickly as possible; now, go on, good sir, and make haste."

The priest went out and returned with the copper. Then the canon took it in his hands and weighed out an even ounce.

My tongue is too inadequate a servant of my wit to describe the duplicity of this canon, root of all wickedness! He seemed friendly to those who did not know him, but he was fiendish in both deed and thought. It wears me out to tell about his falsity, yet I wish to declare it so that men may be warned thereby. That's my real purpose, truly.

He put the ounce of copper into the crucible, which he quickly placed on the fire; then he threw in the powder and told the priest to blow up the fire. The priest had to bend over as low as he had done before—everything was just a trick; the canon made a monkey of the priest, just as he desired! Then he cast the copper in the mold, and finally he placed it in the pan of water and thrust in his own hand. He had a sheet of silver up his sleeve, as you heard me explain before. He slyly pulled it out, this crafty wretch, while the priest knew nothing about the whole trick, and left it on the bottom of the pan. Then he splashed about in the water, very skillfully took out the piece of copper and hid it, also without the priest's knowledge. Next, he grabbed the priest by the coat-front and said to him jestingly, "Stoop down; by God, you are to blame! Help me now as I helped you before. Put in your hand and see what's there."

The priest immediately picked up the sheet of silver, and then the canon said, "Let us go to a goldsmith with these three sheets which we have made and find out if they are worth anything. For, by my faith, I would not by any means use them unless they were pure, fine silver. But that can be tested very quickly."

They went to a goldsmith with the three sheets of silver, and he tested them with fire and hammer. No one could in any way deny that they were all that they should have been.

Who was happier than this stupid priest? There was never a bird happier to see the dawn, nor a nightingale to sing during the May season, nor a lady to sing carols or talk about love and womanhood, nor a knight to do a bold feat of arms to win favor with his dear lady, than was this priest to be learning that sorry science. He said to the canon: "For the love of God, who died for us all, how much does this formula cost, if I deserve it from you? Tell me now!"

"By our Lady," said the canon, "it's expensive, I warn you; for except for me and a friar, there is no man in England who can do this."

"It doesn't matter," said the priest. "Now, sir, for God's sake, how much shall I pay? Tell me, I beg you!"

"Certainly, it's expensive, as I said," replied the canon. "Sir, in a word, if you wish to have it, you must pay forty pounds, so help me God! And if it were not for the friendship you showed me a while ago, you would certainly pay more."

The priest fetched the sum of forty pounds in nobles at once, and gave them all to this canon in return for his formula. All his work was only fraud and deception.

"Sir Priest," he said, "I don't care to be praised for my work, for I wish it kept secret. Therefore, if you love me, don't give away the secret. For if men knew my subtlety, by God, they would have such great envy of me, because of my philosophy, that I would be killed, that is certain."

"God forbid," said the priest. "What are you saying? Why, I would rather spend all the money I have than to see you come to such pass; may I lose my mind if that is not true."

"You have given good proof of your good will, sir," said the canon. "Farewell, and thank you!"

He went on his way and the priest never saw him after that day. But when the priest, having found a suitable occasion, made a test of his formula—farewell! it would not work. See how he was hoodwinked and deceived! That's how that canon worms his way in to bring folk to ruin.

Consider, sirs, how in every rank there is such fighting between men and gold that there is scarcely any gold left. So many people are deceived by this transmutation of metal that, in good faith, I believe it is the principal cause of such scarcity. Philosophers speak so vaguely in this science that ordinary people cannot understand them, for all the wit men have nowadays. But these philosophers might as well chatter like jaybirds and devote their interest and effort to definition of terms, for they will never accomplish their purpose. If a man has money, he can easily learn to transmute his money to nothing!

See, here is the reward in that gay game: it will turn a man's mirth to grief, empty large and heavy pocketbooks, and make folks buy curses against those to whom they lent their money. Oh, fie! For shame! Alas, can't those who have been burned flee from the fire's heat? You folk that practice transmutation, I advise you to give it up before you lose everything; better late than never. Never to prosper would be too long to wait. Though you prowl around forever, you shall never find the answer. You are as bold as blind Bayard, the horse who blunders on, never considering the danger. He is as ready to run against a stone as to pass beside it along the road. So it is with you people who transmute, I say; if your eyes can't see clearly, be sure your mind does not lack its sight. Though you look and search far and wide, you'll win nothing in that business; rather, you'll waste all you can borrow or steal. Take away the fire, lest it burn too fast; I mean, meddle no more with that science, for if you do your thriftiness is completely gone.

I shall tell you right now what the philosophers say about this matter. See, so says Arnold of New Town in his *Rosarium:* "No man can transmute mercury without his brothers knowing about it." Truly, he says exactly that. And he tells how this statement was first made by the father of philosophers, Hermes, who says that without doubt the dragon does not die unless slain by its brother; that is to say, the dragon means mercury, and the brother sulphur, which is made from gold and quicksilver. "And, therefore," he said—take heed of my quotation—"let no man busy himself in search of this art, unless he can understand the meaning and speech of philosophers; if he does, he is a stupid man, for this science, this cunning, is the secret of secrets, by God."

There was also a disciple of Plato who once spoke to his master, as his book *Senior* bears witness, and this was his exact request: "Tell me," he said, "the name of the secret stone."

Plato at once answered. "Take the stone that men call Titanos."

"Which is that?" the disciple asked.

"Magnesia is the same," replied Plato.

"Sir, is that right?" asked the disciple. "If so, it is less clear than your other term. What is Magnesia, good sir, I beg you?"

"It is a water which is made, I say, of the four elements," answered Plato.

"Tell me the basis of that water, good sir," said the disciple, "if you please."

"No, no," said Plato, "I certainly will not. The philosophers each swore that they would reveal it to no one, nor is it in any way written down in any book. For it is so precious and dear to Christ that He does not wish it to be revealed, except where it pleases His divinity to inspire mankind—and to forbid it, too, to whomever He pleases. See, that is all."

So I conclude thus: since God in Heaven does not desire the philosophers to explain how a man shall find this stone, my advice is that it is best to let it go. For whoever makes God his adversary, and works in any way contrary to His will, shall certainly never thrive, though he transmute for the rest of his life. And here I stop, for my tale is ended. May God send every true man help in his misfortune! Amen.

HERE ENDS THE CANON'S YEOMAN'S TALE.

THE MANCIPLE

HERE FOLLOWS THE PROLOGUE OF THE MANCIPLE'S TALE: Don't you know where a little village called Bob-up-and-down stands, overlooked by Blean forest on the Canterbury road? There our Host began to joke and play, and said: "Look, sirs, Dun is in the mud! Is there no one, for prayers or money, who will awaken our friend who has fallen behind? A thief could easily rob him and tie him up. See how he dozes! See how, by God's bones, he will soon fall from his horse! Is that a London cook, worse luck? Make him come forward; he knows his punishment, for he must tell a tale, by my faith, even though it isn't worth a wisp of hay. Wake up, you Cook," he said. "God send you sorrow! What's wrong with you that you are sleeping in the morning? Have you fought fleas all night, or are you drunk? Or did you spend all night with some wench, so that now you can't hold up your head?"

The Cook, who was extremely pale and without any color, said to our Host, "So help me God, such drowsiness has come over me, I don't know why, that I'd rather sleep than drink a gallon of the best wine in Cheapside."

"Well," said the Manciple, "if it will help you, Sir Cook, and if it does not displease anyone else who rides in this group, and if our Host in his courtesy agrees, I shall relieve you of telling a tale now. For, in good faith, your face is very pale, your eyes seem to me to be dazed, and—I know it well—your breath stinks horribly, which indicates clearly that you

331

are indisposed. Certainly, you won't be flattered by me. Look!
See there how he yawns, this drunken one, as if he wanted
to swallow us whole. Shut your mouth, man, by the soul of
your father! May the devil from hell put his foot therein!
Your cursed breath will infect us all. Fie, stinking pig! Fie,
bad luck to you! Ah, sirs, take notice of this fine fellow. Now,
sweet sir, would you like to play a jousting game? It seems
to me that you are well prepared for that! I think that you
have drunk ape-wine, and that is the time when men play
with a straw."

The Cook grew very angry and rough at these words and
began, for lack of speech, to shake his head vigorously at the
Manciple. Then his horse threw him down, where he lay
until he was picked up. That was a fine piece of horsemanship
for a cook! Alas, that he could not help himself up with his
ladle! And before he was in his saddle again, it took great
shoving back and forth, along with many other troubles, to
lift him, so clumsy was this sorry, pallid ghost. And then
our Host spoke to the Manciple:

"Since drink has overcome this man, I believe, by my
salvation, that he would tell a stupid story. For, whether it
was wine or old musty ale which he drank, he speaks through
his nose and wheezes fast, and also he has a cold. In addition,
he has more than enough to do to keep himself and his nag
out of the ditch, and if he falls from his nag again, then
we'll all have enough to do to lift up his heavy, drunken
carcass. Tell your tale; I won't worry about him. But, Man-
ciple, you were really foolish to scold him publicly for his
vice. Some other day he will, perhaps, challenge you and
take you in hand. I mean that he will discuss various little
things, such as finding fault with your accounts, which, if it
came to proof, would not be in your credit."

"No," said the Manciple, "that would cause great trouble!
He could easily bring me into a trap that way. I had rather
pay for the mare which he rides on than to have him angry
with me. I won't anger him, as I hope to thrive! That which
I said was spoken in jest. And do you know what? I have
here in a gourd a draught of wine—yes, wine of ripe grapes—

and right now I'll show you a good joke. This Cook, if I can arrange it, will drink some. Under pain of death, he won't refuse me."

And then, to tell it as it happened, the Cook drank fast from this gourd. Alas! Why did he need to do that? He had drunk enough before. And when he had blown in this horn, he returned the gourd to the Manciple and was extremely happy with the drink. Then he thanked the Manciple the best way he could.

Our Host laughed wonderfully loud at that, and said: "I see clearly that it is necessary, wherever we go, to carry good drinks with us, for they can turn rancor and strife to accord and love, and appease many an insult.

"Oh, you Bacchus, blessed be your name, since you can so easily turn seriousness to sport! Worship and thanks to your deity! Of that matter you shall get no more from me. Tell your tale, Manciple, I beg you."

"Well, sir," said the Manciple, "now listen to what I say."

HERE BEGINS THE MANCIPLE'S TALE OF THE CROW: When Phoebus lived down here on earth, as old books tell us, he was the lustiest bachelor in all the world and also the best archer. One day he slew Python, the serpent, as he lay sleeping in the sun. And anybody can read about many other noble, brave deeds which he performed with his bow.

He could play every instrument, and sing so that it was a joy to hear the sound of his clear voice. Truly, Amphion, king of Thebes, who walled that city by his singing, could never sing half so well as Phoebus. Also, he was handsomer

than any man alive, or who ever lived since the beginning of
the world. What need is there to describe his features? For
nowhere in this world was there a man so handsome. In
addition, he was a model of gentility, of honor, and of great
worth. It was the custom of this Phoebus, the flower among
all young men, both in generosity and chivalry, so the story
tells us, to carry his bow in his hand, to amuse himself, as
a sign of his victory over Python.

Now this Phoebus had a crow in his house which he kept
for a long time in a cage, and he taught it to speak, just as
people teach a jay. This crow was as white as the snow-white
swan, and he could imitate the speech of anyone, when he
wished to talk. In addition, there was no nightingale in all
the world which could sing one hundred-thousandth part so
prettily and well.

Phoebus also had a wife in his house, whom he loved more
than life itself, and night and day he did all he could to please
her and to pay her respect, except that, if I tell the truth, he
was jealous and eager to keep her to himself. For he, like
any man in his position, did not want to be deceived. But
that is always in vain, for it does not help. A good wife, who
is pure in thought and deed, should certainly not be watched;
and without doubt it is a waste of time to watch an evil wife,
for it will not help. I consider it really foolishness to waste
time watching wives; so said ancient writers, in their time.

But now to my story, which I started before: Noble Phoe-
bus did all that he could to please his wife, thinking that be-
cause of this fact, as well as because of his manhood and
his behavior, no man could win her favor from him. But,
God knows, no man can manage to prevent a thing which
nature has placed instinctively within a creature.

Take any bird, put it in a cage, and do all you possibly can
to raise it lovingly with all the daintiest food and drink which
you can imagine, and guard it with the most careful attention.
Though its cage is of the finest gold, still this bird had twenty
thousand times rather be in a rough, cold forest, eating worms
and similar miserable food. Constantly it will do its best to

escape from the cage if possible. This bird will always want liberty.

Take a cat, raise it well on milk and tender meat, and give it a silken bed. Then, just let it see a mouse sneaking along a wall, and it immediately deserts the milk and meat and every comfort in the place, so great is its desire to eat a mouse. You see here that lust dominates and appetite overcomes discretion.

A she-wolf also has a villainous nature. At the time when she lusts for a mate, she will take the most ignorant wolf that she can find, or the one with the worst reputation.

I recite all these examples to show that men are unfaithful, not women; for men always have a wanton desire to find enjoyment with other women than their wives, no matter how beautiful, no matter how true or gay the latter are. Unfortunately, the flesh so loves newfangled things that we cannot for any length of time find pleasure in things which are connected with virtue.

Phoebus, who suspected no tricks, was deceived in spite of all his attractiveness. For, unknown to him, his wife took another man, of little reputation, and in no way to be compared with Phoebus—more was the pity. Frequently it happens that way, and much harm and unhappiness result. And so it happened, when Phoebus was absent, that his wife at once sent for her lover. Her lover? Certainly this is vulgar talk! Forgive me for it, I beseech you.

The wise Plato says—you may read it—that the word must accord with the deed. If a man is to tell a thing properly, the word must be cousin to the act. I am a crude man to say this, but I say truly that there is no real difference between a wife of high rank who is unfaithful to her husband, and a poor wench, except this—if both are adulterous—the gentlewoman will be called her lover's lady, while the other, who is poor, will be called her lover's wench or woman. But, God knows, my own dear friend, that men lay the one as low as the other.

In the same fashion, I say that there is no difference between a usurping tyrant and an outlaw or roving thief. The following distinction was told to Alexander: since the tyrant has greater power because of the number of his followers who can kill, burn homes and houses, and make everyone suffer, he is called a captain; but since the outlaw has only a few followers and cannot do as much harm or bring such great suffering to a country as the tyrant, people call him an outlaw or a thief. But, since I am not a learned man, I care nothing at all for reciting texts. I shall continue my tale as I began it.

After Phoebus' wife had sent for her lover, they soon set about satisfying their wanton lust. The white crow, which always was kept in its cage, saw their doings, but said never a word. Then when Phoebus, the master, returned home, the crow greeted him with "Cuckoo! Cuckoo! Cuckoo!"

"What, crow?" said Phoebus. "What song are you singing? Has it not been your custom to sing so merrily that it gladdened my heart to hear your voice? Alas! What song is this?"

"By God!" said the crow, "I don't sing incorrectly. Phoebus, in spite of all your worth, your beauty, and your gentility—in spite of all your songs and minstrelsy, and all your watching—your eyes are bleared by a man of little reputation, not worth a gnat in comparison with you, as I hope to prosper! For I saw him make love with your wife on your bed."

What more do you wish? The crow then told him with convincing evidence and bold words how his wife had conducted her adultery, to his great shame and dishonor. The crow kept repeating that it had seen the act with its own eyes.

Phoebus turned away; he thought that his grief-stricken heart would burst in two. He bent his bow, set an arrow to the string, and then in his anger killed his wife. That is the fact; there is no more to say. In his grief at losing his wife, he broke his musical instruments—harp, lute, guitar, and psaltery—and he also broke his bow and his arrows. Then he spoke to the crow:

"Traitor, with the tongue of a scorpion," he said, "you have brought confusion upon me. Alas, that I was born! Why was I not dead? Oh, dear wife! Oh, gem of all delight! You who were so steadfast and also so true, now you lie dead, with a pale face, fully innocent, I certainly dare swear! Oh, rash hand, to do so foul a deed! Oh, troubled mind, oh, reckless anger, which foolishly kills the innocent! Oh, distrust, full of false suspicion, where was your sense and your discretion? Oh, every man, beware of rashness! Believe nothing without strong evidence. Do not strike too soon, before you know why, and consider soberly and well before you carry out any act in suspicious anger. Alas! Rash ire has undone a thousand people, and brought them despair. Alas! I will kill myself because of grief."

Then he said to the crow: "Oh, false thief! I will repay you at once for your lying story. Once you sang like a nightingale; now, false thief, you shall give up your song, and also every one of your white feathers. Never again in all your life shall you speak. That is how mankind shall be avenged upon a traitor. You and your offspring shall evermore be black, and never shall you make a pleasing sound; but you shall always cry out against approaching tempests and rain, in token that through you my wife was killed."

Then he leaped upon the crow, pulled out every one of its white feathers, made it black, took away its power of song and also of speech, and slung it to the devil through the door —to whom I consign it. And because of this case, all crows are black.

Ladies and gentlemen, from this example I beg you to beware and to take heed of what I say: Never while you live tell any man how another man has slept with his wife. Without doubt, he will hate you mortally. Lord Solomon, as learned folk tell, teaches a man to hold his tongue. But, as I said before, I am not learned. Nevertheless, my mother taught me in this way:

"My son, remember the crow, in God's name! Hold your tongue, my son, and keep your friends. A malicious tongue is worse than a devil, and everybody should pray to escape the devil. My son, God, in His everlasting goodness, walled in the tongue with teeth and also with lips, so that a man would consider before he spoke. Very often many men have been killed, so teach the clerics, because they talked too much. But no man, generally speaking, has ever been harmed for talking too little. My son, you should restrain your tongue at all times, except when you dutifully speak of God in honor and prayer. The foremost virtue, son, if you wish to learn, is to restrain and guard your tongue. Children learn this when they are small. My son, much harm comes from too much ill-advised talk, where less talk would have sufficed; so I was told and taught. There is plenty of sin in too much talk. Do you know what purpose is served by a rash tongue? Just as a sword cuts and hacks an arm in two, my dear son, so does a tongue sever friendship in two. A prattler is abominable to God. Read wise and honorable Solomon; read the Psalms of David; read Seneca. My son, do not speak, but just nod your head. Act as if you are deaf when you hear a prattler speaking of dangerous things. The Fleming says—take heed if you wish—that a minimum of prattling brings a maximum of peace. My son, if you have not said any malicious word, you need have no fear of being betrayed. But the man who has spoken maliciously cannot, I am sure, in any way call back his words. A thing which is said is said, and away it goes, whether the speaker wishes it to do so or not. The man who has told a tale which he should not have told is the slave of his hearer.

"My son, beware, and do not be the first giver of news, no matter whether it is false or true. Wherever you travel, among poor or rich, guard well your tongue and remember the crow." HERE ENDS THE MANCIPLE'S TALE OF THE CROW.

THE PARSON

HERE FOLLOWS THE PROLOGUE OF THE PARSON'S TALE: By the time the Manciple had ended his tale, the sun had sunk so low that it looked to me less than twenty-nine degrees high. I think it was then four o'clock, for my shadow was eleven feet in length, or a little more or less, there and at that time—that is, double my height of six feet. Also, the moon's exaltation—I mean Libra—was still ascending as we entered a little village. Therefore, our Host, since he was accustomed to guide our jolly company in such matters, said: "Ladies and gentlemen every one, we now lack no more than one tale. My ideas and my decisions have been carried out; we have heard, I think, from each rank, and my supervision is almost completed. I pray God to give very good luck to the man who willingly tells us our next tale.

"Sir Priest," he said, "are you a vicar, or are you a parson? Tell the truth, by your faith! Be whatever you wish, but don't break our rules, for everybody except you has told his tale. Unbuckle, and show us what's in your bag. For from your appearance, it really seems to me that you should be able to work up something worth hearing. Tell us a fable at once, by God's bones!"

The Parson immediately answered: "You shall get no fable from me, for Paul, writing to Timothy, reproves those people who leave truth and tell fables and similar trash. Why should I sow chaff out of my hand when I can sow wheat, if I want to? Therefore, I say that if you wish to hear moral and vir-

339

tuous material, and if you will listen to me, then I am very eager, in reverence of Christ, to please you as best I am able. But you can be sure, I am a Southern man, and I cannot tell a story 'rum, ram, ruf' to the letter. No, God knows, I consider rhyme to be but little above that. And therefore, if you wish—I won't interpret texts—I shall tell you a merry tale in prose to wind up all this game and make an end of it. And may Jesus, in His grace, send me the wit to show you on this trip the way for that perfect, glorious pilgrimage which is called Jerusalem the Celestial. And if you agree, I shall begin my tale at once. Therefore, I ask you to give your decision; I can tell nothing better. But, nevertheless, I wish to make this sermon constantly subject to correction by clerics, for I am not learned; I take only the meaning, be sure. Therefore, I declare myself subject to correction."

After these words, we immediately agreed to his proposal, for it seemed fitting to make an end with virtuous material and to give him time and attention. So we instructed our Host to tell him that we all wished to hear his tale.

Our Host was our spokesman. "Sir Priest," he said, "now good luck to you! Tell your thoughts," he said. "But make haste; the sun is setting. Be fruitful and brief. And may God send you His grace to do well! Say what you like, we shall listen gladly."

After these words, the Parson spoke like this. PROLOGUE ENDS.

THE PARSON'S TALE: [*In spite of the Host's instructions, the Parson does not tell a tale at all; nor is his performance brief. His "virtuous material" takes the dull form of a three-part, two-hour sermon on penitence, with a lengthy digression on the seven deadly sins. Finally, the Parson concludes with the assurance that the kingdom of heaven can be attained by poverty of spirit, humility, work, death, and mortification of sin.*]

HERE THE MAKER OF THIS BOOK TAKES HIS LEAVE: Now I beg all those who hear or read this little treatise to thank our Lord Jesus Christ, from whom comes all wit and all goodness, for anything in it which pleases them. And if there is anything which displeases them, I also request them to attribute it to my lack of skill rather than to my evil intention, for I would very gladly have spoken better if I had been able. For our Book says, "All that is written, is written for our instruction," and that has been my intention. Therefore, I beseech you humbly, for God's mercy, to pray for me so that Christ will have mercy upon me and excuse my sins, particularly my translations and compositions dealing with worldly vanities, all of which I revoke in my retraction, such as the book of Troilus, also the book of Fame, the book of the Nineteen Ladies, the book of the Duchess, the book for Saint Valentine's day of the Parliament of Birds, those of the tales of Canterbury which incline toward sin, the book of the Lion, many another book which I cannot remember, and many a song and many a lecherous poem; may Christ in His great mercy forgive me the sin.

But for the translation of Boethius' *Consolation*, and for the other books of saints' legends, of homilies, of morality, and of devotion, I thank our Lord Jesus Christ, His blessed Mother, and all the saints of heaven, begging them that they send me, henceforth to the end of my life, the grace to bewail my sins and to study for the salvation of my soul; and that they grant me the grace of true penitence, confession, and absolution in this present life, through the benign grace of Him who is King of Kings and Priest over all priests, and who redeemed us with the precious blood of His heart, so that I may be one of those who shall be saved at the day of judgment. *Qui cum patre et Spiritu Sancto vivit et regnat Deus per omnia secula. Amen.*

HERE ENDS THE BOOK OF THE TALES OF CANTERBURY, COM-PILED BY GEOFFREY CHAUCER, ON WHOSE SOUL MAY JESUS CHRIST HAVE MERCY.

AMEN.

THE CANTERBURY TALES

 IN MIDDLE ENGLISH

NOTHING *can delight a translator more than to find that his work has encouraged its readers to turn to the original. For those who wish to refresh their minds and memories with the mild rigors of tasting the delights of Chaucer's own language, the "General Prologue" and one of the most perfect of the tales are here reprinted in Middle English.*

GENERAL PROLOGUE

*Here bygynneth the Book of the
Tales of Caunterbury.*

    Whan that Aprille with his shoures soote
The droghte of March hath perced to the roote,
And bathed every veyne in swich licour
Of which vertu engendred is the flour;
Whan Zephirus eek with his sweete breeth
Inspired hath in every holt and heeth
The tendre croppes, and the yonge sonne
Hath in the Ram his halve cours yronne,

And smale foweles maken melodye,
That slepen al the nyght with open ye
(So priketh hem nature in hir corages);
Thanne longen folk to goon on pilgrimages,
And palmeres for to seken straunge strondes,
To ferne halwes, kowthe in sondry londes;
And specially from every shires ende
Of Engelond to Caunterbury they wende,
The hooly blisful martir for to seke,
That hem hath holpen whan that they were seeke.

　　Bifil that in that seson on a day,
In Southwerk at the Tabard as I lay
Redy to wenden on my pilgrymage
To Caunterbury with ful devout corage,
At nyght was come into that hostelrye
Wel nyne and twenty in a compaignye,
Of sondry folk, by aventure yfalle
In felaweshipe, and pilgrimes were they alle,
That toward Caunterbury wolden ryde.
The chambres and the stables weren wyde,
And wel we weren esed atte beste.
And shortly, whan the sonne was to reste,
So hadde I spoken with hem everichon
That I was of hir felaweshipe anon,
And made forward erly for to ryse,
To take oure wey ther as I yow devyse.

　　But natheless, whil I have tyme and space,
Er that I ferther in this tale pace,
Me thynketh it acordaunt to resoun
To telle yow al the condicioun
Of ech of hem, so as it semed me,
And whiche they weren, and of what degree,
And eek in what array that they were inne;
And at a knyght than wol I first bigynne.

　　A KNYGHT ther was, and that a worthy man,
That fro the tyme that he first bigan
To riden out, he loved chivalrie,
Trouthe and honour, fredom and curteisie.

Ful worthy was he in his lordes werre,
And therto hadde he riden, no man ferre,
As wel in cristendom as in hethenesse,
And evere honoured for his worthynesse.
At Alisaundre he was whan it was wonne.
Ful ofte tyme he hadde the bord bigonne
Aboven alle nacions in Pruce;
In Lettow hadde he reysed and in Ruce,
No Cristen man so ofte of his degree.
In Gernade at the seege eek hadde he be
Of Algezir, and riden in Belmarye.
At Lyeys was he and at Satalye,
Whan they were wonne; and in the Grete See
At many a noble armee hadde he be.
At mortal batailles hadde he been fiftene,
And foughten for oure feith at Tramyssene
In lystes thries, and ay slayn his foo.
This ilke worthy knyght hadde been also
Somtyme with the lord of Palatye
Agayn another hethen in Turkye.
And evermoore he hadde a sovereyn prys;
And though that he were worthy, he was wys,
And of his port as meeke as is a mayde.
He nevere yet no vileynye ne sayde
In al his lyf unto no maner wight.
He was a verray, parfit gentil knyght.
But, for to tellen yow of his array,
His hors were goode, but he was nat gay.
Of fustian he wered a gypon
Al bismotered with his habergeon,
For he was late ycome from his viage,
And wente for to doon his pilgrymage.

  With hym ther was his sone, a yong SQUIER,
A lovyere and a lusty bacheler,
With lokkes crulle as they were leyd in presse.
Of twenty yeer of age he was, I gesse.
Of his stature he was of evene lengthe,
And wonderly delyvere, and of greet strengthe.

And he hadde been somtyme in chyvachie
In Flaundres, in Artoys, and Pycardie,
And born hym weel, as of so litel space,
In hope to stonden in his lady grace.
Embrouded was he, as it were a meede
Al ful of fresshe floures, whyte and reede.
Syngynge he was, or floytynge, al the day;
He was as fressh as is the month of May.
Short was his gowne, with sleves longe and wyde.
Wel koude he sitte on hors and faire ryde.
He koude songes make and wel endite,
Juste and eek daunce, and weel purtreye and write.
So hoote he lovede that by nyghtertale
He sleep namoore than dooth a nyghtyngale
Curteis he was, lowely, and servysable,
And carf biforn his fader at the table.

A YEMAN hadde he and servantz namo
At that tyme, for hym liste ride so;
And he was clad in cote and hood of grene.
A sheef of pecok arwes, bright and kene,
Under his belt he bar ful thriftily,
(Wel koude he dresse his takel yemanly:
His arwes drouped noght with fetheres lowe)
And in his hand he baar a myghty bowe.
A not heed hadde he, with a broun visage.
Of wodecraft wel koude he al the usage.
Upon his arm he baar a gay bracer,
And by his syde a swerd and a bokeler,
And on that oother syde a gay daggere
Harneised wel and sharp as point of spere;
A Christopher on his brest of silver shene.
An horn he bar, the bawdryk was of grene;
A forster was he, soothly, as I gesse.

Ther was also a Nonne, a PRIORESSE,
That of hir smylyng was ful symple and coy;
Hire gretteste ooth was but by Seinte Loy;
And she was cleped madame Eglentyne.
Ful weel she soong the service dyvyne,

Entuned in hir nose ful semely,
And Frenssh she spak ful faire and fetisly,
After the scole of Stratford atte Bowe,
For Frenssh of Parys was to hire unknowe.
At mete wel ytaught was she with alle:
She leet no morsel from hir lippes falle,
Ne wette hir fyngres in hir sauce depe;
Wel koude she carie a morsel and wel kepe
That no drope ne fille upon hire brest.
In curteisie was set ful muchel hir lest.
Hir over-lippe wyped she so clene
That in hir coppe ther was no ferthyng sene
Of grece, whan she dronken hadde hir draughte.
Ful semely after hir mete she raughte.
And sikerly she was of greet desport,
And ful plesaunt, and amyable of port,
And peyned hire to countrefete cheere
Of court, and to been estatlich of manere,
And to ben holden digne of reverence.
But, for to speken of hire conscience,
She was so charitable and so pitous
She wolde wepe, if that she saugh a mous
Kaught in a trappe, if it were deed or bledde.
Of smale houndes hadde she that she fedde
With rosted flessh, or milk and wastel-breed.
But soore wepte she if oon of hem were deed,
Or if men smoot it with a yerde smerte;
And al was conscience and tendre herte.
Ful semyly hir wympul pynched was,
Hir nose tretys, hir eyen greye as glas,
Hir mouth ful smal, and therto softe and reed;
But sikerly she hadde a fair forheed;
It was almost a spanne brood, I trowe;
For, hardily, she was nat undergrowe.
Ful fetys was hir cloke, as I was war.
Of smal coral aboute hire arm she bar
A peire of bedes, gauded al with grene,
And theron heng a brooch of gold ful sheene,

On which ther was first write a crowned A,
And after *Amor vincit omnia.*

    Another NONNE with hire hadde she,
That was hir chapeleyne, and preestes thre.

    A MONK ther was, a fair for the maistrie,
An outridere, that lovede venerie,
A manly man, to been an abbot able.
Ful many a deyntee hors hadde he in stable,
And when he rood, men myghte his brydel heere
Gynglen in a whistlynge wynd als cleere
And eek as loude as dooth the chapel belle.
Ther as this lord was kepere of the celle,
The reule of seint Maure or of seint Beneit,
By cause that it was old and somdel streit
This ilke Monk leet olde thynges pace,
And heeld after the newe world the space.
He yaf nat of that text a pulled hen,
That seith that hunters ben nat hooly men,
Ne that a monk, whan he is recchelees,
Is likned til a fissh that is waterlees,—
This is to seyn, a monk out of his cloystre.
But thilke text heeld he nat worth an oystre;
And I seyde his opinion was good.
What sholde he studie and make hymselven wood,
Upon a book in cloystre alwey to poure,
Or swynken with his handes, and laboure,
As Austyn bit? How shal the world be served?
Lat Austyn have his swynk to hym reserved!
Therfore he was a prikasour aright:
Grehoundes he hadde as swift as fowel in flight;
Of prikyng and of huntyng for the hare
Was al his lust, for no cost wolde he spare.
I seigh his sleves purfiled at the hond
With grys, and that the fyneste of a lond;
And, for to festne his hood under his chyn,
He hadde of gold ywroght a ful curious pyn;
A love-knotte in the gretter ende ther was.
His heed was balled, that shoon as any glas,

And eek his face, as he hadde been enoynt.
He was a lord ful fat and in good poynt;
His eyen stepe, and rollynge in his heed,
That stemed as a forneys of a leed;
His bootes souple, his hors in greet estaat.
Now certeinly he was a fair prelaat;
He was nat pale as a forpyned goost.
A fat swan loved he best of any roost.
His palfrey was as broun as is a berye.

A FRERE ther was, a wantowne and a merye,
A lymytour, a ful solempne man.
In alle the ordres foure is noon that kan
So muchel of daliaunce and fair langage.
He hadde maad ful many a mariage
Of yonge wommen at his owene cost.
Unto his ordre he was a noble post.
Ful wel biloved and famulier was he
With frankeleyns over al in his contree,
And eek with worthy wommen of the toun;
For he hadde power of confessioun,
As seyde hymself, moore than a curat,
For of his ordre he was licenciat.
Ful swetely herde he confessioun,
And plesaunt was his absolucioun:
He was an esy man to yeve penaunce,
Ther as he wiste to have a good pitaunce.
For unto a povre ordre for to yive
Is signe that a man is wel yshryve;
For if he yaf, he dorste make avaunt,
He wiste that a man was repentaunt;
For many a man so hard is of his herte,
He may nat wepe, althogh hym soore smerte.
Therfore in stede of wepynge and preyeres
Men moote yeve silver to the povre freres.
His typet was ay farsed ful of knyves
And pynnes, for to yeven faire wyves.
And certeinly he hadde a murye note:
Wel koude he synge and pleyen on a rote;

Of yeddynges he baar outrely the pris.
His nekke whit was as the flour-de-lys;
Therto he strong was as a champioun.
He knew the tavernes wel in every toun
And everich hostiler and tappestere
Bet than a lazar or a beggestere;
For unto swich a worthy man as he
Acorded nat, as by his facultee,
To have with sike lazars aqueyntaunce.
It is nat honest, it may nat avaunce,
For to deelen with no swich poraille,
But al with riche and selleres of vitaille.
And over al, ther as profit sholde arise,
Curteis he was and lowely of servyse.
Ther nas no man nowher so vertuous.
He was the beste beggere in his hous;
[And yaf a certeyn ferme for the graunt;
Noon of his bretheren cam ther in his haunt;]
For thogh a wydwe hadde noght a sho,
So plesaunt was his *"In principio,"*
Yet wolde he have a ferthyng, or he wente.
His purchas was wel bettre than his rente.
And rage he koude, as it were right a whelp.
In love-dayes ther koude he muchel help,
For ther he was nat lyk a cloysterer
With a thredbare cope, as is a povre scoler,
But he was lyk a maister or a pope.
Of double worstede was his semycope,
That rounded as a belle out of the presse.
Somwhat he lipsed, for his wantownesse,
To make his Englissh sweete upon his tonge;
And in his harpyng, whan that he hadde songe,
His eyen twynkled in his heed aryght,
As doon the sterres in the frosty nyght.
This worthy lymytour was cleped Huberd.

    A MARCHANT was ther with a forked berd,
In mottelee, and hye on horse he sat;
Upon his heed a Flaundryssh bever hat,

His bootes clasped faire and fetisly.
His resons he spak ful solempnely,
Sownynge alwey th' encrees of his wynnyng.
He wolde the see were kept for any thyng
Bitwixe Middelburgh and Orewelle.
Wel koude he in eschaunge sheeldes selle.
This worthy man ful wel his wit bisette:
Ther wiste no wight that he was in dette,
So estatly was he of his governaunce
With his bargaynes and with his chevyssaunce.
For sothe he was a worthy man with alle,
But, sooth to seyn, I noot how men hym calle.

A CLERK ther was of Oxenford also,
That unto logyk hadde longe ygo.
As leene was his hors as is a rake,
And he nas nat right fat, I undertake,
But looked holwe, and therto sobrely.
Ful thredbare was his overeste courtepy;
For he hadde geten hym yet no benefice,
Ne was so worldly for to have office.
For hym was levere have at his beddes heed
Twenty bookes, clad in blak or reed,
Of Aristotle and his philosophie,
Than robes riche, or fithele, or gay sautrie.
But al be that he was a philosophre,
Yet hadde he but litel gold in cofre;
But al that he myghte of his freendes hente,
On bookes and on lernynge he it spente,
And bisily gan for the soules preye
Of hem that yaf hym wherwith to scoleye.
Of studie took he moost cure and moost heede.
Noght o word spak he moore than was neede,
And that was seyd in forme and reverence,
And short and quyk and ful of hy sentence;
Sownynge in moral vertu was his speche,
And gladly wolde he lerne and gladly teche.

A SERGEANT OF THE LAWE, war and wys,
That often hadde been at the Parvys,

Ther was also, ful riche of excellence.
Discreet he was and of greet reverence—
He semed swich, his wordes weren so wise.
Justice he was ful often in assise,
By patente and by pleyn commissioun.
For his science and for his heigh renoun,
Of fees and robes hadde he many oon.
So greet a purchasour was nowher noon:
Al was fee symple to hym in effect;
His purchasyng myghte nat been infect.
Nowher so bisy a man as he ther nas,
And yet he semed bisier than he was.
In termes hadde he caas and doomes alle
That from the tyme of kyng William were falle.
Therto he koude endite, and make a thyng,
Ther koude no wight pynche at his writyng;
And every statut koude he pleyn by rote.
He rood but hoomly in a medlee cote,
Girt with a ceint of silk, with barres smale;
Of his array telle I no lenger tale.

A FRANKELEYN was in his compaignye.
Whit was his berd as is the dayesye;
Of his complexioun he was sangwyn.
Wel loved he by the morwe a sop in wyn;
To lyven in delit was evere his wone,
For he was Epicurus owene sone,
That heeld opinioun that pleyn delit
Was verraily felicitee parfit.
An housholdere, and that a greet, was he;
Seint Julian he was in his contree.
His breed, his ale, was alweys after oon;
A bettre envyned man was nowher noon.
Withoute bake mete was nevere his hous
Of fissh and flessh, and that so plentevous,
It snewed in his hous of mete and drynke,
Of alle deyntees that men koude thynke.
After the sondry sesons of the yeer,
So chaunged he his mete and his soper.

Ful many a fat partrich hadde he in muwe,
And many a breem and many a luce in stuwe.
Wo was his cook but if his sauce were
Poynaunt and sharp, and redy al his geere.
His table dormant in his halle alway
Stood redy covered al the longe day.
At sessiouns ther was he lord and sire;
Ful ofte tyme he was knyght of the shire.
An anlaas and a gipser al of silk
Heeng at his girdel, whit as morne milk.
A shirreve hadde he been, and a countour.
Was nowher swich a worthy vavasour.

AN HABERDASSHERE and a CARPENTER,
A WEBBE, a DYERE, and a TAPYCER,—
And they were clothed alle in o lyveree
Of a solempne and a greet fraternitee.
Ful fressh and newe hir geere apiked was;
Hir knyves were chaped noght with bras
But al with silver; wroght ful clene and weel
Hire girdles and hir pouches everydeel.
Wel semed ech of hem a fair burgeys
To sitten in a yeldehalle on a deys.
Everich, for the wisdom that he kan,
Was shaply for to been an alderman.
For catel hadde they ynogh and rente,
And eek hir wyves wolde it wel assente;
And elles certeyn were they to blame.
It is ful fair to been ycleped "madame,"
And goon to vigilies al bifore,
And have a mantel roialliche ybore.

A COOK they hadde with hem for the nones
To boille the chiknes with the marybones,
And poudre-marchant tart and galyngale.
Wel koude he knowe a draughte of Londoun ale.
He koude rooste, and sethe, and broille, and frye,
Maken mortreux, and wel bake a pye.
But greet harm was it, as it thoughte me,
That on his shyne a mormal hadde he.

For blankmanger, that made he with the beste.
  A SHIPMAN was ther, wonynge fer by weste;
For aught I woot, he was of Dertemouthe.
He rood upon a rouncy, as he kouthe,
In a gowne of faldyng to the knee.
A daggere hangynge on a laas hadde he
Aboute his nekke, under his arm adoun.
The hoote somer hadde maad his hewe al broun;
And certeinly he was a good felawe.
Ful many a draughte of wyn had he ydrawe
Fro Burdeux-ward, whil that the chapman sleep.
Of nyce conscience took he no keep.
If that he faught, and hadde the hyer hond,
By water he sente hem hoom to every lond.
But of his craft to rekene wel his tydes,
His stremes, and his daungers hym bisides,
His herberwe, and his moone, his lode-menage,
Ther nas noon swich from Hulle to Cartage.
Hardy he was and wys to undertake;
With many a tempest hadde his berd been shake.
He knew alle the havenes, as they were,
Fro Gootlond to the cape of Fynystere,
And every cryke in Britaigne and in Spayne.
His barge ycleped was the Maudelayne.
  With us ther was a DOCTOUR OF PHISIK;
In al this world ne was ther noon hym lik,
To speke of phisik and of surgerye,
For he was grounded in astronomye.
He kepte his pacient a ful greet deel
In houres by his magyk natureel.
Wel koude he fortunen the ascendent
Of his ymages for his pacient.
He knew the cause of everich maladye,
Were it of hoot, or coold, or moyste, or drye,
And where they engendred, and of what humour.
He was a verray, parfit, praktisour:
The cause yknowe, and of his harm the roote,
Anon he yaf the sike man his boote.

Ful redy hadde he his apothecaries
To sende hym drogges and his letuaries,
For ech of hem made oother for to wynne—
Hir frendshipe nas nat newe to bigynne.
Wel knew he the olde Esculapius,
And Deyscorides, and eek Rufus,
Olde Ypocras, Haly, and Galyen,
Serapion, Razis, and Avycen,
Averrois, Damascien, and Constantyn,
Bernard, and Gatesden, and Gilbertyn.
Of his diete mesurable was he,
For it was of no superfluitee,
But of greet norissyng and digestible.
His studie was but litel on the Bible.
In sangwyn and in pers he clad was al,
Lyned with taffata and with sendal;
And yet he was but esy of dispence;
He kepte that he wan in pestilence.
For gold in phisik is a cordial,
Therefore he lovede gold in special.

A good WIF was ther OF biside BATHE,
But she was somdel deef, and that was scathe.
Of clooth-makyng she hadde swich an haunt,
She passed hem of Ypres and of Gaunt.
In al the parisshe wif ne was ther noon
That to the offrynge bifore hire sholde goon;
And if ther dide, certeyn so wrooth was she,
That she was out of alle charitee.
Hir coverchiefs ful fyne weren of ground;
I dorste swere they weyeden ten pound
That on a Sonday weren upon hir heed.
Hir hosen weren of fyn scarlet reed,
Ful streite yteyd, and shoes ful moyste and newe.
Boold was hir face, and fair, and reed of hewe.
She was a worthy womman al hir lyve:
Housbondes at chirche dore she hadde fyve,
Withouten oother compaignye in youthe,—
But therof nedeth nat to speke as nowthe.

And thries hadde she been at Jerusalem;
She hadde passed many a straunge strem;
At Rome she hadde been, and at Boloigne,
In Galice at Seint Jame, and at Coloigne.
She koude muchel of wandrynge by the weye.
Gat-tothed was she, soothly for to seye.
Upon an amblere esily she sat,
Ywympled wel, and on hir heed an hat
As brood as is a bokeler or a targe;
A foot-mantel aboute hir hipes large,
And on hir feet a paire of spores sharpe.
In felaweshipe wel koude she laughe and carpe.
Of remedies of love she knew per chaunce,
For she koude of that art the olde daunce.

A good man was ther of religioun,
And was a povre PERSOUN OF A TOUN,
But riche he was of hooly thoght and werk.
He was also a lerned man, a clerk,
That Cristes gospel trewely wolde preche;
His parisshens devoutly wolde he teche.
Benygne he was, and wonder diligent,
And in adversitee ful pacient,
And swich he was ypreved ofte sithes.
Ful looth were hym to cursen for his tithes,
But rather wolde he yeven, out of doute,
Unto his povre parisshens aboute
Of his offryng and eek of his substaunce.
He koude in litel thyng have suffisaunce.
Wyd was his parisshe, and houses fer asonder,
But he ne lefte nat, for reyn ne thonder,
In siknesse nor in meschief to visite
The ferreste in his parisshe, muche and lite,
Upon his feet, and in his hand a staf.
This noble ensample to his sheep he yaf,
That first he wroghte, and afterward he taughte.
Out of the gospel he tho wordes caughte,
And this figure he added eek therto,
That if gold ruste, what shal iren do?

For if a preest be foul, on whom we truste,
No wonder is a lewed man to ruste;
And shame it is, if a preest take keep,
A shiten shepherde and a clene sheep.
Wel oghte a preest ensample for to yive,
By his clennesse, how that his sheep sholde lyve.
He sette nat his benefice to hyre
And leet his sheep encombred in the myre
And ran to Londoun unto Seinte Poules
To seken hym a chaunterie for soules,
Or with a bretherhed to been withholde;
But dwelte at hoom, and kepte wel his folde,
So that the wolf ne made it nat myscarie;
He was a shepherde and noght a mercenarie.
And though he hooly were and vertuous,
He was to synful men nat despitous,
Ne of his speche daungerous ne digne,
But in his techyng discreet and benygne.
To drawen folk to hevene by fairnesse,
By good ensample, this was his bisynesse.
But it were any persone obstinat,
What so he were, of heigh or lough estat,
Hym wolde he snybben sharply for the nonys.
A bettre preest I trowe that nowher noon ys.
He waited after no pompe and reverence,
Ne maked him a spiced conscience,
But Cristes loore and his apostles twelve
He taughte, but first he folwed it hymselve.

    With hym ther was a PLOWMAN, was his brother,
That hadde ylad of dong ful many a fother;
A trewe swynkere and a good was he,
Lyvynge in pees and parfit charitee.
God loved he best with al his hoole herte
At alle tymes, thogh him gamed or smerte,
And thanne his neighebor right as hymselve.
He wolde thresshe, and therto dyke and delve,
For Christes sake, for every povre wight,
Withouten hire, if it lay in his myght.

His tithes payde he ful faire and wel,
Bothe of his propre swynk and his catel.
In a tabard he rood upon a mere.

Ther was also a REVE, and a MILLERE,
A SOMNOUR, and a PARDONER also,
A MAUNCIPLE, and myself—ther were namo.

The MILLERE was a stout carl for the nones;
Ful byg he was of brawn, and eek of bones.
That proved wel, for over al ther he cam,
At wrastlynge he wolde have alwey the ram.
He was short-sholdred, brood, a thikke knarre;
Ther was no dore that he nolde heve of harre,
Or breke it at a rennyng with his heed.
His berd as any sowe or fox was reed,
And therto brood, as though it were a spade.
Upon the cop right of his nose he hade
A werte, and theron stood a toft of herys,
Reed as the brustles of a sowes erys;
His nosethirles blake were and wyde.
A swerd and bokeler bar he by his syde.
His mouth as greet was as a greet forneys.
He was a janglere and a goliardeys,
And that was moost of synne and harlotries.
Wel koude he stelen corn and tollen thries;
And yet he hadde a thombe of gold, pardee.
A whit cote and a blew hood wered he.
A baggepipe wel koude he blowe and sowne,
And therwithal he broghte us out of towne.

A gentil MAUNCIPLE was ther of a temple,
Of which achatours myghte take exemple
For to be wise in byynge of vitaille;
For wheither that he payde or took by taille
Algate he wayted so in his achaat
That he was ay biforn and in good staat.
Now is nat that of God a ful fair grace
That swich a lewed mannes wit shal pace
The wisdom of an heep of lerned men?
Of maistres hadde he mo than thries ten,

That weren of lawe expert and curious,
Of which ther were a duszeyne in that hous
Worthy to been stywardes of rente and lond
Of any lord that is in Engelond,
To make hym lyve by his propre good
In honour dettelees (but if he were wood),
Or lyve as scarsly as hym list desire;
And able for to helpen al a shire
In any caas that myghte falle or happe;
And yet this Manciple sette hir aller cappe.

    The REVE was a sclendre colerik man.
His berd was shave as ny as ever he kan;
His heer was by his erys ful round yshorn;
His top was dokked lyk a preest biforn.
Ful longe were his legges and ful lene,
Ylyk a staf, ther was no calf ysene.
Wel koude he kepe a gerner and a bynne;
Ther was noon auditour koude on him wynne.
Wel wiste he by the droghte and by the reyn
The yeldynge of his seed and of his greyn.
His lordes sheep, his neet, his dayerye,
His swyn, his hors, his stoor, and his pultrye
Was hoolly in this Reves governyng,
And by his covenant yaf the rekenyng,
Syn that his lord was twenty yeer of age.
Ther koude no man brynge hym in arrerage.
Ther nas bailif, ne hierde, nor oother hyne,
That he ne knew his sleighte and his covyne;
They were adrad of hym as of the deeth.
His wonyng was ful faire upon an heeth;
With grene trees yshadwed was his place.
He koude bettre than his lord purchace.
Ful riche he was astored pryvely:
His lord wel koude he plesen subtilly,
To yeve and lene hym of his owene good,
And have a thank, and yet a cote and hood.
In youthe he hadde lerned a good myster;
He was a wel good wrighte, a carpenter.

This Reve sat upon a ful good stot,
That was al pomely grey and highte Scot.
A long surcote of pers upon he hade,
And by his syde he baar a rusty blade.
Of Northfolk was this Reve of which I telle,
Biside a toun men clepen Baldeswelle.
Tukked he was as is a frere aboute,
And evere he rood the hyndreste of oure route.

A SOMONOUR was ther with us in that place,
That hadde a fyr-reed cherubynnes face,
For saucefleem he was, with eyen narwe.
As hoot he was and lecherous as a sparwe,
With scalled browes blake and piled berd.
Of his visage children were aferd.
Ther nas quyk-silver, lytarge, ne brymstoon,
Boras, ceruce, ne oille of tartre noon;
Ne oynement that wolde clense and byte,
That hym myghte helpen of his whelkes white,
Nor of the knobbes sittynge on his chekes.
Wel loved he garleek, oynons, and eek lekes,
And for to drynken strong wyn, reed as blood;
Thanne wolde he speke and crie as he were wood.
And whan that he wel dronken hadde the wyn,
Thanne wolde he speke no word but Latyn.
A fewe termes hadde he, two or thre,
That he had lerned out of som decree—
No wonder is, he herde it al the day;
And eek ye knowen wel how that a jay
Kan clepen "Watte" as wel as kan the pope.
But whoso koude in oother thyng hym grope,
Thanne hadde he spent al his philosophie;
Ay *"Questio quid iuris"* wolde he crie.
He was a gentil harlot and a kynde;
A bettre felawe sholde men noght fynde.
He wolde suffre for a quart of wyn
A good felawe to have his concubyn
A twelf month, and excuse hym atte fulle;
Ful prively a fynch eek koude he pulle.

And if he foond owher a good felawe,
He wolde techen him to have noon awe
In swich caas of the ercedekenes curs,
But if a mannes soule were in his purs;
For in his purs he sholde ypunysshed be.
"Purs is the ercedekenes helle," seyde he.
But wel I woot he lyed right in dede;
Of cursyng oghte ech gilty man him drede,
For curs wol slee right as assoillyng savith,
And also war hym of a *Significavit*.
In daunger hadde he at his owene gise
The yonge girles of the diocise,
And knew hir conseil, and was al hir reed.
A gerland hadde he set upon his heed
As greet as it were for an ale-stake.
A bokeleer hadde he maad hym of a cake.

 With hym ther rood a gentil PARDONER
Of Rouncivale, his freend and his compeer,
That streight was comen fro the court of Rome.
Ful loude he soong "Com hider, love, to me!"
This Somonour bar to hym a stif burdoun;
Was nevere trompe of half so greet a soun.
This Pardoner hadde heer as yelow as wex,
But smothe it heeng as dooth a strike of flex;
By ounces henge his lokkes that he hadde,
And therwith he his shuldres overspradde;
But thynne it lay, by colpons oon and oon.
But hood, for jolitee, wered he noon,
For it was trussed up in his walet.
Hym thoughte he rood al of the newe jet;
Dischevelee, save his cappe, he rood al bare.
Swiche glarynge eyen hadde he as an hare.
A vernycle hadde he sowed upon his cappe.
His walet lay biforn hym in his lappe,
Bretful of pardoun, comen from Rome al hoot.
A voys he hadde as smal as hath a goot.
No berd hadde he, ne nevere sholde have;
As smothe it was as it were late shave.

I trowe he were a geldyng or a mare.
But of his craft, fro Berwyk into Ware,
Ne was ther swich another pardoner.
For in his male he hadde a pilwe-beer,
Which that he seyde was Oure Lady veyl:
He seyde he hadde a gobet of the seyl
That Seint Peter hadde, whan that he wente
Upon the see, til Jhesu Crist hym hente.
He hadde a croys of latoun ful of stones,
And in a glas he hadde pigges bones.
But with thise relikes, whan that he fond
A povre person dwellynge upon lond,
Upon a day he gat hym moore moneye
Than that the person gat in monthes tweye;
And thus, with feyned flaterye and japes,
He made the person and the peple his apes.
But trewely to tellen atte laste,
He was in chirche a noble ecclesiaste.
Wel koude he rede a lessoun or a storie,
But alderbest he song an offertorie;
For wel he wiste, whan that song was songe,
He moste preche and wel affile his tonge
To wynne silver, as he ful wel koude;
Therefore he song the murierly and loude.

Now have I toold you shortly, in a clause,
Th'estaat, th'array, the nombre, and eek the cause
Why that assembled was this compaignye
In Southwerk at this gentil hostelrye
That highte the Tabard, faste by the Belle.
But now is tyme to yow for to telle
How that we baren us that ilke nyght,
Whan we were in that hostelrie alyght;
And after wol I telle of our viage
And al the remenaunt of oure pilgrimage.
But first I pray yow, of youre curteisye,
That ye n'arette it nat my vileynye,
Thogh that I pleynly speke in this mateere,
To telle yow hir wordes and hir cheere,

Ne thogh I speke hir wordes proprely.
For this ye knowen al so wel as I,
Whoso shal telle a tale after a man,
He moot reherce as ny as evere he kan
Everich a word, if it be in his charge,
Al speke he never so rudeliche and large,
Or ellis he moot telle his tale untrewe,
Or feyne thyng, or fynde wordes newe.
He may nat spare, althogh he were his brother;
He moot as wel seye o word as another.
Crist spak hymself ful brode in hooly writ,
And wel ye woot no vileynye is it.
Eek Plato seith, whoso that kan hym rede,
The wordes moote be cosyn to the dede.
Also I prey yow to foryeve it me,
Al have I nat set folk in hir degree
Heere in this tale, as that they sholde stonde.
My wit is short, ye may wel understonde.

   Greet chiere made oure Hoost us everichon,
And to the soper sette he us anon.
He served us with vitaille at the beste;
Strong was the wyn, and wel to drynke us leste.
A semely man OURE HOOSTE was withalle
For to han been a marchal in an halle.
A large man he was with eyen stepe—
A fairer burgeys is ther noon in Chepe—
Boold of his speche, and wys, and wel ytaught,
And of manhod hym lakkede right naught.
Eek therto he was right a myrie man,
And after soper pleyen he bigan,
And spak of myrthe amonges othere thynges,
Whan that we hadde maad our rekenynges,
And seyde thus: "Now, lordynges, trewely,
Ye been to me right welcome, hertely;
For by my trouthe, if that I shal nat lye,
I saugh nat this yeer so myrie a compaignye
Atones in this herberwe as is now.
Fayn wolde I doon yow myrthe, wiste I how.

And of a myrthe I am right now bythoght,
To doon yow ese, and it shal coste noght.
    Ye goon to Caunterbury—God yow speede,
The blisful martir quite yow youre meedel
And wel I woot, as ye goon by the weye,
Ye shapen yow to talen and to pleye;
For trewely, confort ne myrthe is noon
To ride by the weye doumb as a stoon;
And therfore wol I maken yow disport,
As I seyde erst, and doon yow som confort.
And if yow liketh alle by oon assent
For to stonden at my juggement,
And for to werken as I shal yow seye,
To-morwe, whan ye riden by the weye,
Now, by my fader soule that is deed,
But ye be myrie, I wol yeve yow myn heedl
Hoold up youre hondes, withouten moore speche."
    Oure conseil was nat longe for to seche.
Us thoughte it was noght worth to make it wys,
And graunted hym withouten moore avys,
And bad him seye his voirdit as hym leste.
"Lordynges," quod he, "now herkneth for the beste;
But taak it nought, I prey yow, in desdeyn.
This is the poynt, to speken short and pleyn,
That ech of yow, to shorte with oure weye,
In this viage shal telle tales tweye
To Caunterbury-ward, I mene it so,
And homward he shal tellen othere two,
Of aventures that whilom han bifalle.
And which of yow that bereth hym best of alle,
That is to seyn, that telleth in this caas
Tales of best sentence and moost solaas,
Shal have a soper at oure aller cost
Heere in this place, sittynge by this post,
Whan that we come agayn fro Caunterbury.
And for to make yow the moore mury,
I wol myselven goodly with yow ryde,
Right at myn owene cost, and be youre gyde;

And whoso wole my juggement withseye
Shal paye al that we spenden by the weye.
And if ye vouche sauf that it be so,
Tel me anon, withouten wordes mo,
And I wol erly shape me therfore."

This thyng was graunted, and oure othes swore
With ful glad herte, and preyden hym also
That he wolde vouche sauf for to do so,
And that he wolde been oure governour,
And of our tales juge and reportour,
And sette a soper at a certeyn pris,
And we wol reuled been at his devys
In heigh and lough; and thus by oon assent
We been acorded to his juggement.
And therupon the wyn was fet anon;
We dronken, and to reste wente echon,
Withouten any lenger taryynge.

Amorwe, whan that day bigan to sprynge,
Up roos oure Hoost, and was oure aller cok,
And gadrede us togidre alle in a flok,
And forth we riden a litel moore than paas
Unto the wateryng of Seint Thomas;
And there oure Hoost bigan his hors areste
And seyde, "Lordynges, herkneth, if yow leste.
Ye woot youre foreward, and I it yow recorde.
If even-song and morwe-song accorde,
Lat se now who shal telle the firste tale.
As evere mote I drynke wyn or ale,
Whoso be rebel to my juggement
Shal paye for al that by the wey is spent.
Now draweth cut, er that we ferrer twynne;
He which that hath the shorteste shal bigynne.
Sire Knyght," quod he, "my mayster and my lord,
Now draweth cut, for that is myn accord.
Cometh neer," quod he, "my lady Prioresse.
And ye, sire Clerk, lat be youre shamefastnesse,
Ne studieth noght; ley hond to, every man!"
Anon to drawen every wight bigan,

And shortly for to tellen as it was,
Were it by aventure, or sort, or cas,
The sothe is this, the cut fil to the Knyght,
Of which ful blithe and glad was every wyght,
And telle he moste his tale, as was resoun,
By foreward and by composicioun,
As ye han herd; what nedeth wordes mo?
And whan this goode man saugh that it was so,
As he that wys was and obedient
To kepe his foreward by his free assent,
He seyde, "Syn I shal bigynne the game,
What, welcome be the cut, a Goddes name!
Now lat us ryde, and herkneth what I seye."
And with that word we ryden forth oure weye,
And he bigan with right a myrie cheere
His tale anon, and seyde in this manere.

THE NUN'S PRIEST'S TALE

*Heere bigynneth the Nonnes Preestes Tale
of the Cok and Hen, Chauntecleer and Pertelote.*

A povre wydwe, somdeel stape in age
Was whilom dwellyng in a narwe cotage,
Biside a grove, stondynge in a dale.
This wydwe, of which I telle yow my tale,
Syn thilke day that she was last a wyf,
In pacience ladde a ful symple lyf,
For litel was hir catel and hir rente.
By housbondrie of swich as God hire sente
She foond hirself and eek hir doghtren two.
Thre large sowes hadde she, and namo,
Three keen, and eek a sheep that highte Malle.
Ful sooty was hire bour and eek hir halle,
In which she eet ful many a sklendre meel.
Of poynaunt sauce hir neded never a deel.
No deyntee morsel passed thurgh hir throte;
Hir diete was accordant to hir cote.
Repleccioun ne made hire nevere sik;
Attempree diete was al hir phisik,
And exercise, and hertes suffisaunce.
The goute lette hire nothyng for to daunce,
N'apoplexie shente nat hir heed.
No wyn ne drank she, neither whit ne reed;
Hir bord was served moost with whit and blak,
Milk and broun breed, in which she foond no lak,
Seynd bacoun, and somtyme an ey or tweye;
For she was, as it were, a maner deye.
    A yeerd she hadde, enclosed al aboute

367

With stikkes, and a drye dych withoute,
In which she hadde a cok, hight Chauntecleer.
In al the land, of crowyng nas his peer.
His voys was murier than the murie orgon
On messe-dayes that in the chirche gon.
Wel sikerer was his crowyng in his logge
Than is a clokke or an abbey orlogge.
By nature he knew ech ascencioun
Of the equynoxial in thilke toun;
For whan degrees fiftene weren ascended,
Thanne crew he, that it myghte nat been amended.
His coomb was redder than the fyn coral,
And batailled as it were a castel wal;
His byle was blak, and as the jeet it shoon;
Lyk asure were his legges and his toon;
His nayles whitter than the lylye flour,
And lyk the burned gold was his colour.
This gentil cok hadde in his governaunce
Sevene hennes for to doon al his plesaunce,
Whiche were his sustres and his paramours,
And wonder lyk to hym, as of colours;
Of whiche the faireste hewed on hir throte
Was cleped faire damoysele Pertelote.
Curteys she was, discreet, and debonaire,
And compaignable, and bar hyrself so faire,
Syn thilke day that she was seven nyght oold,
That trewely she hath the herte in hoold
Of Chauntecleer, loken in every lith;
He loved hire so that wel was hym therwith.
But swich a joye was it to here hem synge,
Whan that the brighte sonne gan to sprynge,
In sweete accord, "My lief is faren in londe!"
For thilke tyme, as I have understonde,
Beestes and briddes koude speke and synge.

And so bifel that in a dawenynge,
As Chauntecleer among his wyves alle
Sat on his perche, that was in the halle,
And next hym sat this faire Pertelote,

This Chauntecleer gan gronen in his throte,
As man that in his dreem is drecched soore.
And whan that Pertelote thus herde hym roore,
She was agast, and seyde, "Herte deere,
What eyleth yow, to grone in this manere?
Ye been a verray sleper; fy, for shame!"
    And he answerde, and seyde thus: "Madame,
I pray yow that ye take it nat agrief.
By God, me mette I was in swich meschief
Right now, that yet myn herte is soore afright.
Now God" quod he, "my swevene recche aright,
And kepe my body out of foul prisoun!
Me mette how that I romed up and doun
Withinne our yeerd, wheer as I saugh a beest
Was lyk an hound, and wolde han maad areest
Upon my body, and wolde han had me deed.
His colour was bitwixe yelow and reed,
And tipped was his tayl and bothe his eeris
With blak, unlyk the remenant of his heeris;
His snowte smal, with glowynge eyen tweye.
Yet of his look for feere almoost I deye;
This caused me my gronyng, doutelees."
    "Avoy!" quod she, "fy on yow, herteleees!
Allas!" quod she, "for, by that God above,
Now han ye lost myn herte and al my love.
I kan nat love a coward, by my feith!
For certes, what so any womman seith,
We alle desiren, if it myghte bee,
To han housbondes hardy, wise, and free,
And secree, and no nygard, ne no fool,
Ne hym that is agast of every tool,
Ne noon avauntour, by that God above!
How dorste ye seyn, for shame, unto youre love
That any thyng myghte make yow aferd?
Have yo no mannes herte, and han a berd?
Allas! and konne ye been agast of swevenys?
Nothyng, God woot, but vanitee in sweven is.
Swevenes engendren of repleccriouns,

And ofte of fume and of complecciouns,
Whan humours been to habundant in a wight.
Certes this dreem, which ye han met tonyght,
Cometh of the greete superfluytee
Of youre rede colera, pardee,
Which causeth folk to dreden in hir dremes
Of arwes, and of fyr with rede lemes,
Of rede beestes, that they wol hem byte,
Of contek, and of whelpes, grete and lyte;
Right as the humour of malencolie
Causeth ful many a man in sleep to crie
For feere of blake beres, or boles blake,
Or elles blake develes wole hem take.
Of othere humours koude I telle also
That werken many a man in sleep ful wo;
But I wol passe as lightly as I kan.
    Lo Catoun, which that was so wys a man,
Seyde he nat thus, 'Ne do no fors of dremes?'
    Now sire," quod she, "whan we flee fro the bemes,
For Goddes love, as taak som laxatyf.
Up peril of my soule and of my lyf,
I conseille yow the beste, I wol nat lye,
That bothe of colere and of malencolye
Ye purge yow; and for ye shal nat tarie,
Though in this toun is noon apothecarie,
I shal myself to herbes techen yow
That shul been for youre hele and for youre prow;
And in oure yeerd tho herbes shal I fynde
The whiche han of hire propretee by kynde
To purge yow bynethe and eek above.
Foryet nat this, for Goddes owene love!
Ye been ful coleryk of compleccioun;
Ware the sonne in his ascencioun
Ne fynde yow nat repleet of humours hoote.
And if it do, I dar wel leye a grote,
That ye shul have a fever terciane,
Or an agu, that may be youre bane.
A day or two ye shul have digestyves

Of wormes, er ye take youre laxatyves
Of lawriol, centaure, and fumetere,
Or elles of ellebor, that groweth there,
Of katapuce, or of gaitrys beryis,
Of herbe yve, growyng in oure yeerd, ther mery is;
Pekke hem up right as they growe and ete hem yn.
Be myrie, housbonde, for youre fader kyn!
Dredeth no dreem, I kan sey yow namoore."

   "Madame," quod he, "graunt mercy of youre loore.
But nathelees, as touchyng daun Catoun,
That hath of wysdom swich a greet renoun,
Though that he bad no dremes for to drede,
By God, men may in olde bookes rede
Of many a man moore of auctorite
Than evere Caton was, so moot I thee,
That al the revers seyn of this sentence,
And han wel founden by experience
That dremes been significaciouns
As wel of joye as of tribulaciouns
That folk enduren in this lif present.
Ther nedeth make of this noon argument;
The verray preeve sheweth it in dede.

   Oon of the gretteste auctour that men rede
Seith thus; that whilom two felawes wente
On pilgrimage, in a ful good entente;
And happed so, they coomen in a toun
Wher as ther was swich congregacioun
Of peple, and eek so streit of herbergage,
That they ne founde as much as o cotage
In which they bothe myghte ylogged bee.
Wherfore they mosten of necessitee,
As for that nyght, departen compaignye;
And ech of hem gooth to his hostelrye,
And took his loggyng as it wolde falle.
That oon of hem was logged in a stalle,
Fer in a yeerd, with oxen of the plough;
That oother man was logged wel ynough,
As was his aventure or his fortune,

That us governeth alle as in commune.
    And so bifel that, longe er it were day,
This man mette in his bed, ther as he lay,
How that his felawe gan upon hym calle,
And seyde, 'Allas! for in an oxes stalle
This nyght I shal be mordred ther I lye.
Now help me, deere brother, or I dye.
In alle haste com to me!' he sayde.
This man out of his sleep for feere abrayde;
But whan that he was wakened of his sleep,
He turned hym, and took of this no keep.
Hym thoughte his dreem nas but a vanitee.
Thus twies in his slepyng dremed hee;
And atte thridde tyme yet his felawe
Cam, as hym thoughte, and seide, 'I am now slawe.
Bihoold my bloody woundes depe and wyde!
Arys up erly in the morwe tyde,
And at the west gate of the toun,' quod he,
'A carte ful of dong ther shaltow se,
In which my body is hid ful prively;
Do thilke carte arresten boldely.
My gold caused my mordre, sooth to sayn.'
And tolde hym every point how he was slayn,
With a ful pitous face, pale of hewe.
And truste wel, his dreem he foond ful trewe,
For on the morwe, as soone as it was day,
To his felawes in he took the way;
And whan that he cam to this oxes stalle,
After his felawe he bigan to calle.
    The hostiler answerede hym anon,
And seyde, 'Sire, your felawe is agon.
As soone as day he wente out of the toun.'
    This man gan fallen in suspecioun,
Remembrynge on his dremes that he mette,
And forth he gooth—no lenger wolde he lette—
Unto the west gate of the toun, and fond
A dong-carte, wente as it were to donge lond,
That was arrayed in that same wise

As ye han herd the dede man devyse.
And with an hardy herte he gan to crye
Vengeance and justice of this felonye.
'My felawe mordred is this same nyght,
And in this carte he lith gapyng upright.
I crye out on the ministres,' quod he,
'That sholden kepe and reulen this citee.
Harrow! allas! heere lith my felawe slayn!'
What sholde I moore unto this tale sayn?
The peple out sterte and caste the cart to grounde,
And in the myddel of the dong they founde
The dede man, that mordred was al newe.

O blisful God, that art so just and trewe,
Lo, how that thou biwreyest mordre alway!
Mordre wol out, that se we day by day.
Mordre is so wlatsom and abhomynable
To God, that is so just and resonable,
That he ne wol nat suffre it heled be,
Though it abyde a yeer, or two, or thre.
Morde wol out, this my conclusioun.
And right anon, ministres of that toun
Han hent the carter and so soore hym pyned,
And eek the hostiler so soore engyned,
That they biknewe hire wikkednesse anon,
And were anhanged by the nekke-bon.

Heere may men seen that dremes been to drede.
And certes in the same book I rede,
Right in the nexte chapitre after this—
I gabbe nat, so have I joye or blis—
Two men that wolde han passed over see,
For certeyn cause, into a fer contree,
If that the wynd ne hadde been contrarie,
That made hem in a citee for to tarie
That stood ful myrie upon an haven-syde;
But on a day, agayn the even-tyde,
The wynd gan chaunge, and blew right as hem leste.
Jolif and glad they wente unto hir reste,
And casten hem ful erly for to saille.

But to that o man fil a greet mervaille:
That oon of hem, in slepyng as he lay,
Hym mette a wonder dreem agayn the day.
Hym thoughte a man stood by his beddes syde,
And hym comanded that he sholde abyde,
And seyde hym thus; 'If thou tomorwe wende,
Thow shalt be dreynt; my tale is at an ende.'
He wook, and tolde his felawe what he mette,
And preyde hym his viage for to lette;
As for that day, he preyde hym to byde.
His felawe, that lay by his beddes syde,
Gan for to laughe, and scorned him ful faste.
'No dreem,' quod he, 'may so myn herte agaste
That I wol lette for to do my thynges.
I sette nat a straw by thy dremynges,
For swevenes been but vanytees and japes.
Men dreme alday of owles and of apes,
And eek of many a maze therwithal;
Men dreme of thyng that nevere was ne shal.
But sith I see that thou wolt heere abyde,
And thus forslewthen wilfully thy tyde,
God woot, it reweth me; and have good day!'
And thus he took his leve, and wente his way.
But er that he hadde half his cours yseyled,
Noot I nat why, ne what myschaunce it eyled,
But casuelly the shippes botme rente,
And ship and man under the water wente
In sighte of othere shippes it bisyde,
That with hem seyled at the same tyde.
And therfore, faire Pertelote so deere,
By swiche ensamples olde maistow leere
That no man sholde been to recchelees
Of dremes; for I seye thee, douteless,
That many a dreem ful soore is for to drede.

    Lo, in the lyf of Seint Kenelm I rede,
That was Kenulphus sone, the noble kyng
Of Mercenrike, how Kenelm mette a thyng.
A lite er he was mordred, on a day,

His mordre in his avysioun he say.
His norice hym expowned every deel
His sweven, and bad hym for to kepe hym weel
For traisoun; but he nas but seven yeer oold,
And therfore litel tale hath he toold
Of any dreem, so hooly was his herte.
By God! I hadde levere than my sherte
That ye hadde rad his legende, as have I.
  Dame Pertelote, I sey yow trewely,
Macrobeus, that writ the avisioun
In Affrike of the worthy Cipioun,
Affermeth dremes, and seith that they been
Warnynge of thynges that men after seen.
And forthermoore, I pray yow, looketh wel
In the olde testament, of Daniel,
If he heeld dremes any vanitee.
Reed eek of Joseph, and ther shul ye see
Wher dremes be somtyme—I sey nat alle—
Warnynge of thynges that shul after falle.
Looke of Egipte the kyng, daun Pharao,
His bakere and his butiller also,
Wher they ne felte noon effect in dremes.
Whoso wol seken actes of sondry remes
May rede of dremes many a wonder thyng.
Lo Cresus, which that was of Lyde kyng,
Mette he nat that he sat upon a tree,
Which signified he sholde anhanged bee?
Lo heere Andromacha, Ectores wyf,
That day that Ector sholde lese his lyf,
She dremed on the same nyght biforn
How that the lyf of Ector sholde be lorn,
If thilke day he wente into bataille.
She warned hym, but it myghte nat availle;
He wente for to fighte natheles,
But he was slayn anon of Achilles.
But thilke tale is al to longe to telle,
And eek it is ny day, I may nat dwelle.
Shortly I seye, as for conclusioun,

That I shal han of this avisioun
Adversitee; and I seye forthermoor,
That I ne telle of laxatyves no stoor,
For they been venymous, I woot it weel;
I hem diffye, I love hem never a deel!
  Now let us speke of myrthe, and stynte al this.
Madame Pertelote, so have I blis,
Of o thyng God hath sent me large grace;
For whan I se the beautee of youre face,
Ye been so scarlet reed aboute youre yen,
It maketh al my drede for to dyen;
For al so siker as *In principio*,
Mulier est hominis confusio,—
Madame, the sentence of this Latyn is,
'Womman is mannes joye and al his blis.'
For whan I feel a-nyght your softe syde,
Al be it that I may nat on yow ryde,
For that oure perche is maad so narwe, allas!
I am so ful of joy and of solas,
That I diffye bothe sweven and dreem."
And with that word he fley doun fro the beem,
For it was day, and eke his hennes alle,
And with a chuk he gan hem for to calle,
For he hadde founde a corn, lay in the yerd.
Real he was, he was namoore aferd.
He fethered Pertelote twenty tyme,
And trad hire eke as ofte, er it was pryme.
He looketh as it were a grym leoun,
And on his toos he rometh up and doun;
Hym deigned nat to sette his foot to grounde.
He chukketh, whan he hath a corn yfounde,
And to hym rennen thanne his wyves alle.
Thus roial, as a prince is in his halle,
Leve I this Chauntecleer in his pasture,
And after wol I telle his aventure.
  Whan that the month in which the world bigan,
That highte March, whan God first maked man,
Was compleet, and passed were also,

Syn March bigan, thritty dayes and two,
Bifel that Chauntecleer in al his pryde,
His sevene wyves walkynge by his syde,
Caste up his eyen to the brighte sonne,
That in the signe of Taurus hadde yronne
Twenty degrees and oon, and somwhat moore,
And knew by kynde, and by noon oother loore,
That it was pryme, and crew with blisful stevene.
"The sonne," he seyde, "is clomben up on hevene
Fourty degrees and oon, and moore ywis.
Madame Pertelote, my worldes blis,
Herkneth thise blisful briddes how they synge,
And se the fresshe floures how they sprynge,
Ful is myn herte of revel and solas!"
But sodeynly hym fil a sorweful cas,
For evere the latter ende of joye is wo.
God woot that worldly joye is soone ago;
And if a rethor koude faire endite,
He in a cronycle saufly myghte it write
As for a sovereyn notabilitee.
Now every wys man, lat him herkne me;
This storie is also trewe, I undertake,
As is the book of Launcelot de Lake,
That wommen holde in ful greet reverence.
Now wol I torne agayn to my sentence.

A col-fox, ful of sly iniquitee,
That in the grove hadde woned yeres three,
By heigh ymaginacioun forncast,
The same nyght thurghout the hegges brast
Into the yerd ther Chauntecleer the faire
Was wont, and eek his wyves, to repaire;
And in a bed of wortes stille he lay,
Til it was passed undren of the day,
Waitynge his tyme on Chauntecleer to falle,
As gladly doon thise homycides alle
That in await liggen to mordre men.
O false mordrour, lurkynge in thy den!
O newe Scariot, newe Genylon,

False dissymulour, o Greek Synon,
That broghtest Troye al outrely to sorwe!
O Chauntecleer, acursed be that morwe
That thou into that yerd flaugh fro the bemes!
Thou were ful wel ywarned by thy dremes
That thilke day was perilous to thee;
But what that God forwoot moot nedes bee,
After the opinioun of certein clerkis.
Witnesse on hym that any parfit clerk is,
That in scole is greet altercacioun
In this mateere, and greet disputisoun,
And hath been of an hundred thousand men.
But I ne kan nat bulte it to the bren,
As kan the hooly doctour Augustyn,
Or Boece, or the Bisshop Bradwardyn,
Wheither that Goddes worthy forwityng
Streyneth me nedely for to doon a thyng,—
"Nedely" clepe I symple necessitee;
Or elles, if free choys be graunted me
To do that same thyng, or do it noght,
Though God forwoot it er that it was wroght;
Or if his wityng streyneth never a deel
But by necessitee condicioneel.
I wol nat han to do of swich mateere;
My tale is of a cok, as ye may heere,
That tok his conseil of his wyf, with sorwe,
To walken in the yerd upon that morwe
That he hadde met that dreem that I yow tolde.
Wommennes conseils been ful ofte colde;
Wommannes conseil broghte us first to wo,
And made Adam fro Paradys to go,
Ther as he was ful myrie and wel at ese.
But for I noot to whom it myght displese,
If I conseil of wommen wolde blame,
Passe over, for I seyde it in my game.
Rede auctours, where they trete of swich mateere,
And what they seyn of wommen ye may heere.
Thise been the cokkes wordes, and nat myne;

I kan noon harm of no womman divyne.
  Faire in the soond, to bathe hire myrily,
Lith Pertelote, and alle hire sustres by,
Agayn the sonne, and Chauntecleer so free
Soong murier than the mermayde in the see;
For Phisiologus seith sikerly
How that they syngen wel and myrily.
And so bifel that, as he caste his ye
Among the wortes on a boterflye,
He was war of this fox, that lay ful lowe.
Nothyng ne liste hym thanne for to crowe,
But cride anon, "Cok! cok!" and up he sterte
As man that was affrayed in his herte.
For natureelly a beest desireth flee
Fro his contrarie, if he may it see,
Though he never erst hadde seyn it with his ye.
  This Chauntecleer, whan he gan hym espye,
He wolde han fled, but that the fox anon
Seyde, "Gentil sire, allas! wher wol ye gon?
Be ye affrayed of me that am youre freend?
Now, certes, I were worse than a feend,
If I to yow wolde harm or vileynye!
I am nat come youre conseil for t'espye,
But trewely, the cause of my comynge
Was oonly for to herkne how that ye synge.
For trewely, ye have as myrie a stevene
As any aungel hath that is in hevene.
Therwith ye han in musyk moore feelynge
Than hadde Boece, or any that kan synge.
My lord youre fader—God his soule blesse!—
And eek youre mooder, of hire gentillesse,
Han in myn hous ybeen to my greet ese;
And certes, sire, ful fayn wolde I yow plese.
But for men speke of syngyng, I wole seye,
So moote I brouke wel myne eyen tweye,
Save yow, I herde nevere man so synge
As dide youre fader in the morwenynge.
Certes, it was of herte, al that he song.

And for to make his voys the moore strong,
He wolde so peyne hym that with bothe his yen
He moste wynke, so loude he wolde cryen,
And stonden on his tiptoon therwithal,
And strecche forth his nekke long and smal.
And eek he was of swich discrecioun
That ther nas no man in no regioun
That hym in song or wisedom myghte passe.
I have wel rad in "Daun Burnel the Asse,"
Among his vers, how that ther was a cok,
For that a preestes sone yaf hym a knok
Upon his leg whil he was yong and nyce,
He made hym for to lese his benefice.
But certeyn, ther nys no comparisoun
Bitwixe the wisedom and discrecioun
Of youre fader and of his subtiltee.
Now syngeth, sire, for seinte charitee;
Lat se, konne ye youre fader countrefete?"

    This Chauntecleer his wynges gan to bete,
As man that koude his traysoun nat espie,
So was he ravysshed with his flaterie.

    Allas! ye lordes, many a fals flatour
Is in youre courtes, and many a losengeour,
That plesen yow wel moore, by my feith,
Than he that soothfastnesse unto yow seith.
Redeth Ecclesiaste of flaterye;
Beth war, ye lordes, of hir trecherye.

    This Chauntecleer stood hye upon his toos,
Strecchynge his nekke, and heeld his eyen cloos,
And gan to crowe loude for the nones.
And daun Russell the fox stirte up atones,
And by the gargat hente Chauntecleer,
And on his bak toward the wode hym beer,
For yet ne was ther no man that hym sewed.

    O destinee, that mayst nat been eschewed!
Allas, that Chauntecleer fleigh fro the bemes!
Allas, his wyf ne roghte nat of dremes!
And on a Friday fil al this meschaunce.

O Venus, that art goddesse of plesaunce,
Syn that thy servant was this Chauntecleer,
And in thy servyce dide al his poweer,
Moore for delit than world to multiplye,
Why woldestow suffre hym on thy day to dye?

O Gaufred, deere maister soverayn,
That whan thy worthy kyng Richard was slayn
With shot, compleynedest his deeth so soore,
Why ne hadde I now thy sentence and thy loore
The Friday for to chide, as diden ye?
For on a Friday, soothly, slayn was he.
Thanne wolde I shewe yow how that I koude pleyne
For Chauntecleres drede and for his peyne.

Certes, swich cry ne lamentacion,
Was nevere of ladyes maad whan Ylion
Was wonne, and Pirrus with his streite swerd,
Whan he hadde hent kyng Priam by the berd,
And slayn hym, as seith us *Eneydos*,
As maden alle the hennes in the clos,
Whan they had seyn of Chauntecleer the sighte.
But sovereynly dame Pertelote shrighte,
Ful louder than dide Hasdrubales wyf,
Whan that hir housbonde hadde lost his lyf,
And that the Romayns hadde brend Cartage.
She was so ful of torment and of rage
That wilfully into the fyr she sterte,
And brende hirselven with a stedefast herte.

O woful hennes, right so criden ye,
As, whan that Nero brende the citee
Of Rome, cryden senatoures wyves
For that hir husbondes losten alle hir lyves;
Withouten gilt this Nero hath hem slayn.
Now wole I turne to my tale agayn.

This sely wydwe and eek hir doghtres two
Herden thise hennes crie and maken wo,
And out at dores stirten they anon,
And syen the fox toward the grove gon,
And bar upon his bak the cok away,

And cryden, "Out! harrow! and weyl-away!
Ha! ha! the fox!" and after hym they ran,
And eek with staves many another man.
Ran Colle oure dogge, and Talbot, and Gerland
And Malkyn, with a dystaf in hir hand;
Ran cow and calf, and eek the verray hogges,
So fered for the berkyng of the dogges
And shoutyng of the men and wommen eeke,
They ronne so hem thoughte hir hirte breeke.
They yolleden as feendes doon in helle;
The dokes cryden as men wolde hem quelle;
The gees for feere flowen over the trees;
Out of the hyve cam the swarm of bees.
So hydous was the noyse, a, *benedicitee!*
Certes, he Jakke Straw and his meynee
Ne made nevere shoutes half so shrille,
Whan that they wolden any Flemyng kille,
As thilke day wes maad upon the fox.
Of bras they broghten bemes, and of box,
Of horn, of boon, in whiche they blewe and powped,
And therwithal they skriked and they howped.
It semed as that hevene sholde falle.

  Now, goode men, I prey yow herkneth alle:
Lo, how Fortune turneth sodeynly
The hope and pryde eek of hir enemy!
This cok, that lay upon the foxes bak,
In al his drede unto the fox he spak,
And seyde, "Sire, if that I were as ye,
Yet sholde I seyn, as wys God helpe me,
'Turneth agayn, ye proude cherles alle!
A verray pestilence upon yow falle!
Now am I come unto the wodes syde;
Maugree youre heed, the cok shal heere abyde.
I wol hym ete, in feith, and that anon!'"

    The fox answerde, "In feith, it shal be don."
And as he spak that word, al sodeynly
This cok brak from his mouth delyverly,
And heighe upon a tree he fleigh anon.

And whan the fox saugh that the cok was gon,
   "Allas," quod he, "O Chauntecleer, allas!
I have to yow," quod he, "ydoon trespas,
In as muche as I maked yow aferd
Whan I yow hente and broghte out of the yerd.
But, sire, I dide it in no wikke entente.
Com doun, and I shal telle yow what I mente;
I shal seye sooth to yow, God help me so!"
   "Nay thanne," quod he, "I shrewe us bothe two.
And first I shrewe myself, bothe blood and bones,
If thou bigyle me ofter than ones.
Thou shalt namoore, thurgh thy flaterye,
Do me to synge and wynke with myn ye;
For he that wynketh, whan he sholde see,
Al wilfully, God lat him nevere thee!"
   "Nay," quod the fox, "but God yeve hym meschaunce,
That is so undiscreet of governaunce
That jangleth whan he sholde holde his pees."
   Lo, swich it is for to be recchelees
And necligent, and truste on flaterye.
   But ye that holden this tale a folye,
As of a fox, or of a cok and hen,
Taketh the moralite, goode men.
For seint Paul seith that al that writen is,
To oure doctrine it is ywrite, ywis;
Taketh the fruyt, and lat the chaf be stille.
Now, goode God, if that it be thy wille,
As seith my lord, so make us alle goode men,
And brynge us to his heighe blisse! Amen.

Heere is ended the Nonnes Preestes Tale.